William James and the Art of Popular Statement

RHETORIC AND PUBLIC AFFAIRS SERIES

- *Eisenhower's War of Words: Rhetoric and Leadership,* Martin J. Medhurst, editor
- *The Nuclear Freeze Campaign: Rhetoric and Foreign Policy in the Telepolitical Age,* J. Michael Hogan
- *Mansfield and Vietnam: A Study in Rhetorical Adaptation,* Gregory A. Olson
- *Truman and the Hiroshima Cult,* Robert P. Newman
- *Post-Realism: The Rhetorical Turn in International Relations,* Francis A. Beer and Robert Hariman, editors
- *Rhetoric and Political Culture in Nineteenth-Century America,* Thomas W. Benson, editor
- *Frederick Douglass: Freedom's Voice, 1818–1845,* Gregory P. Lampe
- *Angelina Grimké: Rhetoric, Identity, and the Radical Imagination,* Stephen Howard Browne
- *Strategic Deception: Rhetoric, Science, and Politics in Missile Defense Advocacy,* Gordon R. Mitchell
- *Rostow, Kennedy, and the Rhetoric of Foreign Aid,* Kimber Charles Pearce
- *Visions of Poverty: Welfare Policy and Political Imagination,* Robert Asen
- *General Eisenhower: Ideology and Discourse,* Ira Chernus
- *The Reconstruction Desegregation Debate: The Politics of Equality and the Rhetoric of Place, 1870–1875,* Kirt H. Wilson
- *Shared Land/Conflicting Identity: Trajectories of Israeli and Palestinian Symbol Use,* Robert C. Rowland and David A. Frank
- *Darwinism, Design, and Public Education,* John Angus Campbell and Stephen C. Meyer, editors
- *Religious Expression and the American Constitution,* Franklyn S. Haiman
- *Christianity and the Mass Media in America: Toward a Democratic Accommodation,* Quentin J. Schultze
- *Bending Spines: The Propagandas of Nazi Germany and the German Democratic Republic,* Randall L. Bytwerk
- *Malcolm X: Inventing Radical Judgment,* Robert E. Terrill
- *Metaphorical World Politics,* Francis A. Beer and Christ'l De Landtsheer, editors
- *The Lyceum and Public Culture in the Nineteenth-Century United States,* Angela G. Ray
- *The Political Style of Conspiracy: Chase, Sumner, and Lincoln,* Michael William Pfau
- *The Character of Justice: Rhetoric, Law, and Politics in the Supreme Court Confirmation Process,* Trevor Parry-Giles
- *Rhetorical Vectors of Memory in National and International Holocaust Trials,* Marouf A. Hasian Jr.
- *Judging the Supreme Court: Constructions of Motives in* Bush *v.* Gore, Clarke Rountree
- *Everyday Subversion: From Joking to Revolting in the German Democratic Republic,* Kerry Kathleen Riley
- *In the Wake of Violence: Image and Social Reform,* Cheryl R. Jorgensen-Earp
- *Rhetoric and Democracy: Pedagogical and Political Practices,* Todd F. McDorman and David M. Timmerman, editors
- *Invoking the Invisible Hand: Social Security and the Privatization Debates,* Robert Asen
- *With Faith in the Works of Words: The Beginnings of Reconciliation in South Africa, 1985–1995,* Erik Doxtader
- *Public Address and Moral Judgment: Critical Studies in Ethical Tensions,* Shawn J. Parry-Giles and Trevor Parry-Giles, editors
- *Executing Democracy: Capital Punishment and the Making of America, 1683–1807,* Stephen John Hartnett
- *Enemyship: Democracy and Counter-Revolution in the Early Republic,* Jeremy Engels
- *Spirits of the Cold War: Contesting Worldviews in the Classical Age of American Security Strategy,* Ned O'Gorman
- *Making the Case: Advocacy and Judgment in Public Argument,* Kathryn M. Olson, Michael William Pfau, Benjamin Ponder, and Kirt H. Wilson, editors

William James and the Art of Popular Statement

Paul Stob

Michigan State University Press • *East Lansing*

∞ The paper used in this publication meets the minimum requirements of ANSI/NISO Z39.48-1992 (R 1997) (Permanence of Paper).

Michigan State University Press
East Lansing, Michigan 48823-5245

Printed and bound in the United States of America.

19 18 17 16 15 14 13 1 2 3 4 5 6 7 8 9 10

LIBRARY OF CONGRESS CATALOGING-IN-PUBLICATION DATA

Stob, Paul.
William James and the art of popular statement / Paul Stob.
p. cm. — (Rhetoric and public affairs series)
Includes bibliographical references and index.
ISBN 978-1-60917-370-8 (ebook)—ISBN 978-1-61186-083-2 (pbk. : alk. paper) 1. James, William, 1842–1910. 2. Rhetoric. I. Title.

B945.J21S76 2013
191—dc23 2012033879

Book design by Scribe Inc. (www.scribenet.com)
Cover design by John Barnett, www.4eyesdesign.com
Cover portrait of Henry James is owned by Harvard Art Museums/Fogg Museum, Harvard University Portrait Collection, commissioned by the Department of Philosophy for the faculty room, 1910, H111. Photograph of portrait is used with permission of the Imaging Department © President and Fellows of Harvard College.

green press INITIATIVE Michigan State University Press is a member of the Green Press Initiative and is committed to developing and encouraging ecologically responsible publishing practices. For more information about the Green Press Initiative and the use of recycled paper in book publishing, please visit www.greenpressinitiative.org.

Visit Michigan State University Press at www.msupress.org

For Sarah and Elliott

Contents

⌘

Acknowledgments

⌘

When I was still an undergraduate student, two events foreshadowed the writing of this book. First, I began reading William James's work. For the most part I didn't yet understand James, but his thoughts captivated me nonetheless. Second, I heard the word "rhetorician" for the first time, and, for some strange reason, it sounded like something I wanted to be. *William James and the Art of Popular Statement* is, at least in retrospect, the culmination of these two events.

Of course, in the years between my undergraduate education and the publication of this book, numerous individuals have given me their time, guidance, and criticism (in the best sense of the term). Marty Medhurst is not only an extraordinary editor but a longtime teacher, mentor, and friend. Jim Aune has been a profound influence on my life and career, and I owe him more than he'll ever know. John McDermott was really the first to help me understand William James, and his scholarship and teaching continues to inspire me.

At the University of Wisconsin, I was fortunate to study with the best rhetorical scholars in the country. Rob Asen, Erik Doxtader, Sue Zaeske, and Rob Howard were, and continue to be, invaluable scholarly influences. Above all, I am indebted to Steve Lucas, whose unfailing encouragement, guidance, feedback, and friendship helped improve my work in countless ways. He was able to see the shape of this book long before I was, and his editorial abilities strengthened my writing several times over. I should also thank my graduate-student cohort in Madison, who made earning a PhD more fun than it should have been. I am particularly grateful to Pam Conners for her friendship over the years.

Various other individuals are due my sincerest thanks. At Vanderbilt University, John Sloop, Bonnie Dow, Vanessa Beasley, Claire King, Kass Kovalcheck, and John Lachs have been incredibly supportive. Bill Keith, Mike Hogan, Angela Ray, Scott Stroud, Jeremiah Hickey, and Meghan Gilbert-Hickey have provided helpful and incisive feedback on various stages of this project. Participants at the 2010 William James symposium, especially Paul Croce, Robert Richardson, and Lynn Bridgers, shared numerous insights on James's life and work. The staff at Harvard's Houghton Library, which houses the James papers, made archival research a pleasure. At Michigan State University Press, Martha Bates and Kristine Blakeslee, among others, have expertly guided the publication of this book.

Dick and Nancy Stob, my parents, and Andrew Bandstra, my grandfather, have supported me in more ways than I know how to list. Perhaps my largest debt of gratitude is due to my wife, Sarah, and my son, Elliott. Over the last several years they have kindly listened to an insufferable number of anecdotes about William James. Only occasionally did they role their eyes at my enthusiasm.

Introduction

⌘

On May 1, 1903, William James sat at his desk catching up on correspondence. One of the letters he wrote that day was to his close friend and philosophical ally Ferdinand Canning Scott Schiller. James addressed a number of topics in the letter—a recent essay Schiller had published, page proofs of a book notice James had written, gossip about mutual friends, the chance of James teaching at Oxford, and James's plan to retire from Harvard. He also discussed how intellectually rewarding it had been to deliver the Gifford Lectures at the University of Edinburgh. The lectures, which James had completed in the spring of 1902, had led to the publication of one of his masterpieces—*The Varieties of Religious Experience*, a wildly popular book that many deemed an instant classic. Thinking over the success of *Varieties*, James told Schiller something remarkable: "I believe popular statement to be the highest form of art."[1]

This remark, buried in a wide-ranging letter, is more revealing of James's intellectual commitments than scholars have yet recognized. By the spring of 1903, James was one of the most visible and influential scientists, psychologists, and philosophers in the world. Yet he singled out "popular statement" as his intellectual ideal. Not locked away in his study, not behind a desk in academic seminars, not in the pages of professional journals, but in statements to general audiences was where he saw his calling. When thinking about his career and his plans for the future, James turned to the discursive relationships he had fostered with "popular" audiences. Popular statement—the kind of statement that had made *The Varieties of Religious Experience* a smashing success—was the height of intellectual creativity.

James's commitment to the art of popular statement did not go unnoticed during his lifetime. Few, if any, American scholars received the kind of popular coverage that he did. According to a North Dakota paper in 1887, James produced "unusually readable" essays that stood out prominently in an age of scientific jargon.[2] His thoughts on the human mind, summarized a Texas paper in 1888, were "most eloquent, . . . both beautiful and forcible," and accessible to generally interested readers without specialized training in psychology.[3] In 1891, a New Orleans paper explained that *The Principles of Psychology* was filled with "luminous pages," representative of someone with "the rare power of presenting the most abstract ideas in a vivid pictorial form."[4] James was "brilliant and vigorous," opined a Massachusetts paper in 1898, able to treat complex issues "in a way to interest everybody."[5] With a clear sense of his audience, concluded a California paper in 1899, James wrote "so that even the ordinary reader accompanied him without the least difficulty."[6] In 1907, a New York paper summarized James's career by explaining that his work contained "unusual skill and persuasiveness," which enabled him to attract "considerable attention not alone among philosophers by profession, but also among ordinary folk who do not as a rule meddle with philosophy." According to the paper, James skillfully adapted his discourse "for the man (and woman) of the street," using "the concrete example to bring home the abstract proposition. He does not even occasionally disdain the use of the slang of the day to elucidate the problems of all time."[7]

After James's death in 1910, countless tributes echoed these sentiments. The *Los Angeles Times* deemed his writing style "as clear and as fascinating as that of a brilliant novelist," which enabled him "to reduce technical terms to a common language, intelligible to a child."[8] Among all the "pioneers of a new world of thought," concluded the *Chicago Tribune*, James was the "preeminent" intellectual; he "fascinated, aroused, and dominated us by his thought, his marvelous style, and his personality."[9] "No American thinker," the *New York Times* lamented, "could leave a deeper sense of loss in our intellectual life than William James. He was widely read and his influence was widely felt." His death, the paper predicted, would be "an experience of personal regret to multitudes beyond the range of his acquaintance."[10]

As these accounts attest, James operated with a high level of visibility—among scholars and among members of the larger community. His books and essays were read by scientists and philosophers as well as by those who did not typically read scientific or philosophical treatises. His greatest works—*The Principles of Psychology, The Will to Believe, Talks to Teachers on Psychology and to Students on Some of Life's Ideals, The Varieties of Religious Experience, Pragmatism,* and *A Pluralistic Universe*—were among the most-read scholarly publications at the turn of the twentieth century. At a time when many thinkers seemed to turn away from public culture, James wrote in a way that transcended the intellectual divisions of his generation.[11] With "linguistic simplicity and clearness," remarked the *Springfield Daily Republican,* James had done "more to popularize philosophy than any other writer of this generation. It is a delight for the person unfamiliar with philosophic jargon to read him."[12]

It was not by chance that James attracted so many readers. He worked tirelessly to craft texts that would advance modern thought and prove compelling to general audiences. But the art of popular statement was not only integral to James's books and essays; it was also integral to the lectures he delivered across the country year after year. At the lectern, few scholars could match his passion, wit, and eloquence, and even fewer could attract the crowds that he did. James routinely spoke in packed auditoriums. On several occasions, organizers had to move his lectures at the last minute to larger venues to accommodate throngs of attendees. As one onlooker described the typical scene, "breathlessly listening crowds" greeted James "as the messenger of some new gospel." And he did not disappoint, communicating effectively with everyone from "business men" to "matrons and maids" and "merchants and publishers and newspaper men and men in more humble walks of life."[13]

Yet it would be a mistake to make a sharp distinction between James's writings and lectures, for the vast majority of his publications began on the lecture circuit. The chapters that made up *The Will to Believe, Talks to Teachers, The Varieties of Religious Experience, Pragmatism,* and *A Pluralistic Universe,* among others, originated on the public platform. More striking still, James typically did not undertake major revisions when turning his lectures into manuscripts for publication. What he said at the lectern was, by and large, what the American people read when they devoured his texts. He thus enabled readers to perceive, even to feel themselves a part of, the lecture occasion from which a given text emerged. James's oral prose style gave readers the impression that he was in the act of thinking and that they were participants in the unfolding of insight.[14]

When we think of James nowadays, it is easy to overlook the amount of time he spent on the lecture circuit speaking to the American people and crafting accessible texts. We think of him primarily as a scientist, psychologist, and philosopher. And, of course, he was these things. But he was someone who pursued science, psychology, and philosophy in conjunction with those for whom modern thought was often alien and unappealing. This is not to say that we lack a substantial picture of James's life and work. His ongoing influence has led to stacks of scholarship on his biography,[15] his publications,[16] his upbringing,[17] his scholarly development,[18] his role in shaping American philosophy,[19] his involvement in academic debates,[20] even his fascination with the paranormal.[21] Nor is this to say that we have overlooked the fact that James addressed popular audiences. Scholars have long known that he spoke to ordinary Americans and that his way with words was a prominent part of his appeal. Ross Posnock, for example, has noted that "James articulated his social thought in a rhetoric of incomparable moral eloquence and passion, becoming a beloved cultural hero by the last decade of his life and remaining one in our own time."[22] George Cotkin has explained that James "regularly addressed" popular audiences on "issues of the cultural and philosophical moment."[23] Frederick J. Ruf has explored James's work for its stylistic appeal, showing how James's artful prose contributed to the character of his thought.[24] And Gay Wilson Allen, one of James's many biographers, has written that James routinely "impressed others as a man alive to his fingertips—or better, to the roots of his nimble brain and his witty tongue. His charming presence, his informal, conversational lectures, and his clear, vigorous writings on psychology and philosophy were unfailingly stimulating to all who saw or heard or read him. And the aim of all his professional lecturing and writing was to promote more abundant health and pleasurable activity in his audience."[25]

These characterizations, though apt, only begin to elucidate the role that popular statement played in James's overall intellectual endeavor.

Despite the mountain of scholarship on his life and work, we have little understanding of why so many people traveled to lecture halls to hear him speak, why they made his books national and international best-sellers, and why they subscribed to his view of pressing problems of the day. Even Cotkin's admirable treatment of James as a "public philosopher," which is the most complete account yet of James's efforts to link philosophy with American public culture, does not explore the popular relationships he cultivated, the strategies he used to build these relationships, and the reasons his work demanded attention from academics and nonacademics alike.[26] The art of popular statement was far more than an aside in James's career. It was integral to the way he carried himself, to his interactions with colleagues, to his choice of venues for speaking and publishing, to the discursive style he adopted, to the conversations he influenced, and to the intellectual bonds he fostered with his fellow citizens.

This book is an exploration of the role of popular statement in James's life and work. By using the lecture circuit, popular periodicals, and his numerous best sellers to address "the people," James was able to distinguish himself from his colleagues and to assume a place of prominence unequalled by other American thinkers of the day. I use the words "the people" advisedly, fully aware that the label points more to a constitutive fiction than to any actual group.[27] Nevertheless, even if "the people" is a rather generic term, even if there is no unified, overarching public sphere wherein citizens congregate as equals, appeals to "the people" can still be effective in bringing individuals together.[28] Addressing "ordinary Americans" or "the masses" is not a matter of reflecting a reality but of calling people forward and constituting publics around particular ideas and perspectives. For James, addressing "the people" about affairs of the mind was a matter of adopting a discursive posture and drawing upon symbols that would allow different audiences—usually nonacademic audiences—to enter his texts. Orienting his thought toward "ordinary Americans" helped those who thought of themselves as ordinary Americans identify with his intellectual project.

Yet as we shall see, the significance of James's work was not simply that he addressed "the people"; after all, many intellectuals spoke *to* general audiences. The central argument of this book is that James's commitment to popular statement ultimately led him to a different kind of thought, a different epistemology, a view of science, religion, and philosophy that revolved around ordinary people and their experiences and perceptions. James built an understanding of the world around those he addressed, giving them a distinct role in the pursuit of knowledge and, in fact, fostering a new intellectual culture with them. In that regard James did more than speak popularly; he spoke as an intellectual populist. On the lecture circuit and in publications oriented toward general audiences, he confronted aristocrats of the mind—those who had accumulated power through various systems of academic and professional authority—and he argued that intellectual power should be returned to the people. In an age when knowledge was supposedly in the hands of experts, vouchsafed by academically certified specialists, James brought ordinary Americans into the marketplace of ideas. Because of their position outside the strictures of professional inquiry, they were often in the best position to answer life's big questions—questions about God, religion, science, ethics, the nature of the world, the nature of human beings, and the good life.

To be clear, the argument of this book is limited to discursive interactions between James and popular audiences. That is to say, tracing his art of popular statement and the emergence of his intellectual populism is a way of tracing a prominent mode of engagement in his career, but it is not a way of characterizing everything he said and did. The art of popular statement does not provide a comprehensive framework for understanding and analyzing all of James's massive corpus. It does, however, help us see how James committed himself to engaging intellectually disaffected publics, and it helps us understand why these publics responded enthusiastically to his message. The art he developed over the years was an art of attitudes, postures, appeals, and strategies for connecting with individuals who, he believed, deserved to be addressed. James was concerned, from early in his career, with the direction in which the world of thought was moving. In response, he offered popular statement as a kind of corrective, as a way of reconfiguring inquiry so that it better served "the people"—however amorphous and inexact that concept was.

Because the art of popular statement helped James create an alternative to the dominant patterns of thought at the time, this book is also about the transforming world of knowledge at the turn of the twentieth century. James became prominent and influential in part because he often opposed the dramatic fragmentation that defined intellectual culture at the time.[29] Beginning in the second half of the nineteenth century, knowledge became increasingly associated with professional training, narrow academic disciplines, and specialized vocabularies that were more or less inaccessible to outsiders. What counted as knowledge, what was necessary to produce knowledge, who could create knowledge, who could express knowledge, and who could use knowledge—these and similar questions were answered much differently early in the nineteenth century than at the end of it. James proved exceedingly conscious of the "culture of professionalism,"[30] and he often tried to combat what he saw as the insidious tendencies of academic specialization—despite the fact that he was one of the most prominent psychologists and philosophers in America. Thus the story of James's art of popular statement is also a story of competing systems of knowledge, which carried (and still carry) very different consequences for intellectual accessibility, participation, power relationships, and discourse.

If we are fully to understand James's place in intellectual culture at the turn of the twentieth century, it is also necessary to understand the social position he occupied. He was more than a scientist, psychologist, and philosopher. He was, to put it succinctly, a public intellectual. As a public intellectual, he helped define the tradition of "scientists, academics in the humanities and the social and political sciences, writers, artists and journalists who articulate issues of importance in their societies to the general public."[31] For James, working as a public intellectual meant spending significant time on the lecture circuit and publishing in popular venues; it meant crafting discourses that drew the American people into intellectual conversations; and it meant speaking a language that distinguished him from his colleagues.

The label "public intellectual" is not without its problems, however. Over the last twenty years, the idea of the public intellectual has led to particularly active scholarly debates. Since publication of Russell Jacoby's *The Last Intellectuals* in 1987, writers in a variety of disciplines have analyzed the meaning, value, and prevalence of public intellectuals, but they have come to little consensus. For Jacoby, the term captures the spirit of thinkers and writers "who address a general and educated audience" instead of communicating within the borders of specialized academic enclaves.[32] Unfortunately, Jacoby continues, the twentieth century witnessed a precipitous decline in publicly oriented thinkers and writers. Echoing Jacoby's lament, Richard Posner has concluded that "Public-intellectual work is becoming less distinctive, less interesting, and less important."[33] For Jacoby and Posner, the heyday of public intellectualism—the day of William James, W. E. B. DuBois,

John Dewey, Sidney Hook, Reinhold Niebuhr, Hannah Arendt, Jean-Paul Sartre, and others—is but a fleeting memory.

In response to this narrative of decline, a number of scholars have questioned whether there ever was a heyday of public intellectualism. The story, they say, is much more complex than that described by Jacoby and Posner.[34] Other scholars have redirected the debate to an international domain, exploring what seems to be more robust public-intellectual activity in Europe.[35] Still others focus on public intellectuals as oppositional agents—thinkers and writers who challenge power structures and work to abolish the status quo.[36] In addition, there has been extensive work on the role of minority public intellectuals, particularly African Americans, in shaping the social, cultural, and political landscape.[37] The result of these many studies has been a seemingly endless number of opinions on who public intellectuals are, what they do, and why they might be important.

Though scholars seem unable to agree on the current state of public intellectuals—whether they are in decline, abundant, oppositional, or more prevalent internationally—most recognize that debates about intellectual duty vis-à-vis the larger community are nothing new. In fact, one of the reasons it is fitting to treat James as a public intellectual is because he was a central figure in some of the first American discussions of the relationship between intellectual practice and public culture. James struggled with many of the issues that still animate scholarly debates: What is the relationship among experts, specialists, academics, and intellectuals? What responsibilities do these figures have insofar as public knowledge is concerned? What role should specialized languages play in intellectual culture? What is the place of experts in public debates? What can nonacademics contribute to the advancement of thought? These and similar questions presented James with a host of issues he had to work through in his pursuit of popular statement, and they are questions that remain at the forefront of current conversations.[38]

We should also recognize that James was one of the first Americans to use the term "intellectual" as a noun to describe a particular person.[39] While other American thinkers used *intellectual* in its noun form before him—the most notable being Robert Ingersoll[40]—James gave the term cachet, helping to popularize it in the midst of the Dreyfus Affair of the late 1890s and early 1900s.[41] When the French writer Èmile Zola used his literary fame to speak out in national newspapers against the treatment of Captain Alfred Dreyfus, a French artillery officer and Jew wrongly convicted of treason for selling military secrets to the Germans, the word "intellectual" began to assume its modern connotations in France. Zola and the other "Dreyfusards," as they were called, believed it their duty to engage the controversy and to shed light on the injustice of the situation. In America, James followed the affair closely, paying particular attention to how Dreyfus's friends and colleagues discussed the duty of thinkers and writers to speak out on this political problem. The more James reflected on the situation, the more he embraced the French intellectual impulse. In 1899, he wrote to his friend William Mackintire Salter that "we 'intellectuals' in America must all work to keep our precious birthright of individualism, and freedom from these institutions."[42] In 1900, he repeated the sentiment to William Dean Howells, writing: "I think that '*les intellectuals*' of every country ought to bond themselves together into a league for the purpose of fighting the curse of savagery that is pouring over the world."[43] Then, in 1907, he used "intellectual" in a public lecture to define a "class-consciousness" that ought to stand against political corruption. The lecture was subsequently published in *McClure's Magazine* under the title "The Social Value of the College-Bred."[44] The intellectual, James believed, was one who relied upon his or her learned reputation to clarify the meanings and implications of common problems. Though he never put the word "public" in front of "intellectual," he recognized that public commitments were inseparable from significant ideas.

Studying James's art of popular statement will in no way settle questions about public intellectualism writ large, about the function of intellectual discourse in public culture, or about the value of public intellectuals in different time periods. There is no need to position James as the quintessential public intellectual, nor is there a need to extrapolate from his life and work any general theory of the nature, duty, and significance of public intellectuals. The details of the problems with which he grappled were particular to his time, so it is almost impossible to offer normative suggestions based on his life for what public intellectuals should and should not do.

Nevertheless, we can find in James's work important evidence that current conceptions of public intellectualism fall short of capturing his mode of operation in the Gilded Age and Progressive Era. For example, Jacoby's definition of the public intellectual—not to mention many subsequent definitions—discusses the public intellectual as someone who speaks to general audiences.[45] Under this conception, the public intellectual shares knowledge with the masses, offering it to them in a public forum. But if being a public intellectual is nothing more than addressing general audiences and sharing ideas, we could identify most academics as public intellectuals, for countless professors deliver public presentations at some point in their careers. Speaking to or writing for general audiences is nothing unique—in James's day or in our day. Even Charles Sanders Peirce, who never came close to uttering a popular statement, delivered public lectures in Cambridge and elsewhere.[46] But Peirce's thought never connected with the American people, it never led to a shared understanding with general audiences, so it would be strange to call him a public intellectual.

To think of James as someone who simply shared ideas with general audiences fails to capture the appeal, nuance, and power of his thought. As we shall see, he went beyond speaking *to* general audiences by working *with* them on the issues they faced. His work was a matter of collaboration, as he entered into relationships with listeners and readers across the country to confront common problems. James dedicated himself to the art of popular statement specifically because it allowed him to create an intellectual arena that he could occupy with the American people writ large. Public-intellectual practice was a matter of mutually affective relationships—of James and his audiences crafting a shared vision.

Another way of putting it is to say that James's art of popular statement and his public-intellectual persona hinged upon the "micro-situations," to use Randall Collins's term, that constituted his career.[47] In particular lectures and reader interactions, James encountered different kinds of people facing different kinds of problems—and he did his best to confront those problems with them. Over time, these encounters formed a complex chain of associations that connected James to an array of publics and helped move his thought through various networks of individuals.[48] Indeed, one might even argue that the prominence and influence of his ideas emerged directly from his frequent encounters with new and different audiences. The popularly oriented micro-situations of his career fostered countless contexts of reception that made his ideas meaningful for particular people dealing with their own issues.[49]

But how exactly did James's ideas become meaningful in these encounters? After all, simply interacting with popular audiences does not guarantee success; certainly it does not necessarily result in the kind of visibility James achieved. So how was he able to make his statements popular, effective, and influential? His method for doing so, and the primary reason he succeeded as a public intellectual, was his command of the art of rhetoric. Attuned to the power of language, he knew how to turn a phrase to make an idea memorable. He knew how to adapt his lectures for listeners across the country—be they in New England, further down the Eastern Seaboard, in the Midwest, or on the distant West Coast—thereby giving his audiences the sense that his work was significant for their situation. He knew how to help his listeners and readers reach conclusions about pressing problems facing the nation. He knew how to make nonacademics feel intellectually productive. In short, he understood how language could bridge the gaps between individuals in a society. In James's career, language was "a symbolic means of inducing cooperation in beings that by nature respond to symbols."[50] Speaking to packed auditoriums across the country and publishing some of the best-selling intellectual works of the time, he lived by the fine art of "adjusting ideas to people and of people to ideas."[51]

Unfortunately, the term "rhetoric" can be as problematic as the term "public intellectual," yet both are crucial for understanding James's art of popular statement. For millennia, philosophers, politicians, orators, and others have debated what rhetoric means, and each generation—indeed, each thinker—seems to have defined the term anew. From Aristotle's oft-cited definition of rhetoric as "the faculty of observing in any given case the available means of persuasion"[52] to more modern conceptions of rhetoric as "the study of misunderstanding and its remedies,"[53] the term can be perplexing and elusive. In popular discourse, many writers exacerbate the problem by contrasting "rhetoric" with "reality," as though the former is completely disconnected from, and insignificant when compared to, the latter. Others talk about "mere rhetoric," thereby belittling the art in light of what they see as true insight. Still others dismiss rhetoric as a matter of style alone, as though thought and language, form and content, style and substance are easily separable.

Despite the seemingly endless number of ways to define rhetoric, those who study it can generally agree that it involves the way symbols shape perceptions, foster personal and collective judgments, and lead to action.[54] At the very least, rhetoric is a tool for inducing change in the world and for altering our relationships with one another. It is a productive art, assisting with deliberation at a time when no clear answers are in sight. A central component of democratic society, rhetoric "can offer counsel, define problems, suggest solutions, provide meaning when all appears confused and uncertain, or persuade an audience to believe or to act in a fitting and timely manner."[55]

Because rhetoric is an art of building symbolic relationships, because it offers speakers and writers the chance to bridge (or to widen) perceived divisions within or among groups, it is an inexorable part of public-intellectual practice. Indeed, a keen understanding of the constitutive power of language is necessary for those who hope to create "enduring works that broadly influence cultural habits and institutional practices during their lifetimes."[56] Moreover, the rhetorical connections an intellectual makes with different publics greatly influence the way that intellectual is perceived by those publics. That is to say, language use is central to the creation and maintenance of a public intellectual's reputation. As Steven Mailloux explains, "Public intellectuals not only rhetorically engage audiences beyond the academy but are recognized as doing so by both academics and nonacademics."[57] In order to bring together texts, audiences, and ideas in specific situations, in order to create recognition and identification across intellectual divisions, public intellectuals depend upon the art of rhetoric.[58] It is the art of rhetoric that structures the micro-situations of a public intellectual's career.

Scholars have long recognized that James, one of America's greatest public intellectuals, was engaged in a rhetorical project, or at least that his thought was helpful for those thinking about rhetoric. Early in the twentieth century, writers of public-speaking textbooks turned to James's work in psychology, particularly his discussion of attention, to help describe the process by which speakers engage the complex mental makeup of audiences.[59] In the middle of the century, however, scholars of rhetoric seemed to move on from James, leaving his work unexamined and unacknowledged. Across the disciplinary landscape, in fact, not just in the field of rhetorical studies, James's thought fell out of fashion.[60] Eventually, a wave of interest in the relationship between rhetoric and pragmatism brought renewed attention to the classical pragmatists, including James.[61] Steven Mailloux, for one, puts James and other pragmatists in conversation with the sophistic tradition of ancient Greece to create a "rhetorical hermeneutics" that draws upon the antifoundationalism of American pragmatism to analyze historical acts of interpretation. The goal for Mailloux is to use "rhetoric to practice theory by doing history."[62] Focusing more on the sociocultural milieus in which pragmatism was born, Robert Danisch uses James's work, along with the work of John Dewey, Jane Adams, Oliver Wendell

Holmes Jr., and Alain Locke, to show how "a belief in uncertainty, epistemological anthropocentrism, pluralism, community, and the need for practical arts are the grounds for a philosophy that indicates rhetoric's central place in human affairs."[63] James is particularly important in this regard because "the intellectual commitments of James's pragmatism share an orientation to the world with classical rhetoric and open the possibility for a new American rhetoric."[64]

Yet for all the accounts of James's link to the art of rhetoric, we lack a complete picture of James as a rhetorician—that is, as someone practicing the art of rhetoric. Danisch has even argued that "James does not appear to have reflected self-consciously on his own rhetorical practices, and for that reason he was not a rhetorician."[65] James's commitment to the art of popular statement tells quite another story, however. Not only did he reflect upon his rhetorical practices but he engaged specific audiences in specific situations and relied upon specific strategies to influence the character of American discourse. Thus far, the closest we have to an account of James as a rhetorician is Frederick Antczak's *Thought and Character*, which includes a chapter on James's efforts to bring together philosophy and public culture. As Antczak describes, James ranged widely from "calculated formality to offhand folksiness," crafting a "rhetoric of democratic education" that linked philosophy with the American experience. "James's tactical genius," Antczak insists, "consisted in recognizing and addressing the paradoxical task of expounding the conflict in philosophy powerfully enough to convey its significance without making it sound intellectually inaccessible."[66] Antczak's characterization is correct, but it is also brief, glossing over questions of how James crafted his work in particular moments for particular audiences relative to particular ends. Without getting into the micro-situations of James's career, we lack a complete picture of his rhetorical artistry and work as a public intellectual.

Because this book is concerned with James's art of popular statement, it focuses primarily on his rhetorical practices relative to popular audiences. This is not to say that one could not focus on James's rhetoric relative to other kinds of audiences or in other situations. It is simply to say that an art of popular statement required the creation of a rhetorical style capable of animating individuals who stood outside the professional cultures of which James was a part. On the public stage and in the pages of books and essays, James faced many of the same challenges that rhetors throughout history have faced. He had to get listeners and readers interested in problems and ideas—no matter how distant the problems and ideas may have seemed at first glance. He had to ensure that they could follow the progression of his thought. He had to speak a language they could understand, appreciate, and share. He had to bring abstract concepts before their eyes, helping them see what was immaterial. And he had to inspire in them a sense of purpose and agency, or at least the sense that their time with him had been worthwhile. These and similar rhetorical issues stood between James and an effective art of popular statement. But as we shall see, he responded in a way that made him one of America's greatest public intellectuals.

Given the scope of James's writing and the sheer volume of his corpus, it would be well-nigh impossible to cover every time he engaged popular audiences. Consequently, I focus on those instances that functioned as turning points in his development and in his relationship with intellectual culture. I pay particular attention, though not exclusive attention, to James's work on the lecture circuit because it was there that he connected most effectively with specific audiences and crafted the oral style that permeated his publications. Approaching James from this perspective will allow us to see the arc of his popular endeavor, including the practices and strategies that led to his prominence. The visibility and influence he achieved was the result of a long process of negotiation and experimentation. Understanding this process will produce a clearer view of how his thought shaped and was shaped by his place in public culture.

Those familiar with James's work will notice significant absences from what follows, and two of these absences deserve special mention. First, I do not investigate James's civic orations and publications, including his work in opposition to American imperialism. Cotkin, among others, has already treated James's anti-imperialism at length,[67] and approaching the subject with an eye toward the art of popular statement would add little to our overall understanding of what James undertook. Moreover, the art of popular statement was about developing relationships, and few Americans knew James as an anti-imperialist, at least when compared to the other roles he played. In the eyes of the nation and world, he was primarily a scientist, psychologist, philosopher, psychical researcher, and communicator; anti-imperialist was a minuscule part of his reputation.

Second, I do not analyze the "Will to Believe" controversy. While the controversy no doubt attracted significant attention, and while it would certainly be possible to place an analysis of the text in the overall development of James's art, the fact was that James accomplished more by delivering *The Varieties of Religious Experience*. In the scheme of James's career, *Varieties* was more important and influential than *The Will to Believe*. The overall picture this book tries to paint is of James's constantly evolving pursuit of popular statement, and while other texts and case studies could be included, what follows is enough to reveal the contours and substance of his eloquent vision.

Chapter 1 explores the shifting intellectual terrain that propelled James's career and set the stage for his turn to popular statement. James grew up in the presence of some of the most influential thinkers of the first half of the nineteenth century, including Ralph Waldo Emerson and Henry James Sr., who modeled for him a system of knowledge based on eloquence, popular lecturing, and wide-ranging intellectual vision. The "culture of eloquence" in which Emerson and Henry Sr. thrived was a culture in which advanced degrees were not essential, insight was defined by rhetorical prowess, and big ideas were supposed to edify and entertain communities. But around the time James went to college, eloquence was giving way to expertise, technical vocabularies, and exclusive enclaves of inquiry. At Harvard's Lawrence Scientific School, James entered a "culture of professionalism" that was closely linked to the problems and prospects of modern science. He also encountered figures who demonstrated different means of negotiating the demands of science: Benjamin Peirce, Asa Gray, Jeffries Wyman, Louis Agassiz, and Oliver Wendell Holmes Sr. As we shall see, the shift from eloquence to professionalism created a productive tension that animated James's popular efforts. In the process of confronting and working through the challenges of modern thought, he tried to keep alive the spirit of inquiry that had defined his youth.

Chapter 2 investigates James's early efforts to address the intersection of professional inquiry and public culture. As a young scholar his intellectual output consisted primarily of anonymous book reviews in popular periodicals such as the *North American Review*, the *Nation*, and the *Atlantic Monthly*. Thus far, scholars have glossed over these reviews, setting them aside as largely insignificant when compared to his later work. But I treat the early reviews as sites of intellectual invention that allowed James to develop many of the ideas, arguments, and strategies of his subsequent work—such as his 1878 lectures at Johns Hopkins University in Baltimore and the Lowell Institute in Boston. In what became the most significant lectures of his young career, James drew upon the arguments developed in his book reviews to foster a shared perspective with popular audiences on the significance of modern science.

Chapter 3 continues to explore how James worked with specific communities on issues they faced. In particular, I turn to the most-delivered lecture series of James's career—"Talks to Teachers on Psychology," which he presented almost a dozen times during the 1890s. Speaking to primary and secondary schoolteachers on the relationship between psychology and pedagogy, James did not simply share psychological insights with his audiences. Rather, he worked with them on bettering themselves, their professional predicament, and their place in democratic society. "Talks to Teachers" was, I argue, a collaboration between James and the nation's teachers more than it was a set of scientific musings on pedagogy. By the time James finished delivering the lectures at the end of the 1890s, he fully understood how popular interactions could produce useful knowledge.

Chapter 4 explores what was the most controversial aspect of James's career—his work as a psychical researcher. Many scholars treat his dedication to psychical research as a curiosity, simply an extension of his quirky personality and open-mindedness. To the contrary, I present psychical research as a turning point in James's development as a public intellectual. Having dedicated himself to the study of ghosts, mediums, spirit communication, haunted houses, telepathy, automatic writing, and other paranormal phenomena, James encountered significant opposition from academics who saw psychical research as an unfortunate remnant of the premodern era. In response to professional criticism, James took to the popular press and to the public platform to defend himself, his fellow psychical researchers, and the very idea of investigating the paranormal. In 1890 and 1892 articles in *Scribner's* and *Forum*, in an 1896 presidential address before the Society for Psychical Research, and in his 1896 Lowell lectures on "Exceptional Mental States," James did his best to frame psychical research as an important part of modern science and as a way for scientists to help ordinary Americans make sense of their experiences. I argue that James's efforts to defend psychical research resulted in a popular-professional divide that shaped the remainder of his career. In fact, defending psychical research cleared the way for James to develop a populist epistemology.

Chapter 5 explores how James developed this populist epistemology in the context of a specific rhetorical situation. The first American invited to deliver the prestigious Gifford lectures on natural theology, James worked tirelessly to craft his masterpiece, "The Varieties of Religious Experience," which was later published, and widely read, under the same name. Treating "Varieties" as a carefully constructed public performance, I argue that James presented his listeners (and subsequent readers) with a vision of intellectual culture in which the experiences and perceptions of "the people" formed the basis of knowledge. In a complete reconfiguration of the culture of professionalism, which viewed knowledge as extending from the work of specially trained experts, James affirmed everyday experience as the beginning of insight. With "Varieties," then, his work as a public intellectual became mature, for he not only displayed his dedication to addressing ordinary people but also built his thought around them, their beliefs, their feelings, and their perceptions.

Chapter 6 extends the intellectual populism of chapter 5 by turning to what is generally considered James's most important contribution to modern philosophy: pragmatism. As we shall see, pragmatism not only emerged on the lecture circuit but also advanced James's effort to restructure intellectual culture around the primacy of "the people." Best articulated in his 1906 and 1907 lectures at the Lowell Institute and Columbia University, pragmatism was an attempt to overthrow the philosophical aristocracy of the modern era and to call forth a public of lay philosophers who could set the pursuit of knowledge back on track. Although *Pragmatism*, the book that resulted from the lectures, would earn James a number of professional enemies, it would also become one of the most popular philosophical works in American history. Readers hailed it as a new philosophical creed, an American gospel, perfectly attuned to everyday experience at the dawn of the twentieth century.

In the end, exploring James's commitment to the art of popular statement and his corresponding development as a public intellectual will position his work in a new light. As we will see, James tried to carry on an oratorical culture that had defined the life of the mind during the first half of the nineteenth century. What he said was novel for its time, but what he did was familiar and comforting to those who yearned for the intellectual practices of old. We will also see how many reactions to James's work, including popular praise and professional scorn, stemmed from his efforts to engage, edify, and empower ordinary Americans. The art of popular statement was a threat to specialization, expertise, and the in-group languages of academic inquiry. It was, at the same time, a way of creating a vibrant public sphere by inviting people to participate in civil society.

Exploring the art of popular statement will also provide a striking counterpoint to one of the most prominent and long-standing criticisms of James's life and work. Since his death, and even before, scholars have criticized James for being a rugged individualist, even an elitist, who was blind to the social problems of his time.[68] A number of scholars have already answered this criticism,[69] but James's art represents yet another reply. As he toured the country speaking to the American people, as he took their intellectual predicaments seriously and worked with them on common problems, he not only demonstrated his concern for social affairs but also constructed a new community. Far from being an individualist in the negative sense of the term, James embarked on a decades-long project of bringing people together in an alternative intellectual culture.

By 1910, the year of James's death, no other American scholar could match his visibility and influence. None could rival his standing as an intellectual champion of the people. His efforts to speak a popular language, to challenge professional authority, and to reimagine the pursuit of knowledge endeared him to millions. By making the art of popular statement his intellectual ideal during the Gilded Age and Progressive Era, he found a way to speak to the ages.

Abbreviations

⌘

Corr. — *The Correspondence of William James,* 12 vols. Edited by Ignas K. Skrupskelis and Elizabeth M. Berkeley. Charlottesville: University Press of Virginia, 1992–2004.

ECR — *Essays, Comments, and Reviews* (*The Works of William James*). Cambridge: Harvard University Press, 1987.

EP — *Essays in Psychology* (*The Works of William James*). Cambridge: Harvard University Press, 1983.

EPR — *Essays in Psychical Research* (*The Works of William James*). Cambridge: Harvard University Press, 1986.

ERE — *Essays in Radical Empiricism* (*The Works of William James*). Cambridge: Harvard University Press, 1976.

ERM — *Essays in Religion and Morality* (*The Works of William James*). Cambridge: Harvard University Press, 1982.

ML	*Manuscript Lectures* (*The Works of William James*). Cambridge: Harvard University Press, 1988.
MT	*The Meaning of Truth* (*The Works of William James*). Cambridge: Harvard University Press, 1975.
PP	*The Principles of Psychology*, 3 vols. (*The Works of William James*). Cambridge: Harvard University Press, 1981.
Prag.	*Pragmatism* (*The Works of William James*). Cambridge: Harvard University Press, 1975.
PU	*A Pluralistic Universe* (*The Works of William James*). Cambridge: Harvard University Press, 1977.
SPP	*Some Problems of Philosophy* (*The Works of William James*). Cambridge: Harvard University Press, 1979.
TT	*Talks to Teachers on Psychology and to Students on Some of Life's Ideals* (*The Works of William James*). Cambridge: Harvard University Press, 1983.
VRE	*The Varieties of Religious Experience* (*The Works of William James*). Cambridge: Harvard University Press, 1985.

CHAPTER ONE

Eloquence and Professionalism in the Nineteenth Century

⌘

Born in January 1842, William James grew up in uncertain times. Politically, socially, culturally, economically, and intellectually, the world of his youth would little resemble the world of his adulthood. Perhaps Henry Adams—James's contemporary, friend, and fellow intellectual—captured the changes best when he wrote: "The American boy of 1854 stood nearer the year 1 than to the year 1900."[1] The Civil War was the defining event of James's generation, but the war affected his career less directly than did the changes in the pursuit of knowledge that shaped his upbringing.

During the nineteenth century, intellectual culture underwent a striking metamorphosis. This is not to say that the world of thought changed overnight; the metamorphosis took decades.[2] But it is to say that intellectual culture was a different creature at the end of the century than at the beginning. In the most general terms, the metamorphosis involved the shift from a "culture of eloquence" to a "culture of professionalism."[3] In the culture of eloquence, which was prominent for much of the first half of the nineteenth century, the pursuit of knowledge was defined by broad, prophetic visions and efforts to edify the general community. For many Americans of the time, the heart of the nation's intellectual life could be found in popular, relatively accessible, civically focused lecture halls and periodicals, which spread new ideas to middle- and upper-class communities from Maine to Missouri. In the culture of professionalism, which shaped much of the second half of the nineteenth century, the pursuit of knowledge was defined by specialized inquiry, strong disciplinary boundaries, and academically certified experts. After the Civil War, the heart of America's intellectual life moved to universities, laboratories, narrowly focused journals, and other professionally oriented forums. This is not to say that lecture halls and popular periodicals disappeared altogether, of course. But it is to say that people's perceptions about where true knowledge was produced shifted away from the venues that had defined the culture of eloquence.[4]

Scholars have long recognized that James became intellectually prominent during a time of specialization, fragmentation, and scholarly division. Francesca Bordogna has even shown that James's prominence was due in no small part to his ability to work past the academic boundaries of his era.[5] Yet James's place in the era of expertise only tells half the story. His work not only emerged from and helped critique a time of academic professionalism but also kept alive the spirit of eloquence that had defined his youth. If we are to understand the moments of popular interaction that structured James's career, we need to understand how he developed in and through the shift from eloquence to professionalism.

The purpose of this chapter, then, is to lay the groundwork for a claim that will be developed more fully in subsequent chapters. Specifically, the points of tension between the culture of eloquence and the culture of professionalism provided James with a wealth of rhetorical resources for relating to and interacting with popular audiences. Because of his understanding of intellectual life in the first half of the nineteenth century, he was able to reconnect the American people to an increasingly rare yet still appreciated mode of thought and engagement. At the same time, because of his understanding of modern science and the new frontiers of the mind, he was able to help his audiences comprehend, respond to, and participate in patterns of thought in the late nineteenth and early twentieth centuries. In short, the attitudes, appeals, ideas, practices, and commitments James displayed in moments of popular interaction grew out of the intellectual tensions between eloquence and professionalism.

As we shall see below, some of the most significant figures in James's upbringing were giants of the culture of eloquence, modeling for him an artistic, oratorical, visionary, and civically minded form of engagement. Ralph Waldo Emerson and Henry James Sr., William's father, were particularly important in this regard. Their example created a background against which it is necessary to view James's turn to popular statement. Yet even as a young man, James knew that the world of thought was changing, and if he were to thrive, he would need to branch out from these early influences. As a student at Harvard's Lawrence Scientific School and at the medical school, he received an enviable scientific education. He also encountered a number of influential professors—namely Benjamin Peirce, Asa Gray, Jeffries Wyman, Louis Agassiz, and Oliver Wendell Holmes Sr.—who modeled different forms of engagement applicable in the second half of the nineteenth century. By the time James graduated from Harvard in 1869 with a medical degree, he had traversed much of America's changing intellectual landscape. But his journey left him with few answers about how best to live the life of the mind. He soon entered a time of profound uncertainty and depression, which, we shall see, was closely connected to the metamorphosis of inquiry.

Reared in a Culture of Eloquence

The culture of eloquence, which took hold in the 1830s and reached its zenith in the 1840s and 1850s, revolved around the belief that eloquent discourse could transform speakers, writers, listeners, and readers through mutually affective interactions. Out of these interactions would come "the possibility of new movement, power, and efficacy" in rhetors and audiences alike.[6] Thus pervading the era was a robust spirit of public engagement, a resounding affirmation of the "public responsibility of citizenship."[7] The best Americans, at least in the popular imagination, were those who put their personal interests aside and worked for the improvement of their community and nation. Their tool in this project of improvement was the art of oratory, which became "a prime necessity to success in public life."[8] The "good man skilled in speaking" was to lead the nation through the dizzying array of problems that defined antebellum society.[9] Daniel Webster, Henry Clay, John C. Calhoun, Wendell Philips, Edward Everett, and Frederick Douglass, among many others, were giants of the culture of eloquence because they brought rhetorical wisdom to bear on common problems. Together, they created what Edward Parker famously called the "Golden Age of American Oratory."[10]

The spirit of public engagement and the importance of oratory shaped almost all aspects of American life, including the nation's intellectual culture. Indeed, for much of the first half of the nineteenth century, knowledge and eloquence were inexorably linked. Being able to articulate one's ideas compellingly became inseparable from what it meant to be learned, as effective speaking defined the properly cultivated mind.[11] As George Curtis, editor of *Harper's Monthly Magazine,* explained in 1856, the height of intellectual ability was to be found in "the living speaker, commanding subject and audience by fullness of knowledge and potency of will—every muscle and nerve in the service of thought and emotion, every pulse obedient to the intellect."[12] In the culture of eloquence, then, insight and rhetorical artistry were counterparts in the pursuit of knowledge, and the world of thought marched forward through oratorical activity.

The close connection between eloquence and knowledge was accompanied by an important new venue for ideas—the popular lecture, which would prove central to the work of Ralph Waldo Emerson and Henry James Sr., not to mention William James. The popular lecture was a "disinterested act," at once witty, serious, and moral, and directed at "the good of the audience and society."[13] It was, in short, a way for the community to think and grow together. As Thomas Wentworth Higginson, a prominent abolitionist and popular lecturer—as well as a friend of the James family—explained: "Thought must be popularized, execution made broader and rougher, before it can be appreciated in an instant by a thousand minds; but those thousand minds give you in return a magnificent stimulus that solitude can never supply. It is needless to debate which is best: it is the difference between light and heat."[14]

As popular lectures sparked the imaginations of communities across the country, there soon arose a new vocation. For the first time in American history, individuals could earn their keep solely by peddling intellectual wares on the public stage. They could live the life of the mind without the backing of a university or religious order and without a more traditional form of income to supplement public performances. Popular lectures thus offered "occupational identity and prestige, an income, and a public intellectual role."[15] The best example of this new vocational opportunity was the lyceum movement, which structured the art of popular lecturing for much of the nineteenth century. Taking its inspiration partly from the British Mechanics' Institute and partly from Josiah Holbrook, who, in October 1826, published a manifesto stressing the importance of continuing education for all individuals, the lyceum gave lecturers and audiences a forum for entering the marketplace of ideas.[16] Traveling to diverse communities in various locales, lyceum lecturers covered a broad range of topics—from practical matters such as farming, gardening, raising animals, raising children, and making sound investments to more scholarly subjects such as history, art, philosophy, language, and literature. Together, lecturers promoted a new cultural consciousness, giving disparate audiences a similar way of viewing the nation's problems and possibilities.[17]

Although the lyceum movement in particular and the lecture circuit in general were never as egalitarian as some believed—they were too often divided according to race, class, and gender[18]—what really mattered to those participating in the culture of eloquence was the democratic ideal that guided them. Speakers insisted that they were working for the moral and intellectual uplift of the nation. Even though they often addressed a white, middle-class, Protestant audience, lecturers saw themselves as concerned citizens engaging fellow citizens on common problems. They were agents of edification and delegates of culture, providing "society with the means to dispense justice, debate policy, and exalt the beauties of truth and nature."[19] As Edward Channing explained in 1856, lecturers, orators, and debaters were not taking part in a contest for "triumph over each other and an ignorant multitude; the orator himself is but one of the multitude, deliberating with them upon common interests, which are well understood and valued by all."[20]

Channing's sentiment points to perhaps the most important feature of the culture of eloquence, at least if we are to understand James's place in public culture later in the nineteenth century—namely, the primacy of the audience in the intellectual encounter. For Channing and for countless others at the time, speakers and audiences were engaged in a collaborative project, the result of which was the fullest, most important kind of knowledge possible. Lecturers did not impart ideas to the masses; rather, they entered into "a process marked by intellectual and emotional reciprocity" with the communities they addressed.[21] In essence, then, audiences were able to shape the movement of ideas on the lecture circuit right along with speakers. "The people" had remarkable intellectual agency. Because their pocketbooks provided a lecturer's livelihood, they had the power to authorize some speakers to continue their work and to deny others the chance to move forward. As one commentator explained in 1865, "The popular lecture is the most purely democratic of all our democratic institutions. The people hear a second time only those who interest them. If a lecturer cannot engage the interest of his audience, his fame or greatness or learning will pass for nothing."[22]

What audiences demanded above all from speakers was an astute rhetorical prowess, an engaging and inspiring language, as eloquence and knowledge were inexorably linked. A successful lecturer had to entertain at the same time that he or she helped audience members refine their skills or see the world in a new light.[23] Participating in the world of thought meant blending education, edification, and entertainment. Consequently, a lecturer's ability to articulate a compelling vision was far more important than any advanced degree or specialized training. Of course, some level of education or personal experience was implied. But the primary requirement for engaging one's community was rhetorical artistry. Moreover, because advanced degrees and specialized training carried little weight, orators and lectures could be as wide-ranging as they wished. They did not have to live according to disciplinary boundaries, so long as they could articulate an insight eloquently and so long as audiences remained interested. The same lecturer might speak on literature, history, and philosophy before turning to biology, astronomy, and botany. If a speaker was able to inspire, entertain, and enlighten, he or she was in a perfect position to work with popular audiences on crafting a shared vision.

Publicly oriented, wide-ranging, attuned to the language of the community, directed at moral cultivation and the alleviation of common problems—eloquent intellectual practice represented the height of knowledge for several decades. For William James, it represented the tenor of childhood. As a privileged New Englander, he was fortunate to live in the presence of some of the most celebrated thinkers, lectures, and writers of the first half of the nineteenth century—the two most important being Emerson and Henry Sr. Eugene Taylor has argued that Emerson and Henry Sr. played a much more central role in the development of James's thought than scholars typically recognize.[24] Taylor is correct, but the point goes further. Emerson and Henry Sr. showed James the importance of public commitments and popular intellectual practices; they modeled the behaviors and attitudes that would later define his career.

In the culture of eloquence, few names could compare with Emerson's, a man who earned his keep largely on the lecture circuit and who, more than anyone else, defined the intellectual side of American oratory. As the intellectual figurehead of the eloquent generation, he was the perfect expression of his own call for the American Scholar.[25] But Emerson was more than a lecturer and more than a scholar; he was the nation's first public intellectual, a font of ideas who flooded American culture via the public platform.[26] During his career, Emerson delivered more than 1,500 public lectures, speaking in almost every state in the nation. Donning a long black robe, he assumed his place at the lectern between fifty and eighty times a year.[27] Because of the time he spent on the lecture circuit, he had the opportunity to create powerful connections with the American people. Many relished the novelty and eloquence of his vision; others despised his unorthodox, potentially heretical thought. But even those who despised him knew he was making a significant mark on American society. For good or for ill, Emerson demanded attention, and audiences felt compelled to cheer him on, to respond to him, to argue over his ideas, or to defend their beliefs against his.[28]

On the lecture circuit, Emerson was as wide-ranging as he was visionary, greatly contributing to the egalitarian ideal of the culture of eloquence. One night he might speak on English literature, the next on classical poetry, the next on fine art, the next on modern philosophy, and the next on Western history. After that he might move to biology, botany, zoology, travel, or leisure. Like other public lecturers at the time, he was not confined by disciplinary boundaries. As long as audiences were willing to listen—and most Americans were willing to listen to Emerson—he could roam the intellectual landscape as he wished, connecting his listeners to the world of ideas through a striking and sometimes peculiar discursive style. One lecture attendee and future president of the United States, Rutherford B. Hayes, effectively captured Emerson's relationship with the American people when he wrote:

"Logic and method, he has none, but his bead-string of suggestions, fancies, ideas, anecdotes, and illustrations, delivered in a subdued, earnest manner, is as effective in chaining the attention of his audience as the most systematic discourse could be."[29]

Across New England, a generation of aspiring intellectuals looked to Emerson for guidance and inspiration. In his hometown of Concord, the entire community practically organized itself around his influence. Outside of Concord, supporters could be just as enthusiastic. One such dedicated follower was Henry James Sr. Because of Henry Sr.'s interest in emulating Emerson, the young William James would have his most direct connection to the culture of eloquence.

Henry Sr. was both brilliant and spoiled. His father, William James of Albany, was at one point the second richest man in America, behind only John Jacob Astor.[30] Respected across upstate New York at the beginning of the nineteenth century, William of Albany had a difficult time with his son Henry. A rebellious and often irreverent child, Henry drank, gambled, wasted his father's money, ran away from home, and, eventually, studied theology and philosophy. After William of Albany's death, a legal battle ensued over the terms of his substantial estate. Through various legal wranglings, Henry was able to secure a significant portion of his father's wealth.[31] With little need to worry about money, Henry could live in comfort, tour America and Europe with his new wife, Mary Walsh, and devote his time to the life of the mind.

After a year and a half of marriage, Henry and Mary started a family, one that would benefit greatly from Henry's wealth and intellectual appetite. William James was born in New York City on January 11, 1842. The following year, Henry Jr. was born. Two more boys appeared later in the decade—Garth Wilkinson in 1845 and Robertson in 1846. The fifth and final child was a girl, Alice, born in 1848. Together, the James family would spend time in New York, Rhode Island, and Massachusetts as well as in prominent western European countries, as they traversed the globe in search of education and insight. They were, Henry Jr. once recalled, "hotel children,"[32] but they had opportunities available to few others in the mid-nineteenth century.

At the time William was born in 1842, Henry Sr. was struggling to find his own intellectual voice. In searching the annals of modern thought, he experimented widely, most notably with the work of the controversial Scottish theologian Robert Sandeman and the Swedish mystic Emanuel Swedenborg. But Henry Sr. knew that making it in America required a touch of Americanness, and for that he turned to Emerson. Their paths first crossed in March 1842 when Emerson was lecturing in New York City. Speaking on diverse topics including "The Times," "The Poet," "The Conservative," "The Transcendentalist," "Manners," and "Prospects," Emerson tied the lectures together with his characteristic vision of the individual in full possession of the world around him. It was exactly the message Henry needed to hear, and in response, he dashed off a note of thanks to Emerson:

> I listened to your address this evening, and as my bosom glowed with many a true word that fell from your lips & felt ere long fully assured that before me I beheld a man who in very truth was seeking the realities of things, I said to myself I will try when I go home [to see] how far this man follows reality—how far he loves truth and goodness. For I will write to him that I too in my small degree am coveting to understand the truth which surrounds me and embraces me, am seeking worthily to apprehend—or to be more worthily apprehended of—the love which underlies and vivifies all the seeming barrenness of our most unloving world.[33]

James and Emerson met in person the next day, and they became friends instantly. In Emerson's eyes, Henry was "the best apple on the tree" of New York, a "very intelligent person, . . . independent right minded."[34]

What happened next between Emerson and Henry—or, more rightly, between Emerson and Henry's infant son William—was one of the most wonderfully symbolic moments in American intellectual history. While Emerson was visiting the James home at 5 Washington Place during his time in New York, Henry asked the famous lecturer to give a blessing over the new baby. It must have been difficult for Emerson, who had lost his own young son just a month before. Nevertheless, he granted Henry's wish. America's first great public intellectual was, according to Henry Jr., "proudly and pressingly 'taken upstairs' to admire and give his blessing" to the infant who would come to lead the second generation of American public intellectuals.[35]

Inspired by Emerson's visit, Henry Sr. pledged to take up the role of public intellectual. But there was a problem: Eloquence was tough, and he had not yet found his voice. On one of his first attempts to speak in an Emersonian mode, he managed only to turn listeners away. Lecturing in New York on "the supernatural constitution of morality," he watched his audience fall off quickly after the first lecture. Worse, he received "no tidings of having interested one of the sort (the religious) for whom [the lectures] were wholly designated." He then wrote to Emerson for advice: "Shall I get me a little nook in the country and communicate with my *living* kind, not my talking kind—by life only—a word, may be, of *that* communication, a fit word, once a year? Or shall I follow some commoner method, learn science and bring myself first into men's respect, that thus I may the better speak to them?"[36]

Emerson's reply to the letter is not known, but Henry Sr. took time off from lecturing for a few years. To find his voice, he needed first to work out his own system of thought, particularly the relationship between science and religion.[37] The best place to do so, he figured, was in Europe, where he took his family for two years.[38] Traveling across Europe, the James family spent time with some of the leading intellectual figures of the day, including Thomas Carlyle, John Heraud, John Sterling, and John Stuart Mill. In close quarters with these leaders of Western thought, Henry Sr. eventually found the intellectual spark he needed. Recommitted to following in Emerson's footsteps, he returned to New York City because of what he called "the prospect of . . . preaching & lecturing."[39]

Back in New York, Henry Sr. began in earnest his career as a public intellectual, speaking whenever, wherever, and on whatever he could. On December 16, 1845, he addressed the Young Men's Association for Mutual Improvement of Albany on "What Constitutes the State." On December 11, 1846, he addressed the same group on "A True Education." In the winter of 1847 he lectured to the New York Union of Associationists on "The Religious Grounds of Association." In the summer of 1848 he delivered a presentation on "The Divine Life of Man." On November 1, 1849, he spoke to the Town and Country Club of Boston on the topic of socialism, a lecture he repeated in New York on November 18. In December 1849 he twice lectured on "Morality and the Divine (or Perfect) Life." A year later he delivered his most ambitious lecture series yet, speaking at the Mechanics' Institute and Stuyvesant Institute of New York on topics ranging from democracy and private property to art and ghosts (a topic that would also captivate William James).[40] The sweep of the lecture series attested to Henry Sr.'s comfort in the wide-ranging pursuit of knowledge that defined the culture of eloquence.

Over the years, the relationship between Emerson and the James family blossomed. The James children played with the Emerson children, as William, Henry, Wilkie, Bob, and Alice James vacationed in Concord, and Ellen, Edith, and Edward Emerson spent time with the Jameses. Ralph Waldo was also regularly in the picture. Whenever he was in town to lecture, he stayed with the James family.[41] His visits were so important that the guest bedroom became known as "Mr. Emerson's Room."[42]

Nor was Emerson the only figure of note in the James household. Throughout the 1840s and 1850s, the family came into contact with prominent authors, speakers, essayists, activists, and orators: Henry David Thoreau, Bronson Alcott, Margaret Fuller, Franklin Sanborn, Thomas Wentworth Higginson, Henry Ward Beecher, James Russell Lowell, George Ripley, Horace Greeley, Washington Irving, William Thackeray, Thomas Carlyle, and others. The family was also close to leading political figures. One was Martin Van Buren, a relative (through marriage) and a neighbor when the family lived in Albany.[43] General Winfield Scott, hero of the Mexican War and onetime Whig candidate for president, was another friend.[44] And on one memorable occasion in France, the Jameses relaxed with Senator Charles Sumner, who was recovering from the infamous caning incident on the floor of the U.S. Senate.[45]

For the James children, growing up included a parade of cultural celebrities, a world of ideas, oratory, and public engagement. The intellectual milieus surrounding them were particularly important in the case of young William. These thinkers, speakers, and writers strove tirelessly for eloquence, chasing after ideas that would supposedly better American society. Their time on the lecture circuit, not to mention their work on the printed page, bespoke the power of popular statement. Because of the James family's wealth, social status, and network of associations, William had the opportunity to see how the pursuit of knowledge hinged upon the dynamics of eloquence.

As the years went by, the connection between the James family and the culture of eloquence grew stronger, especially as Henry Sr.'s reputation for insight and rhetorical artistry spread across the country. In fact, Henry Sr. largely succeeded in becoming an Emersonian intellectual—or, better, he succeeded in becoming his own type of intellectual. Though Emerson's work would have a more lasting influence than Henry's, during the 1850s they often stood side by side in public estimation, at least according to Henry's biographer. With "many strong opinions on the topics of the day" and a "ripe, commanding, full-voiced eloquence," Henry's career "as civic rhetor and philosopher . . . reached its zenith."[46]

Whether or not people shared Henry's vision of a new religious order, they often admired his skill with a pen and his eloquence on the podium. After he lectured in Albany in 1853, for example, a writer for the *Albany Evening Atlas* described his presentation as "the most brilliant, finished and witty" the town had seen all year.[47] In an 1857 book on American and European culture, Count Adam Gurowski grouped Henry Sr. with Emerson and George Ripley as the Americans with truly "independent philosophical minds," reserving only for Henry, however, the label of "brilliant rhetorician."[48] Some years later, E. L. Godkin remarked that Henry Sr. "was a writer of extraordinary vigor and picturesqueness, and I suppose there was not in his day a more formidable master of English style."[49] William James himself thought his father's prose possessed "the rich vascular temperament of the old English masters."[50]

By the time William James reached young adulthood, Emerson and Henry Sr. had shown him the prospects of public-intellectual practice in the culture of eloquence. In particular, they had shown him that it was possible to succeed without institutional backing—that is, without the support of a university or a religious order. Emerson and Henry Sr. were freelance intellectuals, and their livelihood depended upon their ability to connect with general audiences. Theirs was the business of using rhetoric to create relationships, to build bridges between themselves, the people they addressed, and the ideas they pursued.

A key question remains, however: Was William James cognizant of the type of intellectual engagement around him? Did he understand what Henry Sr. and Emerson were doing? As an adolescent, James did not record his thoughts about their influence on his life. Nor did he muse about eloquent intellectualism—probably because it was not notable; it simply *was*. Yet as he began to struggle over his own path in life, and as the culture of professionalism started to take hold, James also began to reflect on what his father and Emerson had shown him.

Emerson proved to be particularly important in the years immediately after James completed his scientific studies at Harvard. We will explore his time at Harvard in more detail below, but suffice it to say that when he was there, he learned what academic professionalism meant for the pursuit of knowledge. Then in subsequent years he undertook extensive study of Emerson's work. An important step came when, in the early 1870s, James purchased his own copies of Emerson's books.[51] Although this was not his first time reading Emerson's writings, purchasing his own volumes represented a conscious decision to grapple with the Sage of Concord's legacy.[52]

What James found in Emerson's work, particularly in *Nature*, the first book he purchased, was an exposition of eloquent intellectual conduct. When, for example, Emerson discussed the fusion of the individual and nature as the highest form of existence, he had in mind not just the joining of man and the natural world but also the strengthening of communal bonds—exactly what he tried to do when touring the country on the lecture circuit. "All that is separate from us," Emerson explained, "all which Philosophy distinguishes as the NOT ME, that is, both nature and art, all other men and my own body, must be ranked under the name, NATURE."[53] To the extent that nature encompassed "all other men," Emerson directed his thought to the links between individuals. As he saw it, the task was to enter into a harmonious relationship with God and other people. Being fully oneself meant connecting with nature in the broadest sense of the term. It meant drawing others into one's vision of the divine life.[54]

Not only did James encounter in Emerson's work the ideal of a harmonious community involving the self, others, and God, he also found a vision of how eloquence made the harmonious community possible. "This immediate dependence of language upon nature, this conversion of an outward phenomenon into a type of somewhat in human life," he explained, "never loses its power to affect us. It is this which gives that piquancy to the conversation of a strong-natured farmer or backwoodsman, which all men relish."[55] For Emerson, insight and eloquence were available to all—from the literary genius to the farmer and woodsman. In "The American Scholar," he expanded further upon the role of language in society: "In going down into the secrets of his own mind, [the scholar] has descended into the secrets of all minds. He learns that he who has mastered any law in his private thoughts, is master to that extent of all men whose language he speaks, and of all into whose language his own can be translated."[56] The scholar could be anyone, so long as he or she knew how to speak the language that permeated all minds. By finding this language, one acquired the tools for building a divine community.

For Emerson, the eloquent language of the divine community was embodied by the Poet and the Orator. Exemplars of eloquence, their job was to "complement" their audiences, speaking the language of the soul. If the Poet or Orator could effectively complement his audience, Emerson said, then his audience would "drink his words because he fulfills for them their own nature."[57] Through eloquence, speakers and audiences entered into a reciprocal relationship where each affected the other, and both grew as a result. In "Literary Ethics," Emerson explained this dynamic in terms of a civic debate:

> Observe the phenomenon of extempore debate. A man of cultivated mind, but reserved habits, sitting silent, admires the miracle of free, impassioned, picturesque speech, in the man addressing an assembly—a state of being and power how unlike his own! Presently his own emotion rises to his lips, and overflows in speech. He must also rise and say somewhat. Once embarked, once having overcome the novelty of the situation, he finds it just as easy and natural to speak—to speak with thoughts, with pictures, with rhythmical balance of sentences—as it was to sit silent; for, it needs not to do, but to suffer; he only adjusts himself to the free spirit which gladly utters itself through him; and motion is as easy as rest.[58]

Here was a rationale for pursuing the art of popular statement. Intellectual fulfillment, Emerson insisted time and again, emerged from public interactions. At the least, popular statement was essential to the life of the "good scholar," whose job it was to "serve the world as a true and noble man; never forgetting to worship the immortal divinities who whisper to the poet and make him the utterer of melodies that pierce the ear of eternal time." Emerson elaborated: "The man of genius should occupy the whole space between God or pure mind and the multitude of uneducated men. He must draw from the infinite Reason, on one side; and he must penetrate into the heart and sense of the crowd, on the other."[59]

As time went by, Emerson's rationale for pursuing the art of popular statement would become integral to James's own outlook. In fact, years after studying Emerson's work in the 1870s, James described to Henry James Jr. just how much Emerson had shaped his understanding of intellectual duty:

> The reading of the divine Emerson, volume after volume, has done me a lot of good, and, strange to say has thrown a strong practical light on my own path. The incorruptible way in which he followed his own vocation, of seeing such truths as the Universal Soul vouchsafed to him from day to day and month to month, and reporting them in the right literary form, and thereafter kept his limits absolutely, refusing to be entangled with

> irrelevancies however urging and tempting, knowing both his strength and its limits, and clinging unchangeably to the rural environment which he once for all found to be most propitious, seems to me a moral lesson to all men who have any genius, however small, to foster.[60]

It may have taken decades, but James was finally able to understand Emerson's influence on his life. Dedicated to reporting divine truths in "the right literary form"—dedicated to eloquence, in other words—Emerson helped clarify the choices James had made and would continue to make. Emerson's vision, intellectual breadth, and commitment to popular, even universal, speech appeared in retrospect as a guiding star.

But this recognition of Emerson's guidance was still decades away. Back in the late 1860s and early 1870s, James was struggling to find his calling, and for that he turned to his father in addition to Emerson. James made a conscious decision to grapple with Henry Sr.'s publications at the same time he grappled with Emerson's work. He began with *The Secret of Swedenborg*, which Henry Sr. first published in 1869. "I read it," William reported to Henry Jr., "and am very much enlightened as to his ideas and as to his intellectual rank thereby." He then added: "I am going slowly through his other books. I will write you more when I have read more."[61] Although he had much more yet to read, James had come to at least one conclusion about his father's work, a conclusion that signaled his respect for the man despite their differences. "Suffice it," William reported to his brother, "that many points which before were incomprehensible to me because doubtfully fallacious—I now definitely believe to be entirely fallacious—but as this pile accumulates on one side there is left a more and more definite residuum on the other of great & original ideas, so that my respect for him is on the whole increased rather than diminished."[62]

William never specified exactly which ideas he found "great & original," but if he was looking for evidence of how to live an eloquent life, he no doubt found it. Similar to the way Emerson focused on the Orator and the Poet, Henry Sr. focused on the Artist. The Artist was the personification of intellectual eloquence, someone who brought people together through wise speech. The Artist, Henry Sr. explained, "proceeds from within to without," operating as the "embodiment of an idea" and "giving outward form to purely inward conception."[63] The Artist's task was to reveal "nature and society everywhere pregnant with human meaning, everywhere pervaded by a human soul."[64] It was a task that required a powerful grasp of language. To render his or her divine interiority into outward form, Henry Sr. held, the Artist must know the secrets of effective communication, must grasp the "universal unity" that "binds all nature together in the unity of a man"—and he must "give it a perfect expression."[65] For Henry Sr., "perfect expression" was the mechanism by which the Artist joined with others in the realm of the divine.

Studying his father's thoughts about the Artist and the importance of eloquence, James may well have been transported back to July 4, 1861, when he heard his father deliver a Fourth of July oration to the people of Newport, Rhode Island. As the nation began its slow, deadly march through the Civil War, William and the rest of the James family heard Henry Sr. discourse on "The Social Significance of Our Institutions." In the address, he insisted that the Artist had a special duty in times of crisis, for the Artist had the ability to light the way out of the darkness. Connected to a universal divinity, the Artist could use discourse to open people's minds to righteous ways of thinking. As Henry Sr. explained, with as much eloquence as he could muster,

> What is the joy we feel when we see the gifted man, the man of genius, the man of high conventional place of whatever sort, come down to the recognition of the lowliest social obligations—what is it but a testimony that the purest personal worth is then most pure when it denies itself, when it leaps over the privileged interval which separates it from the common life, and comes down to identify itself with the commonest? This sentiment of human unity, of the sole original sacredness of man and the purely derivative sanctity of persons, no matter who they are, *is what we are born to*, and what we must not fail to assert with an emphasis and goodwill which may, if need be, make the world resound.[66]

It was an unabashedly elitist view of the Artist's duty, but Henry Sr. was an elitist through and through. Telling, however, is the fact that his elitism entailed a meditation on intellectual activity and public engagement. With divine insight and a penchant for eloquence, Henry Sr. believed, the Artist could help make society over as God desired.[67]

Reading his father's thoughts on the Artist, James had before him a theory and practice of public intellectualism. Henry Sr., like Emerson, explored intellectual obligations at the same time he tried to live them out. The Artist personified the spirit of public engagement, the wide-ranging vision, the dedication to popular audiences, and the efforts of moral uplift that defined the culture of eloquence. For Henry Sr., being a great thinker meant being a great communicator. One's insights were necessarily a public affair, and the best minds were duty bound to nurture righteousness in others. In such a conception of intellectual effectiveness, vision mattered more than technical precision; eloquence mattered more than the borders of professional enclaves. And wherever the Artist saw a need to enlighten others with a rousing discourse on matters of common concern, he was obligated to do so.

Later in life, James would look back with gratitude on his father's example. Even though he recognized that Henry Sr. would not have Emerson's enduring presence in American culture, he knew his father possessed the type of vision that was much needed in public life. Shortly after Henry Sr.'s death, James opined:

> For me, the humor, the good spirits, the humanity, the faith in the divine, & the sense of his right to have a say about the deepest reasons of the universe, are what will stay with me. . . . Unlike the cool dry, thin-edged men who now abound, he was full of the fumes of the ursprünglich human nature. . . . I hope that rich soil of human nature will not become more rare. I am sure it won't; for if the children of the lettered classes have a thinner blood coursing in their veins, up from unheard-of parents the old generous stream will flow.[68]

James counted himself one of the "children of the lettered classes," and he looked to his father's example to keep his blood thick and his vision clear, especially in the new world of thought.

Why James worried about thin blood and clouded vision had everything to do with the types of thinkers who replaced the intellectuals of the culture of eloquence. As he looked back upon his childhood from the post–Civil War era, the world inhabited by his father and Emerson seemed like a golden age. Eloquence had given way to professionalism, but James hoped that the spirit of eloquence would live on.

Trained in a Culture of Professionalism

The decades surrounding the Civil War involved a remarkable shift in perceptions of how knowledge was and should be produced.[69] The emerging culture of professionalism fundamentally changed the way ideas moved through society, and the close connection between knowledge and eloquence that had defined the pre–Civil War decades was broken. As the nineteenth century marched to a close, explains Burton Bledstein, "the citizen became a client whose obligation was to trust the professional. Legitimate authority now resided in special spaces, . . . and it resided in special words shared only by experts."[70] Thus the "rhetoric of an oratorical culture" was replaced by "the rhetoric of a professional culture of expertise."[71]

The reasons for the shift from eloquence to professionalism were numerous and complicated, but three reasons are especially important for understanding James's intellectual development. First, across America there was a growing belief that "science" represented the future of thought. More than that, science was believed to hold the keys of social progress.[72] Because of electromagnetic induction, the conservation of matter, the laws of thermodynamics, and the relationship between heat and energy—not to mention the telegraph, the railroad, and the camera—the "prestige of positivistic science increased enormously."[73] "Modern empirical scientists taught people not to wonder at natural phenomena," writes David Shi, "but to experiment and reason, to discern and dissect, to classify and compare."[74] Soon, intellectual respectability hinged upon being scientific.

Of course, science itself was undergoing dramatic professionalization at the time. It not only propelled the culture of professionalism but was greatly shaped by processes of specialization.[75] To become modern, science had to juxtapose itself to the kind of intellectual engagement that had defined the culture of eloquence. This was particularly true in the field of psychology—James's field of study—which struggled to emerge as an area of inquiry distinct from philosophy and introspective traditions of the past.[76] Thus while speakers, writers, and thinkers appealed to science, science itself was moving in a shocking array of new directions, making it difficult to know what was involved with claims of scientific authority and insight. The result was a strange mixture of confidence and uncertainty in the pursuit of knowledge.[77]

The second reason for the rise of professionalism in the second half of the nineteenth century involved the influence of German research practices. Many Americans, particularly elite Americans, looked to Europe for indications of the future, often feeling a type of cultural and intellectual envy when they did.[78] Germany seemed to be leading the way forward in the world of thought, and those who could afford a German education paid the price eagerly. In fact, William James was one of the many Americans who traveled to Germany in the 1860s to learn the ways of the German researcher. Aspiring thinkers like James became "enamored of the specialized scholarship, the commitment to speculative research, and, above all, the atmosphere of freedom they had seen" in Germany.[79] What returned to America with these thinkers was a widespread dedication to objectivity, the scientific method, precise terminology, and rigorous research standards. Visionary eloquence did not make the list.

Third, and closely related to the prestige of science and the influence of German scholarship, were fundamental changes in American higher education. During the second half of the nineteenth century, the modern research university effectively supplanted "the quaint 'old-time' college as a dominant institutional model."[80] Just as individual thinkers imported German standards of scholarship to the United States, so too did American universities begin to restructure according to German universities.[81] Administrators worked to modernize, professionalize, and scientize America's leading institutions of higher education. "University leaders adopted the view that science was not primarily a body of knowledge, but a tool for the production of new knowledge. Drawing on this conception of science, they redefined the aims and meaning of educational reform; instead of expanding the breadth of instruction, they sought to make all aspects of university education 'scientific.'"[82] Leading the way in this regard was Harvard and Harvard's trailblazing new president, Charles W. Eliot, who, prior to assuming the presidency, instructed William James on the intricacies of chemistry.[83]

As universities became research institutions, and as university administrators became champions of science and specialized inquiry, the role of the professor changed as well. Earlier in the nineteenth century, a professor was a "master-of-all-disciplines, the traditional polymath who could be relied upon to teach many different subjects and teach them well."[84] Because being learned in the culture of eloquence meant possessing a breadth of knowledge, "the professor who happened to lecture on moral philosophy would be equally qualified to teach mathematics or Greek grammar."[85] But with the German influence and with the rise of science, depth of knowledge took precedence over breadth of knowledge. Scholars now worked to develop "a total coherent system of necessary knowledge within a precise territory."[86] Confident in his area of training but not necessarily confident in others, the new professor was a proud expert. As Daniel Coit Gilman, president of Johns Hopkins University, declared: The best professor is distinguished by a strong devotion to "some particular line of study" and by "the certainty of his eminence in that specialty."[87]

The increasing importance of science, the influence of German research models, and changes in American higher education helped make professionalism the new standard. Many hailed it as necessary for knowledge to progress—and in many ways they were right. But this new model of inquiry did not come without costs. Perhaps the biggest consequence of the rise of professionalism was a waning spirit of public engagement, at least among intellectuals. "Those who sought a more penetrating and rigorous intellectual life," writes Thomas Bender, "rejected and withdrew from the general culture of the city in order to embrace a new model of professionalism. Intellectual purposes were thus clarified and made less complicated."[88] This is not to say that public engagement was absent from the culture of professionalism, but it is to say that scholarly emphasis shifted from civic matters to the pursuit of truth writ large. Contributing to what John Dewey disapprovingly called the "quest for certainty" was more important than participating in the life of the community.[89]

Another consequence of the rise of professionalism involved new criteria for inquiry. Specialization meant expertise in particular areas of knowledge, and soon advanced degrees came to signify intellectual ability. No longer was having an insight enough; one needed academic certification as well. James would later bemoan this part of professional culture as a "Ph.D. Octopus" that had wrapped its tentacles around the university, squeezing the independent spirit out of modern scholarship.[90] Under the new paradigm, scholars were supposed to be objective discoverers of truth, confident in their methodology and dedicated to a well-defined research program.[91] The result was that "Professionals controlled the magic circle of scientific knowledge which only the few, specialized by training and indoctrination, were privileged to enter, but which all in the name of nature's universality were obligated to appreciate."[92]

Still another consequence of the rise of professionalism was the privileging of specialized discourse—precise ways of talking shared by members of a professional enclave but more or less inaccessible to general audiences. With the help of disciplinary jargon, scholars turned to narrower pursuits, and the technical sphere of argumentation assumed a new place of prominence.[93] Public discourse changed as well. "The shared cultural space of early nineteenth-century urban intellectual life" gave way to groups that communicated internally.[94] This led to increasing divergence in the languages of amateurs and professionals, as the "community oriented and popular" discourse of the early nineteenth century was overpowered by the "esoteric and professional" discourse tied to the promises of science.[95]

But perhaps the most striking change to accompany the rise of professionalism had to do with new conceptions of the imagined audience for intellectual discussions. It was no longer necessary for scholars to speak in a way that could edify, educate, and entertain a wide swath of the community. In crafting a text, academics needed to think primarily about members of their enclave, not about filling seats in a lecture hall. Of course, lecture halls and the lyceum circuit persisted throughout the culture of professionalism, but the link between inquiry and the populace was fundamentally altered. True insight was a product of the laboratory, of specialized instruments and technical questions, of meetings among similarly trained experts who could discuss matters precisely. In fact, during the second half of the nineteenth century there was an explosion of professional societies and specialized journals, which promised to make knowledge more exacting, more precise, and more complete.[96] After knowledge was expertly produced, it could be shared with the wider world. But the arrival of professionalism meant that knowledge was first formed and then transmitted. Scholars spoke not as concerned citizens contributing to communal deliberations but as experts who had truths to pass on to the masses.[97]

As specialization, restricted languages, and expertise came to define the world of thought, the lay public that had once been central to the production and movement of knowledge was rendered somewhat passive.[98] The American people became dependent upon expert insights, as they lacked the qualifications and language to question, combat, or challenge specially produced knowledge. Expertise demanded deference on the part of general audiences.[99] Such deference, in turn, fostered uncertainty, frustration, and self-doubt among many Americans. "Symbols of professional authority," explains Bledstein, "reinforced the public's consciousness of its dependence." Many experts played on "the weaknesses of the client, his vulnerability, helplessness, and general anxiety. The client's imagination easily did the rest."[100] In short, professionalism wrested—or appeared to wrest—control of the world of thought from the hands of popular audiences, who, in the culture of eloquence, had been discursive partners with the great orator-thinkers of the day.

For William James, the rise of the culture of professionalism was life changing. Primarily, professionalism meant that the type of intellectual practice Emerson and Henry Sr. had demonstrated was antiquated. Freelance intellectualism—that is, living the life of the mind without institutional backing, particularly the backing of a university—became exceedingly difficult. Some of James's friends would learn this the hard way. John Fiske, Francis Ellingwood Abbot, and Charles Sanders Peirce lacked ongoing institutional support and, as a result, faced tremendous professional challenges, though they displayed remarkable philosophical talents.[101]

James understood the changes under way, at least when it came to the primacy of science in modern inquiry. As a young man searching for his calling, he weighed the options before him, including the life of a painter, and eventually settled on the study of science at Harvard—even as the nation was plunged into the Civil War.[102] Of course, it would have made sense for the teenage James to join the Union Army. He was the eldest son of the family, many of his friends and relatives fought in the war, and he always dreamed of being heroic. But James never took up arms—a decision he would regret for most of his life. Part of the reason for not serving was because his body and temperament were ill-suited for battle. But there was also the issue of his father, who intervened swiftly after James had expressed interest in the army. Essentially, Henry Sr. prohibited both William and Henry Jr. from fighting, even while the two youngest sons would serve.[103] William eventually agreed not to put on a uniform, but only if Henry Sr. allowed him to pursue science at Harvard.[104] In the fall of 1861, then, William began his studies.[105]

First at the Lawrence Scientific School, then at Harvard Medical School, James immersed himself in scientific professionalism during the 1860s. On top of his Harvard education, he traveled to Germany to study physiological psychology, embracing, as many of his generation did, a specialized, rigorous, prestigious German education. But, for the current purposes, the most significant aspect of James's training was what he learned about the pursuit of scientific knowledge during his time at Harvard. Five men were particularly influential in shaping James's view of professional inquiry. Benjamin Peirce was a specialist extraordinaire. Though he tried to bring his thought to bear on common problems, he remained trapped in a narrow discursive universe. In contrast, Oliver Wendell Holmes Sr. made a name for himself as both a man of science and a communicator to the world. Then there were the combatants over Darwinism: Asa Gray, Jeffries Wyman, and Louis Agassiz. Locked in a battle over the truth of evolution, they modeled for James the kind of scientific combat he would later experience, especially when he worked in the 1890s to defend psychical research.[106] Together, Peirce, Gray, Wyman, Agassiz, and Holmes presented James with different ways of navigating the shift from eloquence to professionalism. They were his resources for surviving—and, indeed, thriving—in an era of acute scientism.

Benjamin Peirce, Perkins Professor of Astronomy and Mathematics at Harvard for most of his career, was known across the country as a brilliant mathematician. Harvard President A. Lawrence Lowell once remarked that Peirce had "the most massive intellect" he had ever encountered.[107] Peirce's colleague W. E. Byerly similarly recalled that looking at him was like "looking upon a real live genius, who had a touch of the prophet in his make-up."[108] Members of Phi Beta Kappa remembered him as "the largest natural genius . . . God has given to Harvard in our day."[109]

If James needed a figure to contrast with his father and Emerson, Peirce was it. His style of scholarship signaled the chasm between intellectual discourse in the culture of professionalism and intellectual discourse in the culture of eloquence. Though Peirce would often lecture publicly, he assumed the persona of the expert who stood apart from his audience. At the Lowell Institute, the Concord Summer School of Philosophy and Literature, the Peabody Institute, and Harvard University, he did little to adapt his lectures for his listeners and the occasion. His interest was first and foremost in crafting specialized insights; audience concerns were tangential. For one woman who listened to Peirce lecture at Boston's Lowell Institute, the mathematician was both intriguing and baffling. "I could not understand much that he said," the woman remarked, "but it was *splendid*. The only thing I now remember in the whole lecture is this—'Incline the mind to an angle of 45 degrees, and periodicity becomes non-periodicity and the ideal becomes real.'"[110]

Peirce's students found him similarly baffling and equally intriguing. His greatness, they believed, stemmed from his incomprehensibility. One of Peirce's most notable students, Franklin Sanborn, once remarked that "Few men could suggest more while saying so little, or stimulate so much while communicating next to nothing that was tangible and comprehensible."[111] Another student, George Flagg, recalled an occasion when Peirce went quickly through a lecture, turned to the class and asked: "Do you follow me?" After no one answered, he added: "I'm not surprised. I know of only three persons who could."[112] William James, like Sanborn and Flagg, listened to Peirce's impenetrable soliloquies.[113] Though he did not record his thoughts on Peirce's lectures, he did record the sense of greatness he felt in Peirce's presence and in the presence of Peirce's son Charles Sanders Peirce.[114] These men, James could see, were men of science, men whom he could emulate if he wanted to follow the path of the expert.

James would end up rejecting Peirce's style of scholarship. The unflinching dedication to specialized knowledge would prove too confining for his wide-ranging, popularly oriented aspirations. In fact, as the years went by, James would often argue with Charles Sanders Peirce about the importance of speaking a language that nonspecialists could understand. Like his father, Charles insisted that advancements in knowledge demanded analytical forms available only to a select few. In response, James insisted that knowledge would never advance if analytical forms excluded the American people from conversations.[115] It was an extended argument that harkened back to Benjamin Peirce, one of the first men to show James the commitments—and many of the problems—of academic professionalism.

When it came to influential scientists at Harvard during James's time there, Peirce was one of many. More important in terms of James's development were the three Darwin combatants who essentially "split the school": Asa Gray, Jeffries Wyman, and Louis Agassiz.[116] Darwin's *On the Origin of Species* had appeared in 1859, two years before James enrolled at Harvard. A national debate erupted immediately after the book went on sale, with virtually all quadrants of society arguing over the validity, meaning, and future of evolutionary theory.[117] At Harvard, the Darwin debates were perhaps more intense than at any other American university. Asa Gray was an early supporter of evolution who did his best to see that Darwin's work had a fair hearing in America. Jeffries Wyman was a supporter of Darwin but often played the role of level-headed mediator when disputes became intense. Louis Agassiz, perhaps the most influential scientist in America during the middle part of the nineteenth century, abhorred Darwinism and did all he could to oppose it. So completely did Agassiz despise Darwin and his ilk that Agassiz challenged Gray to a duel, though the challenge never came to pistols.[118]

James was close to Gray, Wyman, and Agassiz, even though they presented him with very different models of scientific inquiry. In their fight, James was able to see one of the central problems of modern science in the culture of professionalism, a problem he would return to repeatedly in his career. Both evolution and antievolution purported to be "true science," but in a world where the truth was supposedly impersonal and singular, evident to anyone properly trained in how to grasp it, there was no room for multiple, incommensurate approaches to knowledge.[119] Because science purported to be precise, verifiable, and virtually unquestionable, the fact that Gray and Agassiz clung to different paradigms threatened the character of science itself. The possibility of different truths made knowledge seem less than ultimate, and those who held to their truths too tightly had no choice but to battle.

Gray, one of the most respected botanists of the nineteenth century, joined the Harvard faculty in 1842 to teach, to direct the botanical garden, and to maintain various plant collections. Over the years, he built a formidable reputation for insightful research and voluminous writing. Some of his favorite venues for discussing modern science were the nation's popular periodicals, including the *American Journal of Science and Arts*, the *Atlantic Monthly*, and, later, the *Nation*. When Darwin's book appeared, Gray was a natural choice to review it. In addition to being known as a scientific leader, he had important personal connections with Darwin. Darwin thought Gray the foremost American botanist.[120] He also believed that "No other person understands me so thoroughly as Asa Gray. If ever I doubt what I mean myself, I think I shall ask him!"[121] As part of Darwin's inner circle, Gray received an outline of *Origin* in 1856, three years before the book was published.

Gray reviewed Darwin's book for the *American Journal of Science* in March 1860.[122] Like most of his scholarship, the review was long and painstaking, spanning thirty-two pages. But the length was an important part of the review's character, for it indicated that evolutionary theory required extensive space to explicate properly. It also allowed Gray to stress the intricacy of Darwin's research and how such research was not heretical. Pleading with readers to receive natural selection with an open mind, Gray described Darwin's project as "strictly scientific," which meant that the "endeavor, whether successful or futile, must be regarded as a legitimate attempt to extend the domain of natural or physical science."[123] The nature of the research, he continued, was not "particularly exposed to the charge of the atheism of fortuity; since it undertakes to assign real causes for harmonious systematic results."[124] According to Gray, it was even possible that Darwin regarded "the whole system of nature as one which had received at its first formation the impress of the will of its Author, foreseeing the varied yet necessary laws of its action throughout the whole of its existence, ordaining when and how each particular of the stupendous plan should be realized in effect, and—with Him to whom to will is to do—in ordaining doing it."[125] Gray concluded by reminding readers that Darwin's work was "a scientific one, rigidly restricted to its direct object; and by its science it must stand or fall."[126]

Gray was making an argument about evolutionary research that James would make repeatedly in the coming years. The argument represented an important connection between the two men, revealing how similarly they handled the transition from old patterns of knowledge to new ones. Both saw Darwin's work as rigorous and scientific but ultimately not fatal to traditional religious perspectives. Darwinism was compatible with religious life, a life that both Gray and James considered foundational. Gray himself was a profoundly religious man, a devout Presbyterian from birth.[127] And James, while not a member of any particular Christian denomination, regularly attended chapel services at Harvard, even though such attendance was not required. Throughout his life, James would affirm the importance of religious belief, and would do so while also affirming the value of Darwin's work. For both James and Gray, then, there was no conflict with religious and scientific commitments. More importantly, both realized that affirming the compatibility of science and religion provided a foray into discussions with the American people. If the theory of evolution, one of the most important scientific advancements in human history, was to receive a fair hearing in America, the nation needed to understand how it did not replace older systems of knowledge but rather supplemented them. "An inevitable and legitimate hypothesis is on trial," Gray wrote, "an hypothesis thus far not untenable—a trial just now very useful to science, and, we conclude, not harmful to religion, unless injudicious assailants temporarily make it so."[128] In time, James would pick up the argument exactly where Gray had left it, connecting with the American people by positioning Darwin's work as a crucial mediation between old and new systems of thought.[129]

While Gray was the most prominent defender of Darwin at the Lawrence Scientific School, Jeffries Wyman also played an important role.[130] In 1847, Wyman joined Harvard to teach at the medical school and the Lawrence school, focusing on anatomy and zoology. He soon thrived, especially when it came to raising funds to build the impressive Museum of Comparative Anatomy.[131] Although not the public figure that Gray was, Wyman was considered a man of impeccable character in Boston's intellectual community—a "preceptor, a role model, . . . a smoother of animosities, and an institution builder."[132] Known as a friend to all and a foe to none, Wyman impressed both Gray and Agassiz. Gray thought Wyman "the ablest anatomist this country has yet produced"[133] and "one of the best lecturers I ever heard."[134] Agassiz welcomed Wyman's assistance in running the Museum of Comparative Zoology. Wyman even managed to sit alongside men like Emerson, Henry James Sr., Oliver Wendell Holmes Sr., and Agassiz at the prestigious Saturday Club, a prominent group of New England thinkers who gathered weekly to dine and to discuss big ideas.[135]

James was closer to Wyman than to Gray. After initially concentrating on chemistry at the Lawrence school, James switched his emphasis to comparative anatomy and physiology under Wyman's direction.[136] In 1863 he began working for Wyman at the Museum of Comparative Anatomy. With "filial feeling towards Wyman," James toiled day and night "in a vast museum, at a table all alone, surrounded by skeletons of mastodons, crocodiles, and the like, with the walls hung about with monsters and horrors enough to freeze the blood."[137] At the museum, James became a steward of professional precision, at least when it came to cataloging specimens.[138]

Like Gray, Wyman taught James about Darwin in the classroom and at the museum. Also like Gray, he imparted to James a defense of evolution that would appear later in James's career. For Wyman, evolution was a matter of good science, but more than that, it was a matter of open-minded inquiry. Darwin's ideas deserved a fair hearing because they were new and intriguing. Even if they threatened religious orthodoxy—and Wyman insisted they did not—they needed to be explored and taken seriously. In the end, he believed, the principles and methods of science would sort out the truth of evolution, but only if scientists worked to ensure that it had a fair hearing.[139] Wyman's argument was one James took to heart, reproducing it in a number of book reviews written during the 1860s and 1870s.[140] Moreover, after Wyman's death in 1874, James published an unsigned note in the *Harvard Advocate* highlighting Wyman's spirit of open-minded inquiry: "The quality which everyone first thinks of in him is his extraordinary modesty, of which his unfailing geniality and serviceableness, his readiness to confer with and listen to younger men—how often did his unmagisterial manner lead them unaware into taking dogmatic liberties, which soon resulted in ignominious collapse before his quiet wisdom!—were kindred manifestations."[141] Open-minded inquiry and the collapse of dogmatism would become central to James's work as well.

If James's time at Harvard had been limited to Gray and Wyman, his life may have turned out differently. But before James could earn his scientific credentials, he had to go through Louis Agassiz. James's relationship with Agassiz was turbulent. After an initial feeling of reverence for the great naturalist, he grew frustrated with Agassiz's antievolution tirades. Yet on the whole he respected Agassiz, and much of his respect had to do with the fact that Agassiz was a master of intellectual combat—something James would have to learn later in his career.

Born in Switzerland and educated in Germany, Louis Agassiz came to the United States in 1846 to explore its natural history; he ended up staying because he fell in love with the country and with the country's love for him.[142] Agassiz was already a scholarly force when he came to America, and his activities around the nation only made him more of one. After spearheading Harvard's push to become a world-class scientific institution, he built an immense museum of zoology and natural history, persuading the nation's wealthy citizens to fund his insatiable hunger for specimen collecting. His talent for fund-raising and institution building greatly contributed to Harvard's growing reputation. So influential was he that before the Darwin debates, science at Harvard was inseparable from his name.

Agassiz stood out from many scholars at the time because of the depth of his knowledge and his proficiency as a lecturer. He knew how to make science an entertaining affair, and as soon as he arrived in America, he assumed a prominent place on the lecture circuit. "Agassiz had all Americans as his students," writes biographer Edward Lurie, and because of his charm, wit, and insight, Americans followed him as their scientific oracle.[143] His lectures were conduits of information for the populace, and to hear him lecture "was to watch a master performance."[144]

On the lecture circuit, in the classroom, and in his writings, Agassiz presented science and religion as inseparable—at least when it came to pre-Darwinian science—and he did so with a zeal and certainty that set him apart from his colleagues. Because of his reputation, many Americans turned to him for guidance on how to think about evolution. Initially, Agassiz dismissed *Origin* as scientific nonsense. Interest in evolution, he believed, would soon pass. But when it did not, he knew he had to act.

In 1861 Agassiz took his case against Darwin to the Lowell Institute in Boston, one of the most prestigious lecture venues in America. Through careful reasoning and detailed evidence, he tried to show that naturalists who accepted evolution were "chasing a phantom, in their search after some material gradation among created beings, by which the whole Animal Kingdom may have been derived by successive development from a single germ, or from a few germs." Material gradation, Agassiz believed, was inconsistent with God's creative power. Every species on Earth was created as it existed in 1861, and the attempt to prove otherwise was nothing but a slap to God's face. Darwin's theory, he insisted, was "contradicted by the intellectual grandeur of the universe; the resources of the Deity cannot be so meagre, that, in order to create a human being endowed with reason, he must change a monkey into a man."[145]

In the audience listening to Agassiz was William James.[146] Along with the other audience members, James sat rapt as Agassiz painted a picture of the natural world as "one great conception and the work of one Mind."[147] Though James did not record his reaction to Agassiz's antievolutionism, he did tell his family about Agassiz's ability to connect with listeners. "He is evidently a great favorite with his audience and feels so himself. But he is an admirable, earnest lecturer, clear as day and his accent is most fascinating."[148] To James, Agassiz perfectly illustrated how one could make science an entertaining affair. And the more he reflected on Agassiz's lectures, the more he thought he would like to study under the great naturalist. Working "with Agassiz 4 or 5 years" would earn him a comfortable position at a university.[149]

Despite his initial excitement about Agassiz, James's enthusiasm soon cooled. The reasons are not fully clear, but James was not the only student at the time who became skeptical of Agassiz and his instruction.[150] Some even started a club called the "Society for the Protection of American Students from Foreign Professors."[151] As James grew closer to Gray and Wyman, Agassiz's unflinching hostility to Darwinism likely seemed less than compelling.

In 1865, however, a once-in-a-lifetime opportunity brought James back to Agassiz. Determined to put the Darwin controversy to rest, Agassiz organized a yearlong trip to Brazil to gather "the facts" against evolution. He hoped to muster all his expertise as a specimen collector to secure the victory of his religiously grounded naturalism. Funded by Nathaniel Thayer, one of Boston's wealthiest businessmen, the Thayer Expedition, as it was known, sailed from Boston on April 1, 1865. It would not return until August 6, 1866.[152]

For a variety of reasons—the opportunity to travel, the opportunity to get away from home, the chance to participate in serious scientific fieldwork—James signed up for the Thayer Expedition. Along with almost a dozen other students connected with the Lawrence Scientific School and the Museum of Comparative Zoology, he became one of Agassiz's foot soldiers in the war against Darwin. Agassiz lectured aboard the ship to Brazil on a daily basis, instructing his army on the fixity of the species and what they would find in the distant, exotic country.[153] Also traveling on the ship was Bishop Alonzo Potter, an influential Episcopal clergyman from Philadelphia who preached on the significance of Agassiz's mission. As James recalled it, Potter instructed him and his fellow travelers "to imitate the simple child like devotion to truth of our great leader. We must give up our pet theories of transmutation, spontaneous generation &c, and seek in nature what God has put there rather than try to put there some system wh. our imagination has devised." James may have rolled his eyes at Potter's sermon, but he did not fail to notice its effect on Agassiz: "The good old Prof. was melted to tears, and wepped [*sic*] profusely."[154]

Once the expedition reached Brazil, the work of proving Darwin wrong got under way. Being in such close quarters and experiencing the old man's zeal on a daily basis, James soon remembered why he had grown apart from Agassiz in the first place. As he explained to Henry Jr., Agassiz was "doubtless a man of some wonderful mental faculties, but such a politician & so self-seeking & illiberal to others that it sadly diminishes one's respect for him."[155] In the grand parlors of Agassiz's brain, there was no room for different interpretations of the world. If science were ultimate, one system of thought had to reign supreme. Later in his career, James would identify the lack of pluralism as the biggest problem with modern science, and he would attack his colleagues for not giving other systems of thought a fair chance.[156] In 1865, Agassiz embodied the need for pluralism in the culture of professionalism.

As the months went by in Brazil, however, James learned to overlook, at least for the time being, Agassiz's self-certainty. "No one sees farther into a generalisation" than Agassiz, James reported to Henry Sr., "and you have a greater feeling of weight & solidity about the movement of Agassiz's mind, owing to the continual presence of his great background of special facts, than about the mind of any other man I know." Having a grand collection of special facts was particularly important for the modern scientist, as a command of hard evidence paved the way for success. "Now that I am becoming more intimate with [Agassiz] & can talk more freely to him," James continued to his father, "I delight to be with him. I only saw his defects at first, but now his wonderful qualities throw them quite in the background. I am convinced that he is the man to do me good."[157]

The Thayer Expedition proved to be a critical time in James's life. Even though he would refer to Agassiz in 1868 as a "scoundrel" for his anti-Darwin views,[158] he learned from Agassiz crucial lessons of how to conduct oneself in public debate. In fact, Agassiz represented an important link between eloquence and professionalism. He was a widely respected scientist who knew how to make science meaningful for general audiences. His was an eloquent intellectual vision, and James made sure to explain as much in an 1896 remembrance. One day, he prophesied, members of the new generation, who were "enriched with the spoils of all our analytic investigations," will truly appreciate Agassiz's "higher and simpler way of looking at Nature. Meanwhile, as we look back upon Agassiz, there floats up a breath as of life's morning, that makes the world seem young and fresh once more."[159] Throughout his career, James would prove to have a soft spot for people like Agassiz, who possessed the same kind of prophetic vision as Emerson and Henry Sr.

Agassiz, Wyman, Gray, and Peirce all made their mark on James in one way or another. But if there was one figure at Harvard who demonstrated the intellectual style that James would later adopt, it was Oliver Wendell Holmes Sr. More than Agassiz, Holmes straddled the divide between eloquence and professionalism in a way that foreshadowed James's own work. Though James never stated that he modeled himself specifically on Holmes, the parallels between the two are striking. Both Holmes and James were medical doctors, and both were influential parts of the nineteenth century's scientific establishment. Yet both used their understanding of modern science to connect with general audiences. They were as successful in the popular lecture hall as they were in scholarly venues, and they both liked the former more than the latter. Above all, Holmes and James were strongly committed to drawing the American people into intellectual conversations, especially when it came to science.

Holmes was a creature of the first half of the nineteenth century, distinguishing himself as a poet, humorist, essayist, and lecturer before distinguishing himself as a scientist. He blended insight and entertainment into a seamless whole, playing "all the roles" and speaking "all the languages, to try to see all the sides" of modern life. Combining "the stances of grave scientist and light humorist, Sage and Jester, traditionalist and progressive, Voice of Reason and confirmed ironist"—the same stances James would assume—Holmes maintained a consistent presence on the public stage.[160] Throughout the 1840s and 1850s, he delivered dozens of lectures a year, earning a reputation for eloquence, wit, and brilliance. With careful preparation and nuanced delivery, he gave "his audiences the comforting illusion that they had received instruction in the midst of their laughter."[161] To those who assembled to hear him, it was clear that Holmes was "having a good time talking."[162]

"A national character, even a national institution," Holmes was known as a man of letters as much as a popular lecturer.[163] He published some of the most celebrated essay collections in the mid-nineteenth century, including *The Autocrat of the Breakfast-Table* (1858), *The Professor at the Breakfast-Table* (1859), and *The Poet at the Breakfast-Table* (1872). "His literary armory," Edward Emerson recalled, "was full of shining weapons wrought by him from physiological and even pathological material."[164] Because of his string of literary successes, he kept company with America's other literary giants, including Emerson, Hawthorne, Longfellow, Whittier, Lowell, Bryant, and Henry James Sr., all of whom respected him for his delightful discourses and engaging conversation.[165] Like most notable writers in New England, Holmes was a fixture of the Saturday Club.

But Holmes had something most literary giants of the nineteenth century did not have—training in modern science. Indeed, what helped him extend his influence, especially as professionalism took hold, was his scientific ethos. At Harvard, Holmes practically embodied the study of medicine, working years ahead of the medical establishment. He spoke out against doctors who prescribed too many drugs to their patients; he advanced microscopic research by suggesting that scientists filter light directly into the instrument; he advocated hand-washing among physicians long before the conservative medical community was ready to acknowledge the need; and he argued that doctors who failed to sanitize themselves between patients were responsible for passing along germs and illness. He also coined the term "anesthesia," proposing it in a letter to Dr. W. T. G. Morton, the man who invented the practice.[166] As Edward Otis wrote in 1909, Holmes was "the Gamaliels of medicine at the Mecca of medical knowledge of his day."[167]

Harvard students relished their time with Holmes. Many waited eagerly to attend his lectures, lining up outside the room well before class started. As soon as the doors to the lecture hall opened, "it was as if a dam had burst and a torrent poured down the steep amphitheatre and flooded its seats. Such a sight was seen at no other lecture."[168] One student recalled the scene this way: "We always welcomed Professor Holmes with enthusiastic cheers when he came into the class room, and his lectures were so brimful of witty anecdotes that we sometimes forgot it was a lesson in anatomy we had come to learn."[169] William James echoed the point, telling his brother Henry that Holmes's lectures "tickled me to death by the perfection of style."[170]

James had an opportunity to reflect more extensively on Holmes's importance in 1868. In a book review of recent advancements in physiology and medicine, James pointed to Holmes as the type of thinker who could help modern science progress properly. While discussing a recent lecture by Holmes—a lecture in which "practical good sense vies with perfection of style and brilliancy of illustration"—James also discussed many of the problems professionalism had created in the practice of medicine: "The amount of baggage which a doctor is now expected to carry in his head is growing too great for the unaided brain. The use of the ever-increasing number of *-scopes* and *-graphs* and *-meters* for diagnosis is alone more than any one man is adequate to; and when we think of the facts he must remember besides, to be considered 'scientific,' we grow fairly dizzy." Believing that Holmes understood the way through this problem, James quoted him prominently: "We must not expect too much from 'science' as distinguished from common experience. There are ten thousand experimenters without special apparatus for every one in the laboratory. Accident is the great chemist and toxicologist. Battle is the great vivisector. Hunger has instituted researches on food such as no Liebig, no Academic Commission has ever recorded."[171] The point was simple enough, and James would echo it loudly in subsequent decades:

Common experience remained a great teacher despite—or, rather, because of—the rise of professionalism.

On a personal level, Holmes and James's relationship was strongest when James was finishing his medical studies at Harvard. In 1869, having taken a year off from medical school to study physiological psychology in Germany, James returned to America to complete his degree, even though he knew he would not practice medicine after graduation. James's mentor through the process of completing the degree was Holmes. "My thesis was decent," James reported to his brother Henry as he hurried to put his medical studies behind him, "and I suppose Dr. Holmes will veto my being plucked no matter how bad my examination may be, but the truth is I feel unprepared."[172] When it came time for the oral examination, Holmes did exactly what James predicted. He did not let James pass unfairly, but he did turn the ten-minute defense into a leisurely chat. After James correctly identified an obscure cranial nerve, Holmes concluded: "If you know *that,* you know everything. Now tell me all about your family and the news at home." For the remainder of the defense, they gossiped about family and friends. Years later, after James had earned a national reputation of his own, this anecdote about Holmes gossiping with James during the oral defense would appear in newspapers across the country.[173] It was an amusing link between two of America's intellectual giants.

James remained an admirer of Holmes for the rest of his life, relishing his penchant for popularity and sophistication. In James's eyes, Holmes represented exactly what professional culture needed—someone who could help science progress but, more importantly, could do so with wit, inspiration, and eloquence. When Holmes passed away in 1894, James reflected on his influence, writing a note of condolence to Oliver Wendell Holmes Jr., who was then serving on the Massachusetts Supreme Court. "One of the great big and important memories of my younger days passes with him," James reflected, "and like so much else now becomes a part of history. How much and how little!"[174] It was a fitting remark, for the elder Holmes had been, as Edwin Hoyt has put it, "the last lingering star of what was a constellation of American genius . . . the centripetal force of genius, [whose] life spanned the second great day of American literature."[175]

For decades James would struggle with the relationship between popular statement and academic inquiry, but in Holmes was someone who blended the two, showing that eloquence was still possible in an age of experts. Even though James and Holmes had different intellectual projects—Holmes was a dedicated physician who also wrote poetry and humorous essays, while James quickly moved from the study of medicine to psychology and philosophy—both expended tremendous energy on speaking a language that nonscientists could understand, appreciate, and share. Simply put, both practiced the art of popular statement.

Conclusion

When James completed his medical degree in 1869, he occupied an enviable position. In the midst of radical changes in the world of ideas, he possessed the connections, credentials, education, and tools necessary for success in the post–Civil War era. Benjamin Peirce, Asa Gray, and Jeffries Wyman had shown him the intricacies of modern science. Darwinism would only become more important over the years, and James had learned evolutionary theory and research from one of Darwin's closest allies. More important, James had in Louis Agassiz and Oliver Wendell Holmes Sr. examples of how to develop an eloquent, engaging, and entertaining science.

Yet despite his education, his socioeconomic status, and his intellectual network, James soon entered some of the darkest years of his life. Depressed and anxious, even suicidal, he was haunted by questions about his future. To be sure, it was not unique for someone of James's privileged position to experience depression and anxiety in the post–Civil War years. Dr. George Beard, a prominent physician at the time, even had a name for the condition: neurasthenia. Beard believed that the transformation of American society after the war was leading middle- and upper-class young adults to feel purposeless despite the tremendous opportunities before them.[176] Fortunate offspring of the Civil War generation had plenty of chances to advance themselves, but the stain left by the war and the daunting challenges of the Industrial Revolution made the nation's prospects seem bleak.

The year 1870 was a particularly low point for James. That year he recorded in his diary two "crisis passages," which many scholars have positioned as central to his intellectual development.[177] What bears noting, however, is that these diary entries grew out of the shift from eloquence to professionalism. The first crisis passage, recorded on

February 1, 1870, moved from a feeling of emptiness to an unavoidable moral crux: "Today, I about touched bottom, and perceive plainly that I must face the choice with open eyes: Shall I frankly throw the moral business overboard, as one unsuited to my innate aptitude, or shall I follow it, and it alone, making everything else merely stuff for it?" James concluded that he would "give the latter alternative a fair trial." To get his life back on track and to find the sense of purpose that was eluding him, he would switch his priorities, treating the practical, utilitarian ends of life "as occasions for my moral life to become active."[178] As James surveyed his options, moral clarity and vision seemed absent, so he took it upon himself to fill the void.

On April 30, 1870, still feeling that his moral life had not become active, James recorded another crisis in his diary. As before, he believed that an intellectual reorientation was necessary to move forward:

> I think that yesterday was a crisis in my life. I finished the first part of Renouvier's second *Essais* and see no reason why his definition of free will—the sustaining of a thought *because I choose to* when I might have other thoughts—need be the definition of an illusion. At any rate, I will assume for the present—until next year—that it is no illusion. My first act of free will shall be to believe in free will. For the remainder of the year, I will abstain from the mere speculation and contemplative *Grüblei* in which my nature takes most delight, and voluntarily cultivate the feeling of moral freedom, by reading books favorable to it, as well as by acting.[179]

This crisis passage, like the first one, signaled the intellectual predicament in which James found himself, and it signaled the rhetorical reorientation he thought necessary for his own advancement.[180] A key part of the culture of eloquence had been the cultivation of the moral character of oneself and one's community. Now, after having been immersed in professional science for almost a decade, James felt that moral purpose was fleeting. His response was to yearn for the characteristics that Emerson had praised in the Poet and Orator and that Henry Sr. had celebrated in the Artist. Implicitly at least, James's crisis passages were pledges to live in accord with the ideals of the previous generation.

In subsequent decades, the tensions between eloquence and professionalism would present James with the rhetorical resources needed to practice the art of popular statement. Discovering the contours of this art was not trivial, of course, but because of his upbringing and training, he would be able to fashion novel ways of relating to popular audiences in the late nineteenth and early twentieth centuries. As professionalism encouraged scholars to orient themselves toward specialized forms of inquiry, James would work tirelessly with listeners and readers on common problems. As people felt frustrated with, uncertain about, and displaced by the new world of thought, James would give ordinary Americans a participatory role in answering the biggest questions of the day. And as the pursuit of knowledge seemed increasingly removed from everyday experience, James would dedicate himself to constructing a system of thought centered on the experiences, perceptions, and predicaments of the man and woman of "the street."[181]

To be sure, James was not interested in the complete destruction of academic professionalism—he was, after all, a prominent figure in the professionalization of psychology and philosophy in America. Moreover, he would benefit greatly from being known as the greatest psychologist and philosopher in the country. At the same time, however, he would work to keep alive the visionary, eloquent spirit of the past. Those elements of professional culture that impeded a wide-ranging, pluralistic, participatory, experientially focused world of thought would prove too bothersome for James to ignore. The art of popular statement would be his corrective.

But a fully developed art of popular statement was still a ways off. James first had to find his own place in intellectual culture. And as we shall see in the next chapter, doing so was closely connected to helping the American people understand their relationship to modern science.

CHAPTER TWO

Engaging Science and Society

⌘

The late 1860s and the early 1870s forced William James to confront one of the prickliest truths about the culture of professionalism: Institutional affiliation was practically necessary for aspiring intellectuals. Because specialized training and academic credibility were considered markers of scholarly ability, the backing of an institution—particularly a research institution—was almost essential.[1] So aside from whatever grand ideas of moral purpose and visionary eloquence James may have had, he needed a job. The practice of medicine was out of the question, as the life of a physician had long repelled him.[2] But ever since studying at Harvard, a professorship had seemed appealing. Some sort of teaching position, even a temporary one, would at least give him something to do and would help pay the bills. In a bind, he knew he could rely upon his wealthy family for support. But he could not live off his father's inheritance forever. He needed a steady paycheck as much as he needed a new outlook on life.

In August 1872, James found what he was looking for. He found, as he put it to his sister, "just the thing to work my salvation in every respect."[3] His salvation came in the form of a job offer to teach physiology at Harvard in the spring of 1873. Appropriately enough, the position once belonged to Jeffries Wyman, who had recently decided to relinquish his teaching duties. Although the job would not pay much—$300 for the semester[4]—it would afford James a sense of value and purpose. More importantly, it would allow him to link his name with Harvard University, America's premier scientific institution. As a teacher of physiology, he could become an official part of the scientific establishment—even if he did not yet know how he fit into the establishment. As one of James's biographers has explained, the Harvard appointment placed James "at the forefront of the all-important emerging field of physiology just when physiology and medicine (and even Harvard) were poised for the sudden jump to modernity."[5]

James was partly right when he said that teaching at Harvard would work his salvation. It was, as many scholars have noted, integral to overcoming his neurasthenia.[6] Nevertheless, teaching at Harvard would introduce an array of new issues into his life, forcing him to confront difficult questions that would surround him for decades. Perhaps the most prominent of these questions was what kind of scholar he wanted to be. As a Harvard student, he had encountered various models of intellectual engagement, but now it was time to fashion his own identity. Would he be a preeminent expert? A true believer in Darwinism? An adamant opponent? A man of both literature and science? Something else entirely? How would he relate to other scientists? How would he relate to nonscientists? What kind of language would he speak—a precise technical language, a popularly oriented language, some combination of the two? If he were going to carry on the tradition of public engagement that his father and Emerson had affirmed, how would he, as part of the scientific establishment, connect with the American people?

In the years and decades after the Civil War, both William James and the scientific community writ large faced what scholars of rhetoric have identified as the most basic discursive issue—that of invention.[7] Inventional considerations are a matter of beginning, of finding and creating the ideas, appeals, arguments, and strategies for speaking and writing. Simply put, the task is to figure out what to say. In the culture of professionalism, scientists had to decide what to argue, how to argue, the grounds for knowledge claims, the procedures for arriving at knowledge claims, and a host of related issues. These were the basic rhetorical problems involved with the creation of disciplinary identity and power.[8] Even as people appealed to science as authoritative and definitive, members of the scientific community were experimenting with the symbols, ideas, figures, and discursive relationships that marked science as intellectually superior to other forms of knowledge. What was emerging, then, was a new, increasingly modern rhetoric of scientific inquiry.[9]

A young scientist in a constantly evolving intellectual culture, James faced the same inventional challenges as the rest of the scientific community. What is notable, however, especially given the arc of his career, is how he responded to questions of science, culture, knowledge, eloquence, professionalism, and invention. On the one hand, he responded according to the parameters of his job—teaching students about anatomy, physiology, and psychology, and conducting experiments that followed the norms of scientific research. On the other hand, he attempted to work through the intellectual problems around him by engaging popular audiences. How James began forging relationships with popular audiences and how these relationships influenced the direction of his thought are the subjects of this chapter.

Even before teaching at Harvard, James was a frequent conversant in the nation's intellectual dialogue. Yet none of his early work bore his name. Between 1865 and 1878, the year that his first signed academic essay appeared in print, James published almost fifty anonymous book reviews and notices in such venues as the *North American Review*, the *Atlantic Monthly*, and the *Nation*. The reviews not only kept a small amount of money in his pocket—earning him anywhere between $5 and $50 each[10]—they also allowed him to keep abreast of the latest developments in different scholarly fields, including physiology, anthropology, woman suffrage, philosophy, biography, pathology, botany, metaphysics, and aesthetics. James even reviewed a book on the bones, ligaments, and muscles of the domestic cat.[11] What's more, the publications in which the reviews appeared constituted a forum for thinking about science and society with general audiences. James's position as a reviewer demanded that he grapple with the nexus of scholarly inquiry and public knowledge.[12] Taken together, the book reviews provided him with his first extended opportunity to develop an art of popular statement.

Those who study James's work have largely neglected his book reviews, especially the reviews from early in his career. Most often, scholars point to the publication of his first journal article in 1878 as the time when he emerged as a thinker in his own right.[13] Prior to 1878, we are told, James produced writings that were of "slight importance" compared to the academic essays he began publishing that year.[14] The one scholar who has discussed the significance of the early book reviews is Paul Croce, who sees the texts as evidence of James's efforts to carve out a place between physiology and philosophy.[15] The early reviews, Croce notes, helped James acquire a "public professional voice" regarding the prevailing intellectual issues of the day.[16]

Croce's discussion effectively captures the main ideas with which James wrestled for most of the 1870s, showing how James's scholarly outlook emerged from his early experiments in invention. What remains to be seen, however, is how the book reviews grounded James in a wide-ranging, popularly oriented intellectual culture that demanded he work through the tensions between science and philosophy in the service of general readers. As an anonymous book reviewer for the nation's popular periodicals, James had the opportunity to shape the perceptions of ordinary Americans on some of the biggest issues of the day—the role of science in society, the authority of specialists, the character of public discourse in the age of expertise, and the relationship between professional and lay perspectives. The result of these efforts was a set of rhetorical strategies for addressing the intersection of modern science and public culture.

As we shall see, these rhetorical strategies came in handy sooner rather than later. In 1878, James undertook his first major forays into the world of public lecturing. At Johns Hopkins University and at the Lowell Institute in Boston, he addressed the role of science in society and employed many of the appeals originally developed in his book reviews, working to give his listeners a better sense of their place in a world increasingly dominated by specialization and expert authority. Examining James's book reviews and his 1878 lectures will thus afford an opportunity to understand how he began drawing upon the symbolic resources of the shift from eloquence to professionalism.

Popular Periodicals and the Art of the Book Review

America's popular periodicals—the weekly and monthly magazines, journals, and literary collections that drew a wide readership during the nineteenth century—developed alongside the culture of eloquence. Changes in the marketplace, various technological advances, new methods of distribution, rising literacy rates, and alterations in copyright law helped foster a vibrant print culture during the 1830s, 1840s, and 1850s.[17] In the decades after the Civil War, the prominence and influence of the nation's periodicals continued to increase, offering a variety of publishing opportunities for established and aspiring writers, including William James. Given that specialized publications did not yet dominate the world of ideas—it would take until the 1880s and 1890s for academic and professional journals to transform the intellectual marketplace[18]—the clearest pathway to publication for James and others like him was the "magazine mania" sweeping the country.[19]

The intellectual ideals that guided such periodicals as the *North American Review*, the *Atlantic*, and the *Nation* were largely the same ideals that animated popular lectures. Though different periodicals targeted different segments of the population—some were national in character, others were regional—editors generally believed that they were engaged in the all-important business of educating the populace. Margaret Fuller, for example, drawing on her experience editing *The Dial* and writing for the *New York Tribune*, insisted that "The most important part of our literature, while the work of diffusion is still going on, lies in the journals, which monthly, weekly, daily, send their messages to every corner of this great land, and form, at present, the only efficient instrument for the general education of the people."[20] Because educating widely was the goal, many periodicals set their sights broadly, moving in and out of topics and subjects in order to give readers an all-encompassing view of the changing world. Any given issue of *Harper's Monthly Magazine*, *Graham's American Monthly Magazine*, *Scribner's Monthly*, and a host of other titles might include a piece of serialized fiction, an essay on natural science, a rich description of a far-off land, discussions of pressing social and political matters, as well as poetry, music, and art. Popular periodicals were a sprawling intellectual feast, "marked not just by the slow pacing of many courses, but also by the spirited conversation and debate of the guests."[21]

More than ever before in American history, the marketplace determined the character of literature.[22] And it was a wide marketplace, at least for the time. Increased literacy rates, due in part to the common school movement, meant that the audience for national periodicals was becoming more diverse in terms of age, gender, socioeconomic background, even race.[23] Moreover, as various technological advancements and new methods of distribution resulted in cheaper publications, an increasing number of Americans could obtain the material.[24] Thus writers and editors had to be ever mindful of the language they adopted and the relationships they worked to develop.[25] Their prose had to be artful and engaging—inspirational to Easterners, Midwesterners, Southerners, men and women, young and old, rich and poor. They had to speak to the common concerns of the nation regardless of the particular subject at hand. As periodicals became "the primary means professional writers used to establish their careers and earn the majority of their income," such writers "consciously shaped their work—its style, subject matter, and format—according to the requirements of the magazine market."[26]

The rise of popular periodicals meant changes for readers as well. People of diverse backgrounds were able to keep abreast of—indeed, to participate in—the latest discussions of politics, science, literature, art, music, philosophy, theology, and a host of other topics. Consider the January 1858 issue of the *Atlantic*, a magazine "founded with the cultural mission of guiding the age in literature, politics, science, and the arts."[27] This particular issue included, but was not limited to, an article on architecture in America; an installment of the story "Maya, the Princess"; a poem entitled "Catawba Wine"; a chapter from the serialized novel *Akin by Marriage*; an essay from Oliver Wendell Holmes's collection *The Autocrat of the Breakfast-Table*; an analysis of the rhetoric of President Buchanan; and a discussion of slavery in ancient Rome. Such topical diversity took readers on a grand tour of modern thought and exposed them to the same breadth and eloquence they encountered in the lecture hall. But unlike popular lectures, periodicals allowed for enlightenment and entertainment in the comfort of one's parlor.

While featured articles set much of a periodical's intellectual tone, there was yet another component that gave readers an opportunity to range widely in the world of ideas. Almost every periodical contained a sweeping overview of the latest books published in America and overseas. In fact, a single issue might contain anywhere from six to a dozen in-depth, critical assessments of the latest treatises. The *Atlantic* of January 1858, for example, included reviews of *Contributions to the Natural History of the United States of America*, by Louis Agassiz; *The Physical Geography of the Sea*, by M. F. Maury; *The Spanish Conquest in America, and its Relation to the History of Slavery and to the Government of Colonies*, by Arthur Helps; *Handbook of Railroad Construction for the Use of American Engineers*, by George Vose; *Sermons of the Rev. C. H. Spurgeon; Roumania*, by James O. Noyes; *Une Eté dans le Sahara*, by Eugene Fromentin; as well as a half dozen other books. As these titles indicate, book reviews were just as broad and wide-ranging as the featured articles. And they were often just as intricate and detailed, running anywhere from a couple paragraphs to over a dozen pages.

Because of the intricacy and depth of the reviews, book reviewers had to be as aware of the periodical's readership as those who penned featured articles. This is not to say that a reviewer had to speak to every constituency when considering the contributions of a new book. But it is to say that he or she had to understand the difference between reviewing a book for a general audience and reviewing a book for a specialized audience. A review of a recent work on physiology, for example, could not be written in the language of the physiologist. The reviewer had to take the insights of the text and recast them for a wider public. Consequently, working as a book reviewer required expert-like command of specialized subject matter plus the literary sensitivity of a citizen concerned about the state of public knowledge.

Yet another factor greatly influenced the character of book reviews and the role of the book reviewer: anonymity. The vast majority of reviews in the nineteenth century were unsigned. When readers picked up popular periodicals and turned to a book review, they encountered only the judgment of a given text, not the person issuing the judgment (or at least not the name of that person). Implicitly, then, the identity of the reviewer did not matter; his or her credentials or professional training were left aside. The reviewer might be an established scholar, an aspiring intellectual, or simply a well-read amateur; the audience had no way of knowing. What readers did know was that the editor of the periodical trusted the reviewer enough to publish his or her judgment. Ideas were more important than the critic's identity.

In crafting their assessments, then, book reviewers borrowed the ethos of the periodical in which their review appeared. They spoke as representatives of the publication rather than as independent experts in particular fields. Unnamed voices in a diverse yet intellectually hungry community, they focused on how a given text would influence the discursive relationships that defined the community as a whole. For young or relatively inexperienced reviewers, this was a beneficial position from which to write. Anonymity meant that writers were more or less shielded from reprisal and recrimination; they could communicate with a level of freedom difficult to find elsewhere. Beholden only to the editor and readers of the periodical, reviewers could praise or condemn a book as forthrightly as they wished, so long as they provided sufficient reasons and evidence to bolster their assessments. They were free to experiment with different arguments, to try out different personas and points of view, and to speak with different voices depending on the situation at hand.

Such was the inventionally rich discursive culture James entered when he became a book reviewer. His life as a reviewer came about partly because of competition with his brother Henry James Jr. and partly because of his desire to do something with his education. Henry Jr. began publishing short stories before William could get anything into print. Given the competitive nature of the James family, the younger brother's success only made the older brother more committed to making his mark.[28] William could not sit by while Henry collected the family's literary accolades. But unlike Henry, William was not interested in writing fiction. He was a scientist—at least his diploma said so—which made science the natural point of entry for his writing career. In fact, by writing on science, he could distinguish himself from both Henrys in his life. Henry Sr. was the eminent writer of religious works; Henry Jr. was the up-and-coming novelist. No one in the family had yet conquered modern science.

James, the aspiring critic, was fortunate to know several of the country's most influential editors, including Charles Eliot Norton, editor of the *North American Review*; James Thomas Fields and William Dean Howells, both editors of the *Atlantic Monthly*; and E. L. Godkin, editor of the *Nation*. These men had given Henry Jr. the opportunity to publish short stories, and William hoped they would give him the chance to address the implications of modern science. For the editors, allowing William to publish a book review was a fairly safe course of action. His training at Harvard and in Germany qualified him to discuss science, and the literary caliber of his family made it likely that he could write with care, flair, and nuance. As a result, he was almost perfectly positioned to mediate between popular and professional scientific knowledge.

The Work of Intellectual Criticism

As one looks across the fifty anonymous reviews James published between 1865 and 1878, a number of themes emerge, but for the purpose of understanding his intellectual development, three stand out prominently: evolution, the relationship between "old" and "new" forms of knowledge, and the place of the expert in society. In addressing these topics, James revealed that he had not yet come to firm conclusions about the benefits and drawbacks of the changing intellectual landscape. Indeed, the young James was, as Croce explains, like a sailboat seeking direction, tacking "to one side and then the other as he sought his own direction while mediating the new scientific and traditionally philosophical sides of the field."[29] Yet such tacking back and forth was more than just James seeking his own direction; it was also James helping readers of popular periodicals understand what modern science meant for their lives.

The weightiest issue James tackled in his book reviews was the same issue that had loomed over his time at Harvard: evolution. In his very first book review, which appeared in the *North American Review* in January of 1865, he explored evolution through a critical assessment of Thomas Huxley's *Lectures on the Elements of Comparative Anatomy*.[30] Running eight pages in one of the nation's most respected periodicals, the review was a significant achievement for a twenty-three-year-old college student. James began it by noting Huxley's "vigor and activity," as well as his "vivacity" of mind, but he quickly turned to the significance of Darwin's challenging idea.[31] For those skeptical of evolution, James turned Huxley into a sympathetic character. Huxley, he wrote, was a scientist who possessed a "great faith in the doctrine of Transmutation of Species," but who aimed ultimately to give the doctrine a "fair and respectful hearing."[32] By framing Huxley's perspective as one of "faith" aimed at a "fair" hearing, James made Huxley's work less an issue of scientific certainty than an issue of personal commitment. If transmutation was a matter of faith, there remained the opportunity for honest disagreement and open debate. In other words, evolution was not a threat but an intriguing idea to consider further.

Yet James also wanted to show readers of the *North American Review* that Darwin's ideas represented a fruitful path for scientific advancement, notwithstanding the arguments of evolution's detractors. When Darwin's theory was "being trampled under foot," James wrote, science itself was threatened. But it was to evolution's credit that the idea persisted, for every time it was "buried in one form," it reappeared in another, thus showing itself to be "more robust and vivacious than before." Nowadays, in fact, "we find that such naturalists as Asa Gray, Lyell, Owen,

Schleiden, Vogt, von Baer, Kölliker . . . [are] coming round, one by one, to espouse it." Because evolution was being endorsed by such prominent scientists, James concluded, the American people should begin contemplating "the possibility of our ape descent now and then." Once we accustom ourselves to the thought, "the dire prospect" of evolution will "appear shorn of some of its novel horrors, and our humanity appear no less worthy than it was before."[33]

Reviewing Huxley's book gave James a chance to do what both Asa Gray and Jeffries Wyman, two of his biggest influences at Harvard, were also trying to do—namely, to give evolutionary theory an ideological home in American public culture. Similar to Gray and Wyman, James wanted to strip Darwinism of its threatening visage and to frame it as an intellectual possibility that should be given a fair hearing. As a matter of "faith," as something to which we should accustom "our imaginations," Darwinism was simply part of the nation's ongoing conversation. It was not what extremists on both sides of the debate insisted—that is, it was not the new truth that Huxley said it was, nor was it the atheistic threat to religion that Darwin's opponents said it was. Overall, the strategy signaled James's sensitivity to the general audience for whom he wrote. If the American people were to give evolution a fair hearing, it needed to occupy a middle ground where reasonable people could gather and contemplate Darwin's big idea. They could hold onto their traditional views of human nature—for humanity was "no less worthy than it was before"—and still bring Darwinism into the discussion.

Also noteworthy is the fact that James's review of Huxley's book appeared in 1865—the same year James traveled with Agassiz to Brazil on the Thayer Expedition.[34] In a sense, James's activities that year illustrated the type of outlook he hoped the American people would adopt. On the one hand, he carefully promoted evolutionary theory in his book review. On the other hand, he worked for Agassiz to collect "the facts" that might prove Darwin wrong. Such approaches may stand in tension, yet they may also represent the kind of critical pluralism James advocated throughout his career. By considering evolution from very different perspectives, James was better able to assess the situation as a whole. More importantly, he was better equipped to speak about evolution's role in American society to supporters and detractors of Darwin's work.

In several other reviews during the 1860s and 1870s, James continued to stress open-mindedness when it came to evolutionary research—a strategy that indicated his respect for the nation's concern over Darwinism and his dedication to making evolution a part of public debate. For those who questioned Darwin's research, James framed evolution as a possibility instead of a certainty, thereby making it something his readers did not have to accept but should consider critically. Even if the American people did not become vehement supporters of evolution, he thought, they should at least understand its value in raising awareness about science and in strengthening the nation's discourse. In a review of Darwin's *The Variation of Animals and Plants under Domestication*, for example, he wrote that evolution's value came in "setting naturalists to work, and sharpening their eyes for new facts and relations. The present book harrows and refreshes, as it were, the whole field of which it treats."[35] Elsewhere, James acknowledged the "startling discoveries that have placed beyond a doubt the fact that man existed at an age remoter than the greyest antiquity which tradition records," but he made a special point to note that the real value of evolutionary research lay in its ability to energize public culture: "The applications which have been made of Darwin's hypothesis to man have been of a nature to arouse the interest of every one, both by reason of the natural wonder and pleasure we all have in contemplating the dim and mysterious."[36] In another review, James stated that Darwin properly turned public attention to the health of society, for "the slow education of the race" was the path to a better future.[37] In yet another review, this one on recent works on "mental hygiene," he insisted that "Darwinism has begun to awaken people's consciences about the responsibilities of breeding in the human race; and we fancy that, before long, nervous brides and bridegrooms without jaws or shoulders will be rarer to meet than they unhappily are now."[38] From the perspective of James's reviews, Darwinism would not yield any firm conclusions about God and spiritual reality, but it could and should draw people further into discussions about human development, science and faith, and the wonders of the natural world.

Perhaps above all, James's handling of evolutionary theory demonstrated his understanding of the art of audience adaptation that the nation's popular periodicals demanded. Entering the carnivalesque intellectual forum of the *Nation*, the *Atlantic Monthly*, and the *North American Review*, James viewed the Darwin debates through the eyes of his readers—or at least through the eyes of the "average American" he envisioned and constructed in his reviews.[39] He knew that many Americans followed Agassiz's lead in seeing evolution as a threat to traditional beliefs. He also knew that evolution was one of the most important scientific advancements in human history. To navigate these tensions, he ultimately argued that individuals did not have to relinquish their traditional beliefs just because evolution had arrived on the scene. "Questions as to the fundamental elements of existence, the fundamental grounds for belief, and the fundamental reasons for action and endurance," James wrote in a review of Herbert Spencer's *The Data of Ethics*, "remain to be discussed as subtly after as before we learned that each phenomenon was evolved and had a peculiar history of its own."[40] Such an argument gave the American people the opportunity to be both conservative and critically engaged when approaching evolutionary theory and research. In turn, it gave evolution the chance of a respectful hearing in society.

James's assessment of Spencer's book concerned not only evolution but also the second major theme of his reviews—namely, the relationship between "old" and "new" approaches to knowledge. While Darwinism was the most controversial scientific subject of the day, it was inexorably linked to questions of professionalism and professionalism's impact on public culture. What did specialization mean for the pursuit of knowledge? Who was qualified to contribute to the development of science? What, if anything, did the deductive systems of the past have to offer the inductive systems of the present? How did the new and evolving "spaces of knowledge" alter the rules, values, and norms of modern intellectual culture?[41] Part of James's concern with "old" and "new" was no doubt due to his own vocational search, which was taking place at the same time that he was publishing many of his early reviews. But he also understood the anxiety among many academics and nonacademics over what was happening in contemporary scholarship. Accordingly, he took it upon himself to discuss with his readers the consequences of professionalism.

For example, to those who feared that new forms of inquiry would completely replace old ones, rendering more traditional perspectives inoperative and leaving behind insights of the past, James emphasized common ground between the old and the new. "Moralists need not be anxious," he wrote in an 1874 review of Henry Maudsley's *Responsibility in Mental Disease*, "when the most advanced positivism comes to practical conclusions that differ so little from those of the 'metaphysically' minded Marcus Aurelius."[42] If positivism were compatible with centuries-old philosophy, then a variety of individuals could work together on problems that transcended specific schools of thought. Both philosophers and scientists were relevant in the post–Civil War era. James made a similar point in another review. Confronting those scientists who seemed to think that knowledge was produced only through the scientific method, he insisted that it was wrong to "bar our personal bias, or the subjective method, from the construction of the ethical standard of right, however fatalistic we may be. For if *what is right* means *what succeeds*, however fatally doomed to succeed that thing may be, it yet succeeds through the determinate acts of determinate individuals; and until it has been revealed what *shall* succeed, we are all free to 'go in' for our preferences and try to make them right by making them victorious."[43] Likewise, he concluded a review of a book on the mediation of science and religion by insisting that "In the physical realm the 'subjective method' of finding truth may be the root of all evil. But the affirmation that this physical world has *also* a moral meaning and a moral plan is one that no argument drawn from purely physical truth can either establish or impugn." Because physical experimentation and personal aspirations have a place in inquiry, James indicated, it is possible, even necessary, to follow science as well as the "inward, free, or moral assent, or rather consent, in which the subjective method consists."[44]

In the process of addressing the relationship between the old and the new, James crafted for himself a compelling intellectual persona. He wrote as someone thoroughly familiar with modern science but also as someone committed to helping general audiences understand what science meant for their lives. He was thus an intellectual mediator, albeit an anonymous one, whose expertise facilitated rather than impeded his ability to engage public culture. James's expert understanding of scientific professionalism did not demand deference on the part of his readers; it encouraged them to approach new systems of thought critically and with an open mind.[45]

In this role of intellectual mediator, James often worked to minimize the magnitude of the changes from old to new systems of thought, giving his readers at least the semblance of stability amid change. Science, he stated in one review, "differs from ordinary knowledge only in being more elementary and exact." It confirms, albeit with precision, what people have long known: "Ordinary experience teaches us that if a man breathes the fumes of burning charcoal, his life is endangered." But science fills in the "complicated series of processes" that makes charcoal fumes dangerous.[46] In another review, James explained that modern science was not so radically new that it left traditional philosophy behind. In fact, the scholar who was both scientific and philosophical would lead the way forward. He thus praised "men engaged in the physical sciences" as the ones who ended up "pressing hard in the direction of metaphysical problems." Such scientists, with their "trained cunning in experiment, their habits of patience and fairness, and their willingness to advance by small steps at a time," would bring to metaphysical speculation "new results of the highest importance."[47]

James's message was not just, not even primarily, for professional scientists and philosophers. It was for the diverse readers of popular periodicals who wondered what the new scientific mania would do to the great philosophic traditions of the past. His message to them was simple, and it was one he would repeat to anxious audiences throughout his career: Have no fear; modern science is important, but it need not fundamentally alter the truths that order your lives. You can remain as active, engaged, and intellectually vested now as before scientific professionalism altered the world of thought. The old and the new can and should work together.

Despite this message of reassurance, however, it would be a mistake to assert that, at this stage in his career, James had a settled view of the intellectual changes under way. Depending on the subject at hand and the target audience for his review, he could express strikingly different opinions. But of course, he was a young scholar writing anonymously, and he took full advantage of the opportunity to experiment with different appeals and perspectives. Perhaps the clearest example of his desire to experiment came in his discussions of "the expert"—the third major theme of his book reviews. A relatively new idea at the time, the expert quickly became a god-term in the culture of professionalism.[48] Expertise meant specialized insights, which meant the ability to stake a claim in the pursuit of knowledge. Yet for many Americans, the expert's place in society was far from obvious. Was the expert to dictate the "right" answers to public problems? Was the expert to define the terms of popular debates? Was the expert a disinterested vessel of science, or did the expert's temperament influence the direction of his or her scholarship? How were the American people to listen to this new figure of professionalism?[49]

Neither James nor the nation had ready-made answers to these confounding questions, but popular periodicals provided an excellent forum for proposing ideas. At times, James insisted that experts needed the help of laypersons to advance scientific inquiry, picturing a collaborative intellectual culture involving amateurs and professionals. In an

1868 review of anthropological investigations in France, for example, he argued that Darwin's work was "of a nature to arouse the interest of every one," which meant that it could bring together experts and non-experts in the pursuit of scientific knowledge. With evolution, James continued, "science has really been furthered. All sorts of amateurs have been set working, and facts and documents dug up or rescued from destruction which otherwise we might have waited for indefinitely."[50] In another review, James discussed "analytic" and "synthetic" practitioners of science—those who worked more rationally, such as trained professionals, and those who worked primarily from experience, such as amateurs—as "indispensable" to helping science achieve a "sublime point of view." Either group, he held, "is infirm alone and needs the other to make up for its shortcomings."[51] Elsewhere, he insisted that it was necessary to "enlist the interest of laymen" to help physicians figure out how to handle "chronic patients" (those in asylums). Dealing with the mentally ill, he concluded, was a matter of "public economy" and required the input of a broad range of individuals.[52]

Just as James positioned lay inquirers as necessary for intellectual advancement, he chastised those who tried to block nonprofessionals from joining important discussions. For example, he faulted Spencer—a man quickly on his way to becoming James's scientific and philosophical nemesis—for denying the value of forms of thinking other than his own. Spencer, he held, wrongly demanded that readers "find the opposite of his First Principles inconceivable." Those who did not agree with him became "'*pseudo*' thinkers," even though Spencer himself "begs the question and appeals to the authority of his personal insight as against ours."[53] According to James, Spencer did not give lay perspectives any credence, and he wrongly blocked non-Spencerians from joining the conversation. In a similar way, James railed against the work of George Henry Lewes, a man who seemed to invent specialized philosophical problems that foreclosed collective deliberation. Lewes's *Problems of Life and Mind* was troubling, he told readers, because "they are not our problems, but only Mr. Lewes's." Crippled by "metaphysical worry," Lewes's book was "superfluous" because it concluded with "common-sense," thereby putting "us in the possession of our old feelings, motives, and duties." The "practical difference" of Lewes's work was "nil."[54]

Appealing to common sense, endorsing humanity's "old feelings, motives, and duties," and insisting that different people can have different first principles, James tried to help readers see their place in contemporary intellectual culture. Because everyone had common sense, everyone had something to add to the storehouse of ideas. Because everyone approached the world from a different perspective, everyone could contribute to the larger picture. No matter what a person's level of training, he or she had a place in the advancement of thought. Here was a call for widespread participation.

Yet for all his intellectual egalitarianism, there was often another James working as a book reviewer. This other James did not bring lay perspectives into the culture of professionalism; instead, he used his expert authority to move nonprofessionals out of certain debates. For example, in an 1868 review he argued that the validity of Darwinism ought to be left to professionally trained scientists. Given the complexity of the theory, the "enormous spaces of time in question," and the fact that it may never be possible "to give a physically strict proof of" evolution, the debate ought to be removed from "the jurisdiction of critics who are not zoologists." Those without zoological credentials were "mere reasoners," he explained, who had "already written nonsense enough about it." Evolution should be left to "the learned tact of experts, which alone is able to weigh delicate facts against each other, and to decide how many possibilities make a probability, and how many small probabilities make an almost certainty."[55]

At the same time that he lauded the authority of experts, James sometimes praised the rise of narrowly academic discourse. Reviewing an anthropological treatise by Paul Topinard in 1876, for example, he defended the "new tendency to stick to matter and facts in scientific writing, even if general phrases have to suffer." Because in many disciplines the "bugbear of appearing pedantic" had given way to an "exceedingly healthy tendency" for scientific precision, Americans could "cheer on" the specialization of academic prose "with a good conscience."[56] James reiterated the same point in a review of William K. Clifford's *Lectures and Essays*, concluding that the world needed "no mere sentimental worshipper of science, but an expert in her ways."[57] Professional discourse, he explained elsewhere, gives the reader the "sense of when he is on terra firma and when he is not." He who "begins with popular literature never properly knows where he is."[58]

Such praise of specialized jargon stood in marked contrast with the many times James lauded lay participation in scientific inquiry. Indeed, it was as though there were two Jameses at work in the reviews—one who promoted a culture of popular participation and one who relegated science to properly trained professionals. Admittedly, James was dealing with different questions and different texts in his reviews, so the point may have been that *at some times* there was a need for public participation while *at other times* specialists needed to settle the matter. And in this regard there was a telling pattern to his critiques. When it came to issues with which he agreed (the validity of evolution, for example), he often wanted those properly trained to settle the matter, instead of allowing uninformed reactionaries to meddle with the debate. But when it came to issues with which he disagreed (Spencer's philosophy, for example), he wanted everyone to have a say and to leave inquiry open for diverse points of view.

We must also recognize that James was a young scholar, writing anonymously, and dealing with a monumental shift in the way knowledge was produced. He was searching for order in the same way the nation was searching for order.[59] He did not offer consistent guidance on the place of the expert because he had no consistent answer. Yet because of his anonymous position, he was able to experiment with various propositions and to explore his own possible roles at the intersection of science and society. Grappling with the social functions of expertise was a way of thinking through the intellectual opportunities before him. Moreover, it was a way of using public outlets to create shared perspectives on common problems.

The Role of Style in Intellectual Discourse

When his career as a book reviewer was in its infancy, James often sent drafts of his work to his brother Henry for comments and suggestions. On one such occasion in 1867, as he was trying to complete a review for the *Nation*, he told Henry something rather surprising: "Style is not my forte, and to strike the mean between pomposity and vulgar familiarity is indeed difficult."[60] Given the accolades for stylistic brilliance James would later receive, his early self-doubt is noteworthy. But the comment reveals more than a juxtaposition between his self-perception and the work he eventually produced; it reveals one of the primary issues that occupied his attention as a book reviewer. Style, James knew, was central to a book's success. A text's level of sophistication, its clarity and precision, its ability to engage and interest readers, its mode of argumentation, its use of metaphor and imagery—these concerns stood at the forefront of James's consciousness when he assessed the latest scholarly treatises. Indeed, in virtually every review he published, he said something about the stylistic effectiveness of the book under consideration. And writing anonymously, he could be as forthright as he wanted in praising a writer's command of language or in condemning a writer's inaccessible prose.

Given the centrality of stylistic assessments in James's book reviews, and given his own stylistic prowess, it would be a mistake to pass over his early career without considering his abiding interest in the relationship between style and intellectual discourse. Fully aware that expertise and specialization greatly altered the nation's discursive landscape, he explored the ramifications of prose at the same time he explored the ramifications of science. In the end, he realized something his career would wonderfully illustrate: Style was not tangential or superfluous to big ideas; it was integral to the march of knowledge.[61]

Across his many reviews, James never dealt with the issue of style in a vacuum. Style was always a matter of relationships—of the connections between writers, texts, ideas, and audiences. Recognizing what rhetoricians have long known, James was keenly aware of language's ability to build bridges with some people while erecting barriers with others.[62] If a recent book spoke across disciplinary boundaries, if it spoke a language that ordinary Americans could understand, *and* if it had something meaningful to say about common concerns, he would quickly recommended it as a must-read. In assessing John Morley's *Voltaire*, for example, he insisted that Morley possessed "a thoroughly sympathetic intelligence" and pursued his craft with "a vehement moral or constructive impulse" as well as "a powerful reasoning faculty, a keen sense of the beautiful, and a command of expression which, if it were somewhat chastened, would place him high among the masters of English rhetoric." Because of Morley's "command of expression," James was able to recommend the book "to our readers as perhaps the most important English *literary* work of the year."[63] In a similar way, he praised Benjamin Paul Blood's self-published pamphlet *The Anesthetic Revelation* for communicating "at home, this side, beneath the feet." Blood, he said, wrote in terms that made his work "thoroughly original and suggestive," marked by "acuteness of thought and often great felicity of style." As James saw it, those who wished to ponder life's big questions, those "real students of philosophy," ought to explore Blood's work.[64] For those same students of philosophy he also recommended Charles Renouvier's *La Critique Philosophique*, which was composed with "marvelous clearness, . . . trenchant logic and condensed vigor of expression." Because Renouvier's command of language would help readers understand the "weight and moral authority" of his ideas, James recommended the book for "all thoughtful minds."[65]

Style was also central in James's assessment of scientific texts. The way a book of science was written could make it indispensable for all thoughtful minds or relegate it to a group of narrow specialists. When it came to Darwin's work, for example, James insisted that both scientists and generally educated readers had to take note. At a time when "so much of scientific industry consists of a mere mechanical cataloguing of immediate results," Darwin's *The Variation of Animals and Plants under Domestication* was refreshing because it was "thoroughly and elaborately composed" and had "a beginning, a middle, and an end." As a result, James could "cordially recommend" the book "to the student" as well as to the "popular reader," even though the latter might not find it as engaging as *On the Origin of Species.*[66] James found William B. Carpenter's *Principles of Mental Physiology* to be similarly refreshing. Not only did Carpenter craft the book with an eye toward "edification" and the application of "physiological laws to moral culture," he also balanced "multitudinous facts" with a whimsical style that merited "commendation in this day of slouchy familiarity." Though students of physiology may find "nothing that is new in the book," wrote James, it was to be commended to general readers, and especially to "clergymen and educators," because of its "sustained polish and refinement."[67]

While effective style usually led to a positive assessment on James's part, ineffective style often raised his ire. He condemned a physiological work by J. Bell Pettigrew because of its confusing structure, lamenting that it offered nothing more than "a good many facts of original observation rather chaotically strung together." Though some of Pettigrew's views were "original," the book ultimately failed because it was "lamely presented and poorly supported."[68] Ernest Renan's *Dialogues et fragments philosophiques* proved to be a similar communicative failure. James told readers of the *Nation* that Renan's book made for "really sad reading." His "mental ruin" came through most clearly in his "insincerity and foppishness" and "an indescribably unmanliness of tone compounded of a sort of historically sentimental self-conceit."[69] Likewise, William K. Clifford's companion volumes *Lectures and Essays* and *Seeing and Thinking* were so poorly put together, so wrecked by "unshapeliness," that they bewildered an "already too perplexed" public. "Splintered ends, broken threads, broken lights, and, at last, broken hearts and broken life!"[70]

It is hard to image James, a young scholar at the time of these reviews, using such a tone had he not been writing anonymously. But his anonymity meant that he could advance his stylistic critiques unabashedly. He lamented that one author "sins by obscurity through a quaint density of expression, and by such verbal monsters as *spacical* instead of spatial."[71] He praised another author's work because it "is extremely concise, dry, and clear, and as the author is as thoroughly at home in the library as in the laboratory, the work is really a cyclopedia of reference."[72] Other books he praised for being "temperate and witty," for moving with "light and elegant composition and easy style," and for containing "neat compression of statement . . . and a dry and ironical humor."[73] Still others he condemned for "diffuseness and sermonizing . . . vagueness and generality," for being "awkward," and for containing "considerable psychological crudity" that left readers wanting.[74] For James, "fluent and varied style, . . . lucidity of thought and expression," made a text meaningful for the "general reader."[75]

Style, James believed, made a difference. It made a difference in the scope and accessibility of modern thought. It made a difference in the way a book reinforced or helped break down the barriers between disciplines. And it made a difference in a text's ability to address common concerns and to advance cultural conversations. Consider his assessment of the "English style" of prose in two very different texts—Horace Bushnell's *Women's Suffrage* and John Stuart Mill's *The Subjection of Women*. James told readers that he appreciated British writing's "atmosphere of homely splendor, of familiar pomp, of surcharged association."[76] Yet he slammed Bushnell's work because it left "a strong impression that rhetoric—the mere delight of listening to one's self making sweet music—was an important motive in its production."[77] Bushnell failed, in other words, because he simply spouted ideas with little concern for his readers. Mill's work was another story entirely. "Mr. Mill's sentences," James explained, "clean, weighted, and going straight to their mark, would, if translated literally, sound as natural and forcible to French, German, or Italian ears as they do to ours."[78] Mill was dealing with the same subject as Bushnell, but Mill's prose was capable of affecting readers across the globe. His writing brought people and ideas together, whereas Bushnell's floated into obscurity.

The more James worked as a book reviewer, the more he focused on the importance of style. Over time, style became so important to his outlook that he started critiquing the stylistic abilities of friends and family. To those in the Metaphysical Club, most notably Charles Sanders Peirce and Chauncey Wright, James did not hesitate to chastise work that he saw as too scientific or positivistic, too disconnected from the lives of "average Americans."[79] When their writing became too pedantic, he insisted that they were harming themselves and harming public culture. Peirce was perhaps the most grievous stylistic sinner. By speaking and writing in a way that made sense to him alone, he remained intellectually isolated, cut off from the relationships he needed to succeed. In an age of specialization, Peirce proved that professional discourse could erect almost insurmountable barriers.[80]

While Peirce may have been the best example of a scientist who spoke and wrote with little regard for effective communication, closer to home was someone who, in James's mind, needed even more stylistic guidance. The trouble, however, was that many commentators considered this person to be a literary genius. But that did not stop William from giving his brother Henry as much stylistic advice as he could. When the subject of Henry's writing came up in correspondence, William became an incisive critic, almost as though he were writing a review for a popular periodical. After reading Henry's short story "Poor Richard" in 1868, for example, he sent Henry a rather backhanded compliment, thanking him for writing with "hardly a trace of that too diffuse explanation of the successive psychological steps wh. I remember attacking you for when you read it to me."[81] By linking the style of the published version of "Poor Richard" to the advice he had originally given Henry, William took credit for the final product. As he saw it, he had intervened, set the story on the right track, and made it more appropriate for readers of the *Atlantic Monthly*, where it was first published.

Though backhanded, William's response to "Poor Richard" proved to be one of his kinder assessments of Henry's literary abilities. As the years went on, his critical posture hardened. "Your own tendency," William complained in 1872 after reading "A European Summer," published serially in the *Nation*, "is more and more to over-refinement, and elaboration. Recollect that for Newspaporial purposes, a broader treatment hits a broader mark; and keep bearing that way as much as you can with comfort."[82] In another letter, he complained that Henry's "style ran a little more to *curliness* than suited the average mind, or in general the newspaper reader. In my opinion what you should *cultivate* is directness of style. Delicacy, subtly and ingenuity will take care of themselves."[83] In still another letter, William condemned Henry's "constant use of french phrases," as they separated Henry from his readers and made him sound "cold, thin blooded & priggish."[84] "Keep watch and ward," he cautioned elsewhere, "lest in your style you become too Parisian and lose your hold on the pulse of the great american public to which after all you must pander for support."[85]

Over subsequent decades, Henry became more successful and William became more biting. When William read *Wings of the Dove*, he told Henry that Henry's style was "perverse."[86] When he read *The Golden Bowl*, he balked at Henry's "method of narration by interminable elaboration of suggestive reference."[87] The contrast between the brothers came out most fully in 1907 after William read *The American Scene* and complained:

> You know how opposed your whole "third manner" of execution is to the literary ideals which animate my crude and Orson-like breast, mine being to say a thing in one sentence as straight and explicit as it can be made, and then to drop it for ever; yours being to avoid naming it straight, but by dint of breathing and sighing all round and round it, to arouse in the reader who may have had a similar perception already (Heaven help him if he hasn't!) the illusion of a solid object, made (like the "ghost" at the Polytechnic) wholly out of impa[l]pable materials, air, and the prismatic interferences of light, ingeniously focused by mirrors upon empty space. . . . In this crowded and hurried reading age, pages that require such close attention remain unread & neglected.[88]

William was wrong, of course; Henry's pages were not unread and neglected. Indeed, he was a literary giant of the late nineteenth and early twentieth centuries. But that did not stop William's unrelenting criticism. There was certainly jealousy involved in his advice, as William felt threatened by his younger brother's success. There was also the fact that criticism was a way of life among members of the James family; Henry Sr. had trained his children to criticize without hesitation.[89] But in terms of William's intellectual development, what stands out in his advice to Henry is the same concern for effective communicative relationships that dominated his book reviews. In their correspondence, William said little about Henry's characters or plots. Setting these issues to the side, he most wanted to draw Henry's attention to the way prose style facilitated and impeded relationships among writers, readers, and ideas. Whether one was a novelist or a scientist, William was interested in the art of building connections in public culture.

Of course, one could object that William was judging his brother's work by the wrong set of stylistic standards. Works of fiction are supposed to sound different than scholarly tracts or commentaries in popular periodicals. Yet William's advice was not completely off base. When he criticized his brother in the 1860s and 1870s, he was actually working far ahead of the literary curve. As the nineteenth century wore on, many authors began to rebel against Henry James's writing style, panning his work as overly sentimental and psychological, excessively intricate and indirect. In an interesting twist, many novelists ended up sounding less like Henry James and more like William James, adopting the same directness and forcefulness that distinguished William's scientific and philosophical works.[90] Though William may have been too harsh on Henry, his criticism was a prelude to America's embrace of realism.

The 1878 Baltimore and Boston Lectures

Having spent over a dozen years working as an anonymous book reviewer, James was ready to expand his intellectual activities. Harvard's increasing research demands were a big part of his motivation to publish original scholarly essays under his own name.[91] But in addition to working on academic articles, he began to lecture publicly. In 1875, James gave a talk to the Harvard Natural History Society.[92] He also spoke on March 1, 1877, in Harvard's Sanders Theater on "Recent Investigations on the Brain."[93] Unfortunately, notes from these lectures have not survived, making it difficult to assess how he crafted his talks. Moreover, the lectures received little attention and were given to largely academic audiences.[94] It was not until 1878, when James lectured on "The Senses and the Brain and Their Relation to Thought" at Johns Hopkins University in Baltimore and on "The Brain and the Mind" at the Lowell Institute in Boston, that he was able to demonstrate his oratorical prowess beyond the academy.

Public lecturing marked a shift in James's intellectual development. As a lecturer he could no longer work anonymously, meaning that he had to come to more definite answers about the questions with which he struggled as a book reviewer. But book reviews had prepared him to speak insightfully at the lectern. Writing for popular periodicals had given him the chance to experiment, to craft a compelling speaking position, to mediate between old and new as well as popular and professional forms of knowledge, and to better understand what made for an effective intellectual style. Overall, speaking to the people of Baltimore and Boston gave James the opportunity to select from and extend the ideas, arguments, appeals, and strategies he had first developed as a book reviewer.

This is not to say that James could speak to the people of Baltimore and Boston exactly as he had spoken to periodical readers. Not only were the printed page and the public platform markedly different discursive forums, but by the time James spoke in 1878, the relationship between science and society had become even more precarious. The Darwin controversy had not abated; it had grown more divisive. Inside the academy, the fight centered on the teaching of evolution. At Yale, for example, President Noah Porter and Professor William Graham Sumner clashed publicly over Sumner's textbook selection of Herbert Spencer's *The Study of Sociology*. The clash pitted the religiously minded Porter, who represented the pre–Civil War university tradition, against the positivist Sumner, who represented the post–Civil War new science.[95] The debate soon embroiled them in one of the nation's earliest cases of academic freedom.[96]

At Johns Hopkins, which had only opened its doors in 1876, two years before James would speak there, similar problems ensnared the community. President Daniel Coit Gilman, who had generally "shown great eagerness to avoid offending religious sensibilities,"[97] hosted lectures by Thomas Huxley in 1876. A close ally of Darwin's, Huxley had a remarkable ability to attract controversy, particularly of the religious sort. After he spoke at Johns Hopkins, a public debate erupted, and Gilman soon found himself mediating the concerns of the Baltimore community with the commitments of a modern research university.[98]

At Harvard, James underwent an evolution-related struggle of his own. In 1876 he taught Natural History 2: Physiological Psychology, a course he had designed with the approval of Charles William Eliot.[99] Hoping to keep his nineteen students abreast of the latest developments in the topic area, James assigned Spencer's *Principles of Psychology* for class discussion. Even though he was not defending Spencer,[100] the mere presence of Spencer's ideas outraged James's colleague Francis Bowen, who tried to stop the textbook from entering the classroom.[101] An ardent foe of Darwinism, Bowen thought evolution a "dirt-philosophy, . . . baseless and false."[102] Some faculty members sided with James, others with Bowen, and something of a schism emerged between the two camps. With President Eliot's blessing, however, James taught the course and used Spencer's book, providing students with "a clear explanation of the theory" of evolution that, according to the *Harvard Crimson*, was invaluable to the "many who have been puzzled by the conflicting opinions they have read."[103]

James's confrontation with Bowen and the antievolutionists at Harvard provided the impetus he needed to look for work at another university. James had been thinking of leaving Harvard for a couple of years already; his growing unhappiness with the tone of physiology and psychology at the university, combined with his desire to move into a philosophy department, led him to consider employment elsewhere. And the more he thought about his situation, the more Johns Hopkins seemed appealing. It was an up-and-coming research institution that defined itself by the promise of academic freedom. In 1877, then, James wrote to Gilman about securing a philosophy position at Johns Hopkins.[104] Interested in bringing James to the new university, Gilman arranged for him to give a series of public lectures in Baltimore in February 1878.[105] Though James would be paid $500 for the lectures, they were, in essence, a job interview—albeit one conducted in a public forum.[106]

The lectures were popularly and professionally significant for James. Because they were tied to the prospect of employment, he had to strike a professional tone, keeping in mind Johns Hopkins's strong commitment to research. Yet because the lectures were open to the Baltimore public, which had just emerged from the Huxley controversy, he had to be careful with subject matter steeped in evolutionary theory. Though few reports of the lectures survive, those that do suggest James was successful in balancing popular and professional concerns. The *Fourth Annual Report of the Johns Hopkins University* mentioned the lectures and reported an average attendance of sixty-two people.[107] Francis Child, Boylston Professor of Rhetoric and Oratory at Harvard, attended the series and wrote to James Russell Lowell that James "made a decided impression" on the audience, laying out clear reasons "for not accepting the theory that we are automatons unreservedly."[108] James himself must have thought the lectures went well, for he corresponded with Gilman over the following years about returning to Baltimore to speak.[109]

Despite the success of the lectures, James ultimately decided to stay at Harvard.[110] President Eliot promised him a philosophy appointment in the coming years, and being in Cambridge would allow him to remain by family and friends. The Boston area was his home and, despite its shortcomings, offered a number of venues for intellectual engagement, not the least of which was the Lowell Institute. Because James was still intent on moving his scholarly activities in new directions, Lowell seemed the perfect place to repeat the Johns Hopkins material. The prestigious institute offered him visibility, especially among the people of Boston. On May 19, 1878, he sent Augustus Lowell, chairman of the institute, a number of testimonials about his success in Baltimore. He also explained his firm grasp on the delicacies of discussing a controversial scientific subject; he was confident, he told Lowell, that he could "make the course both entertaining to the many by its abundance of new facts and illustrations, and instructive to the few by its theoretic conclusions." He was also sure that he could avoid coming off as either "a materialistic partisan" or "a spiritualistic bigot."[111] Lowell seemed to agree, scheduling James for a course of lectures on "The Brain and the Mind" to be delivered October 15–29.

Unlike the Johns Hopkins lectures, the Lowell lectures received significant attention in the press, marking the first time commentators wrote about James's oratorical abilities. According to the *Boston Daily Advertiser*, "Dr. James kept the attention and interest of his audience by his evident mastery of his subject, and quite as much by his clear, lucid and unpretentious way of presenting what he knows about it."[112] A week later, the same paper reported that James spoke "in a familiar way" about very technical scientific subjects.[113] Because of the stylistic choices he made, James's ideas hit their mark, creating a point of contact between him and the audience. The *Worchester Daily Spy*, covering the news from Boston, wrote that James came off as "a singularly pleasing lecturer on a fascinating subject, clear and simple in his statements, and entirely interesting."[114]

In terms of content, the 1878 Lowell lectures were a condensed version of the Johns Hopkins lectures. In Baltimore, James presented a series of ten lectures; in Boston, he presented six. Complete manuscripts of neither set have survived. What has survived are drafts of some of the lectures and outlines for both sets.[115] The drafts contain mostly full sentences and substantive paragraphs, providing a sense of the internal development of the talks as well as the tone James hoped to create. The outlines are sparser, containing a mixture of fragments and full sentences, but they provide a good sense of the overall structure of the lectures as well as the larger points James wanted to make. Taken together, the drafts and outlines paint a clear picture of how James approached the art of lecturing. As would become his typical mode of operation over the years, he began by writing the lectures in prose form. He then used the prose to develop a set of speaking notes, composed of both full sentences (for points he had to word precisely) and sentence fragments (for points he could deliver extemporaneously).[116] Speaking from these notes allowed him to balance the concerns of the academic and lay portions of his audience.

Scholars have thus far paid scant attention to James's Baltimore and Boston lectures. One notable exception is Francesca Bordogna, who has shown how James used the lectures to position himself as a scientist and philosopher as well as "an impartial, responsible teacher who could help students carefully sift through the philosophical implications of physiology and the new naturalistic science of man."[117] Bordogna is right to see the lectures as one of James's early attempts to work across the boundary between science and philosophy, but it is also important to recognize that the lectures were a culmination of James's work and experience up to that point. Book reviews had prepared him to address science and society in a way that could ease the nation's anxieties about the intellectual changes afoot. Moreover, the chance to lecture publicly was also the chance to draw upon what he had learned from his father and Emerson as well as from Louis Agassiz and Oliver Wendell Holmes Sr., both of whom knew how to make science exciting and relevant. Ultimately, the message James hoped to leave with his listeners in Baltimore and Boston was the same one he had tried to communicate to readers of the nation's popular periodicals. While modern science seemed to deny the importance of individuals, while natural selection and chemical processes seemed to determine the character and direction of human life, the American people retained control of their destiny.

Both the Johns Hopkins and Lowell lectures began with the division between modern science (which James often discussed in terms of physiology) and traditional forms of inquiry (which he discussed in terms of philosophy). The fight between the old ways of philosophy and the new ways of physiology, he told his listeners, had turned America's intellectual landscape into a battlefield. The "sectaries of physical science" claimed to "explode and render obsolete the old views of mental action all based on a priori speculation and metaphysics," he explained, while traditional thinkers found "the most brutal materialism lurking behind what the former call enlightenment and scientific progress, like some hideous heathen idol whose form is dimly seen through the glare of fireworks and golden dust and dazzling vapors of incense with which its followers continually fill the air before it."[118] Though James's imagery may seem extreme today, it reflected the intellectual divisions of his time. After all, Louis Agassiz had challenged Asa Gray to a duel, and Huxley had managed to stir up controversy wherever he went, including at Johns Hopkins. By emphasizing the chasm between the two extremes in the Darwin debates, James made a middle-ground perspective seem all the more attractive.

But the middle ground he had in mind was not just for the warring scientists and philosophers; it was also for those members of the community who had traveled to the lecture hall to listen to him. Speaking to them in particular, James turned metaphorical. Consider, he said, owners of adjoining lots whose properties are separated by a fence. Where the lots run against each other, "we find each owner disposed to push back the fence" and claim more land for himself.[119] Each "wishes to shove back the fence and reduce the size of his neighbor's lot for the benefit of his own and the disputed boundary leads to the jealousies we have seen." Like the landowners, James continued, specialists try to secure their own sizable lot in "the field of human knowledge" and cultivate the intellectual land "conscientiously."[120] But they begin to feud when they see themselves primarily as specialists instead of pursuers of truth in general. If physiologists think truth comes primarily through physiology, and if philosophers think truth comes primarily through philosophy, conflict is inevitable. Where truth is monistic, James counseled, battles will surely follow.

To avoid a war, scholars should think of themselves as coproprietors of a common land. He explained, "I think we ought . . . to aspire to the attitude of one who should own both lots. He does not care where the fence stands and being master of all the land tries to cultivate every square foot of it impartially." The argument was directed at both academics and nonacademics, because "We are each alike proprietors of a body and a mind." Because our bodies (a term of physiology) and our minds (a term of philosophy) are forever interconnected, both are necessary for better understanding ourselves and our world.[121] In the end, physiology would "corroborate, confirm the wisdom of the past and make us feel again that there is no such breach" between the new science and traditional inquiry.[122]

The argument that old forms of inquiry (philosophy) and new forms of inquiry (physiology) shared the same field of knowledge was one that James had made repeatedly in his book reviews.[123] In both contexts, the argument underscored the possibility of reconciliation between warring factions. It also spoke to skeptical members of the audience, as the wisdom of the past found fuller expression in modern science. To create the most complete picture of the world, James argued, Americans needed both the insights of philosophy and the exactness of physiology. As coproprietors, we have a "common share in human nature."[124]

To the extent that James spoke to both academics and members of the larger community, he occupied the same speaking position that he had occupied in his book reviews. James was a mediator of knowledge, a reconciler of epistemological differences, an "intellectual translator,"[125] helping different people understand the contours of a common project. Addressing science and philosophy as well as American society, he portrayed himself as someone thoroughly familiar with the specialized issues at hand but also as someone who cared deeply about the public consequences of the issues. In that way, James was ready to tend the entire field of knowledge—philosophic, scientific, and public. As he explained to the people of Baltimore and Boston, his work was spread "rather thin over a broad surface," but such breadth helped him "form responsible opinions concerning a variety of matters about which irresponsible opinions are very frequently and loudly expressed." In the philosophical and physiological wars, he was as "impartial as possible in a field where partizanship has too often held sway."[126] For the Lowell audience, he went into even more detail:

> I have for some years past in thinking of my duties as teacher in Cambridge, been inclined to deplore the rather wide surface over which my instruction had to be spread. . . . I have been obliged to teach a little Anatomy, a little Physiology, a little Psychology; and I have felt that where one's wisdom tried to cover so much ground it must needs be thin at any given spot. But in standing before you now I feel that my misfortune has had its good side. A teacher must form responsible opinions; a reader need not. But the difficulties of deciding a question are not often felt by one who is not responsible for his decision.[127]

Given the increasing specialization of the era, this description made James distinctive. His breadth of learning, in an age where depth was the ideal, gave him a unique perspective. Connected to science and philosophy, he could see past intellectual boundaries. And because he presented himself as a teacher above all, he was in a perfect position to teach the audience how to work through the tensions between the old and the new.

Even when it came to the divisive issue of Darwinism, James insisted that reconciliation was possible and that he knew the best way forward. Evolutionary research, he told the people of Boston, "has made us understand so much about animal and vegetable forms and how in particular the physiologists by the deep insight they have been acquiring into the nervous system and the brain, have to a great extent banished the mystery which used to hang about the action of the mind."[128] At the same time, he was quick to point out that Darwinism did not have all the answers. While evolutionary theory provided a new way of viewing important physiological issues, it did not provide ultimate truths about human beings. At best, evolutionary research entailed "only the large and vague v[alue] of circumstantial evidence."[129] With evolution, there was "no fulcrum of certainty."[130] And without a fulcrum of certainty, there remained room for honest disagreement and open debate about life's biggest questions. Pluralism was possible; more than that, it was necessary.

James's argument that evolution was valuable but not ultimate—an argument that first emerged in his book reviews[131]—was important for creating common ground between himself and his audience, particularly that part of the audience who remembered the uproar Huxley had caused two years prior. Though James was a scientist and knew how to speak the language of physiology, he was not an ardent materialist. Instead, he knew full well that materialism could not be a "*rational* explanation of everything," and he stood firmly against "all that is repugnant or objectionable in materialism."[132] By pulling evolution back from claims of epistemological finality, he left the issue of larger philosophical truth alone, giving more traditional thinkers a place in the culture of inquiry. Because physiology provided only "circumstantial evidence," philosophy could still help people reach higher rungs on the ladder of knowledge.

To make the point even clearer, James turned to recent work on consciousness, showing how philosophy and physiology could work profitably together. Evolution, he insisted, accounted "for mind as a product"; first there were nervous systems, then there arose consciousness.[133] In other words, the mind was a product of its environment. But because the mind was a product of its environment, and because the environment was constantly changing, as evolutionists proclaimed, then consciousness was not predetermined. It was, rather, molded by the dynamic currents swirling around it. "A sensation," James explained, "is the most fluctuating and indefinite of mental occurrences. So far is it from being the stable and solid foundation of knowledge, that it is wholly plastic in the hands of our thoughts of things."[134]

James's physiological view of the mind retained important aspects of traditional philosophy. To the extent that sensations were "wholly plastic" in human hands, individuals had power over natural processes. It was not just that environments shaped people; it was also that people shaped environments through the way they handled sensations and thoughts (a point he would make emphatically in *The Principles of Psychology*).[135] Individuals both molded and were molded by their world. It was a view, as James described it, that "wakens the mind from its slumber"—an important allusion to Immanuel Kant—"and when the mind puts forth its power it may do so in the way of overriding, altering or ignoring altogether the sensation."[136] With attention turned one way instead of another, individuals focused on specific sensations and ignored countless others. Thus the sensations attended to became active parts of the flux of experience, which meant that people were able to direct their lives according to practical ends.

James's vision of personal power within an evolutionary scheme—which, again, had appeared several times in his book reviews[137]—meant that even the philosophical traditionalists in his audience, those who wanted to hang on to the notion of free will, for example, could embrace the new science of Darwinism. "Persons who are fearful of the reduction by physiology of higher to lower powers of the mind," he said, should be aware that physiological research "has been hailed by followers of Kant as the most striking experimental verification ever made of a doctrine originally deduced a priori, the doctrine of innate potentialities in the mind which sensations merely awaken into exercise."[138] By linking the new science of physiology to Kant's philosophy, he let his listeners know that the work of the past remained integral to the work of the present. He also let them know that questions about morality were still paramount. "Our organizations are the literal resultants of our past sins and good deeds," he explained. Natural selection "at this moment [is] literally [the] moulded result of our past acts. If they be acts of virtue, [that is] well. If [they be] sins, woe unto us. The great thing is to form habits which then leave [the upper hemisphere of our brains] free for higher flights and in forming habits, to keep them unbroken."[139]

The overall point was one of empowerment: Individuals could still find meaning and be effective in the world despite the upheavals around them. As he explained at the end of the lecture series:

> I, for one, as a scientific man & a practical man alike, deny utterly that Science compels me to believe that my conscience is an *ignis fatuus* or outcast, & I trust that you too after the evidence of this evening will go away strengthened in the natural faith that your delights & sorrows, your loves & hates, your aspirations & efforts are real combatants in life's arena, & not impotent, paralytic spectators of the game.[140]

This was the same powerful appeal to personal relevance that had appeared in James's book reviews, and it would recur throughout his career.[141] By declaring his faith in individual worth, in addition to his faith in science, and by inviting the audience to adopt the same faith, James brought himself and his listeners together in a clearer view of the relationship between philosophy and physiology. Though modern science often seemed to threaten traditional belief structures, the audience could rest assured that life as they knew it, including their moral responsibilities and personal fancies, would continue unabated.

Conclusion

The 1878 Baltimore and Boston lectures carried on the intellectual threads first spun in James's early book reviews. The lectures were the culmination of more than a decade of invention and experimentation, a time in which James tested ideas, postures, arguments, and appeals to navigate the shift from eloquence to professionalism. Not all of these ideas, postures, arguments, and appeals would stay with him during his career, but they were integral to the formation of his public-intellectual identity and his still-emerging art of popular statement.

The most telling aspect of James's early inventional efforts, at least if we are to understand his pursuit of popular statement, was his public orientation. Uncertain of his own place in the world of thought, uncertain of the kinds of inquiry he would embrace, James nevertheless experimented in full view of general audiences. More than that, he experimented *through* general audiences—through the perspectives, predicaments, and concerns that seemed to pervade public culture, at least with regard to the intersection of science and society. By interacting with the American people in periodicals and lecture halls, James saw the outlines of his intellectual niche. These were not the only forums he turned to, of course; he launched a research program and began publishing in academic outlets as well. But on the whole, his early efforts centered on public engagement and finding an eloquence representative of he who "does not care where the fence stands and being master of all the land tries to cultivate every square foot of it impartially."[142]

Even though this eloquence was in its infancy, James had discovered a sentiment that would help structure his popular interactions for decades to come. The need for mastery, for cultivation, for the directed efforts of the farmer and landowner, spoke to the importance of individual initiative. In response to the often contentious relationship between science and society, James reaffirmed personal choice, reminding ordinary Americans that their aspirations, decisions, and endeavors remained relevant in shaping the character of their lives. This, in fact, was the central message of "Talks to Teachers on Psychology"—the lecture series that, more than any other in James's career, turned popular statement into a practical art.

CHAPTER THREE

Talking to Teachers

⌘

By the end of the 1870s, William James had realized how much he enjoyed discussing science and society with the American people. In fact, in February 1879, a few months after completing his first series of lectures at the Lowell Institute, he wrote to Augustus Lowell about giving another course of lectures there. Hoping to address "the Theory of Evolution as applied to Mind," James proposed talks that would be "expository and critical of recent speculations in mental evolution, especially Mr. Spencer's. They will contain a considerable amount of entirely original material, and . . . their tendency will be decidedly 'conservative.'"[1] Even though James would end up not delivering the lectures, the fact that he wanted to speak about evolution in a "decidedly 'conservative'" manner signaled his ongoing desire to mediate between "old" and "new" systems of knowledge. His goal would likely have been to help his listeners understand that they remained in control of their lives.

Whatever James may have said at the Lowell Institute in 1879, perhaps it was best that he did not deliver the lectures, considering that his hands were already full with a project that would change his career and, in the process, change the study of psychology in America. In June 1878, James had received a letter from publisher Henry Holt inquiring whether he would be interested in writing a psychology textbook for Holt's American Science series. James was interested, but told Holt he would need two full years to complete the manuscript. "I am a little staggered by the length of time which you think it would take to write the Psychology," Holt replied. "This delay, however, does not incline me to seek any other author in preference to yourself."[2]

The book, James's first, would become the revolutionary *Principles of Psychology,* and it would take twelve years, not two years, to complete. From 1878 to 1890, James would labor to describe the progress and future of modern psychology. When finally in print, the book established him as one of the most original and insightful psychologists—indeed, scientists—in the nation. Newspapers began referring to him as "the eminent psychologist of Harvard," "the brilliant writer on psychological subjects," and someone who possessed "the rare power of presenting the most abstract ideas in a vivid pictorial form."[3] In classrooms across the country, professors and students explored the many scientific vistas offered by "Big James," as *Principles* was nicknamed because of its length—over 1,300 pages spread across two volumes. When James published a condensed version of the book a couple years later, titled *Psychology: Briefer Course,* it was given the nickname "Little Jimmy" to distinguish it from "Big James." Both "Big James" and "Little Jimmy" were triumphs, defining the study of psychology in America for decades to come. In 1917, one of James's intellectual rivals praised *Principles* as "a declaration of independence, defining the boundary lines of a new science with unapproachable genius."[4] In 1969, a group of prominent psychologists insisted that, "without question," *Principles* was "the most literate, the most provocative, and at the same time the most intelligible book on psychology that has ever appeared in English or in any other language."[5]

As these psychologists recognized, *Principles* was as much a literary achievement as an academic one. To readers and reviewers alike, the book seemed to represent what intellectual discourse could be, even in the culture of professionalism. William Dean Howells praised the "charming spirit, the delightful manner, and the flavorous and characteristic style" of James's prose. The work, said Howells, contains "passages which may be read aloud to the tenderest female, so lightly and agreeably are some of the most difficult problems of the soul handled in them."[6] George Santayana called *Principles* a "rich and living" book "in which a generous nature breaks out at every point, and the perennial problems of the human mind are discussed so modestly, so solidly, with such a deep and pathetic sincerity."[7] James himself knew it was a significant accomplishment. The year 1890, he told his brother Henry, with the usual immodesty that characterized their correspondence, "will be known as the great epochal year in American literature" because of three groundbreaking works: Henry's *The Tragic Muse,* Howells's *A Hazard of New Fortunes,* and his own *Principles of Psychology.*[8]

With the publication of *Principles,* then, James found himself atop America's scientific community. Admittedly, it was not *Principles* alone that built his reputation. Between 1878 and 1890, he had published over thirty signed articles in various forums and had lectured more than a dozen times to various audiences.[9] But *Principles* was his masterpiece, the work that gave him enough scientific credibility, enough professional ethos, to speak in virtually any auditorium across the country. After 1890, James was a representative of modern psychology, considered far and wide to be a brilliant scientist who could entertain at the same time he educated.[10]

The most significant lecture opportunity to emerge from the success of *Principles* was "Talks to Teachers on Psychology." Presented almost a dozen times from 1891 to 1898, "Talks to Teachers" put James in contact with different communities across the nation. Eventually, the series would become a wildly successful book, further connecting him to a diverse mix of Americans. Since its publication in 1899, in fact, *Talks to Teachers on Psychology and to Students on Some of Life's Ideals* has never been out of print.[11] Although exact sales figures for the book are not available, it is reasonable to estimate that James sold well over 100,000 copies during his lifetime, and hundreds of thousands, if not millions, more in subsequent decades.[12]

Despite the enormous success of the book and the lecture series from which it emerged, *Talks to Teachers* has received little scholarly attention. A group of educational psychologists revisited the work a hundred years after it was first published, focusing largely on the validity of James's psychological insights after a century of further research, but they had nothing to say about how the text functioned in its historical moment.[13] Perhaps the best characterization of *Talks* as a lecture series comes from Linda Simon, who writes that James offered "more than a translation of the new psychology. . . . He wanted [his audience] to consider, or reconsider, the purpose of education."[14] But Simon's treatment of the lectures is brief, which is unfortunate considering that "Talks to Teachers" was the most-delivered series of James's career.

Given the success of the lectures and the number of times they were delivered, one may rightly ask why *Talks to Teachers* is frequently set aside, mentioned in passing, or treated in brief. Part of the reason, it seems, involves the perception that *Talks* falls naturally in the shadow of *Principles*. Because of the success of the textbook, James was asked to speak on what his work might say about pedagogy. The historical relationship between the two works thus encourages the view that James simply deployed or recast his psychological insights for audiences of teachers. This is precisely how Gerald Myers describes *Talks*—as "lectures to teachers on the application of psychology to pedagogy, much of it a direct adaptation of *Principles* for the use of the classroom teacher."[15] If *Talks* is simply a targeted version of *Principles,* it is reasonable to focus on the masterpiece instead of the side project.

This chapter takes a different view, however, demonstrating that *Talks* was far from a teacher version of *Principles*. To be sure, it dealt with many of the themes that appeared in *Principles*. But the lectures were fundamentally different from the textbook, addressing distinct audiences, problems, situations, and ideas. Unlike *Principles*, *Talks* dealt with the predicament America's schoolteachers faced amid the dizzying changes of the late nineteenth century. The delivery of the lecture series during the 1890s, not to mention the publication of the book in 1899, brought James into contact with tens of thousands of primary and secondary educators from a variety of socioeconomic backgrounds. These "school marms," as he affectionately called them, stood far beyond the walls of the academy and the world of professional psychology. They occupied a professional culture of their own, and specialized research in scientific subjects was largely alien to them. To connect successfully with these individuals, James had to do far more than simply recast his psychology. A new, unique intellectual encounter had to take place.

As we shall see, James's frequent interactions with educators in the East, the Midwest, and across the Mississippi helped him appreciate the problems that teachers faced in their struggle for professional respectability. The lecture series, in turn, became an extended moment of identification—in Kenneth Burke's sense of the term[16]—that resulted in a text less about pedagogical psychology (although that was certainly part of it) than about the place of teachers in a democratic society. Moreover, this extended moment of identification enabled James to develop one of the key aspects of his art of popular statement—namely, adopting the problems of his audience as his own and working with them on effective solutions. As a way of relating to and building a relationship with America's teachers, James indicated that he was laboring on their behalf, acting not as a bringer of psychological truth but as a servant in their struggle for professional advancement. The goal was to provide a relatively marginalized and disaffected public with an urgent, important conception of its continuing relevance and new possibilities at the turn of the twentieth century.

The Professional Predicament of America's Schoolteachers

One way to talk about American culture during the Gilded Age and the Progressive Era is to talk about a widespread desire for professional esteem. As specialization transformed the nation's workplaces, people began to think of themselves increasingly in terms of their "special role in an industrialized society."[17] In fact, one's work was often more central to one's identity than the community in which one lived.[18] Those who demonstrated their expertise and command over a particular area of knowledge could be confident in their contributions to society. Those who failed to demonstrate their expertise and command over a particular area fell behind the times. For many individuals, groups, organizations, and professions, the project was to enhance the status of their work.

Occupational alliances were particularly important for this project. Lawyers, doctors, engineers, architects, field workers, factory workers, union members, and countless others created work-specific organizations to distinguish their contributions from the contributions of others and to declare their mastery over a particular body of knowledge.[19] Even within a given profession, specialized associations sprung up throughout the post–Civil War era. In the field of medicine, for example, the years 1864 to 1888 saw the creation of the American Ophthalmological Society, the American Otological Society, the American Neurological Association, the American Dermatological Association, the American Gynecological Society, the American Laryngological Association, the

American Surgical Association, the American Association of Genito-Urinary Surgeons, the American Orthopedic Association, and the American Pediatric Society.[20]

Another way that Americans tried to secure professional esteem was through new forums for group interaction.[21] At specialized lyceum lectures, university extension programs, summer-school institutes, public-library information services, cooperative settlement houses, and more, individuals met to enhance their work and to stake their claim in an increasingly fragmented society. These meetings were crucial to promoting cohesion within professions, to reinforcing occupational identity, to defining technical knowledge, and to erecting the barriers that separated specialties. The goal was to "organize and gain respectability" by defining professional space within the nation's "history and political economy."[22]

On top of these in-person meetings, profession-specific publications helped workers stay abreast of developments in their field. Even though popular periodicals were still considered leading repositories of knowledge, professional journals were quickly gaining intellectual authority.[23] Inside the academy, journals devoted to economics, the law, biology, history, literature, language, and philosophy—not to mention subspecialties in these disciplines—cropped up across the country. Outside the academy, architects, engineers, doctors, mechanics, farmers, and others created their own publications to disseminate the ideas that would enhance the ethos of their labor. Even with workers thousands of miles away in different parts of the country, professional publications helped solidify group identity.

The widespread push for professional esteem in the second half of the nineteenth century put America's schoolteachers in a difficult situation. For decades already, teachers had faced a problem of respectability, which only worsened with the rise of professionalism. Often seen as "Ichabod Cranes and fussy schoolmarms," they embodied the "apparent paradox of exceptionally low prestige in a land that acclaimed universal education."[24] Moreover, despite the "increasing requirement that job applicants" in a host of occupations "possess formal educational certificates or diplomas, teachers still did not have to possess many academic credentials, and in fact very few did."[25] The result was a fairly widespread perception that teachers were not professionals, which could be exceedingly problematic in the culture of professionalism. To make matters worse, methods of teaching seemed antiquated in light of new, proudly scientific systems of knowledge. The quality of education varied wildly from community to community and from schoolroom to schoolroom, which did little to promote cohesion and group identity among pedagogues.

The National Education Association, founded in 1857 as the National Teachers Association, fostered some sense of professional identity, as did many state and regional organizations. But as the nineteenth century wore on, it became clear that teachers needed more than occupational associations to shake the negative perceptions associated with their work.[26] Essentially, teachers needed to become pedagogical experts and to seize the cultural authority that accompanied expertise. In countless professional publications at the time, the call went out for teachers to modernize, specialize, and demonstrate the value of their labor. Albert Bushnell Hart argued for "The Teacher as Professional Expert."[27] Walter Ballou Jacobs insisted that "teaching ought to be a profession; that its work in importance is second to none; that while the other professions restore—medicine to health, law to justice, theology to righteousness—teaching is the science by which evil is anticipated by prevention; by which the bad never exists, because of the development of the good."[28] E. E. Higbee, superintendent of schools in Pennsylvania, declared that teachers should "use every opportunity within their reach to advance their professional zeal and skill. Well-conducted teachers' institutes are exceedingly valuable for this purpose; indeed, in our judgment, indispensable."[29]

Higbee was not alone in his belief that teacher institutes and other professional-development courses were essential to the advancement of education in America. By meeting together to discuss common problems and possible solutions, many believed, teachers could learn state-of-the-art techniques, standardize their methods of instruction, solidify their associations, and gain a better sense of their social value. Moreover, professional-development courses allowed teachers to learn a common language, an in-group vocabulary that separated pedagogy from other practical arts. Writing in the *Southern Education Journal* in 1897, Henry Hayes explained that "The institute has no more important office than that of developing professional spirit and enthusiasm among the teachers. Most teachers live and labor in narrow spheres. . . . Above all things else, the institute ought to be a source of inspiration, filling the teachers with an earnest zeal for educational progress and professional advancement."[30]

In addition to promoting a new professional identity, teachers' institutes offered schoolteachers the opportunity to learn the insights, lessons, and promises of modern science. Because "science" was "the basic word that every school of thought claimed and worshipped," it enabled educators to put pedagogy on a seemingly solid foundation.[31] Infusing the art of teaching with the supposed rigor and certainty of science would, hopefully, bring education in line with the rest of industrial America. In turn, teachers could earn the respect they desired and find their place alongside other modern professions. Thomas Morgan put the point succinctly in his advice to young teachers in 1892: When you understand pedagogy as "the science of developing the human soul to its highest degree," when you draw upon "every science or branch of knowledge which throws light upon man in any of his relations, stages of development, or activities," then "those whom you teach will feel the quickening influence of your presence, catch your enthusiasm for truth, imitate your methods of work, imbibe your philosophy of life, and take on the stamp of your character. Your services will be in demand, your labors rewarded, your own self-respect satisfied."[32]

Of all the branches of science that teachers could use to advance themselves and their work, psychology seemed to hold the most promise. "The science of psychology would revolutionize education," writes Vernon Hall, characterizing the popular belief of the day, "and many educators at all levels were willing to give the new science a chance."[33] In particular, psychology presented the opportunity to know the minds of students and to control what happened in the classroom. For some, in fact, pedagogy was little more than applied psychology.[34] James McKeen Cattell, a prominent psychologist and a frequent rival of William James, aptly summarized the promise of psychology for pedagogy in an article in *Popular Science Monthly.* When the rigors of modern psychology are applied to pedagogy, Cattell explained, "we may hope to replace vague surmises with exact knowledge. In our laboratories of psychology we can test the senses and faculties of children. We can determine whether the course of study is developing or stunting fundamental characteristics. . . . Above all, our tests and measurements will demonstrate the value of learning itself, and tell us whether under given circumstances it is secured by the development or sacrifice of more essential qualities, such as health of body, serenity of mind, common sense, honesty, and kindliness."[35]

Despite Cattell's insistence, bringing psychology to bear on pedagogy was seldom an easy task. At the same time the study of psychology was differentiating and distancing itself from philosophy, carving out an "independent realm in the academic landscape,"[36] it was also constructing a new technical discourse, which often functioned as a barrier to those outside the discipline. Essentially, psychologists and teachers lacked a common language, which often led to confusion, frustration, apathy, and boredom on the part of educators. As one commentator described the problem, "Teachers as a body are by no means fond of being talked to on psychology. . . . It is doubtless a sad fact that an overwhelming majority of teachers either never have had their attention attracted to psychology, or have been repelled from it by a formal and uninteresting presentation of the subject."[37]

Nevertheless, the final decade of the nineteenth century witnessed the rise of a veritable cottage industry of lectures and texts aimed at the intersection of psychology and pedagogy.[38] Psychologists, lecture organizers, book publishers, and editors all seemed excited about the opportunity to bring together the laboratory and the classroom. In 1881, for example, Granville Stanley Hall, a young psychologist trained under James, gave a series of lectures in Boston on the importance of applying modern science to the work of teachers. "The great change which has been brought about in the modern systems of education," reported the Boston *Daily Advertiser* in summarizing Hall's final lecture, "has resulted from a better understanding of the nervous system. . . . The ideal system of marks and punishments which ought to be constantly in view, however we may fall short of attaining it, is to have them conformable to those rewards and those adverse or retributive influences which the pupil will inevitably encounter when he engages in the affairs of life."[39]

Hall was just one of many scientists who saw an important opportunity to talk about psychology with America's schoolteachers. Another was William James.[40] Taking part in "a great fermentation in 'paedagogy' at present in the U.S.," as James told a friend, he made talking to teachers a priority in his life.[41] In cities and towns across the country, educators wanted to know more about modern science, about the changing world of knowledge, and about how psychology could benefit their work. But they needed someone who understood their predicament, who spoke their language, and who could help them navigate the often-bewildering dynamics of science, professionalism, and industrial society. Among all the psychologists in the country, James was perhaps in the best position to speak to the nation's schoolteachers. Because of the success of *Principles of Psychology* and because of his reputation for compelling presentations, he could, if he wanted, spend a decade or more talking to teachers.

Life on the Lecture Circuit

Touring the country during the 1890s to address America's schoolteachers, James became painfully familiar with life on the lecture circuit. Homesickness, exhaustion, nagging social obligations, boredom, health problems—he experienced them all. But he never stopped what he was doing. Year after year, he returned to the circuit to speak with new audiences in different parts of the country. Money played a role in his commitment, as he earned upwards of an extra $1,000 a year—approximately one-fourth of his Harvard salary—by delivering "Talks to Teachers."[42] But money was only part of the equation. After all, he could have earned just as much by lecturing in and around Boston, and he could have avoided many of the issues that accompanied extensive travel. James found something besides money on the lecture circuit. What was it? Engaging a relatively marginalized group of people struggling for professional esteem provided him with a new perspective on the American experience. Moreover, it allowed him to practice the highest form of art.

James's first chance to talk with teachers came after Harvard hired Paul Henry Hanus as assistant professor of the history and art of teaching. Hanus's job was to launch a course of instruction for aspiring educators—professionalizing them as best he could.[43] When Hanus and Harvard president Charles William Eliot thought about how to get the pedagogy program off the ground in Cambridge, they could think of no better contributor than James. They figured he, if anyone, could deliver insightful and entertaining lectures for local teachers. At first, James hesitated to accept the lecture offer, unsure that he had anything original to say. He did not know "what pedagogic psychology means," he wrote to Hanus, "except the habit, association, apperception, and attention chapters of common psychology." Eventually, however, James agreed to "sacrifice" himself and help Harvard advance its pedagogical offerings.[44] From October 27, 1891, to January 21, 1892, he gave ten lectures in a series he called "Topics in Psychology of Interest to Teachers."[45]

By all accounts, the first iteration of "Talks to Teachers" was a success. Though the lectures were originally scheduled to be delivered in Upper Dane Hall Laboratory on Harvard's campus, the turnout was so great that organizers had to move the presentation to the large lecture room in Upper Dane and open it to the public. During the talks, at least two of James's listeners wrote him notes praising the lectures and asking him to pursue various ideas further for the benefit of the audience as a whole.[46] Another listener took careful notes and published his summaries in several consecutive issues of the *Journal of Education*.[47]

James himself did not comment much on the lectures; he likely had no intimation of how often he would repeat them. But a couple years after the Harvard course, two more opportunities to talk with teachers came his way. The first was at the Brooklyn Institute of Arts and Sciences, a prominent lecture venue at the end of the nineteenth century. Not much is known about this iteration of the series. In fact, scholars of James's work have thus far been unsure whether James even spoke at the Brooklyn Institute in 1894.[48] However, recently uncovered lecture announcements and reports from the venue confirm the talks.[49] Beginning on October 6 and ending on November 17, he delivered six lectures on what he called "The Applications of Psychology to Teaching."[50] James did not comment on the effectiveness of the lectures, but in publicizing the series, a writer for the *Catholic World* predicted what was likely to transpire: While James was "one of the ablest philosophical scholars in the United States," he would not "befog the subject" of pedagogical psychology with "high-sounding words."[51]

James's second opportunity to talk with teachers in 1894 took place at a schoolhouse on the corner of St. Botolph and Cumberland streets in Boston. The series, now titled "Psychology as Applied to Teaching," ran from November 12 through December 24. Although it is not clear how this iteration may have differed from the first two, it is clear that the lectures were a hit. They were "crowded," James reported to his brother Henry, and he was "gaining great *desinvolture* in their delivery."[52] Perhaps he had something original to say to teachers after all.

Sometime around the 1894 lecture series, although the precise time is not clear, James composed a "Talks to Teachers" speaking notebook that he would use repeatedly during the 1890s.[53] The contents of the notebook and the way James likely used it at the lectern provide an important glimpse into his habits as a lecturer. James did not speak from a full-sentence manuscript when delivering "Talks to Teachers."

Instead, he relied on succinct fragments, which allowed him to lecture in a conversational yet intellectually stimulating manner. The goal was to talk with listeners about important ideas rather than to speak at them with fully formed sentences. Consider some of his points for the fourth lecture in the series: "Psychology can't direct. Horse to water. Make him thirsty. Herbartian preparation. Rewards & punishments. *Voluntary attention*—interest remote." James knew what the fragments meant; they indicated where he was going in the lecture, but they did not dictate the sentences that would come from his mouth. As a result, he could improvise, adapt as needed, and provide a view of thought unfolding.

With speaking notebook in hand, James made plans for the following summer, which included a "lecturing tour of a minute sort."[54] First up was Norwich, Connecticut, where he spoke to teachers at the Norwich Free Academy, July 15–17, 1895. One of many teacher institutes in operation across the country that summer, the Norwich Free Academy was designed to aid a teacher's professional development and to provide a detailed introduction to modern science.[55] For James, the institute was an opportunity to develop the lecture series further. Because the academy's summer session allowed him only a brief visit, he had to compress the ten-lecture series down to only three. But that seemed agreeable enough to his audience—some "350 (young women mainly)" in a beautiful country setting.[56] Both the "school-marms," as James called them, and the town were "'sylvan' to the last degree."[57] Were it not for the "vile hammock-like 'woven wire mattresses'" at his hotel, the trip would have been perfect.[58] When it was time for James to depart, his hosts asked him to repeat the series the following summer.[59]

After Connecticut, James returned to Cambridge to deliver the lectures at Harvard's summer school. Though his audience was not as big as it had been previously—only 30 people this time around—he nevertheless thought his listeners "a very fine lot, very mature, strong looking, and attentive and responsive, one grandmother, and 8 male school superintendents among them."[60] He also expanded the number of lectures in the series, speaking six times instead of three. Over the next few years, speaking half a dozen times at Harvard's summer school would become a tradition.

The final stop in the 1895 miniature lecture tour allowed James to put more money in his pocket but also, and more important, to engage a community far away from home. George Turnbull, principal of Colorado

Springs High School and director of the Colorado Summer School, had heard nothing but praise of James's lectures, and early in 1895 he asked James to visit Colorado Springs.[61] James leaped at the idea, both for intellectual reasons and because the trip would allow him to visit the great American West, a place he had long wished to see. After finishing his lectures at the Harvard summer school, he boarded a train that took him through New York to Detroit, then to Chicago and Kansas City before rolling into Colorado. When the train pulled into the station, George Turnbull was there to greet him.[62]

In Colorado Springs, James stayed at the home of a Mrs. Goddard, whom he described as "a widow, and woman of the world."[63] He was particularly grateful that she gave him space to relax and to work on his lectures, the first of which took place on August 2 in the Coburn Library Chapel of Colorado College. The turnout was large, and the lecture went off "well enough," but James was struck by the character of his audience. Allowing his New England elitism to show through, he told his wife that "the western woman of the poorer classes has a long way to make to reach the level of her new england homologue." Because they seemed like backwoods small-towners, James thought his audience members "of an inferior quality" when compared "to those I had previously given the same course to."[64]

James's elitist remark, not atypical when he was feeling homesick, signaled the distance he felt from his audience at the beginning of the lecture series. Socially, culturally, intellectually, even geographically, he occupied a different world than that of small-town schoolmarms in Colorado. But a great distance between speaker and audience meant that James had an opportunity to change the relationship. And as the lecture series proceeded, he began to feel a remarkable kinship with Colorado, its people, and the intellectual work being done. "Things are reeling off splendidly, and I am feeling very well as I get more acclimated," he told his wife.[65] Toward the end of his visit he remarked that he was glad he made the trip, "for [it] keeps one more in tune with one's fellow country men. Uncouth and crude as most of these school teachers are, it touches one's sympathies to see their dead seriousness and 'struggling towards the light' attitude."[66] Despite referring to the audience as "uncouth and crude," James understood the importance of what was happening in the lecture hall. The focus of the talks was not on any new psychological insights or on James's research program. The focus was on helping teachers in Colorado, who were desperately "struggling towards the light," find professional esteem.

This moment of identification between James and his audience continued through the close of the lectures. By the end, he felt himself "a better american" for having talked with Colorado's schoolmarms.[67] The label "American" was especially significant. At first, James had seen himself as an elite New Englander towering over the unkempt ladies of a backwards town. But by the end of the series, he used a label that transcended geographic and cultural differences. They were all Americans. "The great marvel of [the lectures] to the school-marms," James elaborated, "seems to have been that they were *intelligible*. Such a thing was not to be expected of psychology, according to their previous experience."[68]

At the end of the summer, James reflected on the development of "Talks to Teachers" and turned his attention toward the future. He lamented that the edges of his speaking notebook were "getting worn off . . . by repetition," and he feared that "they won't stand much more delivery." He had made some good money, and along the way he had done what other psychologists seemed unable or unwilling to do: He had helped America's teachers in their struggle for professional identity by crafting lectures that were intelligible, engaging, and entertaining. The more he thought about it, the more he figured his frayed lecture notes could "make a saleable booklet with no great trouble in composition."[69] Money, again, was important, but a book could also reach thousands more people than lecturing alone.

The published version of "Talks to Teachers" was still a few years away, however. In the meantime, the lecture circuit beckoned—promising more money, more teacher audiences, and more opportunities to feel like a better American. First up in 1896 was the Harvard summer school, where James spoke in early July. It was easy to repeat what he had said the previous summer, and his lectures seemed as effective as ever.[70] But Harvard was just a prelude to his subsequent engagements. After Harvard, he hopped on a train for the University of Buffalo, where his hosts were "a young medical man & his wife in a charming new house on a charming street." The community, James thought, was lovely, but he was burdened once again with a dreaded wire mattress; he told his wife that he would probably just sleep on the floor instead of endure another night on such a vile invention.[71]

Despite the mattress, the lectures in Buffalo were a hit. James delivered the first on July 16, pleasantly surprised by "the spirit with which it was delivered, and by the approbative gestures etc which it received from the audience" of 100 to 150 people.[72] In fact, James thought the lecture "the best I *ever* gave."[73] It was a significant statement, given the accolades he had already received for his speaking. But it proved that repeating the material in town after town, year after year, strengthened the work.

In between talks in Buffalo, James decided to take in some local color. At the top of his list was a visit to Niagara Falls. He was particularly amused by a six-year-old boy's reaction to the falls. Staring at the magnificent vista before him, the boy stood in silence until his mother asked: "Well! what do you think of them?" The boy replied in amazement: "Is that the kind of spray I spray my nose with?"[74] Heartily amused, James thought it an excellent example of "apperception," one of the concepts he was exploring with his audience at the University of Buffalo. He would even incorporate the anecdote into the published version of *Talks*.[75]

As the series in Buffalo came to a close, James found himself "quite astonished" by the lectures, especially that "the old stuff is not yet worn out." The material seemed revived in part because he had to strip it "down to its fighting weight, and talk with the energy of despair." Because he spoke five times for forty-five minutes at a stretch, he could include only the essential material.[76] In the end, James was taken by the same sentiments of the previous summer. He was pleased to talk with "so many good fellow country people" and to visit their communities.[77] While the beautiful mountain views of Colorado had made him feel connected to nature, the up-to-date urban cityscape of Buffalo also brought a smile to his face. He described the scene as "200 miles of asphalt pavement—and pretty as a picture throughout."[78]

However, James was not nearly as excited about the Chautauqua Institute in western New York, where he stopped on his way home. At Chautauqua, he spoke to some 500 people on "Psychology and Relaxation," and he came away with a good sense of his growing intellectual celebrity.[79] Yet he was dissatisfied with the tone of the institute. The identification he had felt with teacher audiences stood in stark contrast to his disconnection from Chautauqua's sterile ways of life. The institute was bland, artificial, inauthentic, and divorced from the world that most Americans experienced. It was *too* perfect. Upon leaving, James craved signs of human depravity: "The flash of a pistol, a dagger, or a devilish eye, anything to break the unlovely level of 10,000 good people, a crime, murder, rape, elopement, anything would do."[80] Whereas talking to teachers had presented James with a sociocultural gap to bridge, the Chautauqua Institute revealed the banalities of privilege. Sadly, the most dangerous thing he experienced there was "ice cream soda," which perfectly illustrated the place's "mediocrity."[81]

Two weeks after returning from the Chautauqua Institute, James boarded a train for Chicago. From September 1 to 4, 1896, he spoke at the University of Chicago to a crowd that averaged around 500 people per lecture. The audience, he reported, was interested and appreciative, but he was a little disappointed at "the absence of special praise from anyone, such as I have had before."[82] Once again, however, the distance he felt from the audience was soon overcome. Lecturing reminded him just how "pure, noble, well meaning and intelligent through & through" the American people were.[83] Unlike the Chautauqua Institute, but just like Colorado and Buffalo, Chicago was authentic. The schoolteachers of Illinois were authentic. And when the lectures came to a close, James once again felt himself a "better American."[84]

James also used his time in Chicago to make progress on turning "Talks to Teachers" into a book. He knew he was getting close to the day when the material would be worn out, so publishing it seemed the best way to proceed.[85] To that end, he hired a stenographer to attend his Chicago lectures and to record what he said, which would save him the trouble of turning his fragments into full-sentence prose. Though he was somewhat disappointed with what the stenographer produced,[86] it was significant that he thought hiring a stenographer the best course of action. By recording the talks stenographically, James had the opportunity, and the apparent desire, to capture the energy and authenticity—the Americanness—of the lecture hall. In essence, he wanted to publish his lectures, rather than a book based on the material used in the lectures. It was an impulse that would define much of his work. *The Varieties of Religious Experience*, *Pragmatism*, and *A Pluralistic Universe*, among others, exemplified James's desire to publish his lectures qua lectures instead of more traditional academic texts.

The summer of 1897 brought less lecturing and more publication preparation. James did deliver "Talks to Teachers" at the Harvard summer school, as he had done the previous two years. And as before, the lectures were a hit. The "ladies of the summer school" even held a reception for him at the Harvard faculty club.[87] He also repeated what he had done the previous summer by hiring a stenographer to get the lectures down on paper.[88] At the same time, he drummed up correspondence with Walter Hines Page, editor of the *Atlantic Monthly,* about publishing a few of the lectures in the *Atlantic*. Doing so would not only thicken his wallet—the *Atlantic* would end up paying $600 for four of his talks—it would also whet the public's appetite for more pedagogical morsels.[89]

Eighteen ninety eight marked the final year of the "Talks to Teachers" lecture series. By the fall, the manuscript would be in the hands of the printer, but not before James embarked on his longest western jaunt to date. California had been calling to him for a number of years. No doubt his friend, colleague, and philosophical foil Josiah Royce, a native of California, had increased his desire to visit the West Coast. But the shores of the Pacific also offered him the opportunity to work with teachers in still another community—one very different than those in the East, the Midwest, and Colorado. Beginning in early 1897, James corresponded with George Holmes Howison of the University of California, Berkeley, about delivering lectures in northern California.[90] He hoped to speak on a number of topics to fund the trip: "Talks to Teachers"; a series on psychology and paranormal phenomena entitled "Exceptional Mental States," which he had delivered at Boston's Lowell Institute in 1896; and a couple popular lectures dealing with philosophical questions of interest to the general community.[91] Though he would end up not repeating "Exceptional Mental States," he would deliver "Talks to Teachers" and the other lectures. In negotiating with Howison, James singled out the success of "Talks to Teachers" as a primary reason to bring him to California: "I have given such courses before pedagogical audiences many times during the last three years, and have no doubt of their success. In Chicago last winter they were given before the public school teachers, to a constantly increasing audience of over 600."[92] James and Howison went back and forth for a number of months before settling on August 1898 for James's trip.[93]

In late July, James boarded a train for California, choosing his route based primarily on scenery—one of his favorite aspects of life on the lecture circuit. He spent the night in Montreal, saw the gorgeous banks of Lake Superior, gazed upon the open prairies of Manitoba, and stopped in Seattle and Portland before rolling into San Francisco. In California, he spoke first at the University of California's Philosophical Union. "Philosophical Conceptions and Practical Results," as the talk was titled, would go down in history as the discourse that first brought pragmatism to the world's attention. He then spoke in Berkeley at a

Harvard Club dinner before moving to Stanford to answer the question "What Makes a Life Significant?" He delivered "Psychology and Relaxation" on September 12 to a general audience at Berkeley, then headed to the Teacher's Institute of Alameda County to present "Talks to Teachers" for the final time.

In Alameda County, James hoped to "dispel their mystifications" about science and psychology, as he put it to Howison.[94] Interest in James's talks grew steadily as the start date approached. A circular advertising the series insisted that "We are assumed, from Prof. James' well-known reputation, that these lectures will be an inspiration to all."[95] The *San Francisco Call* wrote that James's lectures would be a "novel innovation" compared with what teachers in the area were accustomed.[96] J. P. Garlick, superintendent of Alameda schools, thought the lectures so important that he required every teacher in the district to pay 50¢ for a ticket.[97] Not only did he need to raise enough money to pay James, but he also believed the lectures would be a defining moment in the advancement of pedagogy in northern California.

On September 12, James stepped to the lectern at First Congregational Church on the corner of Twelfth and Clay streets in Oakland.[98] His audience was "good looking and attentive," around 700 people, but somewhat "inanimate."[99] As had happened many times in the past, however, the lectures ended with a palpable connection between speaker and audience. The final lecture, he told his wife, "went off splendidly, the matter finding its due order, and the language being tip-top; and there can be no question of the hearty appreciation of the audience, many of whom, men and women, expressed it to me with shining eyes & faces."[100] As he wrote to his brother Henry, "The main thing is that the trip has done me a world of good, morally and intellectually, & made me see this world's affairs—I think also a bit the next world's—in a simpler broader light." Before a crowd of almost 800 people, he ended "in a blaze of glory, with many thanks for having emancipated the school teachers' souls."[101]

James was being somewhat cute with his remark about having saved the souls of his audience members. But there was some metaphorical truth to the comment. The most important part of the lectures concerned the relationships he cultivated. The teachers of Alameda County, he realized, had learned something new about the culture of professionalism—namely, that the pursuit of knowledge did not have to be limited to specialized enclaves isolated by peculiar jargon and exclusionary credentials. As he explained to Henry, teachers were too often prey "for systematic mystification and pedantification on the part of the pedagogic authorities who write books for them." At the lectern, James did his best to take the opposite approach: "When one talks plain common sense with no technical terms, they regard it as a sort of revelation."[102] At the end of the "Talks to Teachers" series, then, James was able to see modern psychology through the eyes of his audience—spurning scientific jargon and lauding the art of popular statement because it properly served America's educators.

After stepping off the podium in California, James proceeded with plans for publishing the lectures. He sent four of the talks to the *Atlantic* and began thinking of which publisher he should use for the full volume. Knowing, as he told his wife, that the book would "make us rich,"[103] he wondered whether Scribner, Longmans, or Henry Holt would send the most money his way. He was intent, as one commentator has put it, on squeezing "every penny of profit" from the book.[104] Of course, money alone did not motivate James's desire to publish the lectures, but it is necessary to recognize that James was—or at least thought himself to be—a shrewd businessman when it came to his books. In his mind, popular statement and personal profits were not mutually exclusive.

Confident the book would be a hit, James formulated a fairly novel publishing arrangement. He wrote to Henry Holt that "the lectures have stood very well the test of repeated audiences to whom they were delivered. Suspicious at first of anything so unpedantic, the teachers at the close of the course have always been enthusiastic in their thanks and praise."[105] He then laid out the plan. To increase his own profits, he would have the book printed by a friend in Boston and pay Holt 10 percent of the list price to advertise and ship it. Holt had never heard of such a scheme, and he initially balked at the proposal. But as the publisher of *Principles,* Holt knew that James could sell a lot of books, so eventually he acquiesced. "Have it all your own way," Holt said, "but for God's sake, don't get stuck; for if you do, all sorts of devils—incarnate and excarnate—will whisper to you that it was because your publishers ran no risk of failure, and had small temptations to success, and therefore neglected the book."[106]

Holt's words of warning made James even more determined to publish a successful volume. On the lecture circuit, James had organized his talks around eight general topics, though he shaped the specific content depending on the number of lectures he had to deliver on any given occasion. The topics consisted of an overview of psychology and pedagogy, the psychology of the student, the association of ideas, memory, attention, habit, the process of learning, and the will. When it came to the book, however, he spread the eight topics across fifteen chapters, breaking the content into more manageable units. Shorter chapters would lead to a more popular text, as more people could pick up the book and move briskly to chapter divisions. To make the volume even more attractive to readers, James included three lectures he had delivered to different student organizations over the preceding few years. He called this section, which came at the end of the book, "talks to students on some of life's ideals." Though "Talks to Teachers" and "Talks to Students" were thematically different, James wanted to include the latter to make the book heftier and to justify its price, which would end up being $1.50—a substantial amount for a short book in 1899.[107]

Over the next few years, James's peculiar publishing arrangement with Holt would strain their relationship. James would even accuse Holt of cheating him out of profits.[108] But the arrangement did not stop the book from becoming an instant success. Because the lectures were both "practical and popular, and entirely free from technicalities," wrote *Publisher's Weekly* in announcing the publication, *Talks to Teachers* was bound to make its mark on readers across the nation.[109] The *Boston Evening Transcript* remarked that the text was "fundamental without being abstruse, patient without being wearisome, and both allures and enlightens by charity of expression and by fitness of example."[110] The *School Review* focused on the importance of the book for teachers: "It will be a revelation to many who read this book to find that psychology is really interesting. It will be still more of a revelation to find that the psychologist can be delightfully entertaining in talking about so frightful a subject as the application of psychology to pedagogy. . . . Rare are the qualities of charm and attractiveness in pedagogical literature, and these this work possesses in fullest measure, while the truth of its content is vouched for by the eminent scholarly rank of its author."[111]

The writer for *School Review* was right in predicting the success of *Talks* among teachers. In short order, James's lectures became required reading for various groups of educators. In January 1900, Holt informed James that the Indiana Teachers' Reading Circle, one of the largest such circles in the country, had made *Talks* one of its two required texts. This single adoption ensured sales of between 10,000 and 14,000 copies in Indiana alone.[112] In addition to Indiana, Holt later told James, reading circles in Ohio and Illinois, as well as other unnamed states, were adopting the book.[113] Groups in Minnesota, Iowa, Kansas, and Missouri were considering it, Holt informed James later still.[114] The Colorado Department of Education insisted that teachers in that state study James's book as a matter of "professional reading and training."[115] Teachers in Pennsylvania were told the same.[116] *Talks to Teachers,* James reported to a friend, was "booming,"[117] largely because reading circles were ordering "15,000 copies at a stroke."[118] By 1903, the book's reach extended far beyond the nation's borders, having been translated into Japanese, German, and Italian.[119] The lectures had become a central component of pedagogical advancement, nationally and even internationally.

A Note on Oratory and Orality in James's Prose

Both "Talks to Teachers" (the lecture series) and *Talks to Teachers* (the book) enhanced James's public-intellectual standing. His reputation spread far and wide as someone who knew how to speak and write with that rare blend of entertainment and edification. Yet the success of the lecture series and the book raises important textual questions about James's habits as a speaker and author. What was the relationship between what James said at the lectern and what people read? Was the book simply a published version of James's lectures? Did he significantly alter the talks for publication? Should we treat the lectures and book as the same text?

Definitive answers to these questions are difficult to provide, but the available evidence points to the intellectual persona James hoped to advance. It is necessary to remember that James hired a stenographer on more than one occasion to record what he said at the lectern, but he was displeased with what the stenographers produced, complaining to his wife that he would have to rewrite everything for the printer.[120] In late summer 1898, on his way home from California, he did rework at least some of what he had dictated for the book.[121] But because the stenographer's notes have not survived, the extent of his rewrite is not clear. His speaking notes do survive, and they contain most of the same points and phrases that appear in the book. Yet on the lecture circuit James altered the content of the series for different occasions, sometimes compressing lectures to fit time requirements, sometimes excluding whole talks.

As a result, it would be difficult to call *Talks to Teachers* a straightforward reproduction of the lectures, if for no other reason than that there never was just one set of lectures.

However, the fact that the book was not a reproduction of the lecture series misses the point of how James presented the text to readers. Even though he rewrote parts of the lectures for publication, he made sure their oratorical character remained intact. James wanted his readers to feel themselves a part of the lecture occasion, to assume their place in a virtual lecture hall alongside those who listened to the rhythmic intonations of his voice. Consider how he framed *Talks* in the preface: "In 1892 I was asked by the Harvard Corporation to give a few public lectures on psychology to the Cambridge teachers. The talks now printed form the substance of that course, which has since then been delivered at various places to various teacher-audiences." In underscoring the oratorical genesis of the book, James directed the attention of readers to the relationships he had cultivated with listeners across the country. Such relationships, he suggested, determined the character of the book. "I have found by experience that what my hearers seem least to relish is analytical technicality, and what they more care for is concrete practical application. So I have gradually weeded out the former, and left the latter unreduced; and now that I have at last written out the lectures, they contain a minimum of what is deemed 'scientific' in psychology, and are practical and popular in the extreme."[122] Not only did James want readers to imagine themselves in the lecture audience, he also wanted them to understand that for many years he had been working *for* America's teachers, helping them pursue a new professional identity. "So far as books printed like this book force the fluidity of the facts upon the young teacher's attention," he summarized, "so far I am sure they tend to do his intellect a service."[123]

James underscored the oratorical beginnings of *Talks* as a way of preparing readers for the style of the text that would follow. For James, as we saw in the previous chapter, the style of intellectual discourse determined the character of the relationship between writer, reader, and ideas. And *Talks* was going to work toward a distinctive relationship—at least when compared to most pedagogical psychology—so James felt compelled to foreground the book's style. Schoolteachers (and generally interested readers) had to know that they would encounter sentences that were, or were made to seem, originally delivered to live audiences. Indeed, the book contained what Walter Ong has called "high oral residue," as James's mode of thought proceeded through oral patterns of discourse.[124] This would prove true of most of James's prose, especially of his books that began as lectures. It seems fitting, then, to consider briefly the oral characteristics of his prose and the general functions of an oral style.

The elements of James's oral style were largely the same elements of orality—or, better, "secondary orality"—that scholars have identified in texts stretching back hundreds, even thousands, of years.[125] To be sure, orality predates and evades textuality in human history, but the markers of orality can nevertheless shape the character of a written text. This is especially true when texts emerge from oratorical performances and are designed more for ears than for eyes. As Carroll Arnold explains, "Where orality is the mode of rhetorical discourse, exposure of the self in a personalized relationship with another specially modifies the creative and responsive experiences of both makers and listeners."[126] On the lecture circuit and in the printed version of *Talks,* James's aim was indeed interpersonal interactions, or what Arnold calls "confrontations of active beings, . . . not confrontations of impersonally symbolized concepts."[127] Rather than simply pointing his audience to important concepts in pedagogical psychology, James wanted to initiate a discursive confrontation with listeners and readers.

At the most basic level, James's discursive confrontation proceeded through personal pronouns. *Talks to Teachers,* as well as most of his work, was replete with "you," "I," "we," "our," and similar references that allowed listeners and readers to understand themselves as part of an ongoing exchange. For example, in the chapter on the will, James declared: "You perceive now, my friends, what your general or abstract duty is as teachers. . . . Your task is to build up a *character* in your pupils; and a character, as I have so often said, consists in an organized set of habits of reaction."[128] While such references may seem unimportant, they enabled readers to perceive themselves in the movement of ideas.

Yet the elements of James's oral style go much further than personal pronouns to include what scholars have long recognized as discursive patterns crafted for the ear, for those who do not have a text in front of them.[129] Throughout *Talks,* James was careful to signpost his claims, such as when he insisted: "In these talks with you, I shall entirely neglect the questions that come up on the explanatory level."[130] He helped listeners and readers follow the structure of the lectures by reminding them of what they had already discussed, such as when he summarized: "In our foregoing talk we were led to frame a very simple conception of what an education means. In the last analysis it consists in the organizing of *resources* in the human being, of powers of conduct which shall fit him to his social and physical world."[131] He wrote and spoke with a rhythmical balance that helped his audience parse the development of ideas, such as when he commented on the native interests of children: "Novel things to look at or novel sounds to hear. . . . The grimace that Johnny is making, the spitballs that Tommy is ready to throw, the dog-fight in the street, or the distant firebells ringing—these are the rivals with which the teacher's powers of being interesting have incessantly to cope."[132]

It should also be noted that James's colloquialisms and commonplaces, which were often noteworthy to reviewers of his books, were powerful markers of his oral style. Indeed, colloquialisms and commonplaces have been integral to oral discourse for thousands of years.[133] So when James talked of "the alpha and omega of the teacher's art,"[134] when he mentioned "some little pepper-corn of new truth,"[135] when he spoke of students growing "full of zest,"[136] when he pointed to his audience's "flights of fancy,"[137] when he explained lives "shot through with engrossing significance,"[138] when he highlighted habits "organized for our weal or woe,"[139] and when he described properly educated students as those who will "stand like a tower when everything rocks around" them,[140] his phrases may not have been novel, but they were eminently relatable and understandable, particularly for those who stood outside the psychological establishment.

Also central to James's oral style were, as many scholars have noted, vivid and carefully developed metaphors and images.[141] In speaking to groups of people assembled in lecture halls and in addressing readers of his work, James sought to do what rhetors have sought to do for thousands of years—namely, help the audience "see" what was not immediately before their eyes. Metaphors, at least as James employed them, brought abstract ideas into the audience's field of vision, animating and vivifying concepts that might otherwise have remained distant and obscure. In *Talks to Teachers,* for example, he encouraged his audience to think of the minds of students as some kind of gelatin dessert, a "fluid jelly, in which impressions may be easily made, but are soon closed over again, so that the brain reverts to its original indifferent state. But it may occur here, just as in other gelatinous substances, that an impression will vibrate throughout the brain, and send waves into other parts of it."[142] He saved some of his most incisive imagery for a point about the importance of free, unrestrained conversation: "Where mendacity, treachery, obscenity, and malignity find unhampered expression, talk can be brilliant indeed; but its flame waxes dim where the mind is stitched all over with conscientious fear of violating the moral and social proprieties."[143]

More important than the elements of James's oral style, however, especially when considering his evolving art of popular statement, was the function of his "high oral residue." Orality, as Ong has noted, signifies "person-interactive contexts" rather than "object-attentive contexts."[144] Thus when James made the choice to retain the markers of oral performance in his published texts, he worked more for moments of interaction than for the construction of symbolic and conceptual objects. Concepts were important, of course, but his prose aimed above all at fostering relationships in the unfolding of ideas. *Talks* was crafted with and for America's schoolteachers, as James's direct addresses to listeners became direct addresses to readers. In the end, the book became, to use Arnold's phrase, "markedly other-directed."[145]

Another way of putting it is to say that James's oral style fostered what orality usually fosters—namely, participatory discourses. Whereas modern writing tends to promote "distance and objectivity" around symbolic objects, orality tends "to be empathetic and participatory."[146] Audiences in the contexts of orality are "called to listen in, to participate in a conversational exchange."[147] As a participatory text, *Talks* gave America's schoolteachers a role in the production of knowledge; they had an active part in the creation of pedagogical psychology. In James's hands, orality created a picture of thought in the making—a picture that included educators searching for a sense of their significance in modern society.

While reviewers did not explicitly address the dynamics of orality in *Talks,* they did note the importance of James's style. Perhaps the most significant stylistic comment came from a reviewer for the *Southern Education Journal,* who well understood how James's prose worked across professional boundaries:

> The thinking world is again indebted to Mr. James for a book so clear, understandable and helpful. These days so much clap-trap finds a publisher through the plea that it is addressed to teachers, and so is sure of a considerable sale, that one of the profession expresses mingled feeling of surprise and gratitude in following an author who through chapter after chapter furnishes matter sound from the scientific standpoint and pleasing

> from the literary point of view—matter which refreshes the memory and stimulates the ardor of the earnest pupil, while not beyond the comprehension of any intelligent beginner.[148]

For readers, as for lecture attendees, there was something exciting about America's most prominent psychologist leaving behind the conventions of psychology to refresh the memory and stimulate the ardor of nonacademics. To teachers who felt displaced by the culture of professionalism, James's work represented new possibilities.

Of course, the success of *Talks to Teachers*—both the lecture series and the book, which we will treat as more or less the same text, if for no other reason than that James wanted readers to think of them as the same text—was due not just to the way it was written. While James's oratorical prose was integral to the work, *Talks to Teachers* also managed to strike the right chord at the right time, saying what listeners and readers hoped—and needed—to hear in their search for professional esteem.

The Science of Psychology, the Art of Teaching, and the Requirements of Democratic Society

Talks to Teachers covered extensive ground, so any attempt to analyze it in full is bound to fall short. But if we approach it in relation to James's pursuit of popular statement, we can begin to see how the success of the text emerged from the way James incorporated America's schoolteachers into the movement of ideas. Three rhetorical strategies were crucial in this regard. First, James effectively played into the audience's concern that modern psychology was confusing, unhelpful, even detrimental to effective pedagogy. Second, to distinguish his own psychology from most academic psychology and to position himself as the audience's helper in navigating the world of thought, James relied upon a rhetoric of simplicity, which made his work appear as the easiest, most effective way for teachers to advance themselves. Third, in response to the audience's anxiety about the value and significance of educators in industrial society, James positioned teachers as central to the future of the nation, showing them how they—and not the experts of modern thought—possessed the tools necessary for their professional advancement.

James's first strategy—playing into the audience's frustrations about modern psychology and teachers' professional development—was key in showing that he was different from other psychologists and academics. But he went further than simply distinguishing his work from that of his colleagues; he condemned modern psychology for its excessive professionalism and close-mindedness, which helped him create common ground with the audience of nonacademics. Their frustration was his frustration, and, as a result, they could work together on combating a common foe. At the beginning of the lecture series, for example, James praised the desire of teachers for "completer professional training" and for trying to infuse a more "'professional' spirit in their work." Immediately thereafter, he condemned psychologists for impeding the efforts of teachers, lamenting that educators were too often "plunged in an atmosphere of vague talk about our science, which to a great extent has been more mystifying than enlightening." He continued: "Altogether it does seem as if there were a certain fatality of mystification laid upon the teachers of our day. The matter of their profession, compact enough in itself, has to be frothed up for them in journals and institutes, till its outlines often threaten to be lost in a kind of vast uncertainty."[149]

In disparaging the unnecessary froth that accompanied most pedagogical psychology, James began his lectures with a promise: He would not add to the sea of uncertainty that engulfed the nation's teachers. Instead, he would "dispel the mystification" that impeded their efforts and stick to "the fundamental conceptions of psychology which are of real value to the teacher."[150] By positioning most modern psychology as an obstacle to teachers' professional development, James made it possible for him to become the remover of the obstacle, working on behalf of his audience. Whatever he had to say about psychology, whatever clarity he offered, would be done for America's schoolteachers.

James continued his critique of academic psychology by explaining that other psychologists had approached the subject of pedagogy from the wrong direction. By treating pedagogy as a rigorous science—which was exactly what G. Stanley Hall, James McKeen Cattell, and other scholars had done—psychologists denied its true status as a practical art. James's words were harsh for those who put science over art in the classroom: "You make a great, a very great mistake, if you think that psychology, being the science of the mind's laws, is something from which you can deduce definite programs and schemes and methods of instruction for immediate school-room use. Psychology is a science, and teaching is an art; and sciences never generate arts directly out of themselves." Chastising what educators found frustrating (professional science) and praising what they no doubt found exciting (art, or the creativity of the teacher in the classroom), James indicated that he understood the audience's predicament. He also understood that "An intermediary inventive mind, must make the application" of ideas to specific situations "by using its originality."[151] Teachers were the "intermediary inventive" minds; they were the ones in control of the classroom.

Despite the crowd-pleasing appeals of James's opening lecture, there was profound tension in the way he critiqued modern psychology. Because of his reputation, the audience knew him as a professional psychologist, but his introductory message was essentially that modern psychology was a confusing mess—or at least it was given to America's schoolteachers in the form of a confusing mess. This tension was strategic, however, as it created a gap between the potential of psychology and the current ineffective state of the science. Moreover, it positioned James as someone poised to bridge the gap. He was, unlike most members of the psychological establishment, ready to do things differently for the audience.

The best example of James's contrarian approach came when he discussed "apperception," a concept that, he said, "cuts a great figure in pedagogics of the present day." Often trumpeted as a revolutionary new idea, apperception was supposed to reveal important secrets about effective pedagogy. Most often, James explained, publishers and authors used it as a way to sell books, suggesting that if only teachers understood it, they would improve in the classroom. To illustrate, he quoted from an advertisement for a psychology textbook aimed at teachers, which, he believed, perfectly represented the "insidious mystification" that defined academic psychology. The advertisement was for "Blank's *Psychology*," offered to teachers for only $1, and presented under the heading "What is Apperception?" The advertisement stated that "Many teachers are inquiring" about the concept, which "is making a revolution in educational methods in Germany."[152] For just $1, the ad announced, American teachers could discover the grand secret of this new pedagogical tool; they could catch up with their counterparts in Germany and effect a revolution here at home.

James called the advertisement a "disgrace to all concerned." He also let the audience know that his frustration was, like their frustration, palpable: "The conscientious young teacher is led to believe that it contains a recondite and portentous secret, by losing the true inwardness of which her whole career may be shattered." Not one to remain passive while book publishers tried to mystify young teachers, James explained that "apperception" was really no big secret at all—"meaning nothing more than the manner in which we receive a thing into our minds."[153] By providing this simple definition, he showed teachers that he was enough of a psychologist to explain the idea, but he was not so much a psychologist that he had to pretend it contained some all-important secret of the mind.

James demonstrated the same posture when he explained the "stream of consciousness" to his audience. He presented the concept, which he had famously popularized in *Principles of Psychology,* as the best way for teachers to understand the minds of their students. It was the best way, he explained, because it was "secure from positive error and free from admixture of conjecture or hypothesis." James's sights were thus set on his psychological rivals, those who had "tried to make things appear more exact and scientific by making" their work unnecessarily jargon-filled. Pledging that he would "steer clear of [that psychology] altogether," as it was "only conjectural," he presented his approach as bound to the audience's concerns: "For your practical purposes as teachers, the more unpretending conception of the stream of consciousness, with its total waves or fields incessantly changing, will amply suffice."[154]

The fact that James personified modern psychology while at the same time opposing it (or at least the way it was typically carried out) resulted in a powerful intellectual speaking position: He was in touch with the world of the psychologist and the world of the teacher, but ultimately dedicated to the teacher. In fact, this position constituted one of the most crucial aspects of James's art of popular statement. Though he exuded expertise, stepping to the lectern as the most prominent psychologist in the nation, his allegiances lay with his audience—not with other experts. James was willing to buck the trend of professional culture in service of his listeners and readers, joining with them to address their own intellectual problems. In the case of *Talks to Teachers,* he demonstrated that he knew enough about psychology to explain it, even to critique it; but he wanted above all to overcome professionalism's insidious mystification and to arrive at a position that benefited educators.

At times, James's attempt to demonstrate his distance from the psychological status quo seemed to border on anti-intellectualism, such as when he decried the "crass artificiality" of academic psychology, which too often "chopped up" life into "supposed 'processes' with long greek and latin names" that were unhelpful and confusing.[155] Yet it would be a mistake to characterize James's strategy as anti-intellectual, for he was playing the part of the intellectual and working to connect with those who did not normally consider themselves intellectuals. The art of popular statement was not a matter of speaking popularly as opposed to intellectually. It was a matter of pursuing ideas in a way that drew popular audiences into intellectual conversations. James tried to show ordinary Americans that the creation of knowledge did not have to be off-putting. It could, instead, serve what James called "the deeper springs of human personality"—springs that everyone shared.[156]

The second controlling strategy of *Talks to Teachers* was a direct response to the confusing state of academic psychology. Attuned to his audience's frustrations, James endeavored to present his own psychological scheme as simple enough that any teacher could master it, which meant that any teacher could participate in modern intellectual culture. He promised the audience, for example, that "the elements of the mental machine can be clearly apprehended, and their workings easily grasped." In fact, psychology was so simple that it "might almost be written on the palm of one's hand."[157] Later, he declared that the audience should "hold fast to the ultra-simple point of view"—the view that began with biological sensations and then built to higher functions of the mind—when thinking about the mental activity of their students.[158] The simple point of view was beneficial because it led to a "simple conception of what an education means"—namely, the "organizing of *resources* in the human being, of powers of conduct which shall fit him to his social and physical world."[159] Later still, James explained that underneath the vast range of the student's experience, underneath all the "memories and associations and substitutions" that make up the higher functions of the mind, were "the outlines of our simple psychophysical scheme."[160] That scheme—James's scheme—would help teachers understand the constantly shifting interests of their pupils, especially the relationship between "acquired" and "native" interests. "There is," he said, "a very simple law that relates the acquired and the native interests with each other," a law he italicized so readers could not miss it: "*Any object not interesting in itself may become interesting through becoming associated with an object in which an interest already exists. The two associated objects grow, as it were, together.*"[161] On the next page, James used the simplicity of the law of native and acquired interests to present, again with italics, "*a very simple abstract program for the teacher to follow in keeping the attention of the child: Begin with the line of his native interests, and offer him objects that have some immediate connection with these.*"[162]

The language of simplicity—which contrasted greatly with professionalism's tendency toward complication, systematization, and technical precision—made good on James's promise that he would cut through the confusion of modern psychology. It also allowed him to break down his ideas into manageable blocks of information that teachers could take with them into the classroom. But the rhetoric of simplicity was not for the benefit of the audience alone. With it, James was able to reinforce his public-intellectual ethos. He became the audience's guide in bringing the lessons of psychology into the classroom. Where others had created confusion, James created a space for standing with America's schoolteachers and addressing the challenges they faced. "Elicit interest from within," he summarized, "by the warmth with which you care for the topic yourself, and by following the laws I have laid down."[163]

At times, James's dedication to the rhetoric of simplicity went to such lengths that he seemed more like a motivational speaker than the nation's greatest psychologist. Although we risk cheapening James's work by linking it to the rhetoric of motivational speaking, it is nevertheless the case that James wanted to throw off whatever academic pretensions may have followed him to the podium. "In almost any subject," he advised, sounding like a self-help guru, "your passion for the subject will save you. If you only care enough for a result, you will almost certainly attain it. If you wish to be right, you will be right; if you wish to be learned, you will be learned; if you wish to be good, you will be good. Only you must, then, *really* wish these things, and with exclusiveness, and not wish at the same time a hundred other incompatible things just as strongly."[164] Later in the series, James continued this motivational speaking style by providing three simple steps the audience could take to "save" their students: "Thus are your pupils to be saved: first, by the stock of ideas with which you furnish them; second, by the amount of voluntary attention that they can exert in holding to the right ones, however unpalatable; and third, by the several habits of acting definitely on these latter to which they have been successfully trained."[165] Pedagogical salvation had seldom been this clear.

Salvation, motivation, and inspiration were also central to the conclusion of *Talks*. James hoped to leave America's schoolteachers with a clear sense of their power and effectiveness, which, he plainly suggested, resulted from the intellectual system he offered, as opposed to the exclusionary system offered by the mystifiers:

> If to some of you the things I have said seem obvious or trivial, it is possible that they may appear less so when, in the course of a year or two, you find yourselves noticing and apperceiving events in the school-room a little differently, in consequence of some of the conceptions I have tried to make more clear. I cannot but think that to apperceive your pupil as a little sensitive, impulsive, associative, and reactive organism, partly fated and partly free, will lead to a better intelligence of all his ways. Understand him, then, as such a subtle little piece of machinery. And if, in addition, you can also see him *sub specie boni,* and love him as well, you will be in the best possible position for becoming perfect teachers.[166]

The rhetoric of simplicity provided an appropriate, motivational conclusion to the lecture series. Perfection was possible because of the simple system James had laid out. And if the nation's teachers adopted the system, they could become masters of the classroom.

There are at least two ways of looking at James's motivational speaking style in *Talks*. The first is to view it as pandering to the audience. No self-respecting psychologist, one might argue, should dumb down his or her work to the point where he or she becomes a self-help guru. Such a view, however, misses the point of the lectures. *Talks* was not about advancing psychology; it was about helping America's schoolteachers. Thus the second way to view James's motivational speaking style is to view it in terms of the relationships he hoped to foster. One of America's most brilliant thinkers was so committed to his audience, so interested in helping ordinary Americans with the problems they faced, that he chose to speak in a way that animated them. James took America's teachers so seriously that he wanted to get them excited about their ability to contribute to modern intellectual culture. Indeed, this latter view best reflects James's work on the lecture circuit year after year. Because he had learned to identify with his audience's professional predicament, he adopted a vocabulary and attitude that would draw listeners and readers into a motivational, participatory conversation.

In traveling the country engaging audiences of teachers, James had also realized that they were searching for answers to questions that had little to do with modern psychology. In fact, one of the biggest questions teachers faced in the rapidly industrializing world of the Gilded Age and Progressive Era was essentially a sociological question: What role did schoolteachers play in modern society? What was their value and significance in the late nineteenth century? It was a question tied to the widespread push for professional esteem that shaped American culture at the time. To earn the respect they so craved, the nation's teachers needed to be able to articulate their place in the world. James believed he could help in this regard, and his attempt to answer the sociological question constituted the third controlling strategy of the lecture series. America's schoolteachers, he insisted throughout *Talks,* were not only in control of their classrooms but also in control of America's future. As a result, they were socially indispensable.

Early in the lecture series, James defined education as "*training the pupil to behavior.*" But he meant "behavior" in the broadest sense—not only as it applied to children but also as it applied to future citizens. Teachers, he believed, had to appreciate their duty to equip students for handling "the vicissitudes of life" and for imparting the "assortment of habits that shall be most useful . . . throughout life."[167] For James, education pointed far beyond the walls of the schoolhouse, far beyond the lives of children; it pointed to the character of society as a whole. "Make freemen of your pupils," he begged the audience, "by habituating them to act, whenever possible, under the notion of a good."[168] Students would thus be able to live effectively as productive parts of the citizenry. Yet such effectiveness, James underscored repeatedly, began with teachers. "*Feed* the growing human being, feed him with the sort of experience for which from year to year he shows a natural craving, and he will develop in adult life a sounder sort of mental tissue."[169]

When James put teachers in control of the next generation of Americans, he fulfilled the promise he had established at the beginning of the lecture series—namely, that he would help his audience members in "striving to enlighten and strengthen themselves" relative to "the nation's probabilities of advance in all ideal directions."[170] With his gaze focused on the nation's development, James wanted the teacher to feel "a healthy sense of the importance of his mission" and to know "how exclusively dependent upon his present ministrations in the way of imparting conceptions the pupil's future life is probably bound to be."[171] To that end, he gave his audience various strategies for training future citizens and assisting with the development of the nation. One strategy was to promote a healthy rivalry among students—a competition to earn the best grades and to set the proper example for the rest of the class. According to James, "The feeling of rivalry lies at the very basis of our being, all social improvement being largely due to it." Rivalry, he said, was "essential to a spirited and enterprising character," which would end up strengthening society as a whole.[172] A second strategy was to promote relaxation among students, for "ceaseless over-tension" had become a "grievous national harm." The teacher was thus in a position to mitigate one of America's biggest problems. Indeed, both rivalry and relaxation were necessary for nurturing "a better set of personal ideals," with which students could tackle future challenges.[173] Teachers were not just masters of the classroom; they were masters of social progress.

Of all the ideas James hoped his audience would take away from his lectures, the most important for training future citizens was the role of habit. Habit was a central psychological concept for James, and when he discussed it with teacher audiences, the idea assumed a decidedly civic tone. If only America's teachers could help their students to develop the right habits, James believed, the future of the nation would be more secure. As he explained,

> The physiological study of mental conditions still remains on the whole the most powerful ally of hortatory ethics. The hell to be endured hereafter, of which theology tells, is no worse than the hell we make for ourselves in this world by habitually fashioning our characters in the wrong way. Could the young but realize how soon they will become mere walking bundles of habits, they would give more heed to their conduct while in the plastic state. We are spinning our own fates, good or evil, and never to be undone. Every smallest stroke of virtue or of vice leaves its never-so-little scar.[174]

He then added:

> Let no youth have any anxiety about the upshot of his education, whatever the line of it may be. If he keep faithfully busy each hour of the working day, he may safely leave the final result to itself. He can with perfect certainty count on waking up some fine morning to find himself one of the competent ones of his generation, in whatever pursuit he may have singled out. Silently, between all the details of his business, the *power of judging* in all that class of matter will have built itself up within him as a possession that will never pass away. Young people should know this truth in advance.[175]

In James's scheme, education was about creating the "competent ones" of the next generation, and it was about putting teachers in a privileged position relative to the nation's development. The teacher stood between a life of hell or a life of heaven for the student, which translated into hell or heaven for America. Amid the upheavals of the modern world, educators could—indeed, they had to—push the nation toward a better version of itself. The future of the country hinged upon their work.

It must be noted, however, that James's discussion of education as citizen training was remarkably unoriginal. In fact, it was as old as the Western world. Isocrates, Cicero, and Quintilian, among many others, promoted "education as citizen training" as part of their vision of an enlightened society.[176] But the point of *Talks* was not James's originality; the point was to discuss pedagogy in a familiar and empowering way, putting America's teachers back in possession of the world around them. Since the founding of the Republic, American schools had been focused on inculcating individual and social virtues in the nation's youth. As one historian of education has remarked, for much of the nineteenth century the nation's schools functioned as a "crucible of character," dedicated to "the creation of the diligent worker, the responsible citizen, and the man or woman of virtue."[177] Particularly with the advent of the common school movement in the 1830s, which, by the end of the nineteenth century, had spread across the country, classrooms were seen as sites "for social improvement through education," with countless advocates championing "the importance of education in a republic."[178] When James stressed citizen training, then, he stressed a view of education as it existed before the onslaught of modern science. His audience did not need to worry about their role in society because it had not changed, despite what other psychologists, and professional culture writ large, had told them.

Underlying James's presentation, then, was a subtle point, but perhaps the most powerful one he made in the lectures: Science remained secondary to the efforts of the individual teacher. Because teaching was an art, the audience could use the lessons of psychology as they wished, but psychology, even James's psychology, would always be less important than artistry in the classroom. As James explained, truly effective teaching depended upon seizing "the proper pedagogic moment" to connect with students and upon knowing when "the hour is ripe" for the point of the lesson to emerge.[179] Because there was no way for science to determine when the hour was ripe, it was up to the individual teacher, the artist of the classroom, to make the right connection at the right time. "The teacher must himself be alive and ready," insisted James, "and must use the contagion of his own example" to inspire students. As far as inspiration goes, "psychology and general pedagogy here confess their failure."[180] Yet when psychology and general pedagogy admit their limits, the teacher becomes free to effect real change: "Success depends mainly on the native genius of the teacher, the sympathy, tact, and perception which enable him to seize the right moment and set the right example."[181]

James's point was a very unscientific one, but it reconnected the audience to what they already knew. The job of the teacher had not changed much. Psychology might help explain the student's state of mind, but its value was slight compared to the value of "teachers with eyes in their heads and common sense, and some feeling for the concrete facts of human nature in their hearts."[182] Sidestepping the determinism of modern science, James harkened back to classical notions of pedagogy and civic engagement that were familiar to his audience and still relevant to democratic society. When it came to self-improvement, when it came to professional development, America's teachers needed to listen less to scientists and more to the muses of old.

Conclusion

Talks to Teachers on Psychology dealt with many of the themes and ideas that had made *Principles of Psychology* a groundbreaking work. Yet one of the most striking aspects of *Talks* is that it ended on a remarkably nonpsychological, nonscientific note. Above all, James tried to empower his teacher audiences, giving them a stake in modern intellectual culture and helping them see their value in democratic society. Traveling the lecture circuit and visiting people in markedly different communities helped him identify with America's schoolteachers and their struggle for professional esteem. Over time, he grew accustomed to viewing the intersection of psychology and pedagogy through the eyes of a teacher—someone who often felt bewildered and frustrated with modern science but who also genuinely wished to enhance his or her work. The book that emerged from James's time on the lecture circuit was thus an extension of his relationships with America's schoolteachers.

At a more general level, *Talks to Teachers* reveals one of the central aspects of James's pursuit of popular statement—namely, his dedication to creating a new kind of intellectual community. For years, teachers had been told that modern psychology, and the experts who controlled psychological knowledge, held the secrets to pedagogical advancement. Under such a model, professional development for teachers had to proceed through scientific authorities and the insights they possessed. James did his utmost to alter this system of power. Where other psychologists had been mystifying, he was clear and simple, showing how any teacher could learn the so-called secrets of modern psychology. More than that, however, James let teachers know why psychology was not the pedagogical panacea it had been made to seem. Psychological knowledge, even the psychological knowledge James offered, was simply less important than the artistry of the classroom. "A knowledge of such psychology as this which I am recalling," James concluded, "can no more make a good teacher than a knowledge of the laws of perspective can make a landscape painter of effective skill."[183] What teachers needed to hear at the end of the nineteenth century was something they had long known: Effective teaching was a matter of getting students excited, of compelling performance in the classroom, and of using a little common sense when conducting a lesson. For both James and America's teachers, artistry trumped specialized insights, which meant that the mystifiers and the obtuse experts were much less important than they claimed, at least when it came to pedagogical acumen.

The success of *Talks to Teachers,* not only in terms of sales but also in terms of the intellectual community the text promoted, helped James's reputation spread in new directions. The more he traveled the country and the more he pursued the art of popular statement, the more he was known as someone whose ideas and discourse were different from those of other scholars. By the end of the 1890s, the promise of clarity, orality, insight, edification, and entertainment followed him wherever he went. Yet before we see James's career as one long, successful climb to the top of the intellectual world, it is necessary to recognize that his reputation, and hence his ability to speak effectively to the American people, often teetered on a precipice. Working as a public intellectual is rarely a trouble-free enterprise. In fact, as Edward Said has said, it may well be that public intellectuals define themselves more by controversy than by triumph.[184]

Controversy, as we shall see in the next chapter, was central to James's work as a psychical researcher. During the 1890s, at the same time he was finding success talking to teachers, he was trying to legitimize the study of ghosts, mediums, life after death, haunted houses, telepathy, automatic writing, and more. He quickly found himself locked in heated debates about modern science and the possibility of paranormal phenomena. These debates not only threatened James's intellectual reputation, they also pushed him further away from the culture of academic professionalism.

CHAPTER FOUR

Speaking Up for Spirits

⌘

On July 9, 1885, Herman James, the eighteen-month-old son of William James, died as a result of complications from whooping cough. Two days later, James and his wife buried the child, whom they had affectionately called "Humster" during his short time on earth. His death was devastating to the entire James family, and William lamented that he "had hardly known or seen" the boy "at all."[1]

Although the child was dead, a peculiar turn of events raised the possibility that little Humster was not so far away after all. In September 1885, William James's mother-in-law, Elizabeth Gibbens, visited a Boston psychic named Leonora Piper, whose abilities to channel the departed seemed remarkable. While deep in a trance, Piper provided Mrs. Gibbens with "a long string of names of members of the family, mostly Christian names, together with facts about the persons mentioned and their relations to each other, the knowledge of which, on her part, was incomprehensible without supernormal powers."[2] Mrs. Gibbens was overcome with enthusiasm at the medium's abilities, and she reported the events to her son-in-law. Upon hearing the news, James could not hide his skepticism, as this was not his first time listening to exciting tales of supernormal powers. For the past three years, he had been a member of the Society for Psychical Research, an organization that undertook scientific investigations of mediums, psychics, ghosts, haunted houses, telepathy, automatic writing, life after death, and more. Thus far, the Society for Psychical Research had uncovered nothing impressive; the vast majority of paranormal reports were rubbish. So when Mrs. Gibbens came to James with stories of Piper's abilities, he thought it another trick being played by a money-hungry peddler of the occult.[3]

Skepticism, however, did not stop James from paying Piper a visit. Settling into chairs in the parlor of Piper's house on Beacon Hill, James and his wife watched as the medium entered a trance, her eyes drifting shut, her head turning from side to side, her skin covered with goose bumps, her voice much deeper than normal. Though James and his wife had given the medium no personal information—they were trying to be as objective and scientific as possible[4]—Piper pursued Alice James's maiden name through the fog of the trance. "Niblin," she said first, then "Giblin." Eventually she got it right: Gibbens. After that, Piper repeated the same list of names she had given to James's mother-in-law. Then the meeting took a much stranger turn: Piper asked about a dead child. Many couples at the time lost children to illness, so it was a fairly safe guess, but the medium became eerily specific. The dead child was a small boy, and his name sounded something like "Herrin."

"Herrin" was not exactly "Herman," but it was close enough to pique James's interest. In fact, the names and details Piper provided on that first visit made it "impossible," James later recalled, "not to recognize the particular individuals who were talked about."[5] Confronted with the possibility of legitimate paranormal activity, he visited the medium at least a dozen times over the next several months. The more he studied her, the more she impressed him, as she seemed to know information that she should not know, at least by any conventional means. After repeated investigation, James found two explanations before him: either Piper's abilities amounted to "some lucky coincidence," or she possessed "supernormal powers."[6]

Eventually, Leonora Piper became William James's "white crow"—the proof that he and other psychical researchers needed to put their paranormal investigations on more solid ground. Explaining her status as a "white crow" with the language of the "professional logic-shop," James stated: "A universal proposition can be made untrue by a particular instance. If you wish to upset the law that all crows are black, you mustn't seek to show that no crows are; it is enough if you prove one single crow to be white. My own white-crow is Mrs. Piper. In the trances of this medium, I cannot resist the conviction that knowledge appears which she has never gained by the ordinary waking use of her eyes and ears and wits."[7] Piper was the key to advancing the study of paranormal phenomena, James believed. If she legitimately possessed supernormal powers, then psychical researchers could pursue their projects with confidence.

The trouble for psychical researchers came in convincing others to share their confidence. In other words, James and his colleagues faced a decidedly rhetorical problem. Their task was to find the language, ideas, appeals, arguments, and evidence that would legitimize their work before a skeptical world. To earn academic and professional respect, they needed to demonstrate that they were properly scientific; they needed to fashion a rhetoric of inquiry that linked psychical research with the evolving discourse of late-nineteenth-century science.[8] Psychical researchers thus "took on the methodology of more orthodox science in an attempt to appear as professional—and thereby as credible—as their sister disciplines. . . . Their reports, lengthy and detailed, drew conclusions based on scientific possibility rather than supposition based on faith."[9]

Despite—or perhaps because of—the attempt by psychical researchers to link their work to scientific professionalism, many prominent scientists, particularly in America, were adamant on distancing their own research from the study of paranormal, occult-like phenomena. This was especially true in the emerging field of psychology. For much of the nineteenth century, psychology and the occult were seen as kindred fields of knowledge, at least in the eyes of the general public. When ordinary Americans thought about psychology, they thought about "phrenology, mesmerism, hypnotism, and spiritualism," which resulted in dismay and "embarrassment for the new generation of experimental psychologists."[10] In response, the new generation of psychologists worked on fashioning a discourse that would separate their research from what they saw as the unfortunate investigations and associations of the past. "To win acceptance for their discipline in institutions of higher learning" and "to displace the amateurs—among them, spiritualists and phrenologists—who had captured public attention with their supposed insights into the functioning of the human mind," experimental psychologists began crafting the ideas, arguments, and languages that would earn them respect and scientific standing.[11] They thus turned inward—to members of their specially trained and properly certified group—to solidify the discourse that would structure their professional identity.

The late-nineteenth-century attempt to professionalize psychology led many of James's colleagues to argue that psychical research was a distraction at best and a detriment at worst to truly scientific inquiry. Those who wasted their time listening to ghost stories were, according to the Harvard psychologist Hugo Münsterberg, pursuing "the most vulgar trivialities" and impeding "the truth of science."[12] Joseph Jastrow, a psychologist at the University of Wisconsin, complained that psychical researchers were "simply repeating in new costumes and with improved scenic effects the tragic comedy of former times," thereby detracting from "the moral mission of science."[13] Charles Sedgwick Minot, a professor of comparative anatomy at Harvard, echoed Jastrow's criticism: "It is foolish to search for marvels. The wise search for truth. Yet there are many who have done and are still doing the former, and in so far as they are seeking to find marvelous faculties of the human mind they are performers in the psychical comedy."[14]

James was painfully aware of psychical research's poor standing in much of the scientific community. Yet he was also aware that paranormal phenomena were fascinating subjects for people outside the scientific community. The sheer amount of newspaper coverage psychical research received in America was evidence of a public appetite for discussions of ghostly forces. Strange as it may seem today—especially given James's reputation as a brilliant psychologist, an astute writer on religious life, and the eminent founder of pragmatism—no facet of James's career received more ink in the general press than psychical research, at least during his lifetime. One paper, for example, reporting "bits of gossip" on "men of newspaper fame," revealed that James was "going to try to revive the fashion of experimenting with planchette"—that is, the nineteenth century's equivalent of a Ouija board.[15] Another paper led a story on James and psychical research with the sensational headline "Still They Believe in Ghosts in Boston."[16] Other papers described James's psychical research with such headlines as "Modern Ghosts," "Wonders of the Trance State," "Facts on Phantoms," "A Trio of Ghost Stories,"

"Hypnotism as a 'Fad,'" and "Temporary Absence of the Soul."[17] These characterizations were designed to raise the eyebrows of general readers and to provide a closer look at the curious connection between one of the country's most prominent scientists and the ethereal world beyond the grave.

Nowadays, it is rare to pick up an analysis of James's work and encounter an extended discussion of his psychical research.[18] Biographers have long noted the importance of the subject, at least since Ralph Barton Perry called it "central and typical" to James's worldview.[19] But those interested primarily in James's ideas often set psychical research aside as tangential to his other contributions. The most extended treatment of James as a "public philosopher," for example, says nothing of the subject.[20] In considering James's evolving place in intellectual culture, however, his attempts to legitimize psychical research become pivotal to the trajectory of his career. He sincerely believed that psychical research was a serious and potentially world-changing area of inquiry. But how could he convince others of its value? Moreover, whom should he try to convince?

As we shall see, the art of popular statement became one of James's most-used tools in the project of legitimizing psychical research. That is, when trying to make the subject more respected and secure in intellectual culture, James turned to general audiences. This was not the only place he turned, of course; he also defended psychical research in his correspondence and in more professional forums. But it is significant that James believed addressing popular audiences was crucial for advancing the work of the Society for Psychical Research (SPR). In his eyes, popular audiences were still central to the world of thought; they were worthy of being addressed on pressing issues of intellectual concern.

Unfortunately, James's psychical advocacy led to a host of professional problems, as many academic scientists, particularly those turning inward to distance their research from an occult past, chided his legitimization efforts. The more James tried to bolster the SPR's public standing, the more his reputation suffered among his colleagues. As a result, psychical research tended to divide popular and professional opinion about his work. Nonacademics were generally supportive of his discussions of what paranormal investigations added to humanity's understanding of the mind and the great beyond. Academics were generally suspicious, even dismayed, with his advocacy, deeming it unscientific and unprofessional. The division was not absolute, of course, but it greatly influenced James's intellectual standing and the subsequent direction of his scholarship.

After exploring the spiritualist movement of the 1850s and the emergence of the Society for Psychical Research in the 1880s—both of which shaped James's rhetorical predicament in trying to advance psychical research—we will turn to four strategies James employed as part of his psychical advocacy. First, in two popular articles, "The Hidden Self" and "What Psychical Research Has Accomplished," he sought to position psychical research as unflinchingly scientific, able to provide the hard evidence needed to explain paranormal phenomena. Second, after such evidence was slow in coming (and ultimately unpersuasive), James used his widely read presidential address to the Society for Psychical Research to make psychical research less a matter of gathering scientific evidence and more a matter of carrying out the scientific method. Third, after this strategy met with little success among James's fellow scientists, he delivered a course of lectures on "Exceptional Mental States" that positioned psychical research as part of abnormal psychology in general. His aim, essentially, was to bring psychical research into the world of modern science through the back door.

None of these strategies worked as James had hoped. But close to the end of his life, he adopted a fourth approach, one that illustrated the direction in which his thought had moved. Knowing that his contributions to intellectual culture had been significant and that his place in the annals of history was secure, he published a popular article describing his "confidences" as a psychical researcher. While he had no hard evidence to prove the reality of paranormal phenomena, he did have faith in the world of the unseen—faith that he wanted to share with the American people. Ultimately, this faith was the best evidence he could provide for the existence of spirit influences and a realm beyond that which modern psychology could describe.

Spiritualism and Psychical Research in the Nineteenth Century

Interest in paranormal phenomena is as old as human history, and in that regard spiritualism has been around for millennia. But Spiritualism—the immediate precursor to psychical research—refers to a specific social, scientific, and religious movement that attracted widespread attention in the mid-nineteenth century.[21] The beliefs, ideas, and practices of the Spiritualists seemed to overtake American society in the span of a few years, but almost as quickly as the movement appeared, it receded into the background. Moreover, it would greatly complicate James's advocacy of psychical research.

According to most accounts, Spiritualism began in 1848 in Hydesville, New York, with the paranormal demonstrations of teenage sisters Margaret and Kate Fox.[22] With a firm grasp on effective performance and an interest in capitalizing on their routines, the Fox sisters purported to elicit strange rappings or knocks from beyond the grave. After performing in Hydesville, the girls joined their older sister in Rochester and attracted spectators willing to pay to witness communication with the dead. Although these "Rochester Rappings" turned out to be a hoax—at least according to most accounts[23]—they marked the beginning of a movement that would spread throughout the nation.

As soon as word of the Fox sisters got out, Spiritualist phenomena sprang up far and wide. In 1850, the daughter of magazine publisher LaRoy Sunderland became the first to hold public séances in Boston. In 1851, Horace Greeley wrote in his *Tribune* that Providence, Rhode Island, was overcrowded with mediums who reported rappings. In Philadelphia in 1851, between fifty and sixty séance circles existed in the city. After the Fox sisters traveled to Cincinnati in 1851, a local writer estimated that upwards of 1,200 mediums offered their services in the town. Even out West, mediums, séance circles, and reports of rappings were common.[24] "For consolation, for entertainment, and for assurance of a purpose behind life," Americans became enamored with spirit manifestations.[25] And within a decade, devotees of Spiritualism numbered in the millions.[26]

Although the beliefs of individual Spiritualists could vary widely, most agreed on a few basic propositions. First, they believed in the fact of communication with the dead—or at least communication with a world that existed beyond people's traditional senses.[27] The reality of otherworldly communication was both exciting and comforting, especially as the nation marched ever closer to civil war. Second, Spiritualists agreed on the need to promote a new religious tradition.[28] Calvinism in particular, perhaps the most dominant religious tradition in nineteenth-century America, seemed personally and socially damaging. By overthrowing Calvinist influences and by uniting individuals across this world and the next, Spiritualists hoped to "resacralize a society and cosmos that they feared was spiritually empty."[29] Third, Spiritualists were committed to spiritual equality, a state of affairs in which even the lowliest individuals could receive guidance from spirits who had learned the ultimate lessons of the universe. Every human being could find comfort from an "invisible pastorate" circling around the natural world.[30] Having progressed partway through the "heavenly spheres" of the afterlife, spirits offered a transcendent perspective on how to handle the vicissitudes of existence.[31]

Over and above these defining characteristics, one of the most telling aspects of Spiritualism in the mid-nineteenth century was the insistence that communicating with the dead was a matter of natural science. Spiritualists clung to the belief that their work was truly, emphatically scientific. In fact, had they been forced to call their efforts either religious or scientific, they would have "declared themselves in intent and method on the side of science."[32] As they saw it, spiritualist beliefs adhered to the natural laws of the universe, even though those laws were not yet fully discovered. The fact that mainstream scientists did not agree with them was of little concern. Just as the world had been proven to be other than great minds had originally assumed, Spiritualists believed they could gather the evidence necessary to prove the existence of a spirit world.[33]

Because of their dedication to the idea of a scientifically provable spirit world, most Spiritualists embraced a decidedly scientific style of discourse. With matter-of-fact bravado, similar to the way a naturalist would present a newly discovered species, they laid out evidence for ghosts, mediumistic powers, talks with the departed, and more. Prominent Spiritualist Joel Tiffany, for example, argued in 1856 that Spiritualist claims could be proven in the same way mathematical equations were proven. "If we will adopt the same process that we do in mathematics," Tiffany declared to a conference of New York Spiritualists, "we can have the same certainty upon all other questions that come within the sphere of man's perceptions and affections."[34] Communication with the dead, in other words, was as basic, self-evident, and certain as the addition problems children learned in grammar school. Tiffany and his fellow Spiritualists thus eschewed "the mystical in favor of the empirical."[35]

In presenting their supposed proof of the spirit world, Spiritualists regularly turned to the largest store of evidence available: testimony from people who believed they had spoken with souls beyond the grave.

According to Spiritualists, widespread firsthand accounts of spirit communication went a long way in establishing the reality of the movement's beliefs. Conversations with departed spirits, they proclaimed to the wider world, happened just as regularly and plainly as conversations between family, friends, and neighbors. One of the most respected Spiritualists, John Edmonds, a former New York state judge who lost his place on the bench because of his convictions, recorded his trance communications with Francis Bacon and Emmanuel Swedenborg, among others, with the same straightforwardness that a court reporter would transcribe the testimony of an eyewitness.[36]

For Spiritualists, then, testimonial evidence was authoritative and persuasive. But for critics of Spiritualism, such evidence was dubious and unreliable. Testimony about spirit communication from people who believed in spirit communication smacked of bias, deceit, and fraud. Naturalists did not establish the existence of a new species simply by collecting reports from people who said they saw something strange in the woods; naturalists needed a specimen before they had their proof. Why, then, could Spiritualists claim that their work was scientific simply by relying on firsthand accounts? For all their clamoring of scientific respectability, their "proof" seemed susceptible to manipulation by those who wanted to make a quick buck.[37]

Over time, most onlookers concluded that scientifically sound evidence of the spirit world was lacking, and soon the Spiritualist movement foundered. Of course, interest in paranormal phenomena continued as it had continued for millennia. But Spiritualism as a social, religious, and scientific movement quickly lost its place of prominence in public culture. By the mid-1870s, it was clear that "spiritualism was not going to gain the scientific credentials it sought."[38] Widespread reports of fraud and deception had given the movement a bad name. "The Fox sisters had retired from public mediumship; spiritual manifestations had lost their novelty; the public had become apathetic and skeptical."[39] In short, Spiritualists lost the scientific ethos they had worked hard to establish. Because they could not provide the proof they promised, the nation turned its attention elsewhere.

Just because Spiritualism lost its status as a movement did not mean that Spiritualists and those interested in paranormal activity completely disappeared. Reports of ghostly happenings persisted, leaving onlookers with a familiar set of questions about the reality of the supposed phenomena. In England, a group of British scientists and writers banded together in the early 1880s to explore these reports, founding the Society for Psychical Research.[40] The organization's name would hopefully create distance from the Spiritualist movement of the previous generation. So too would the reputations of the organization's members. The SPR counted among its ranks Edmund Gurney, Frederic Myers, Sir William Barrett, Henry Sidgwick, Eleanor Sidgwick, Arthur Balfour (a future prime minister), William Gladstone (another future prime minster), Alfred Russell Wallace, Couch Adams, Lord Rayleigh, Oliver Lodge, Balfour Stewart, Alfred Lord Tennyson, William Ruskin, and Charles Lutwidge Dodgson, otherwise known as Lewis Carroll. Their object of study was the "ordinary occult"—dreams, premonitions, déjà vu, trances, telepathy, invisible forces, hauntings, and the like[41]—and their aim was to corroborate or falsify whatever reports came their way.

At first blush, psychical research seemed like Spiritualism in new garb, especially given that both groups clung to the promises of science. But a number of important differences separated the two enterprises. First, science had progressed dramatically since 1850, becoming more rigorous and exacting in the culture of professionalism. The type of science that psychical researchers embraced was considerably more refined and specialized than the Spiritualist science of midcentury.[42] Second, unlike Spiritualists, psychical researchers welcomed tricksters and frauds. They wanted to debunk so-called paranormal phenomena as much as they wanted to verify it—or so they insisted. Following science wherever it led meant a victory for truth.[43] Third, whereas Spiritualists were dedicated to a new vision of heaven, psychical researchers did their best to leave religious questions aside; they were interested more in documenting the fringe of human consciousness than in detailing a new metaphysics.[44]

Six months after the Society for Psychical Research was founded in London, William James traveled to England to work on his psychology textbook. He had been to the country many times as a child, and his brother Henry now called London home, so it seemed a good place to make progress on *Principles.* One evening, James was invited to dine with "the Scratch Eight," an exclusive philosophical club of the day. The invitation came from Edmund Gurney, who was also a founding member of the SPR. Dinner conversation that evening consisted primarily of philosophy and psychology, though James and Gurney also seem to have touched on psychical research.[45] In any event, they soon began corresponding about spirit communication, mediums, thought transference, automatic writing, and other paranormal phenomena.

For James, meeting Edmund Gurney rekindled an interest in the spirit world that had been a significant part of his childhood. Henry James Sr. believed in influences from beyond the grave, though he often disagreed with aspects of the Spiritualist movement. When his children suffered from unexplainable maladies, he occasionally blamed their problems on spirits.[46] He used the public platform to defend one of the earliest proponents of Spiritualism, Andrew Jackson Davis, who had come under attack in various periodicals.[47] Passionate about exposing the problems of Calvinist religious orthodoxy, Henry Sr. was also one of the most vocal followers of Emmanuel Swedenborg, a Swedish scientist, philosopher, and mystic whom Spiritualists viewed as their philosophical godfather.[48] Then there was Joseph Curtis, a prominent New York physician and close friend of Henry Sr. who believed himself hounded by spirit voices. So tormented was Curtis that in 1857 he bought a pistol and shot himself in the heart. To the James family, Curtis's suicide was an example of how belief in otherworldly spirits could change people's lives in very real ways.[49]

Given William James's childhood connection with spirit phenomena, his dinner with the Scratch Eight and his correspondence with Edmund Gurney in the months that followed helped revive an old interest in the bizarre and mysterious. After returning to America in 1883, James helped establish the American Society for Psychical Research (ASPR). The organization, said one of the early circulars James composed, was founded to investigate phenomena "not to be ignored by scientific men, especially where the alleged facts would, if real, permit verification, and the conditions allow control." Members of the ASPR, the circular continued, pledged to conduct "exact study" of the "borderland of human experience," which was an "urgent scientific need" that respectable scholars had to pursue.[50]

James's growing scholarly prominence positioned him as the public face of psychical research in America, and newspapers across the country identified him at the center of the new organization. In 1885, for example, the *Boston Daily Advertiser* reported that James was leading a committee of scientists "to collect evidence regarding 'mediumistic phenomena.'" The paper was particularly confident, given James's reputation and given the reputations of the other committee members, that psychical researchers were "in search of truth" and were "not men to be easily imposed upon."[51] In 1890, the *Springfield Daily Republican* called James the "chief spirit of the society."[52] That same year, dozens of papers published James's request for people to send him firsthand accounts of ghostly hallucinations. As leader of the so-called "Census of Hallucinations" in America, he hoped to gather "a mass of facts about hallucinations which may serve as a basis for a scientific study" and which would allow scientists to "ascertain approximately the proportion of persons who have had such experiences."[53] It was important for James to emphasize the scientific angle. His credibility as a researcher, as someone who could investigate ghostly hallucinations without bias and in accord with rigorous standards, was key to convincing the American people of the legitimacy of his work.

In retrospect, it was not coincidental that James's work as a psychical researcher emerged alongside his work in mainstream psychology and his growing intellectual celebrity. As Eugene Taylor has pointed out, it was during the 1890s that James's efforts as a psychologist became largely inseparable from his efforts as a psychical researcher.[54] Publication of *Principles of Psychology* enabled him to pursue paranormal subjects with more credibility than he would have had otherwise—something James himself understood. His reputation, he wrote to fellow investigators, amounted to "a very good pedestal for carrying on psychical research *effectively,* or rather for disseminating its results effectively."[55] By publicizing the work of the SPR, he hoped to "do good to its reputation"[56] and to establish it as "a branch of legitimate science."[57]

As these statements reveal, James knew that the success of psychical research depended on the reputations of the people who undertook it and on the way others perceived it. He also knew that he was in a better position than most, at least in America, to legitimize paranormal investigation as a form of scientific inquiry. Even though James was concerned with many aspects of modern science and professional psychology—*Talks to Teachers,* for example, revealed his frustration with exclusionary jargon and academic mystification—he knew how powerful "science" was as a rhetorical tool. People revered science, even if they found it off-putting. They believed it signified the height of knowledge. For James, then, legitimizing psychical research would begin with the discursive resources of science. If he could help the American people see psychical research as a scientific enterprise, then paranormal investigations could become an accepted part of modern intellectual culture.

Psychical Research, Modern Science, and the Question of Results

Prior to 1890, James's published work on psychical research had been primarily a matter of organizing and directing the American Society for Psychical Research. He had published a few book reviews on psychical subjects, he had helped produce the ASPR's circulars soliciting donations, and he had written a few research reports that appeared in the *Proceedings of the Society for Psychical Research,* the SPR's official journal. Then the ASPR ran into trouble. In the late 1880s, the organization folded due to financial difficulties. However, American psychical researchers remained committed to the mission of their work, and soon they established an American branch of the British SPR.[58]

In the early 1890s, after he had secured his place among America's leading psychologists, James went on the offensive with regards to psychical research, turning his attention to popular forums and the audiences who seemed fascinated by tales of the paranormal. His first popular article on psychical research was titled "The Hidden Self" and appeared in 1890 in *Scribner's Magazine.*[59] His second popular article was titled "What Psychical Research Has Accomplished" and appeared in 1892 in *Forum.*[60] The first article laid the groundwork for the importance of paranormal investigations in general; the second built upon the first by turning to the SPR specifically. The fact that both articles appeared in popular periodicals meant not only a large readership but also that psychical discourse was moving in new directions. Whereas most of the SPR's previous work had been confined to publications that circulated among self-proclaimed psychical researchers—such as the society's *Proceedings* and more marginal periodicals like *The Banner of Light*—James's articles were extensions of the evolving art of popular statement.

The 1890 and 1892 articles worked together to establish a rationale for viewing psychical research as part of modern science. In both publications, James suggested that psychical research was valuable to science because it opened new horizons and revitalized old terrain. "*Anyone,*" he insisted in "The Hidden Self," "will renovate his science who will steadily look after the irregular phenomena."[61] In "What Psychical Research Has Accomplished," he held that the novel discoveries of psychical research could further strengthen science's "positive place" in the world of thought. As "new facts burst old rules" and "newly divined conceptions bind old and new together into a reconciling law," he explained, traditional science could turn to psychical research for intellectual leadership.[62]

James's mention of "new facts" signaled the aspect of psychical research he most wanted to highlight. Psychical research was central to modern science because it could gather evidence that other scientists neglected. Because the SPR collected reports of paranormal phenomena, James explained in "What Psychical Research has Accomplished," "We should end ere long by having a mass of facts concrete enough to found a decent theory upon."[63] Psychical research would lead, he insisted in "The Hidden Self," to a "rapid accumulation of new knowledge."[64] Essentially, James was making a promise to his readers, but it was a promise that demanded something from them: Psychical research would be able to gather important evidence and to create new scientific knowledge, but only if people approached it with intellectual respect and an open mind. In the future, he prophesied, the SPR's "exactitude about evidence and its timidity in speculating" would give it "a position of extraordinary influence."[65]

By dedicating psychical research to the gathering of evidence and the production of new knowledge, James did exactly what many Spiritualists had done at midcentury: He tied the future of paranormal investigations to the scientific results researchers would obtain. For the time being, he left religious questions aside, which was fortunate given that the mixture of religious and scientific appeals in Spiritualist discourse had created a number of problems. But James was unflinching in his dedication to science. Even though he acknowledged that "no conclusive results of any sort" might emerge in the short term, he wrote with confidence that the SPR would eventually be able to verify or falsify paranormal phenomena in general.[66] Researchers would make "a distinct step onward in our knowledge of the truth."[67] They would secure a "crowd of other facts" that "prove" the existence of a mysterious realm of consciousness.[68] In fact, the SPR was already in the process of founding "a department of empirical natural history worthy of all encouragement and respect."[69] By claiming that the SPR had uncovered a new domain of natural science—a claim that Spiritualists had made time and again regarding their own work—James pledged himself and his fellow researchers to obtaining scientifically persuasive evidence for paranormal phenomena, evidence that would supposedly meet the standards of other scientists.

Further building the scientific ethos of psychical research, James introduced members of the SPR and took his readers on a tour of recent psychical experiments, which, he tried to show, had already begun to garner impressive results. In his introduction of SPR members, he focused primarily on their credentials, for if they were scientific people, it followed that the SPR was a scientific organization. In "What Psychical Research Has Accomplished," James explained that Henry Sidgwick was the "most incorrigibly and exasperatingly critical and skeptical mind." He called Arthur Balfour and J. P. Langley "hard-headed" men of science. Oliver Lodge was "an eminent English physicist," and Charles Richet was an "eminent French psychologist."[70] Richard Hodgson possessed "a balance of mind" and an "uncommon keenness in detecting error."[71] These men conducted "systematic experimentation" and collected important "evidence concerning apparitions, haunted houses, and similar phenomena."[72] Their work made psychical research "indispensable in the scientific organism."[73] Furthermore, James concluded, "Were I asked to point to a scientific journal where hard-headedness and never-sleeping suspicion of courses of error might be seen in their full bloom, I think I should have to fall back on the *Proceedings* of the 'Society for Psychical Research.'"[74]

James bolstered his coverage of hardheaded scientists with coverage of hardheaded experiments. In "The Hidden Self," he discussed recent investigations by Pierre Janet and Alfred Binet into "the comparative science of trance-states." In their experiments, James explained, Janet and Binet properly tested their subjects through the scientific process of falsification, using common theories to test hypotheses and to modify conclusions as needed. So carefully did Janet and Binet design their experiments, so thoroughly did they control for error, that readers could confidently accept their conclusions about the "hidden self" of human beings. "It must be admitted therefore," James wrote in the passive voice, suggesting an unavoidable conclusion, "that, in certain persons at least, the total possible consciousness may be split into parts which coexist, but mutually ignore each other and share the objects of knowledge between them."[75]

In "What Psychical Research Has Accomplished," James continued his tour of psychical experiments. Edmund Gurney's work on automatic writing, he stated, proved "that below the upper consciousness the hypnotic consciousness persists, engrossed with the suggestion and able to express itself through the involuntarily moving hand." The result signaled "a new era in experimental psychology."[76] James also praised Frederick Myers's experiments on "the subliminal self" as models of scientific research. These experiments represented the first "thoroughly *inductive* attempt in any language" to explore "the phenomena of hallucination, hypnotism, automatism, double personality, and mediumship as connected parts of one whole subject."[77] In addition, James cited his own work collecting "some five hundred cases of 'hallucination'" as revealing "that we all have potentially a 'subliminal' self, which may make at any time irruption into our ordinary lives."[78]

By piling on example after example of the scientific character of psychical research, James hoped to convince readers that psychical researchers could obtain persuasive results. So impressive would their results be that James, at the end of "The Hidden Self," proclaimed his own acceptance of psychical activity:

> I know a non-hysterical woman who, in her trances, knows facts which altogether transcend her *possible* normal consciousness, facts about the lives of people whom she never saw or heard of before. I am well aware of all the liabilities to which this statement exposes me, and I make it deliberately, having practically no doubt whatever of its truth. My *own* impression is that the trance-condition is an immensely complex and fluctuating thing, into the understanding of which we have hardly begun to penetrate, and concerning which any very sweeping generalization is sure to be premature. *A comparative study of trances and sub-conscious states* is meanwhile of the most urgent importance for the comprehension of our nature.[79]

The "non-hysterical woman" whom James mentioned was Leonora Piper, his white crow. Although he was not ready to make sweeping generalizations about mediumistic abilities, he was confident enough in Piper's powers to endorse her publicly.

In publicly endorsing the abilities of the non-hysterical woman, James made himself a model for ordinary Americans. If a prominent scientist had few difficulties accepting psychical powers, surely others could find their way to accepting them as well. He made a similar move in "What Psychical Research Has Accomplished," proclaiming: "Facts are facts, and the larger includes the less; so these trances make me the more lenient to the other facts recorded in the *Proceedings*. I find myself also suspecting that the thought-transference experiments, the verdical hallucinations, the crystal-vision, yea, even the ghosts, are sorts of thing which with the years will tend to establish themselves."[80] James was a man of science, and he followed the facts wherever they led, including to the world of ghosts. He hoped others would follow his lead and give "the facts" the opportunity to "establish themselves." Accordingly, he rested his case with confidence in the results the SPR would obtain.

As James had hoped, "The Hidden Self" and "What Psychical Research Has Accomplished" garnered coverage in various newspapers and periodicals. By and large, the coverage was positive, especially in popular publications. After "The Hidden Self" appeared, several writers noted James's affirmation of belief in "a non-hysterical woman who, in her trances, knows facts which altogether transcend her possible normal consciousness." Calling the article "striking," "highly interesting," "charmingly written," and part of an "all-prevailing mania" on paranormal subjects, many news outlets reprinted James's paragraph about the woman's abilities.[81] Responses to "What Psychical Research Has Accomplished" sounded a similar note, reinforcing James's optimism about the future of psychical research. The *New York Times* printed a lengthy account of the article, insisting that there was "perhaps no one better qualified" than James to address the progress of psychical research. "Prof. James is himself inclined to believe in the occult," the *Times* told its readers, though, as a good scientist, he was awaiting further evidence.[82] The *Daily Picayune* called James's article "entertaining, instructive, and suggestive," and it identified the SPR's business as "the collection and examination of evidence touching occult mental phenomena, hypnotism, mediumism, clairvoyance, apparitions, haunted houses and the like." Leading the way was James, "a cautious man of science" who refused "to accept the hypothesis of deception as an explanation of all" paranormal phenomena.[83] Several other papers across the country made essentially the same point.[84]

For the time being at least, James could be happy that popular publications accepted his positive framing of psychical research. Yet underlying his argument was a rhetorical problem that James never properly addressed. He had, in fact, created a logic for deeming the SPR a failure. In both "The Hidden Self" and "What Psychical Research Has Accomplished," James argued that psychical research was a scientifically astute organization that would secure compelling evidence and explanations for paranormal phenomena. Psychical research was about obtaining results. Of course, if the SPR had been able to secure positive proof of paranormal phenomena, it would have been responsible for one of the most important scientific discoveries in human history. But James's results-based argument moved in another direction as well:

What if the SPR was unable to supply the persuasive evidence it promised? If the SPR was tied to its results, then a lack of results would be a good reason to dismiss psychical research. The SPR could, by its own standards, be judged a failure. In the coming years, several prominent psychologists would make this very argument.

Psychical Research, Modern Science, and the Appeal of Method

In the fall of 1893, Frederic Myers approached James "informally" about becoming president of the SPR, citing James's "position as a psychologist" and the prestige he could bring to psychical research in America.[85] At first, James declined, telling Myers that ill health prevented him from accepting the job. But Myers persisted, joking that "an eternity of happiness and glory" awaited James if he led the organization.[86] Besides, Myers said, the presidency was largely ceremonial, and James's official duties would be few. The SPR wanted James because of the respect his name engendered. By mid-December 1893, Myers's cajoling had worked; James accepted the presidency, joking that psychical researchers were "bent on having a king-log, so they shall be humored."[87]

James's tenure as president of the SPR began in 1894, and, as Myers had suggested, his official duties were few. He presided over a couple meetings in America and advised fellow researchers about the best strategies for publishing the organization's pamphlets and announcements. At the end of the year, Myers nominated James for a second term, and James accepted.[88] Back-to-back terms as president of the SPR further strengthened the link between James's name and psychical research in America, which may not have been a problem except for the fury that erupted over Italian medium Eusapia Palladino.

Already in the fall of 1894, James knew something peculiar was happening with investigations into Palladino's supposed abilities. Prominent European psychical researchers, including Frederic Myers, Oliver Lodge, and Cesare Lombroso, had studied her extensively and were convinced that she possessed real powers. Lombroso was the most enthusiastic supporter, theorizing that Palladino could tap into "the ether" with her mind and move material objects around a room. James thought Lombroso's theory foolish, referring to him as "the vastest donkey of the age."[89] He also warned Oliver Lodge not to publish a report in a popular periodical on Palladino's supposed powers, as doing so would only give the SPR "an appearance of excitability and eagerness, the absence of which is now among its chief decorations."[90]

Lodge's report did not end up in a popular venue; it ended up in the *Proceedings of the Society for Psychical Research*. But even there it attracted negative attention, creating a number of skeptics about Palladino's abilities. One of the biggest skeptics was Richard Hodgson, the American secretary for the SPR and a close friend of James. After studying Leonora Piper for several years, Hodgson was convinced of the reality of psychic abilities. But Palladino was another story, and Lodge's report did not help her case. After reading the report carefully, Hodgson became convinced that she was a fraud. Hoping to persuade others of the same thing, he wrote an article explaining, in painstaking detail, exactly how the medium could have deceived those who studied her. Hodgson's article appeared in the April 1895 issue of the *Proceedings* and enraged Palladino's supporters, creating a division between American and European members of the SPR.

Determined to prove Hodgson wrong, a number of European researchers, including Frederic Myers and Henry Sidgwick, launched another round of experiments on the medium. They took every precaution to ensure she could not cheat. In the past, Palladino had been able to "move" objects around a room by performing in darkness and by directing attention away from her. This time, however, researchers conducted their experiments in a carefully controlled environment. They caught her freeing her hands from tie-downs and using her fingers to manipulate what was on a table in front of her. She was a fraud, just as Hodgson had said. Myers, Sidgwick, and other investigators were dismayed. But they were also committed to honest science, so they had no choice but to publish their findings. Palladino, they announced, perpetrated "systematic fraud" at every turn, and "there was no adequate reason to suppose any supernormal agency whatever."[91]

Coverage of Palladino's trickery appeared in a number of popular and professional outlets, including the *Boston Medical and Surgical Journal*, which mocked the SPR's gullibility and unscientific ways. "The whole affair," the journal concluded, "is certainly pitiable, and it tends to discredit true scientific investigation in the minds of the multitude."[92] Morale among psychical researchers soon sank to a new low, and donations to the SPR quickly dropped off. After looking at the financial state of the organization over which he presided, James estimated that the SPR's monetary deficit for 1895 was $1,000. He told Henry Sidgwick that the SPR was in shambles and that his own enthusiasm was waning: "I fear the Eusapia business may prove a blow to our prosperity for a while. . . . It has been a bad blow to my own faith in expertness and the effects of education in these matters."[93]

So concluded James's tenure as president of the Society for Psychical Research. As was customary, however, he wrote a farewell address to members of the organization. The address gave him an opportunity to take stock of the SPR as well as to revisit psychical research's role in the scientific world. On January 31, 1896, his remarks were read in London by Frederic Myers.[94] On the same day, James himself read the address to psychical researchers in Boston; the following day, he traveled to New York to speak to researchers there.[95] In both cities, he spoke to "full houses."[96]

James's immediate audience for the address consisted mostly of psychical researchers, but his remarks ended up circulating much farther. In June 1896, the farewell address was published in the *Proceedings of the Society for Psychical Research*.[97] That same month, it also appeared in *Science* at the request of the editor, James McKeen Cattell, an outspoken critic of the SPR.[98] The opportunity to publish the address in *Science,* one of the most respected intellectual forums of the day, seemed "a very good piece of luck," James told Frederic Myers.[99] It would give him another chance to shape perceptions about the importance of paranormal research.

As one reads the presidential address, it becomes clear that James had learned a valuable lesson since the publication of "The Hidden Self" and "What Psychical Research Has Accomplished," and since the Palladino debacle. In particular, he realized that pinning the success of the SPR on the results it would obtain was ill-advised. Legitimizing psychical research required a new strategy, one that could breathe life back into the SPR and help it occupy scientific ground despite its dearth of results. Accordingly, James shifted his advocacy away from results and toward the link between psychical research and the scientific method. If the SPR was conducting its research according to the proper procedures of science, its work was scientific, even if it did not ultimately verify or falsify paranormal phenomena. Thus switching to method was a way for James to sidestep the issue of results and still drape psychical research with the mantle of respectability.

At the beginning of the presidential address, James did what most good public speakers do—he got the audience excited and engaged. He explained how important psychical research was, especially since the SPR did not have the support of the larger scientific community. While the SPR's "active workers" were few compared to those "engaged in more familiar departments of natural learning," psychical researchers could take pride in the "solid progress" the organization had made. To be sure, progress had not been made in proving or disproving a spirit world. Those who expected "definite corroboration or the final *coup de grâce,*" James explained, were undoubtedly disappointed by the SPR's achievements.[100] Nor was the evidence the SPR had gathered strong enough "to convince coercively the sceptic."[101] So what kind of progress had been made? Progress had come, James said, through the "large collection of records" and "first-hand evidence" that appeared in the *Proceedings* of the society. "I should like emphatically to express my hope," he stated, "that the impartiality and completeness of record which has been" the distinguishing character of the *Proceedings* in the past "will be held to even more rigorously in the future. It is not as a vehicle of conclusions of our own, but as a collection of documents that may hereafter be resorted to for testing the conclusions and hypotheses of *anybody,* that they will be permanently important."[102]

James tied the future of the SPR to impartial research because such research would insert the SPR into the experimental processes that defined scientific inquiry at the time. Indeed, late-nineteenth-century science distinguished itself by a dedication to specific processes, guidelines, and safeguards.[103] The belief was that experiments, when properly conducted, could be replicated by any competent researcher, who could then corroborate or falsify previous research. Thus more important than the product of the investigation—which could always be revisited later—was the way it was undertaken. As James insisted, "Science means first of all a certain dispassionate method."[104] If paranormal investigation was an affair of method—of rigorous, hardheaded, replicable method—then psychical researchers could legitimately participate in modern science's conversation with the natural world.

Even when it came to the "white crow," Leonora Piper, James shifted his focus toward method. He admitted that he believed in Piper's abilities and looked favorably upon paranormal phenomena—"ghosts and all"—because of Piper's demonstrations.[105] But, he stressed, he came to his conclusion not because of any preexisting ideas but because research on her was guided by "a certain dispassionate method." Insofar as research on Piper was concerned, he was on the side of method, not the side of results; to suppose that science "means a certain set of results that one should pin one's faith upon and hug forever, is sadly to mistake its genius."[106]

If James could distance psychical research from the issue of results, he could, hopefully, dampen memories of the SPR's recent failures. The Palladino incident was problematic because researchers had gotten excited about their findings, which were soon debunked. If they had embraced method instead of results, they likely would not have endorsed Palladino in the first place. Though James did not mention Palladino by name in the presidential address, the audience knew about the referent when he described the SPR's work as "heterogeneous." "In some cases," he elaborated, "the conditions" of psychical experiments "were not faultless," while in other cases "the observations were not prolonged."[107] Embracing the scientific method more completely would overcome these deficiencies.

James's shift to method was rhetorically adept, as it provided two key advantages. First, it allowed him to give psychical researchers hope for the future. If they embraced method, they could claim to be part of the larger scientific community, even if they lacked persuasive proof of paranormal phenomena. Second, and perhaps more important, shifting to method allowed James to put the foes of psychical research on the defensive. If opponents of the SPR rejected the SPR's work, then they rejected the scientific method, which meant that they rejected science itself. When conventional scientists belittled psychical research without bothering to replicate psychical experiments, they showed themselves to be in favor of a particular result—namely, the nonexistence of paranormal phenomena—and against the dispassionate method of science. "Science may keep saying 'such things are simply impossible,'" James explained to his audience, stressing the bind that the SPR's opponents were now in, "yet, so long as the stories multiply in different lands, and so few are positively explained away, it is bad *method* to ignore them."[108] In fact, James charged, when people embraced predetermined results instead of the scientific method, they reduced themselves to "the status of a sect."[109]

To underscore the sect-like status of those who opposed the SPR, James began to capitalize the word "Science." In so doing, he hoped to show that many scientists had embraced "a certain fixed general belief, the belief that the deeper order of Nature is mechanical exclusively, and that non-mechanical categories are irrational ways of conceiving and explaining even such a thing as human life." Modern Science, he suggested, had moved away from "science" and had become a religion of mechanical rationalism. Its followers were true believers, worshipping the god of matter and reason at the expense of human understanding. By forsaking "the personal view of life," modern Science gave up on helping people understand their actual experiences.[110]

Unlike modern Science, James held, psychical research followed the scientific method in whatever direction proved useful. When it was useful for collecting the "*facts of experience*," psychical researchers had no problem departing from the dominant paradigm of mechanical rationalism.[111] Even when experience included ghosts, mediums, telepathy, communication with the dead, and more, the SPR was interested in being true to science—the noncapitalized version—which meant being true to method. James predicted that when historians looked back on the end of the nineteenth century and saw the cult that Science had become, they would condemn it for neglecting the personal side of life. "When our Science once becomes old-fashioned," he explained, it will become old-fashioned because of "its omissions of fact" and "its ignorance of whole ranges and orders of complexity in the phenomena to be explained." The "systematic denial on Science's part of personality," the unwavering belief that "in its own essential and innermost nature our world is a strictly impersonal world," will cause people in the future to shake their heads disapprovingly at the late nineteenth century.[112]

James himself was a scientist, interested in conducting scientific research in a way that included the American people writ large. The flip side of this interest, however, was that he had little patience for Scientists—for those who conducted their research according to a narrow, exclusionary, rigidly professional paradigm. Mechanical rationalism left no room for psychical research; it left no room for pluralism, which meant that it harmed the advancement of knowledge. "It is the intolerance of Science," he explained in the presidential address, "for such phenomena as we are studying, her peremptory denial either of their existence or of their significance except as proofs of man's absolute innate folly, that has set Science apart from the common sympathies of the race." He then insisted: "I confess that it is on this humanizing mission that our Society's best claim to the gratitude of our generation seems to me to depend. We have restored continuity to history. We have shown some reasonable basis for the most superstitious aberrations of the foretime. We have bridged the chasm, healed the hideous rift that Science, taken in a certain narrow way, has shot into the human world."[113]

James's claim that the SPR had accomplished these tasks was overly optimistic. Psychical researchers were no doubt trying to heal what he called the "hideous rift" that divided the intellectual world, but they had not yet vanquished their foe Science. James discovered as much when his presidential address appeared in print. Oddly enough, the strongest response to it came from James McKeen Cattell, the same editor who had published the address in *Science.* Writing in the September 1896 issue of *Psychological Review,* Cattell defended the foes of psychical research by placing the burden of proof back on James and the rest of the SPR. Though he praised James's abilities as a writer and said that James reviewed the SPR's work with "skill and moderation," Cattell's initial praise was meant only to soften the impending blow. James, he said, had failed to see the real point of the so-called "evidence" the SPR had collected. "When we have an enormous number of cases, and cannot find among them all a single one that is quite conclusive, the very number of cases may be interpreted as an index of the weakness of the evidence." Focusing on the quantity of unpersuasive evidence for paranormal phenomena helped Cattell sidestep James's efforts to make the debate about method. For Cattell, the real issue was always results, a point he reiterated when discussing Leonora Piper. What James and his fellow psychical researchers had found was not one "white crow" but a "great many gray crows," none of which proved that psychic phenomena warranted further investigation. In fact, said Cattell, it was because psychical researchers continued to frolic in a field of gray crows that conventional scientists looked at them askance. Devoted to ideas that were ultimately unprovable, psychical researchers were just like quacks of the past who "have followed alchemy and astrology, have worshiped strange gods, have consulted witches and burned them."[114]

Cattell's response was effective insofar as it forced James to return to the question of results, which he did in the November 1896 issue of *Psychological Review.* At first, James tried to be fair in weighing the possibilities at hand, writing that psychic phenomena "*may* be malobservation, illusion, fraud, or accidental coincidence," but also that the phenomena "*may* be good and true."[115] He explained further that the most ardent critic of psychical research had only been able to conclude, "'I can't believe you're right,' whilst at the same time he has been unable to show how or where we were wrong, or even except in one or two cases to point out what the error most probably may have been."[116] But James's levelheadedness disappeared the more he considered Cattell's affront. Noting that in the past he had been "too fair-minded" in dealing with his critics, he claimed that "the concrete evidence for most of the 'psychical' phenomena under discussion is good enough to hang a man twenty times over. The scientist's objections, on the other hand, are either shallow on their face . . . or else they are proved to be shallow by further investigation."[117] He continued: "Our reports are not of gray crows; at the very worst they are of white crows without the skins brought home, of sea-serpents without the corpse to show; and where there are such obvious reasons why it must be easier to see a wild beast than to capture him, who can seriously maintain that continued reports of merely seeing him tend positively to decrease the probability that he exists?"[118]

James had landed a number of key blows in responding to Cattell, especially with his comparison of psychical research and wild-beast hunting. But to members of the scientific community who were already skeptical of psychical research, and who were extremely interested in severing psychology's historical associations with occult-like phenomena, the fact remained that the SPR lacked white-crow skins and sea-serpent corpses. Psychical researchers did not necessarily need to capture wild beasts alive, mainstream scientists held, but some sort of physical evidence would be nice. Without such evidence, there was simply no reason to take psychical research seriously, especially in the wake of the Palladino debacle. As much as James had tried to make the debate about method, professional scientists in the United States could not get past the fact that the SPR's subject matter was the same subject matter that Spiritualists had trifled over in the middle part of the century. The burden of proof remained on the SPR.

Psychical Research, Modern Science, and the Promise of Abnormal Psychology

With every justification of psychical research James offered, he met significant resistance, even scorn, from prominent scientists. He was, of course, not fighting for psychical research on his own. A number of respected intellectuals in Europe and America were actively supporting, or at least open to, the efforts of the SPR.[119] Nevertheless, psychical research faced much greater opposition in America than it did elsewhere, particularly England.[120] Moreover, James had become the most visible and otherwise-respected psychical researcher in the United States. So criticism of the SPR in America was, at least indirectly, criticism of James's efforts and advocacy. While James turned to popular audiences to generate support for the SPR, mainstream science was becoming more rigorous and, in the case of psychology, more focused on laboratory experimentation. It was becoming clearer and clearer that professional psychology had "a Cattellian scientific future."[121]

Despite the fact that many American psychologists seemed unwilling to change their minds about psychical research, James had managed to strike the right chord with popular audiences. Articles about the SPR continued to appear in newspapers across the country, and James's name was usually prominent in the story. So the more James thought about generating support for psychical research, the more committed he became to using popular statement as a tool for legitimizing his work and that of other researchers. In April 1896, less than three months after delivering his presidential address to the SPR, James had a new idea buzzing about in his head. He wrote to August Lowell—head of the Lowell Institute and the man who, in 1878, had given James one of his first chances to lecture publicly—about a course of "timely and interesting lectures" that had "great practical and historical importance."[122] Knowing of James's ability to draw a crowd, Lowell accepted the proposal, and in the fall of 1896, James delivered a series of lectures on "Exceptional Mental States."

The phrase "Exceptional Mental States" referred to the emerging field of abnormal psychology—a field that James believed held tremendous promise for psychical researchers. For several years prior to 1896, he had been teaching courses on abnormal psychology at Harvard. They were some of the first such courses in America, and students seemed enthralled with the material—not just because of the in-class instruction but also because James complemented his lectures with trips to insane asylums across Massachusetts.[123] Though James knew abnormal psychology encompassed more than just "psychical" events, it was all a matter of paranormal phenomena, of the unexplored areas of human experience.[124] For James, understanding the human mind meant understanding an expansive continuum with conventional psychology on one end and abnormal psychology and psychical research on the other.[125]

Lecturing at the Lowell Institute offered James the opportunity to advance abnormal psychology and to speak about psychical subjects in the language of an emerging scientific field. Yet he knew full well that a lecture series on "Exceptional Mental States" could raise a number of red flags in the minds of skeptics, one of whom was Augustus Lowell. In proposing the lectures, then, James tried to distance his proposed talks from explicitly psychical subjects. He told Lowell that he had "been giving a good deal of attention" to abnormal psychology in previous years, and he insisted that he could bring his thoughts together "in an instructive way." He also promised that he would keep the lectures impartial and "on lines as scientific as possible," adding in a postscript that "thought-transference, the question of 'spirits' in dealing with mediumship, and other peculiarly 'psychical research' matters would not be included in the course as I should give it. It should stick to the solidly ascertained parts of the subject."[126]

Although James gave Lowell the impression that "Exceptional Mental States" would eschew psychical research, the content of the series tells another story. The appeals James made, the scholars he cited, the way he positioned the outer reaches of the mind—all reveal his focus on the same issues he had dealt with in his earlier articles and in his presidential address. "Exceptional Mental States" allowed James to pursue psychical research as part of abnormal psychology, which, in turn, allowed him to distance his presentation from whatever preconceptions his audience may have held about paranormal investigations. At the Lowell Institute, James could talk science with a general audience, he could get them excited about an up-and-coming area of inquiry, and, in the process, he could legitimize psychical research.

James delivered "Exceptional Mental States" on Wednesdays and Saturdays for four weeks, beginning on October 21, 1896, and ending on November 14. The size of the audience fluctuated from 100 people to several hundred people, beginning and ending with several hundred in attendance.[127] Though a full-sentence manuscript of the lectures does not exist, James's speaking notes do survive, and they are complete enough to allow us to draw conclusions about the content of the series. Moreover, summaries of the lectures that appeared in Boston newspapers correspond almost exactly with the surviving notes, which, in turn, allowed Eugene Taylor to reconstruct much of what James said.[128] Beginning with the subject of "Dreams and Hypnotism," moving through "Automatism," "Hysteria," "Multiple Personality," "Demoniacal

Possession," "Witchcraft," and "Degeneration," and concluding with "Genius," James crafted a subtle yet powerful argument as to why psychical research demanded respect.

Although legitimizing psychical research was one of his main goals, James began the lectures by repeating what he had said to Augustus Lowell: There would be "No S. P. R." in the talks. Distancing "Exceptional Mental States" from psychical research was crucial in helping audience members set aside whatever negative perceptions they may have held about the topic. Yet at the same time he pushed the lectures away from the SPR, he introduced an idea that would allow him to bring psychical research back into the fold later in the series. He told the audience that in his talks he would blur the line between "'healthy' & 'morbid'" states of mind. He continued: "A life healthy on the whole must have some morbid elements" in it.[129] When James insisted that "healthy" and "morbid" states of mind coexisted together, he laid the groundwork for turning to mediums, telepathics, ghost hunters, and those who could perform fantastic feats. If, as James said, "What we call normal consciousness is but a fragment" of the human mind, then there was no reason to exclude paranormal phenomena from human psychology.[130]

The point with which James opened the lectures also served as his concluding point. Because "abnormal" was more normal than most people realized, James begged his audience to remain open-minded when it came to the unknown: "Who shall absolutely say that the morbid has no revelations about the meaning of life, that the healthy-minded view so called is *all?* A certain tolerance, a certain sympathy, a certain respect, above all a certain lack of fear seem to be the best attitude we can carry in our dealings with these regions of human nature."[131] For James, dealing with "exceptional mental states" meant approaching seemingly peculiar phenomena with tolerance and respect. He hoped his listeners would agree.

For most of the first half of the lecture series, James dealt with the same issues psychical researchers were exploring, but he was careful not to mention psychical research explicitly. The goal was simply to link psychical subjects to the more respected and more general field of abnormal psychology. Accordingly, he cited the same scholarship he had used to defend the SPR in previous years, praising the work of Pierre Janet, Alfred Binet, Edmund Gurney, and Frederic Myers for showing the fruitfulness of studying the darker corners of the human mind.[132] He mentioned automatic writing and the planchette, both of which, James said, became "more plausible" with Myers's notion of the "Subliminal Self."[133] He then discussed research into split consciousness, a forerunner to work on split-personality disorder, which psychical researchers hypothesized was a way of explaining people's experience of spirit communication.[134] He even returned to the phenomenon of automatic writing in his discussion of hypnosis and the mind-cure movement, weaving a tapestry of powerful but abnormal mental activity.[135]

For three full lectures, James danced around the idea of psychical research without addressing it by name. But by the fourth lecture, the connection between abnormal psychology and paranormal investigations had become so palpable that he had to confront it directly. All along, James announced to the audience, they had been discussing "consciousness *beyond the margin*," and now that they had covered enough ground, they stood at "the portal of P. R., into which I said I would not enter." Nevertheless, James felt compelled to bring psychical research out in the open because he did not want to "disappoint" those who knew psychical research was all around them. For their sake, he insisted, he would speak "frankly" about the relationship between abnormal psychology and "supernormal cases."[136]

What is particularly striking about this point in the lectures is the change in James's speaking notes. For most of the series, he employed the same outline format he had used for "Talks to Teachers" and other lectures. Full sentences were rare; rarer still were finely tuned paragraphs of prose. When turning directly to psychical research, however, James moved to paragraph-length prose. It was as though he needed to get his words just right and offer his appeals with precision and care. This was the turning point of the series.

"The only thing I am absolutely sure of," James announced, is "the extreme complication of the facts." In admitting that the facts were complicated, he may have disappointed those members of the audience who wanted him to speak boldly about the reality of paranormal phenomena. Yet his "great diffidence," as he described his attitude, played masterfully into the unfolding of the lectures. James wanted to present himself as a levelheaded, rational psychologist whose judgments emerged from the facts at hand. And because the facts of psychical research were extremely complicated, he had no easy answers. In that way, he was unlike those who uncritically embraced paranormal phenomena and unlike those who dismissed it out of hand; he occupied a conservative middle-ground. "Some minds would see a marvel in the simplest hypnosis," James explained. "Others would refuse to admit that there was anything new even if one rose from the dead. They would either deny the apparition, or say you could find a full explanation of it in Foster's physiology." In response to both extremes, James appealed to science. "Whether supernormal power of cognition in certain persons may occur," he said, "is a matter to be decided by evidence." He himself was "convinced of supernormal cognition," but his conviction was the result of scientific research, not "a vestige of a theory."[137]

James's explicit handling of psychical research, his discussion of his own tempered conviction, and his presentation of a middle course for the audience to adopt facilitated a more direct confrontation with paranormal topics. During the second half of the lecture series, he spoke openly about "mediumship," explaining in his lecture on demoniacal possession that "History shows that mediumship is identical with demon-possession." Moreover, he continued, "No one regards" demon possession "as insanity"—the implication being that no one should regard mediumship as insanity either.[138] Later in the same lecture, he explained that the "supernormal powers" of present-day mediums were just a continuation of phenomena that had occurred throughout history, such as the work of ancient "oracles."[139] In his lecture on degeneration, he explained how "looking directly at the facts" of paranormal phenomena could make "the Devil's sphere seem less broad and deep."[140] As opposed to the extremists, James wanted to take the "humaner view" and to show how people who supposedly had a "screw loose" actually shared a "normal germ" with everyone.[141] These colloquial, commonplace phrases, which were central to James's oral style, helped make psychical issues seem all the more familiar.

James also used the second half of the series to continue his assault on modern Science. Though he did not capitalize Science as he had done in his 1896 presidential address, his target in the Lowell lectures was the same. To make the case against Science, James relied on the lessons of history to condemn the narrowness of the present. In the lecture on witchcraft, he constructed an analogy between those who burned witches in the past and those who opposed explorations of the unknown at the end of the nineteenth century. Both witch-burners and foes of paranormal investigations, he suggested, were reactionaries who ultimately harmed human understanding. After moving through a number of historical examples involving witchcraft, including Salem, James arrived at a pointed conclusion: "Not witches but accusers were insane."

In other words, at fault in Salem were not the people who believed in the power of unseen forces but those who burned them because of their beliefs. In fact, James stated, those who accused the so-called witches were themselves either "possessed persons" or "hysterics." Their relentless pursuit of witches ended up demonstrating only the horrible results of human prejudice.[142]

If one were to substitute "psychical researchers" and "mediums" for those who believed in unseen forces in Salem, and substitute "foes of psychical research" for those who accused witches, James's point would become clear. Because of their blind commitment to mechanical rationalism, followers of Science chased after psychical researchers without first looking at the evidence. Even if they thought they were doing good work and rooting out error, their prejudices were an "example of the good intentions with which hell is paved. . . . There is no worse enemy of God & Man than zeal armed with power and guided by a feeble intellect." It was a harsh conclusion, but the foes of psychical research were nothing if not zealots for mechanical rationalism. James elaborated, again in full-sentence prose:

> I believe it does one good in one's carelessness to stop now and then and realize what human life really has been, and may be again if the best men do not keep up a constant fight not against an imaginary satan but the real devil of intolerance and ignorance inflamed with the lust of power, and the conceit that they alone can save the world, and getting all the legitimate professional & legal authority into their hands. Strange as it may sound there can be little doubt that a good natured scepticism, and willingness to let the devil have his head a bit, is for public purposes a better state of mind than too exalted a notion of one's duty towards the world.[143]

In James's view, Scientists—those who pursued "all the legitimate professional" authority—demonstrated "intolerance and ignorance" in their attempts to stifle the work of others. Even if psychical researchers could gather no hard evidence of paranormal phenomena, the Scientific powers-that-be should "let the devil have his head a bit"; they should relinquish their imaginary "duty towards the world" and leave the SPR alone to explore the everyday occult.

James did not mention psychical research by name in his chastising of modern Science, but those in the audience who knew about James's work with the SPR would likely have gotten the point. In fact,

James's implicit justification of psychical research was, in some ways, more powerful than his explicit advocacy earlier in the 1890s, for it made psychical research less an issue to be debated scientifically and more a matter of open-minded inquiry. Full-throated advocacy invited counterarguments, while subdued reasoning allowed the audience to draw its own conclusions based on the principle of pluralism. Furthermore, linking psychical research to abnormal psychology made it less a matter of gaining definitive proof of paranormal phenomena—which was unlikely to occur anytime soon—and more a matter of exploring the many ways the human mind operated. If psychical research was primarily a matter of the wonderful complexity of the human mind, then there was little need to show that spirits, mediums, ghosts, and psychic forces were "real" in the conventional sense of the term.[144] Psychical research was justified because paranormal phenomena were intriguing parts of human experience, not because spirit forces were rigorously demonstrable.

By all accounts, James's 1896 lectures succeeded in making the abnormal seem more normal, at least for those who sat in the audience at the Lowell Institute. Newspaper coverage suggested that James effectively created a space for nontraditional investigations in modern intellectual culture. Noting that "Not since Dr. Drummond lectured before the Lowell Institute in the winter of 1893 have such audiences been known as those attracted by Professor James," the *Daily Inter Ocean* explained that the lectures were of a quality "which communicated new gems of thought and new problems for the hearer to work out for himself."[145] The *Boston Evening Transcript,* which published summaries of almost every lecture in the series, concluded that James conveyed "new ideas" and shed "more light upon what have formerly been regarded as very morbid subjects." His treatment of bizarre aspects of human life was "eminently sane and above all hopeful." In the end, the paper opined, "Boston may well be thankful for the privilege which she has enjoyed in listening to scholarly, carefully prepared addresses upon these intensely interesting subjects, by one whose authority is unquestioned."[146]

James never published "Exceptional Mental States," nor did he continue explicitly to pursue psychical research as abnormal psychology (although aspects of this approach would appear beneath the surface of his subsequent work).[147] To be sure, James was pleased with his Lowell lectures, but while preparing them for publication, he received a lecture invitation that would divert his attention for several years. The invitation was to deliver the prestigious Gifford Lectures on Natural Theology in Scotland, and with that opportunity before him, James let "Exceptional Mental States" fall by the wayside.[148]

Because "Exceptional Mental States" was never published and never had the chance to reach an audience beyond listeners at the Lowell Institute, it is impossible to know how James's strategy of "psychical research as abnormal psychology" would have gone over with members of the scientific community. We do know, however, that eighteen months after the Lowell lectures, James was once again dragged into a fight with the foes of psychical research. Regardless of how successful he was in persuading popular audiences, many scientists were not content to sit idly by while he and other members of the SPR impeded the progress of science. In April 1898, James McKeen Cattell published a piece in *Science* attacking Leonora Piper and those who supported her. He complained about the "trivial character of the evidence" supporting Piper's abilities, and then quoted the observations of "five well-known men of science" as to the unpersuasiveness of Piper's supposed trances.[149] Piper was a fraud, Cattell insisted, and James was foolish for calling her his "white crow."

Unsurprisingly, James felt personally accosted, and he responded in the May 1898 issue of *Science*. "The scientific mind," James wrote with palpable frustration, "is by the pressure of professional opinion painfully drilled to fairness and logic in discussing orthodox phenomena. But in such mere matters of superstition as a medium's trances it feels so confident of impunity and indulgence whatever it may say, provided it be only contemptuous enough, that it fairly revels in the untrained barbarians' arsenal of logical weapons." James then parodied the voice of his foes: "In our dealings with the insane the usual moral rules don't apply. Mediums are scientific outlaws, and their defendants are quasi-insane. Any stick is good enough to beat dogs of that stripe with."[150] The editor of *Science* adjoined a final note by Cattell after James's response. It said, in part: "I fear that our disagreement is hopeless. . . . I believe that the Society for Psychical Research is doing much to injure psychology."[151]

In 1898 and 1899 James also exchanged words in the pages of *Science* with E. B. Titchener of Cornell University regarding Titchener's claim that "no scientifically-minded psychologist believes in telepathy." Identifying himself with the "straight scientific path," Titchener praised the work being done in "scientific psychology" to demolish psychical theories.[152] James responded by marveling at Titchener's "hardness of hearing" as far as listening to the evidence was concerned, and he concluded, with no small amount of bitterness: "May the consciousness of his fidelity to correct scientific principles console him in some degree both for his deafness and for his isolation."[153]

Contrary to what James insisted, Titchener was not isolated. In fact, James's debates with Cattell and Titchener illustrated the degree to which mainstream science was moving away from James and other psychical researchers. Though James managed to find popular success in his Lowell lectures, crafting what was perhaps his most promising justification of psychical research, his continuing feuds with academics furthered the perception that he was becoming less of a "true scientist." Had he pursued psychical research as abnormal psychology more completely, he may have been able to change the debate with Cattell and Titchener. Then again, professional prejudices against psychical research were deeply ingrained, so there may have been nothing James could have done to make Scientists—those of the capitalized persuasion—think psychical research anything other than an unfortunate remnant of the superstitious past.

Psychical Research and Faith Near the End of Life

James's fight over psychical research during the 1890s strengthened his commitment to the art of popular statement. In his efforts to defend paranormal investigations, popular periodicals and lecture auditoriums responded as he had hoped. At the same time, he found mostly failure when engaging his colleagues. The more arguments he made—about hoped-for results, about the propriety of method, about the possibilities of abnormal psychology—the more he saw his distance from the evolving culture of professional science.

James's response to this distance was to shift his intellectual focus. By and large, he tried to stay out of the spotlight as far as psychical research was concerned. He occasionally worked behind the scenes for the SPR, he responded briefly when professional psychologists accosted him, and his name continued to appear in newspaper articles discussing psychical research. But he was no longer on the offensive. New projects, including *The Varieties of Religious Experience* and *Pragmatism,* came to occupy his attention. Given the prominence of these projects, James remained at the center of American intellectual culture. But he was largely uninterested in advocating psychical research as he had done in the 1890s.

However, in the summer of 1909, a year before his death, James made headlines because of an account he published in the *Proceedings of the Society for Psychical Research.* The detailed, careful account described his communication, through Leonora Piper, with his dead friend and fellow SPR member Richard Hodgson. Newspapers across the country made James's spirit communication fodder for public gossip. "Harvard leader talks to spirit?" the *Chicago Tribune* questioned. "Prof. James writes of the alleged spirit messages from Dr. Hodgson. He thinks them real," the paper reported.[154] "Prof. James bets 'twas Dr. Hodgson," wrote the *New York Times,* which proceeded to reprint a large portion of the transcript between James and the supposed ghost.[155] The *Times,* in fact, thought James's communication important enough to make the front page. The following day, an anonymous critic complained to the editor that James was a "victim" of Leonora Piper, who was either a "rank impostor" or "a neurotic person subject to self-hypnosis." The commentator continued: "The unseen ghosts of the Psychological Researchers are a poor, aimless lot, occasionally droll, but never convincing to anybody who has not made up his mind to the honesty of the medium."[156]

A few months later, seemingly energized by the controversy, James tried one last time to legitimize psychical research. And once again, popular statement was his tool. "Confidences of a 'Psychical Researcher'" appeared in *American Magazine* and was both a response to criticism of the Hodgson conversation and an attempt to redirect memories of James's work with the SPR.[157] Yet the most significant aspect of the article was the intellectual disposition James displayed—a disposition strikingly different than that of his earlier pieces. Reflecting on his extensive work with the SPR, he averred that he was no closer now than "at the beginning" to figuring out what was really going on with reports of paranormal phenomena. As he saw it, "The creator has eternally intended this department of nature to remain *baffling*. . . . Although ghosts, and clairvoyances, and raps and messages from spirits, are always seeming to exist and can never be fully explained away, they also can never be susceptible of full corroboration."[158]

When James acknowledged that reports of paranormal phenomena could never be "susceptible of full corroboration," he broke from the scientific appeals of his past. It was as though he wanted nothing to do with the quandary in which he had found himself during the 1890s. Accordingly, he stated that the aim of his 1909 article was "Not to convert readers, but simply to *put my own state of mind upon record publicly.*" No doubt most readers already had an inclination as to his state of mind concerning psychical matters, but the statement was significant insofar as it moved the debate in a new direction. By turning to his own state of mind, James shifted psychical research away from scientific verifiability and empirical argument and toward his personal faith in an unseen world. Even though he might be "dooming" himself "in the eyes of better-judging posterity," James wanted readers to focus on his own commitments.[159]

Why was James's state of mind so important? It was important because his reputation and influence had grown dramatically since the late 1890s. Popular audiences had devoured *Pragmatism* and *The Varieties of Religious Experience,* among other works. So, James figured, readers of *American Magazine* may well be interested in his opinions, even if he had no definitive scientific proof to support them. He thus wanted "*to go on the record for the commonness*" of paranormal phenomena. He wanted to express his belief in "*the presence,* in the midst of all the humbug, *of really supernormal knowledge.*" There was, he wrote, "a cosmic environment of *other consciousness*" beyond the normal consciousness of this world. Admitting that "the only certainty is that the phenomena are enormously complex" and can never be fully verified, he left his readers with a conclusion that hinged not on hard data but on a pair of intriguing metaphors. "We with our lives are like islands in the sea," he explained, "or like trees in the forest. The maple and the pine may whisper to each other with their leaves, and Conanicut and Newport hear each other's fog-horns. But the trees also commingle their roots in the darkness underground, and the islands also hang together through the ocean's bottom. Just so there is a continuum of cosmic consciousness, against which our individuality builds but accidental fences, and into which our several minds plunge as into a mother-sea or reservoir."[160]

Close to the end of his life, after he had studied paranormal phenomena for decades, James's "confidences" as a psychical research came down to metaphors about trees and islands. This was a radical departure from his earlier attempts to legitimize the SPR's work; it was certainly not the hard evidence members of the larger scientific community had been demanding. But in the year before his death, James seemed not to care. He had spent the last decade moving in new directions, directions that went away from the confines of stuffy academic science. By and large, he had spent his time on the lecture circuit, further developing the art of popular statement. So when he returned to psychical advocacy, he wrote with both eyes focused on the general public, hoping to inspire ordinary Americans with his belief. Hard evidence was beside the point; inspiration was the key. His own faith, he believed, would help readers see a mystical world lurking beneath the trees and the islands.

Conclusion

"Confidences of a 'Psychical Researcher'" did little to change people's perceptions of James's work and legacy. Those who accepted his appeal to open-minded inquiry continued to believe that paranormal investigations were intriguing and important. After all, reports of ghosts, spirits, mediumistic abilities, and similar phenomena persisted, just as they had throughout human history. At the same time, those who decried psychical research saw James's final appeal as yet another instance of his unfortunate curiosity. A commentator for the *New York Times,* writing immediately after James's death, believed that psychical research left an ugly black mark on his otherwise impressive legacy. To the "common mind," the commentator wrote, James was "an investigator of the claims of spiritualism." Like "many other learned men," he was unfortunately sidetracked by the occult and "wasted valuable time" exploring psychical subjects. The writer further lamented: "It is a pity that Prof. James ever went so far afield," and it is to be hoped that his work as a psychical researcher can "be speedily forgotten."[161]

This backhanded eulogy perfectly captured the popular-professional divide that emerged from James's work as a psychical researcher. To be sure, the idea of a "popular-professional" divide is somewhat misleading, given that many nonacademics viewed psychical research with suspicion and many academics thought it important. But the popular-professional divide speaks less to a strict separation between large groups and more to the discursive split that surrounded James's work from the late 1890s until his death. James pursued the art of popular statement in divisive rhetorical milieus. His work tended to prompt enthusiastic coverage in popular outlets and skeptical coverage in professional outlets. This division was not universal, of course, but it was familiar and predictable during the final decade of James's life.

Yet we must recognize that James himself had much to do with the emergence of the popular-professional divide. His success as a public intellectual stemmed in part from his ability to juxtapose his ideas with the status quo in academia. He called into question entire philosophical and scientific traditions as a way of drawing general audiences into his lectures, essays, and books. Even when he deployed the markers of science to legitimize psychical research, he did so in a way that cast aspersions on much scientific research being done at the time. James set his sights on Science, hoping that he could turn people away from impersonal, monolithic, confining, illiberal intellectual pursuits. Frustrated with Cattell, Titchener, and those who denied psychical research a place in modern systems of knowledge, James dedicated himself to remaking the world of thought around him.

"Confidences of a 'Psychical Researcher'" was a good illustration of where James ended after attempting to remake the world of thought. The question, of course, is how he got there. To answer that question, we must turn to the lecture invitation James received shortly after delivering "Exceptional Mental States." As we shall see in the next chapter, James's Gifford lectures, famously titled "The Varieties of Religious Experience," attempted to reconfigure intellectual culture around the popular audiences who had responded so favorably to him over the years. In positioning religious experience as a primary source of knowledge, James would call into question the systems of power and authority that defined academic professionalism. Ultimately, he would argue for an intellectual culture built around "the people."

CHAPTER FIVE

Religious Experience and the Appeals of Intellectual Populism

⌘

William James was agitated in May 1898. Confrontations over psychical research were fresh in his mind, prompting him to tell James McKeen Cattell just how he felt: "I must say that the 'Scientist' mind seems to me to be characterized by as sectarian a spirit as any. . . . It suggests to me the priggish sectarian view of science, as something *against* religion, *against* sentiment, etc." He was particularly upset with the priggish Scientists who "proceeded to demolish psychical researchers."[1] Cattell's response to the letter is not known, but James's agitation did not abate. A mere four days later, he shot off another letter:

> Your state of prejudice is so *absolute,* that quite naively and unconsciously you perpetrate acts of insolence quite as remarkable as your lapses of logic,

> as if I were some minor or child making a nuisance in the psychological neighborhood. You surely would not adopt that tone in regard to any other difference of scientific opinion, least of all where the adversary had 15 years firsthand acquaintance with the facts and you had never seen them. No! my dear fellow, it is as I say, all the virtues have to be drilled into us afresh in each special matter, and the day for psychical research has not yet come.[2]

James was perturbed with Cattell, but the real focus of his agitation was the system of knowledge Cattell affirmed as exclusively legitimate. Psychical research, according to Cattell and other prominent psychologists of the era, simply did not fit within the strictures of professionalism. Real knowledge would never emerge from trifling in the vagaries and fraudulence of supposed paranormal phenomena. For James, this unwavering opposition was maddening. The professional mind had become too narrow, too confining, perpetrating acts of intellectual insolence against more open-minded inquirers. Scientists, the capitalized version, had become blind to the mysteries, novelties, and possibilities of experience. Dedication to professionalism had gone too far.

This was not a wholly new realization for James. The intensity was new, but he had been concerned for decades about the direction in which intellectual culture was moving. While academic professionalism was not all bad—after all, it had helped him become one of the most prominent American psychologists and philosophers—it often led to unnecessary antagonism in the pursuit of knowledge. When studying at Harvard in the 1860s, he had seen how a lack of pluralism could lead to vicious scientific battles, even to the proposal of a duel. When speaking in Boston and Baltimore in 1878, he had lamented that disciplinary boundaries often created territorial disputes—hence James's metaphor of the farmers and the fence dividing their properties—which discouraged collaboration and the sharing of ideas. When talking to teachers during the 1890s, he had berated scientific mystification and its imposition on people struggling to find their place in modern society. Hostility to psychical research was, then, yet another example of the problems plaguing intellectual culture.

These problems were especially noteworthy when juxtaposed to the relationships James had forged with popular audiences. By the end of the nineteenth century, he stood at the forefront of American thought, and generally educated middle- and upper-class audiences recognized him as doing so. Publishers wanted to publish his books, editors wanted to share his writing with their readers, and lecture planners worked hard to bring him to their venues. Every year his reputation as an engaging speaker became more formidable. In announcing his arrival in town to lecture, for example, one newspaper displayed a prominent photo of James and described him as a psychologist and philosopher of "international fame" whose work had the merit, unlike that of other scholars, of communicating "in brilliant, entertaining style."[3]

Had James wanted to, he could have made a living solely from the lecture circuit. By the end of the nineteenth century, he received hundreds of offers to lecture every year. In 1899, his wife estimated that at least one offer arrived in the mail every day.[4] As a result, he could have quit his job at Harvard and traveled the country addressing packed houses. But travel was hard on him, the social obligations associated with lecturing were often annoying, and he relished his time at home in Cambridge and at his summer house in New Hampshire. James was a firm believer in what he called "The Gospel of Relaxation."[5] Not wanting to spend his whole life on the lecture circuit, he declined the vast majority of invitations he received.

But some offers were too tantalizing to decline. One such offer arrived in January 1897, only two months after James had completed "Exceptional Mental States." William Sorley of the University of Aberdeen inquired as to whether James would consider delivering the Gifford Lectures on Natural Theology, a series in Scotland that was on its way to becoming one of the world's most prestigious intellectual engagements. It was the first time an American had been offered the lectureship. Although James had lectured outside of the United States before, it was always in academic settings. Thus the Gifford offer gave him the chance to deliver a high-profile, well-paying series for people far outside the academy. It also gave him the chance to spend significant time on a subject that had been drawing his attention for years: the religious dimensions of human life.[6] In Scotland, he could pursue his interest in religious inquiry for a popular, public occasion—the kind of occasion that had served him so well in the past.

What emerged from James's exploration of "natural theology," the topic prescribed by the Gifford lectures, was *The Varieties of Religious Experience.* More than any single work, *Varieties* established his standing as a thinker of international influence. One reviewer called it "one of the great books of our time."[7] Another predicted that it would "unquestionably exert a great, a very great influence on the thought of our time."[8] Still another reviewer concluded that James "has taken us many strides in advance of anything we have known in understanding the phenomena of the spiritual life, and he has given an account of religion so profound that any serious attempt in the future must square itself with his conclusions."[9]

Looking back on James's career as a whole, most scholars agree that he produced two masterpieces: *The Principles of Psychology* and *The Varieties of Religious Experience*. The former revolutionized psychology; the latter revolutionized religious thought. Yet *Varieties* was eminently more popular than *Principles*. *Principles* was a textbook that redirected the study of psychology; *Varieties* captured a religious impulse that was—and is—a cherished part of human life. Today, *Varieties* stands as one of the most influential scholarly works in American history. In 1999 a committee assembled by the Modern Library ranked *Varieties* as the second-best nonfiction book of the twentieth century, just behind *The Education of Henry Adams*.[10] The "clearest expression of James's tripartite metaphysics of pragmatism, pluralism, and radical empiricism,"[11] it continues to claim the "interest and the imagination of several generations of readers, in the United States and abroad."[12]

Because of the book's significance, scholars have repeatedly explored its pages, and each time they do, they seem to come away with new insights. Indeed, the number of well-documented interpretations of the text illustrates the depth and richness of James's prose.[13] For all the interpretations of the book, however, little attention has been paid to the lecture occasion from which it emerged. Of course, scholars have long recognized that *Varieties* (the book) came from James's 1901–1902 Gifford lectures, but no one has accounted for the lectures in their historical moment. "The Varieties of Religious Experience" (the lecture series) was undoubtedly one of the most significant performances of James's career, and what he said in Scotland was intimately linked to the audience before him and the intellectual forces around him.

This chapter aims to explicate "Varieties" as central to James's constantly evolving art of popular statement. More specifically, the chapter argues that the lectures marked the emergence of what we might call James's "intellectual populism." In response to the frustrations he felt with many aspects of academic professionalism, James offered "Varieties" as an alternative to the exclusionary tendencies of Science, Philosophy, and Theology. To challenge the problems of intellectual culture he had witnessed and experienced over the years, he crafted a system of knowledge built around the perceptions, beliefs, and experiences of ordinary people. According to the logic of the lectures at least, "the people" were as entitled as academics to claim knowledge and authority in the realm of religious inquiry. In fact, because of their nonprofessional status, they were often in the best position to perceive, feel, and judge the character of reality. Intellectual populism thus challenged the basic structure of the culture of professionalism, returning intellectual power to the ordinary individuals from whom it had been wrested.

It should be noted that "intellectual populism" has no necessary connection to the sociopolitical Populism that grew in the early 1890s and bled into the Progressive Era.[14] That is to say, James was not, by any stretch of the imagination, a Populist in the political-party sense of the term. However, populism—the lowercase version of the word—extends far beyond the People's Party of the late nineteenth century. Indeed, it is best understood as an attitude, a posture, "a language whose speakers conceive of ordinary people as a noble assemblage not bounded narrowly by class, view their elite opponents as self-serving and undemocratic, and seek to mobilize the former against the latter."[15] As a form of rhetorical engagement, populism offers speakers and writers a variety of appeals: an affirmation of "the people," a denunciation of "elites," a call for widespread participation, an opposition to "the system," a prompt for confrontation and radical or revolutionary change, an embrace of individualism and individual liberty, and a respect for tradition and cultural heritage, among others.[16] As a discourse, then, populism constitutes a way of relating to people in specific instances and for specific ends. It enables speakers and writers to construct relationships according to a sense of empowerment for "the people"—however amorphous, inexact, and misleading that term may ultimately be.

Empowering "the people" in the realm of ideas was the basis of James's intellectual populism, and it shaped his primary mode of engagement in "The Varieties of Religious Experience." To be clear, I am not claiming that James became a populist through and through, nor am I claiming that all his subsequent texts fall under the populist heading. Rather, my claim is that for the purposes of the Gifford lectures, he deployed a populist discourse to question the world of academic professionalism so prominent at the time and to affirm the widely participatory, eminently pluralistic intellectual culture he envisioned. "Varieties" was a popular masterpiece because it gave ordinary people a sense of their agency and effectiveness in the pursuit of knowledge. Intellectual authority, James argued, did not rest solely, even primarily, with academic experts. It was, rather, available to the masses—in Scotland, America, and everywhere else.

The Road to Edinburgh

James's Gifford lectures began in a striking confluence of historical factors. Transatlantic intellectual tensions, great expectations, debilitating health, the deaths of close friends, mystical mountaintop experiences, Josiah Royce, and the desire to deliver something identifiably American—all played crucial roles in the development of "Varieties." Indeed, all played crucial roles in James's effort to advance the art of popular statement along more radical lines.

Lord Adam Gifford died on January 20, 1887. His substantial estate was the topic of much conversation, and even before his death, the terms of his will made headlines.[17] Blessed in life with opportunity and wealth, Gifford thought it his duty in death to give back to the community, and the best way to do so was by supporting public scholarship. He believed that "natural theology" was a subject about which every Scotsman needed to know, for knowledge of God, Gifford said in his will, was "the means of man's highest well-being." Establishing public lectures on religion would, he hoped, better "the whole population of Scotland." Open "not only to students of the Universities, but to the whole community," the Gifford lectures were designed to help bridge the knowledge gap between academics and the populace.[18]

Lord Gifford thought the subject of natural theology so important that he established not one series of Gifford lectures but four. His will called for lectures at each of Scotland's most prestigious universities: Edinburgh, Glasgow, Aberdeen, and St. Andrews. Also, because the subject of man's relation to God and the natural world required careful exploration, Gifford thought it impossible for anyone to treat the matter in fewer than twenty lectures, or even "many times that number." Lecturers thus had to spread their talks over two years, giving ten lectures one year and ten more the following year. Fortunately, speakers were paid handsomely for their commitment, but they were also encouraged to be as detailed and intricate as possible. Lord Gifford wanted them to get to the bottom of life's deepest questions, treating theology as "a strictly natural science" and pursuing concrete answers to "Infinite Being."[19]

In 1888, only a year after Lord Gifford died, the Gifford lectures were officially initiated. Friedrich Müller, a German philologist and pioneer of comparative religion, opened the Glasgow series. After Müller came other prominent European thinkers: Edward Taylor, James Stirling, Andrew Lang, Edward Caird, George Stokes, Andrew Fairbairn, William Wallace, Otto Pfleiderer, John Caird, Alexander Fraser, Lewis Campbell, Cornelius Tiele, James Ward, and Alexander Bruce. These men spoke on grand topics designed to fulfill Gifford's hope for "true knowledge of God, that is, of the Being, Nature, and Attributes of the Infinite, of the All."[20] Müller, for example, spoke on "Natural Religion"; Lang spoke on "The Making of Religion"; Edward Caird spoke on "The Evolution of Religion"; John Caird spoke on "The Fundamental Ideas of Christianity"; Pfleiderer spoke on "Philosophy and Development of Religion"; Fraser spoke on "Philosophy of Theism"; Ward spoke on "Naturalism and Agnosticism"; and Bruce spoke on "The Providential Order of the World" and "The Moral Order of the World." Because of the prominence of the lecture series and the scope of the subject matter, delivering the Giffords quickly became a badge of scholarly honor. Lecturers comprised a sort of elite fraternity, and, in turn, Scotland's reputation as a source of Western thought grew to new proportions.

For over a decade, the Gifford fraternity was restricted to Europeans. It was not until James's invitation in January 1897 that an American was asked to join. At first, James was delighted with Sorley's offer to lecture at Aberdeen, but the more he thought about it, the more he wanted to speak at Edinburgh.[21] Aberdeen was not a poor destination, but if James was going to make his popular mark on Europe, he wanted it to be in the "Athens of the North."[22] So with Aberdeen offer in hand, James queried a friend at Edinburgh, Andrew Seth Pringle-Pattison, who was also a member of that venue's planning committee. "The emoluments would seem greater at E[dinburgh]," James wrote, "and the glory, if possible, more transcendent. So, chances being equal, I had rather run for luck with you than with Sorley."[23] He wanted his "last will and testament on religious matters" to be as noteworthy as possible.[24]

James had a good feeling about securing the Edinburgh appointment, and in February 1897 he decided to withdraw his name from consideration at Aberdeen.[25] At the same time, he took it upon himself to recommend his replacement. Considering the nature of the Gifford lectures and the climate of thought in Scotland at the time, he could think of no better candidate than his friend, neighbor, and Harvard colleague Josiah Royce.

"Royce *ought* to be the Harvard man chosen," James told Pringle-Pattison. "Beside his superior ability, he needs the money and opportunity more than I, and has been working methodically for years on the subject."[26] Royce was a fitting recommendation. He was an American, but his mind worked like that of a European. Along with many of Europe's leading philosophers, including the leading philosophers of Scotland, Royce was a proponent of Absolute Idealism—or what James called the "a priori" creation of "warranted systems" of thought, designed to be "all-inclusive, yet simple; noble, clean, luminous, stable, rigorous, true."[27] Absolute Idealism entailed grand, universal knowledge claims, which were exactly what Lord Gifford had wanted. Acting on James's recommendation, Sorley invited Royce to deliver the Gifford lectures at Aberdeen. Royce was elated and began working immediately on his all-inclusive system.[28]

James had declined the Aberdeen invitation without receiving a formal invitation from Edinburgh, and as the months passed, his prospects of becoming a Gifford lecturer seemed to grow dim. Alice James was particularly upset that her husband had turned down Aberdeen and recommended Royce. The result, she believed, would be "our missing the Gifford lectureship altogether. It is hardly probable that so rare a prize will be given to an American two years running."[29] For almost a year, James hung in Gifford limbo. Then finally, in January 1898, he received word that he would lecture at Edinburgh.[30] In addition to being "quite happy" about the honor, he told his brother Henry that he was surprised by the amount of money he would receive: "about 700£ for each of the 2 courses of 10 lectures each." At that rate, James figured, he would earn $350 per lecture (more than $9,000 in today's values). "I never knew before how much my time was worth an hour!"[31]

Soon after receiving the official Edinburgh invitation, James began to work on his lectures. At first, he had a difficult time formulating his arguments, but something of a breakthrough came in July 1898. One night, while on vacation in Keene Valley, New York, with the Adirondack mountains surrounding him on all sides, James was enveloped by "perfect" air temperature. Then "the moon rose and hung above" him, "leaving only a few lingering stars visible." What came next was one of the most powerful religious experiences of his life, which he described in a letter to his wife:

> I got into a state of spiritual alertness of the most vital description. The influences of Nature, the wholesomeness of the people round me, . . . the thought

> of you and the children, . . . the problem of the Edinburgh lectures, all fermented within me till it became a regular Walpurgis nacht. I spent a good deal of it in the woods, where the streaming moonlight lit up things in a magical checkered play, and it seemed as if the gods of all the nature-mythologies were holding an indescribable meeting in my breast with the moral gods of the inner life. . . . The intense *significance* of some sort, of the whole scene, if one could only *tell* the significance; the intense inhuman remoteness of its inner life, and yet the intense *appeal* of it; its everlasting freshness and its immemorial antiquity and decay; its utter americanism, and every sort of patriotic suggestiveness, and you, and my relation to you part and parcel of it all, and beaten up with it so that memory and sensation all whirled inexplicably together; . . . it was one of the happiest lonesome nights of my existence.[32]

For James, that mystical moment in the woods was indicative of a distinct kind of knowledge. It was a knowledge he had a difficult time describing precisely, but it was knowledge nonetheless. It was also gained only through personal experience. These kinds of mystical moments, he soon realized, were exactly what made people's religious lives so meaningful. And as a result, "The Edinboro lectures made quite a hitch ahead."[33]

Although James had found his theme for the Gifford lectures, he soon discovered that finishing the series would be daunting. It was not so much the material that stood in his way, although that was part of it. The bigger issue was his health. Sickly for much of his life, James underwent one of his longest bouts of illness while working on the Gifford lectures. The *New York Times* reported the problem as a severe "enlargement of the heart," and it was bad enough that James had to stop writing.[34] After a year of health troubles, he complained that he had made "almost no headway at all."[35] Unable to deliver the lectures in 1899, the planned start date, James asked the Edinburgh committee to accept his resignation or, if they still wanted him, to grant an extension.[36] The committee agreed to postpone the series until 1901.[37]

Meanwhile, Royce was hard at work on his own Giffords, which would commence in 1899, thereby making Royce the first American to deliver the prestigious lectures, even though James was the first to be invited. An incredibly hard worker, Royce tried to juggle a number of projects at once, but the Gifford lectures began to consume him.[38] "If I cannot do them rightly," he fretted in 1898, "I shall do much more than fail; I shall be a false servant of Harvard, whose honor in a way any lecturer to foreign audiences has in such a case to guard in his own way and range."[39] Wanting to honor Harvard and his own vision of the world, he strove to make his lectures "in a purely technical or academic sense the effort of my life."[40] For Royce, the prestige of the Gifford lectures demanded technical precision, and as an Absolute Idealist, he aimed at nothing less than capturing the universal, transcendent, logical basis of Religion. The lecture series, titled "The World and the Individual," was Royce's way of speaking the language of idealism to other idealists.

Royce began his lectures on January 11, 1899. His hosts, he wrote to James, were welcoming and hospitable, but it was James they most wanted to hear: "You are unquestionably by far the best known of all American philos'rs here, and your lectures will be eagerly awaited, and glowingly received."[41] When the people of Scotland imagined American thought, they imagined James, not Royce. They hoped not for the same Absolute Idealism that defined European philosophy, but for a new, distinctly American take on natural theology. "Everywhere they ask about you," Royce wrote to James, "and regard me only as the advance agent of the true American Theory. *That* they await from you. I received endless kindness; but they have still far more, I am sure, in store for you if only fate would permit them to get at you."[42] The people of Scotland, Royce predicted, would be "ten times as good" to James as they were to him.[43]

As a lecturer, Royce stood worlds away from James. In terms of physical appearance and vocal quality—which play a part, however large or small, in a lecturer's success—Royce faced several challenges. He was short and stout, adorned with freckles, and topped with blazing red hair and a head too large for his body. According to James, an "obscene exposure" of forehead made Royce look like an illustration in an old medical book—a caricature of a real person. Added to this physical appearance was a high squeaky voice that made his lectures difficult to endure.[44]

On top of his physical appearance and vocal quality, Royce's ideas were often impenetrable, especially for nonphilosophers. One of his students at Harvard said his lectures were like a "private soliloquy publicly continued."[45] Essentially, his presentations matched his philosophical outlook: grand, intricate, and all-encompassing to the point of being unrelatable. This is not to impugn Royce's credentials as a philosopher. In academic circles, he was considered a dialectician who could effortlessly point out flaws and contradictions in the arguments of others. But that dialectical ability resulted in discourse that was "difficult to read sympathetically" and "archaic even for his time."[46]

"The World and the Individual" was no exception to Royce's convoluted manner of thought and presentation. "The scope and volume" of the lectures, writes Royce biographer John Clendenning, "were tremendous. The two series into which it is divided command more than a thousand pages, and together they undertake the construction of a complete system."[47] The opening lecture in the series gave the audience a taste of what was to come. After going into detail on three general ways of studying Natural Religion, Royce explained: "Our own business, in these lectures, is with the most neglected and arduous of the methods of studying the relations between religion and the ultimate problems of the Theory of Being. From the first, to be sure, we shall be concerned, in one sense, with human nature, as every philosophy has to be concerned. And in the latter half of this course the Philosophy of Nature will play a part in our investigation. But the central problem of our discussion will be the question: What is Reality?"[48] The lectures, Royce admitted, would be difficult to follow but necessary for true understanding. They aimed at nothing less than a God's-eye view of Absolute Reality.

Most of Royce's audience responded to his arduous method of investigation by exiting the lecture hall. When Royce first spoke, he addressed a group of around sixty people.[49] After that, fewer and fewer took their seats before him. By the time the series concluded in 1900, only about fifteen people remained in Royce's audience. What began as an inquiry into natural theology with dozens of people ended like a graduate seminar on the metaphysics of Absolute Idealism. Royce had produced his masterwork, but it was far from a popular statement.

While Royce was having problems with attendance at the Gifford lectures, James continued to battle illness. Seeking relief from his heart condition, he traveled to Europe for medical treatment. Getting away from his duties in Cambridge, he figured, would help him rest and focus whatever energy he could muster on completing the Gifford lectures. President Eliot gave him a year off from teaching, and when James's condition did not improve, Eliot granted a second sabbatical. For a while, James stayed with his brother in England, doing his best to relax and recuperate. When he found the strength, he split his time between working on his lectures, sightseeing, and socializing with some of the literary intelligentsia of the English-speaking world—among them Stephen Crane, Joseph Conrad, H. G. Wells, and, of course, Henry James Jr.[50]

James also paid special attention to Royce's progress at Aberdeen. In letters, he and Royce debated religion, the Absolute, and the future of philosophy.[51] Then in 1900 the first volume of *The World and the Individual* was published, and James read it with great interest. He thought the book a grand philosophical vision, and he admired Royce's intellect. At the same time, James knew he would approach his own Gifford lectures from a much different direction. With "one eye on the page, and one on you," James told Royce, he would strike a new tone in Scotland.[52] Royce had striven for technical precision in the hope of capturing the Absolute; James cared little for grand systems and all-encompassing philosophies. He even questioned whether he had anything important to say about "natural theology" in general. He was sure, however, that his lectures would be a hit, as he was working to infuse his talks with as much "variety and vitality" as possible.[53] So confident was he in the widespread appeal of his lectures that he told Pringle-Pattison, organizer at Edinburgh, that "Varieties" was "pretty certain to be more popularly entertaining than most previous Gifford courses have been."[54] Pringle-Pattison replied by noting his confidence that the lectures would "stimulate the most jaded palate" by being both "popularly entertaining" and "one of the best courses under the foundation."[55]

After settling on the exact dates for the lectures—May and June 1901 for the first set of ten, the same months in 1902 for the second set[56]—James traveled to Italy for further respite. There he experienced another breakthrough on what he would say in Edinburgh, but it was an unfortunate kind of breakthrough. In Rome at the end of 1900, James reunited with Frederic Myers, who would soon pass away from pneumonia, less than six months after Henry Sidgwick, another prominent psychical researcher and friend of James's, had died.[57] James was particularly saddened by Myers's death because he thought Myers's inquires into the "subliminal self" held the keys to the future of psychology and psychical research. After Myers passed away, James found his days filled with melancholy. But he also found an important connection with his ongoing work. As he researched and composed the Giffords, a series devoted to exploring God, the unseen world, and the afterlife, he felt his own connection to spiritual possibilities increase. According to one account, James sat outside Myers's death chamber with notebook in hand, waiting for spirit communication from his just-departed friend.[58] Although no communication came, James nevertheless thought that Myers's ability to face death with courage demonstrated "the practical influence of a living belief in future existence."[59] In a few months, he would make the same point to his listeners at Edinburgh.

On May 14, 1901, after visiting with his brother Henry in England, James boarded a train for Scotland. With preparation of the lectures finally complete, he grew anxious about the occasion, knowing that great expectations surrounded his performance. James seemed to worry about anything and everything, including what clothes to wear. He feared that he did not own suitable garb for addressing the prestigious Edinburgh audience, and he joked that he might "have to lecture in my pajamas," which would certainly provide "a cachet of american originality."[60] It was an offhanded comment, but it perfectly captured the international dynamics of the situation. James knew that he arrived in Edinburgh as the representative of American thought; Royce had told him as much. So lecturing in pajamas could be yet another mark of American intellectual novelty.

Finally, on May 16, 1901, James took his seat behind a large oak table on a small stage at the front of Edinburgh's largest auditorium. Because of his health, he had to speak sitting down—not his normal practice during lectures. He also had to speak from a full-sentence manuscript, as opposed to employing his usual speaking-outline approach. On this occasion, however, using a manuscript was the right choice. Because the lectures contained many extensive quotations, manuscript delivery allowed him to convey his testimonial evidence with precision. It also helped ease his nervousness, as he had just finished writing the lectures and had not yet grown accustomed to the material. Speaking ten times over a span of four weeks, he delivered what would become the first half of *The Varieties of Religious Experience.*[61]

By all accounts, the first ten lectures were a hit. According to *The Scotsman,* "Numerous clergymen of various denominations, . . . a considerable body of students, and a large sprinkling of ladies" sat rapt as James mused eloquently on the religious dimensions of human life. The audience was "greatly indebted" to him for the material, the paper concluded, showering him with hearty applause.[62] James himself reported the heartfelt praise he received. The audience, which was "more numerous than had been expected," consisting of around 300 people, proved "very attentive & sympathetic and gave protracted and solid applause at the end, the likes of which they give at Harvard, and which one gets from no other sort of audience known to me."[63] As *The Scotsman* explained after the tenth lecture, "Professor James, who was accorded quite an ovation, said his lectures had been attended by far larger numbers than he had dared to hope, and that encouraged him to feel that in the subject he had treated he had chosen one that the high-minded founder of the lectures might have approved of."[64]

With the first ten lectures complete, James had almost a year to write the second ten. After relaxing with Henry in England and seeking further medical treatment in Germany, he returned to the United States in September 1901. Work on the second course of lectures proceeded more smoothly than had work on the first, which allowed James to arrange for publication of the book. Because he wanted *Varieties* to be ready as soon as he finished delivering the lectures, he began sending completed manuscript pages to Riverside Press in Cambridge. This practice continued through the end of 1901 and into 1902 as he went back and forth between writing new lectures and correcting page proofs from the printer. By March 1902, he had a mostly complete text in hand; he would even use some of the page proofs to deliver the second set of lectures.[65]

On April 1, 1902, James sailed for England to deliver the remainder of the Gifford series. Before the lectures commenced, however, he attended Edinburgh's graduation ceremony, where he and Jacob Schurman, president of Cornell, received honorary degrees.[66] Soon James found that much of the previous year's anxiety had melted away. "The ease of the whole thing is a measure of my improvement last year," he remarked to Henry.[67] When he returned to his oak table at the front of the auditorium, *The Scotsman* returned to its coverage, describing the audience as "a large number of professors" and students as well as "a considerable portion" of ladies.[68] At first, James felt a little "humdrum," worried that "excitement never strikes twice in the same place."[69] But he soon found his rhythm and remembered why Edinburgh audiences were "splendid."[70]

If there was any doubt in James's mind about the effectiveness of the second set of lectures, the final lecture, which took place on June 9, settled the matter. The audience had swelled to around 400 people, which made for a standing-room-only crowd, as the auditorium had seats for only 300 people.[71] "The room," said one report, "from corner to corner was crammed to the point of discomfort."[72] Listeners lined the walls, sitting wherever there was space, even perching on window sills to catch a glimpse of the famed American thinker. When James delivered the final line of the lectures, the audience erupted in applause and honored him with a rousing rendition of "For He's a Jolly Good Fellow." A correspondent for the *Boston Evening Transcript* captured the scene:

> It has been a remarkable series of lectures delivered by a remarkable man and to an audience as rare in the standard of its intellectuality and culture as could be found. . . . Through twenty lectures he has kept his audience on tenterhooks, and the simple, manly way in which this much honored and deeply learned man expressed his views, after delving through an incredible mass of scientific investigations, won for him the plaudits of all his hearers.[73]

On the same day he received the plaudits of all his hearers, *The Varieties of Religious Experience* went on sale in England. A week later, it went on sale in America.[74]

As with many of James's books—*Talks to Teachers* being the most notable example—we are left with questions about what James may have said on the podium and what appeared in print. Did he simply publish his lectures? Did he share with the world the same sentences he had shared with the people of Edinburgh? Were his readers treated to the same inspirational vision that had prompted his listeners to break into song? By and large, even though surviving evidence is ambiguous in certain respects, it is safe to conclude that *The Varieties of Religious Experience* (the book) and "The Varieties of Religious Experience" (the lecture series) were substantially the same. The primary difference between the two was the inclusion of a postscript in the book, where James tried to clarify his own religious position—calling himself a "supernaturalist" whose beliefs did not align with "popular Christianity," "scholastic theism," or "the current of thought in academic circles."[75] In terms of the twenty lectures, full-sentence manuscripts for only two have survived, but the handwritten text corresponds closely with what was published. While James appears to have made some changes to the lectures after galley proofs arrived from the printer, they were minor, leaving the overall tone, arguments, evidence, and strategies unaffected. Moreover, we know that James used many typeset pages from the printer when delivering the second half of the lecture series, though he reduced the length of some quotations when speaking.[76] In terms of structure, the book's chapter divisions did not correspond precisely with the divisions between lectures, but James indicated when a given chapter contained more than one lecture.[77]

Ultimately, despite the minor differences that set the lectures and the book apart, James wanted readers to feel as though they were sitting in the lecture hall listening to him. "It is with no small amount of trepidation," he explained at the start of *Varieties,* "that I take my place behind this desk, and face this learned audience."[78] Inclusion of this statement was a way of preparing readers for the oral style of what followed. Indeed, the same elements of James's oral style in *Talks to Teachers* pervaded *Varieties.*[79] And as with the earlier work, orality enhanced the participatory character of what people read. Readers became actors in the unfolding of ideas; they became interlocutors with James rather than mere receivers of his thought.

So engaging was James's style that almost every review of *Varieties* discussed it, regardless of whether the reviewer agreed with James's overall argument. George Coe, for example, wrote for *The Philosophical Review* that reading *Varieties* was "like walking in a great forest—one enjoys the foliage, the light and shade, the vistas of mountain and valley, and even the tantalizing sense of not knowing exactly whither one's feet are tending."[80] The Catholic publication *American Ecclesiastical Review* relished the "lightness of touch," the "wealth of illustration," and the "happy absence of all controversial bitterness that make [*Varieties*] a pleasure, and not a task, to read."[81] The *New York Times* sounded a similar note: "Writing more fresh and vivid cannot easily be conceived, and there are many passages in which the expression, rising to the level of the thought, is of a striking force and beauty."[82]

Of course, the importance of the text went far beyond its oral style. As we shall see below, *The Varieties of Religious Experience*—a label I now use to refer to the lectures and the book, given that they were close in content and that James wanted us to think of them as identical—illustrated the extent to which James was willing to push the art of popular statement. In Edinburgh, popular statement morphed into populist appeals.

Intellectual Populism in The Varieties of Religious Experience

When James took his seat before the people of Edinburgh, part of his project was to address a prescribed topic, natural theology, which Lord Adam Gifford had considered essential for true knowledge. James acknowledged the importance of the topic at the start of the lecture series, but he wanted the audience also to know that he was "neither a theologian, nor a scholar learned in the history of religions, nor an anthropologist"—titles that could be used to characterize previous Gifford lecturers.

"Psychology," he continued, "is the only branch of learning in which I am particularly versed."[83] Over twenty lectures, spread across two calendar years, James tried to put on display the novelty of this psychological perspective. He began with "Religion and Neurology" and a "Circumscription of the Topic." He then dove into "The Reality of the Unseen"; "The Religion of Healthy-Mindedness," which he discussed over two lectures; "The Sick Soul," also spread over two lectures; "The Divided Self, and the Process of Unification"; "Conversion"; "Conversion—Concluded"; "Saintliness," spread over three lectures; "The Value of Saintliness," covered in two lectures; "Mysticism," also covered in two lectures; "Philosophy"; "Other Characteristics"; and "Conclusions."

James took his seat before the people of Edinburgh with the project of addressing natural theology, and he ended up founding what scholars have called "the psychology of religion"[84]—or the striving "for insight into the empirical phenomena that go together under the label of religion."[85] However, James himself saw his goal somewhat differently. His aim, he told listeners and readers, was to shed light on the religious experiences of "individual men in their solitude."[86] This interest in individual men, or "common men" and "common people," as he would also characterize them, pointed ultimately to the striking, even radical, intellectual culture he hoped to advance.[87] It was, as I have already suggested, a populist culture, defined by a populist discourse aimed at remaking the world of ideas. In general, we can understand this discourse by exploring three strategies James employed throughout *Varieties*. First, he repeatedly underscored the deficiencies of religious inquiry according to the standards of academic professionalism. Doing so helped him connect with the popular portion of the audience, and it effectively called into question the dominant intellectual culture. Second, James made "experience" the starting and ending points of inquiry. Because everyone could experience the divine in his or her own way, everyone could contribute to the general storehouse of religious knowledge. Third, James fulfilled the audience's expectations for "true American theory" by linking *Varieties* with international perceptions of American culture—a rustic, individualistic, democratic, and egalitarian culture. In the end, the Americanness of the text further reinforced the novelty and populism of the system of knowledge James envisioned.

While these three strategies were not inclusive of everything James did in the text—*Varieties* is too expansive to be characterized fully in a single analysis—explaining them will help us understand how the lectures extended his art of popular statement. Intellectual populism not only structured his interactions in Edinburgh but also fostered a sentiment that would captivate successive generations.

The Deficiencies of Academic Professionalism

James's foes in *Varieties* went by many names—scientists, philosophers, theologians, materialists, dogmatists, and more—but they all shared a dedication to exclusionary practices. As James presented the matter, experts had accumulated professional power and had, in the process, taken religious insight out of the hands of ordinary people. To be sure, the problem was not with science, philosophy, and theology per se; it was with the rigid, impersonal, monistic, unimaginative versions of these fields. But that was disconcerting enough for individuals striving for religious understanding. James's project, then, was to combat the pretensions of epistemological privilege that many academics claimed for their work.

In the opening lecture, for example, James distanced himself from the "haunts of special erudition" and the "medical materialists" who tried to discredit religious experiences out of hand.[88] Unflinchingly committed to a naturalist paradigm, medical materialists deemed Saint Paul an epileptic whose vision on the road to Damascus was "a discharging lesion of the occipital cortex"; Saint Teresa was nothing more than "an hysteric"; Saint Francis of Assisi was "an hereditary degenerate"; and George Fox had "a disordered colon." By reducing religious experiences to physiological states, medical materialists insisted that "the spiritual authority of all such personages is successfully undermined."[89] In the hands of these experts, specialized physiological inquiry became a weapon for rejecting claims of divine connection. Moreover, those interested in divine connection were disempowered in conversations about God, theology, and spiritual life.

It was a rhetorically brilliant beginning. If James was interested in securing the favor of the people of Edinburgh, who had arrived at the lecture hall to hear his thoughts on natural theology, there was likely no better way to commence than by assaulting those who belittled the great figures of religious history. Accordingly, James chastised the methods of the medical materialists as "illogical and arbitrary," holding no weight for those who were interested in "spiritual significance."[90] And because

James and his audience were committed to exploring the significance of religious life, they could leave medical materialism behind. Indeed, materialist methods were incapable of understanding "our own more exalted soul-flights."[91]

As the lecture series progressed, James branched out from medical materialists to confront other narrow thinkers, thereby distancing himself further from the kinds of academics the audience had come to know over the years. In the second lecture he bemoaned that the "theorizing mind" tended to oversimplify its object of study. Such a mind, James insisted, was "the root of all that absolutism and one-sided dogmatism by which both philosophy and religion have been infested."[92] Later, he explained that scientists and positivists "will tell you that religious thought is a mere survival, an atavistic reversion to a type of consciousness which humanity in its more enlightened examples has long since left behind and outgrown."[93] Theologians could be just as out of touch. With their "fixed definitions" and "positive dogmas," James said when discussing "The Value of Saintliness," theologians turned away from the spiritual center of life and instead devised "clean-cut and scholastic" arguments for God, building a "special *a priori* theological system" to justify whatever conclusions they favored.[94] Philosophers were similarly disconnected from religious life, as they attempted to "construct religious objects out of the resources of logical reason alone, or of logical reason drawing rigorous inference from non-subjective facts."[95]

James's assault on scientists, theologians, and philosophers amounted to a kind of antielitist appeal that defines populist discourse writ large.[96] By distancing himself from the academic establishment, which seemed uninterested in taking people's religious aspirations seriously, he gave listeners and readers a reason to join with him in creating a new intellectual culture. In fact, unlike the academics who belittled the soul-flights of "common men," James shared the audience's religious propensities. Throughout *Varieties* he referenced "we Christians" as a way of pitting himself and his audience against the spiritual vacuousness of the elitist professionals. "Our practice is the only sure evidence, even to ourselves, that we are genuinely Christians," he said in the opening lecture.[97] Later, he praised "our best rooted contemporary Protestant social ideals,"[98] and he lauded "our Protestant and modern education."[99] In affirming religious belief despite the objections of modern science, and in embracing the personal aspects of religion despite the propensities of modern philosophy, James declared that "God is the natural appellation, for us Christians at least, for the supreme reality, so I will call this higher part of the universe by the name of God. We and God have business with each other; and in opening ourselves to his influence our deepest destiny is fulfilled."[100]

As many commentators have noted, James's repeated references to "us Christians" were somewhat peculiar, given that he wrote in the postscript about his "own inability to accept either popular Christianity or scholastic theism."[101] That postscript, however, was not delivered as part of the lecture series. When speaking to the people of Edinburgh, James understood the need to find common ground, and appealing to "us Christians" was a perfect way to align himself with his audience. In fact, in letters to friends written shortly after the Giffords concluded, James acknowledged his attempt to connect with the people of Edinburgh by engaging their Christian propensities.[102] This is not to say he was disingenuous, but it is to say that he was conscious of how his appeals functioned rhetorically.

For all his assaults on scientists, philosophers, and theologians, James's main goal was not to denigrate specific groups of people but to disparage the type of knowledge they produced. In fact, *Varieties* rested upon two general arguments against narrowly professional approaches to knowledge—one about the problem of intellectual absolutism and the other about the problem of academic discourse. The first argument, which James made repeatedly throughout the lectures, was essentially that scientists, philosophers, and theologians approached religion with the idea that there was only one way to acquire true knowledge. This was the "one-sided view" of the subject to which James objected in his second lecture.[103] When dealing with religious phenomena, however, "there is not a single conception that can be sharply drawn. The pretension, under such conditions, to be rigorously 'scientific' or 'exact' in our terms would only stamp us as lacking in understanding of our task."[104] Intellectual absolutism was problematic, James explained further, because religious life "plainly shows the universe to be a more many-sided affair than any sect, even the scientific sect, allows for. . . . The world can be handled according to many systems of ideas, and is so handled by different men, and will each time give some characteristic kind of profit."[105]

The second general argument James offered against narrowly professional approaches to religious knowledge focused on the tendencies of academic discourse. When scientists, philosophers, and theologians undertake their work, James explained in various ways, they do so in the language of logic and reason as opposed to the language of life—that is, the way people actually experience religious phenomena. The rationalist perspective, for example, "insists that all our beliefs ought ultimately to find for themselves articulate grounds. . . . Vague impressions of something indefinable have no place in the rationalistic system."[106] Rationalism may offer "prestige" and "loquacity," James reported further, "it can challenge you for proofs, and chop logic, and put you down with words. But it will fail to convince or convert you all the same, if your dumb intuitions are opposed to its conclusions." Under such a system, one might achieve an impressive, impersonal, logically exacting argument, but such an argument would be far less significant than "your whole subconscious life, your impulses, your faiths, your needs, your divinations. . . . Something in you absolutely *knows* that that result must be truer than any logic-chopping rationalistic talk, however clever."[107] James leveled a similar argument against the discursive tendencies of modern philosophy, which "lives in words, but truth and fact well up into our lives in ways that exceed verbal formulations."[108] As a result, "We must conclude that the attempt to demonstrate by purely intellectual processes the truth of the deliverances of direct religious experience is absolutely hopeless."[109]

In arguing against the discursive norms of academic professionalism, James constructed his sentences in a way that pitted himself and his audience against the reigning systems of intellectual power. Rationalism in particular was an assault on the way ordinary people lived their lives and experienced the divine. The people of Edinburgh, not to mention readers of *Varieties,* were being "put down" by professional argumentation. The image was of an oppressive system that was "absolutely hopeless" for understanding "our lives." James and his audience thus stood together against the elitist professional forces of the day.

How should James and his audience respond to these professional forces, particularly to the arguments and languages that seemed to miss the importance of religious life? The answer to this question was relatively straightforward but incredibly powerful in James's overall populist project. The answer was simply to sidestep the confines of academic discourse. People interested in religious life should just go around the argumentative impositions of the scientists, philosophers, and theologians. When it came to defining religion, James himself had no interest in constructing some grand new definition in response to other academics. He had no interest in quibbling over terminology or in attending to "systematic theology and the ideas about the gods themselves." "Rather than prolong such a dispute," James said, dismissing the entire affair, "I am willing to accept almost any name for the personal religion of which I propose to treat. Call it conscience or morality, if you yourselves prefer, and not religion—under either name it will be equally worthy of our study."[110] He then defined religion "arbitrarily" as "*the feelings, acts, and experiences of individual men in their solitude, so far as they apprehend themselves to stand in relation to whatever they may consider the divine.*"[111] James was content with this arbitrary definition because he had no interest in debating theologians. If they did not like the definition, that was fine by him; they could debate it all they wanted. In the meantime, he would move forward and explore the lives people actually lived.

James demonstrated a similarly dismissive attitude when he discussed the issue of feeling versus reason in philosophical inquiry. Among philosophers, he explained, feeling was "valid only for the individual," whereas reason was considered "valid universally." In an attempt to engender skepticism about the supposed universality of reason, James explained that if the standards of reason led inevitably to truth, philosophers would universally agree on basic propositions. That is to say, they would accept the same arguments because reason was universal. So, James asked, do philosophers believe the same thing? "I need not discredit philosophy by laborious criticism of its arguments," he responded. "It will suffice if I show that as a matter of history it fails to prove its pretension to be 'objectively' convincing. In fact, philosophy does fail. It does not banish differences; it founds schools and sects just as feeling does."[112] As James saw the matter, the proper response to philosophy was not to offer some grand counterargument and quibble over technicalities; it was simply to note that philosophers disagreed, thereby sidestepping the debate.

James's dismissive attitude contributed much to his intellectual populism, for it showed nonacademics how they could circumvent expert authority. James gave the people of Edinburgh a rationale for going around science, philosophy, and theology, and for focusing on what made their religious lives meaningful. They could and should participate in the pursuit of religious knowledge, but they could and should do so apart from the requirements of academic argumentation. To make the point clear, James presented Tolstoy as someone to emulate: "His trouble had not been with life in general, not with the common life of common men, but with the life of the upper, intellectual, artistic classes, the life which he had personally always led, the cerebral life, the life of conventionality, artificiality, and personal ambition. He had been living wrongly and must change. To work for animal needs, to abjure lies and vanities, to relieve common wants, to be simple, to believe in God, therein lay happiness again."[113] Tolstoy had gone around intellectual, cerebral, aristocratic demands and had succeeded; James's audience could do the same.

Religious Experience as Populist Knowledge

Fomenting opposition to the reigning systems of knowledge and to the culture of academic professionalism was the first part of James's intellectual populism. Those members of his audience hoping to better understand their religious propensities now had a host of good reasons to disregard the impersonal logic-chopping of the experts. The project then became articulating an alternative to the entrenched powers. Having questioned mainstream scientific, philosophical, and theological inquiry, James had to explain a mode of inquiry that would meet the needs of ordinary people. To that end, the second component of his populist engagement involved making personal experience the epicenter of religious understanding.

An obvious question, however, is what James meant by "experience." He used the term liberally throughout his writings and often resisted systematic definition of the concept.[114] This refusal to engage experience systematically has led some commentators to question the value of the idea itself. Richard Rorty, for one, has argued that the central problem of *Varieties* was James's inconsistent discussions of experience and his lack of appreciation for the philosophical problems the concept introduced.[115] Other scholars have pointed out that James's reliance upon experience, however he deployed it, linked him to an expansive tradition of experientially focused philosophy.[116] Yet whatever one concludes about James's use or misuse of experience, we should note that that concept did important rhetorical work in the lecture hall. Specifically, it formed the persuasive core of his new approach to knowledge.

Religious experience, generally understood, amounted to an individual's perception of his or her relation to the divine or whatever he or she considered to be divine.[117] Immediate sensations and feelings were key to this notion of experience, as were the relations that emerged from these sensations and feelings. But more intriguing, at least for the current purposes, was the role of perception in religious experience. For James, whatever "the individual feels impelled to respond to solemnly and gravely, and neither by a curse nor a jest," constituted a religious experience.[118] It did not matter whether this thing eliciting a response was "real," at least in the traditional sense of the term. What mattered was the individual's perception of what was real. To understand religious experience, then, one had to uncover

> that curious sense of the whole residual cosmos as an everlasting presence, intimate or alien, terrible or amusing, lovable or odious, which in some degree everyone possesses. This sense of the world's presence, appealing as it does to our peculiar individual temperament, makes us either strenuous or careless, devout or blasphemous, gloomy or exultant, about life at large; and our reaction, involuntary and inarticulate and often half unconscious as it is, is the completest of all our answers to the question, "What is the character of this universe in which we dwell?" It expresses our individual sense of it in the most definite way.[119]

Several aspects of this passage deserve mention. First, James began with sensation and perception and ended with knowledge—that is, with the "completest" answer to the question about the character of the universe. In contrast to most of the Western philosophical tradition, he argued that perception and appearance were not obstacles to be overcome but integral to understanding the world. Second, the movement from perception to knowledge took place at the level of the individual. Every individual could answer the question "What is the character of this universe in which we dwell," and every answer could be legitimate because of the individual's "sense of the world's presence." Put somewhat differently, everyone was on the same epistemological plane. Specialized training mattered little when anyone could form the "completest" answer about the universe's character. Of course, this did not mean that everyone had to arrive at the same "completest" answer, or that all answers were equally beneficial; subsequent experience helped sort out levels of benefit. But it did mean that everyone had a right to answer in his or her own way, and that those answers counted as knowledge, no matter what a person's scholarly qualifications. "By being religious," insisted James, "we establish ourselves in possession of the ultimate reality at the only points at which reality is given us to guard."[120]

This sentiment expressed the core of James's intellectual populism. Indeed, it was the epistemological version of the uprising that is pictured in most populist discourse.[121] James's argument was not just that knowledge resulted from idiosyncratic religious experience; it was that religious experience produced the fullest, most penetrating, most meaningful knowledge possible. Feelings of religious reality, he explained, "are as convincing to those who have them as any direct sensible experience can be, and they are, as a rule, much more convincing than results established by mere logic ever are." Once again, the logic of obtuse academics was pushed aside. James continued: "If you have" religious experiences, "and have them at all strongly, the probability is that you cannot help regarding them as genuine perceptions of truth, as revelations of a kind of reality which no adverse argument, however unanswerable by you in words, can expel from your belief."[122] "If a person feels the presence of a living God," he stated elsewhere, "your critical arguments, be they never so superior, will vainly set themselves to change his faith."[123]

When James presented religious experience as the road to true knowledge, he often co-opted the vocabulary of academic methodology and redeployed it in the service of his populist project. Further wresting intellectual control from mainstream scientists, philosophers, and theologians, he made personal experience the best way to "verify," "corroborate," and "prove" religious ideas. In explaining the connection between happiness and religion, for example, he explained that "it is perhaps not surprising that men come to regard the happiness which a religious belief affords as proof of its truth."[124] Such proof was fuller and more meaningful than any proof theologians could muster. Similarly, James upheld practitioners of mind-cure as people whose "practical experience" had "corroborated" their religious beliefs,[125] and he insisted that personal experience leads to "propositions which your whole bodily and mental experience will verify. . . . Believing that a higher power will take care of us in certain ways better than we can take care of ourselves, if we only genuinely throw ourselves upon it and consent to use it, it finds the belief, not only not impugned, but corroborated by its observation."[126] In describing the idea of saintliness, James made the argument more explicit: "One can never fathom an emotion or divine its dictates by standing outside of it. In the glowing hour of excitement, however, all incomprehensibilities are solved, and what was so enigmatical from without becomes transparently obvious. Each emotion obeys a logic of its own and makes deductions which no other logic can draw."[127]

The populist logic of religious experience was above all empowering. Because personal experience could produce its own valid logic, it gave ordinary people a trump card against the rigid, impersonal logic of academics. Those who felt disempowered by expert authority and professional discourse could turn to religious experience as "an absolute addition to the Subject's range of life" and a "new sphere of power."[128] Unlike dogmatic theology and philosophy, experience entailed "an omnipotent excitement," including "heroic opportunity and adventure."[129] It contained the potential for a "second birth, a deeper kind of conscious being than" before.[130] Liberated and freed, "we float and soar and sing" through our religious aspirations.[131] We "feel that other kingdom to be close at hand, within our reach."[132] In the final lecture, James explained the point of it all:

> You see now . . . why I have seemed so bent on rehabilitating the element of feeling in religion and subordinating its intellectual part. Individuality is founded in feeling; and the recesses of feeling, the darker, blinder strata of character, are the only place in the world in which we catch real fact in the making, and directly perceive how events happen, and how work is actually done. Compared with this world of living individualized feelings, the world of generalized objects which the intellect contemplates is without solidity or life.[133]

What kind of evidence could James possibly provide to support this conclusion? How could he persuade the audience that religious experience functioned as the avenue to the fullest kind of knowledge available? He could not chop logic or offer some grand deduction, seeing that he had already dismissed the propriety of such modes of inquiry. He therefore turned to the most compelling kind of evidence for showing the primacy of religious experience—namely, religious experience itself, or at least people's testimony about their own religious experiences. Over the course of the lecture series, James provided no fewer than 200 accounts of people's intercourse with the unseen world. The length of these accounts ranged from a single sentence to several paragraphs. At times, he simply strung together pages of testimony with a couple sentences of his own to transition from one example to the next. It often seemed to be "a rather indiscriminate reportage of random and widely dispersed 'raw materials' punctuated by James's respectful commentary," as David Hollinger has written. But there was a good reason for the approach. "If we read these chapters as literary texts," Hollinger explains, "with attention to his selection of quotations and their dynamic relation to one another, we gain greater access to James's center of religious gravity."[134] We also gain greater understanding of James's populist appeal. Paragraph after paragraph, page after page, he quoted the testimony of people who gained new knowledge based on their sentiments, feelings, and perceptions of the divine—not on their scientific, philosophical, and theological expertise. The result was an army of voices endorsing James's new egalitarian intellectual culture.

Voices throughout history became proof of the value of James's experiential system of knowledge. In the very first lecture, for example, James quoted Saint Teresa's reflection on her own heavenly visions: "All those who knew me saw that I was changed; . . . this improvement, palpable in all respects, far from being hidden, was brilliantly evident to all men. . . . I saw clearly that a single one of these visions was enough to enrich me with all that wealth."[135] In the third lecture, James quoted his friend Richard Hodgson on feeling the presence of an invisible force and achieving new knowledge as a result: "After I had got into bed and blown out the candle, . . . I *felt* something come into the room and stay close to my bed. . . . It stirred something more at the roots of my being than any ordinary perception. . . . Something was present with me, and I knew its presence far more surely than I have ever known the presence of any fleshly living creature."[136] Still later James quoted a Christian mystic who found a pathway to a new reality: "The great central fact in human life is the coming into a conscious, vital realization of our oneness with this Infinite Life, and the opening of ourselves fully to this divine inflow. In just the degree that we come into a conscious realization of our oneness with the Infinite Life, and open ourselves to this divine inflow, do we actualize in ourselves the qualities and powers of the Infinite Life, do we make ourselves channels through which the Infinite Intelligence and Power can work."[137]

In pointing to the experiential pathway to knowledge, James strategically varied the sources of his quotations. Sometimes he drew from the experiences of prominent religious figures; other times he turned to the soul-flights of unnamed individuals. But by weaving different sources together, he made the case that giants of religious history and ordinary people could achieve the same level of religious understanding. When, for instance, James quoted George Fox, Jonathan Edwards, Martin Luther, John Wesley, John Woolman, Saint Paul, Saint John, Ignatius

Loyola, and others, he quoted them not because of their insight into doctrine but because their intercourse with the divine could throw "a wholly new light upon our natural constitution."[138] Similarly, it was not as though Marcus Aurelius, Goethe, Emerson, Walt Whitman, Leo Tolstoy, John Bunyan, and Mary Baker Eddy were valuable because of their theological arguments; they were valuable because their words illustrated "effective occupation of a place in life, with its dynamic current passing through your being."[139] Alongside these notable figures James included testimony from "common men," showing his listeners that they, too, could effectively occupy a place in the world. An unknown clergyman, a twenty-seven-year-old man, a boy of seventeen, a little-known Swiss writer, different female correspondents of James's, practitioners of mind-cure, an unnamed French writer (who happened to be James himself),[140] people who experimented with mescal and nitrous oxide, and many more—all possessed religious knowledge of the caliber that notable figures possessed. Because experience was the epicenter of insight, it did not matter whether the individual was Saint Paul or an unnamed teenager; both could transact with "unseen powers" and "do things which no enlightened man can nowadays believe in."[141]

James's hundreds of pieces of personal experience amounted to what scholars of rhetoric call "argument by example," wherein "particular phenomena are invoked one after the other" in order to reach a larger conclusion.[142] Moreover, the length of James's examples and the fact that they were pieces of testimony—or what one scholar has called "reported speech"[143]—created a powerful rhetorical effect throughout the lectures. When James spent several minutes quoting a person's intimate religious experience, he effectively gave that person a voice in the lecture itself. That is to say, he gave the individual a chance to contribute to the content and direction of ideas. In his lecture on the religion of healthy-mindedness, for example, James quoted a couple hundred words from Theodore Parker, then several hundred from Walt Whitman, then a full page of prose from an unnamed source, then a page from Henry Wood, then almost a page from R. W. Trine, then a page from one unnamed woman before moving to a page from a second unnamed woman. And these were only some of the quotations James recited in the lecture. This cacophony of voices, this army of reanimated spirits, offered a new sphere of power.

Furthermore, even when James did not recite each quotation word for word, we may speculate on how he likely delivered the evidence. To make lengthy quotations compelling, James would have had to inhabit the experiences of the people he incorporated into the lectures. If the audience was going to feel a connection with the intimate nature of religious experience, he would have had to adopt the personae of prominent religious figures and unnamed individuals. We can only imagine how he may have delivered the words of Mrs. Jonathan Edwards, but as an experienced and proficient lecturer, James would likely have tried to bring her to life: "All night I continued in a constant, clear and lively sense of the heavenly sweetness of Christ's excellent love, of his nearness to me, and of my dearness to him; with an inexpressibly sweet calmness of soul in an entire rest in him. I seemed to myself to perceive a glow of divine love come down from the heart of Christ in heaven, into my heart, in a constant stream, like a stream or pencil of sweet light."[144]

Performing this quotation, as well as all of the quotations, would also have been rhetorically advantageous, putting James's opponents in a bind. How does one argue against the experience of another? How does one prove that Mrs. Jonathan Edwards did not experience Christ's love in her heart? How does one conclude that the army of voices James called forth did not actually undergo their purported transactions with the divine? Scientists could attempt to discount such testimony by saying that James's sources were simply dreaming, or that they were afflicted by some physiological malady. Philosophers and theologians could say that such experiences were too subjective and personal to be of much value in creating a system of religious knowledge. But James had already dealt with such arguments; he had set them aside and authorized the people of Edinburgh to do the same. Scientists, philosophers, and theologians could argue all they wanted, but their arguments would not change the fact that Mrs. Jonathan Edwards believed, in the deepest recesses of her being, that Christ had entered her heart. She did not have to listen to academic counterarguments, and neither did James's listeners and readers.

There was yet another consequence of James's turn to experiential evidence, one that was closely related to his personal frustrations with the forces of academic professionalism. To the extent that James was able to sidestep the arguments of mainstream scientists, philosophers, and theologians, he was also able to provide a new justification of psychical research. In fact, *Varieties* was, in many ways, the culmination of what James had worked so hard to accomplish in the 1890s. The unseen world of religious experience was remarkably similar to the unseen world of paranormal phenomena, as both dealt with the way "spiritual" forces influenced human life. And because *Varieties* was about personal experience as opposed to scientific verifiability, James did not have to show that God, angels, heaven, or hell were "real" in the traditional sense; he only had to show that they made a difference in people's lives. The simple fact that people believed in spiritual forces and experienced them as real was enough to legitimize study of them. James knew he had an excellent argumentative opportunity on his hands. If personal experience became the source of true knowledge, the personal experiences of mediums, members of séance circles, people who saw spirits, automatic writers, telepathics, and those who were possessed became legitimate parts of the intellectual conversation.

When James quoted people who felt the hand of God, who were haunted by angels, who saw visions of the afterlife, and the like, he brought religious and paranormal experience close together. In his third lecture, on "The Reality of the Unseen," he quoted Edmund Gurney's firsthand account of being visited by a spirit; the words of a French woman, Madame Ackermann, who felt "haunted" by "ephemeral and incomprehensible" beings; and the statement of his friend Theodore Flourney, who recalled being transformed "by the presence of a *spiritual spirit*."[145] In other lectures, he cited people who heard voices from unknown origins, who were "haunted" by Scripture, and who became possessed by the Holy Spirit.[146] The link between religious experience and paranormal phenomena became most clear when he discussed the process of conversion: "Voices are often heard, lights seen, or visions witnessed; automatic motor phenomena occur; and it always seems, after the surrender of the personal will, as if an extraneous higher power had flooded in and taken possession."[147] Because of the similarities between religious and paranormal experience, James was able to make much the same point he had made in more explicit defenses of psychical research, but he was able to do so apart from the demands of professional argumentation. "It is as if there were in the human consciousness a *sense of reality, a feeling of objective presence, a perception* of what we may call *'something there,'* more deep and more general than any of the special and particular 'sense' by which the current psychology supposes existent realities to be originally revealed."[148]

Not only did James give his discussion of religious experience a decidedly paranormal tone, he also drew upon psychical researchers to testify in the lectures. He cited Frederic Myers, Pierre Janet, Alfred Binet, Edmund Gurney, and other members of the SPR to shed psychological light on religious experience. He presented the "subliminal self," which originally appeared in the pages of *The Proceedings of the Society for Psychical Research,* as the concept that best explained the value of individual religious experience. "*If there be* higher spiritual agencies that can directly touch us," James said, they touch us through "our possession of a subconscious region which alone should yield access to them. The hubbub of the waking life might close a door which in the dreamy Subliminal might remain ajar or open."[149]

Taken together, testimony from people who experienced religion in a paranormal way and scholars who studied psychical subjects made *Varieties* a powerful justification of psychical research. In fact, after publication of the book, members of the SPR could see the upshot of James's argumentative strategy. "The greatest of living psychologists," explained F. C. S. Schiller, who reviewed *Varieties* for *Proceedings of the Society for Psychical Research,* used psychical evidence to back conventional scientists into a corner, removing "the chief difficulties with which the S.P.R. has had to contend in its dealings with academic psychologists." Schiller further declared: "It seems impossible that psychologists will be able to evade much longer the consideration either of [the subliminal self] or of the evidence on which it is based."[150] In short, James's Gifford lectures rejuvenated the bruised and battered SPR.

An American Performance

James was unlike previous Gifford lecturers, he was unlike the prominent idealists who shaped European thought at the time, and he was unlike the only other American to deliver a series of Giffords. Royce had argued like the great idealists of Europe. James, however, told his listeners that they could, if they wanted, dismiss the kinds of arguments made by many previous Gifford lecturers. They could, in fact, acquire true religious knowledge through their own experience. This was James's central populist appeal, and it gave the audience exactly what they were hoping to hear—namely, "true American theory." Indeed, his intellectual populism and his reputation for quintessentially American thought were mutually reinforcing. In the end, James's lecturers were not just distinctive; they were distinctly American.

Easy to overlook when discussing *Varieties* is the fact that the lectures were delivered to a live audience, meaning that those who first encountered the work received it through the sound vibrations in the air. It was James's voice—which his contemporaries described as "peculiarly attractive" and "singularly sweet" with "resonant tones" that made for a "brilliant, high-strung, dynamic, vivacious, resilient, unexpected, unconventional, picturesque" manner of presentation—that delivered the news of experiential truth.[151] Sitting in the auditorium week after week, across the span of two years, Gifford attendees heard someone who sounded different from them and from most Gifford lecturers. They experienced a speaker whose vocal qualities, mannerisms, pacing, and personable delivery reinforced the appearance of distinctive thought.

But James's manner of presentation was only one aspect of his American performance. Immediately upon taking his seat at Edinburgh, he acknowledged the "trepidation" he felt before such a "learned audience," explaining that, as an American, the phenomenon of "talking whilst the Europeans listen" was strange.[152] He felt humbled by the opportunity to lecture in Edinburgh, which called forth so many "illustrious names" and produced in him "a sense of dreamland quite as much as of reality." He then laid out his vision of intellectual exchange in the future: "As the years go by, I hope that many of my countrymen may be asked to lecture in the Scottish universities, changing places with Scotsmen lecturing in the United States; I hope that our people may become in all these higher matters even as one people; and that the peculiar philosophic temperament, as well as the peculiar political temperament, that goes with our English speech may more and more pervade and influence the world."[153]

Although James spoke of Americans and Scotsmen becoming "one people," united by the English language, the mere mention of nationality reminded the audience of James's unique position. As the lectures progressed, he built upon this opening statement by deploying strategies that made clear the importance of his American perspective. One strategy involved the use of testimony from American thinkers who had something important to say about religious experience. According to James, Jonathan Edwards helped put the fruits of religious life into perspective.[154] Ralph Waldo Emerson spoke convincingly about the impotency of abstract theology.[155] Theodore Parker and Walt Whitman demonstrated the healthy-minded side of religious life.[156] Charles Finney, Colonel Alexander Gardiner, Henry David Thoreau, Mrs. Jonathan Edwards, John Woolman, William Ellery Channing, Edward Everett Hale, Cotton Mather, Charles Sanders Peirce, Joseph Smith—all were Americans contributing to the world's intellectual conversation.

Essentially, it was a plea for recognition. James hoped to expose his audience to the tradition of American religious thought and, in turn, to instill in them appreciation for the American intellectual voice.

But the Americanness of *Varieties* came not only from great American thinkers. Indeed, the "common man" in James's lectures was often an American. Many of his quotations came from the manuscript collection of Edwin Starbuck, a former student of James's and a Stanford scholar who collected hundreds of religious histories from average Americans.[157] Through correspondence, the distribution of surveys, and "statistical inquiry," James explained, Starbuck was able to paint a detailed picture of the religious lives of the American people.[158] James regularly cited Starbuck when borrowing from the manuscript collection, and he made clear that the number of examples he cited "might be greatly multiplied."[159] The point was to give average Americans the chance to testify to the people of Scotland. An unnamed clergyman, a Christian man "aged forty-nine," a man "twenty-seven years old," a woman of unspecified age, a man of unspecified age, one of "Starbuck's correspondents," people who witnessed heavenly light during conversion experiences, people who heard disembodied voices, and a slew of unnamed people who devoted their lives to serving others because of their conversions—these were the voices of ordinary Americans. *Varieties* did not contain only American voices, of course. But the prominence of American testimony indicated that religious insight could come from anyone, anywhere.[160]

On top of the other American elements of the lecture series was the basic fact that James's discussion of experience seemed American. James was not, of course, the first to put experience at the heart of a philosophical project. Emerson had done so in the nineteenth century, and Emerson himself had borrowed heavily from European romanticists. Moreover, experience has "played a role in virtually every systematic body of thought" since the Greeks.[161] Yet at the turn of the twentieth century in Europe, a time when philosophical idealism marched proudly forward, James's unabashed embrace of experience was distinctive. Because most professional philosophers at the time had little respect for personal experience as a source of knowledge,[162] James had the opportunity to give "experience" a tinge of Americanness.

When addressing the topic of "Philosophy," for example, James acknowledged, then reinforced, the audience's belief that his thought was largely a presentation of American individualism. "You suspect that

I am planning to defend feeling at the expense of reason, to rehabilitate the primitive and unreflective, and to dissuade you from the hope of any Theology worthy of the name." He continued: "To a certain extent I have to admit that you guess rightly. I do believe that feeling is the deeper source of religion, and that philosophic and theological formulas are secondary products, like translations of a text into another tongue."[163] It was not as though "feeling" was an American term and "reason" a European one. Rather, when James engaged the audience's expectations, he underscored his opposition to the philosophical systems they knew best. Proud of his practically minded, individualistic embrace of feeling over reason and "primitive and unreflective" intuition over theology, James donned American garb in the philosophical temples of Europe.

So thoroughly did James hope to occupy distinctly American intellectual ground that *Varieties* culminated with an endorsement of a new philosophy, one that had been carefully cultivated on the other side of the Atlantic. In lecture 18, he explained that he hoped to share the work of "an American philosopher of eminent originality," Charles Sanders Peirce, whom James presented as the father of "the principle of *pragmatism*."[164] Peirce had proposed pragmatism in the early 1870s, but he had done so among a small group of friends, one of whom was James. Even though Peirce was the first to formulate pragmatism, it was James who, in 1898, had brought it to the world's attention.[165] Some in the audience, particularly professional philosophers, had no doubt heard of pragmatism prior to *Varieties,* and they knew James as the champion of it. For those who had not yet encountered the term, James made clear that it was the work of an American mind, one who possessed "eminent originality," similar to the originality James was trying to display in his lectures.

Pragmatism was a philosophy for common people, James insisted. It defined beliefs as "rules for action," arguing that the life of the mind ought to be directed at discovering "what conduct" an idea "is fitted to produce; that conduct is for us its sole significance." "This," James reiterated, "is the principle of Peirce, the principle of pragmatism."[166] To show the audience exactly how the principle of pragmatism worked, he applied it to theological discussions of the attributes of God, attributes such as "aseity," "necessariness," "immateriality," "simplicity," "indivisibility," and "actualized infinity." Looking at such attributes according to the principle of pragmatism and asking what conduct they were fitted to produce, James concluded: "I must frankly confess that even though these attributes were faultlessly deduced, I cannot conceive of its being of the smallest consequence to us religiously that any one of them should be true. Pray, what specific act can I perform in order to adapt myself the better to God's simplicity?"[167]

Not only did such a conclusion represent James's dismissive attitude toward academic argumentation, it represented an attitude grounded in the American experience. Using Peirce's principle, James asked to know the "cash value in terms of particular experience" of theological arguments.[168] With economic calculation as his guide, he stepped forward as a proud capitalist of the mind, interested in investing his time and energy only in what would return an intellectual profit. Such an interest may have sounded crass to European ears, but it was crassly American, and James relished it.[169]

He further bolstered the Americanness of pragmatism by telling a story from his childhood. As a young boy, he explained, he used to read books by the novelist Mayne Reid, whose work typically explored life in the American West. Reid championed "out-of-door adventure," such as the adventures of frontiersmen moving across the United States, and he was "forever extolling the hunters and field-observers of living animals' habits." In addition to praising outdoorsmen, James continued, Reid kept up "a fire of invective against the 'closet-naturalists,' as he called them, the collectors and classifiers, and handlers of skeletons and skins." To Reid, closet naturalists purported to know about nature but never got their hands dirty, forever avoiding the mud of the frontiersman's trail. Reid, James stated, thought closet naturalists "the vilest type of wretch under the sun." James then made the point of his story clear:

> Surely the systematic theologians are the closet-naturalists of the deity, even in Captain Mayne Reid's sense. What is their deduction of these metaphysical attributes but a shuffling and matching of pedantic dictionary-adjectives, aloof from morals, aloof from human needs. . . . One feels that in the theologians' hands, [God's attributes] are only a set of titles obtained by a mechanical manipulation of synonyms. . . . What keeps religion going is something else than abstract definitions and systems of concatenated adjectives, and something different from faculties of theology and their professors. All these things are after-effects, secondary accretions upon those phenomena of vital conversation with the unseen divine, of which I have shown you so many instances, renewing themselves *in saecula saeculorum* in the lives of humble private men.[170]

James's approach to religion was the same approach Mayne Reid had taken to describing the American West. Following in Reid's footsteps, James presented himself and his approach to knowledge as part of an American intellectual frontier, where everyone—not just the specially trained experts—could come to religious understanding through the mud and dirt of the outdoors. James himself had done as much in the woods of Keene Valley, New York, in July 1898. In Edinburgh, he hoped his audience would join him in the woods, reconnecting with the nature of their experience and shunning metaphysical argumentation as "an absolutely worthless invention of the scholarly mind."[171] The dogmatic scientists, philosophers, and theologians, James knew, would scoff at this egalitarian community of inquiry, but there was a populist multitude who would seize the opportunity to cut their own paths through the fields of religious experience. "That unshareable feeling which each one of us has of the pinch of his individual destiny as he privately feels it rolling out on fortune's wheel," James proclaimed, "may be disparaged for its egotism, may be sneered at as unscientific, but it is the one thing that fills up the measure of our concrete actuality, and any would-be existent that should lack such a feeling, or its analogue, would be a piece of reality only half made up."[172]

If concrete actuality was comprised of unsharable, individualized feelings rolling out on fortune's wheel, religious truth, in James's sense of the term, was available to anyone who proceeded to live life. In other words, it was available to everyone—technical, academic logic-chopping be damned.

Conclusion

James's populist appeals distanced him from academic elites (or perceptions thereof) and connected him to those in his audience who saw themselves as "common men." How did these "common men" respond? By bursting into a rendition of "For He's a Jolly Good Fellow." And once *Varieties* went on sale, readers proved just as enthusiastic. Seven months after it hit the market, James reported to one of his sons that he had sold 10,000 copies, earning him a "net profit of $2400"—a figure that translates into almost $62,000 in today's values.[173] *Varieties* was, James said elsewhere, a "first rate market-success," especially considering that it cost $3.20 per copy.[174] Soon he began making arrangements with friends around the world to translate the book into other languages. Several translations appeared over the next few years, increasing James's visibility and fattening his pocketbook.

But sales figures were not the best evidence of the book's influence. Those who reviewed *Varieties* for popular publications found James's work exciting and inspirational. A reviewer for *The Dial* concluded that it was "a work of genius, admirable alike for the thoughts expressed and the manner of their expression." Particularly important were the records of personal experience, which constituted "the true origin of religion, that inward and spiritual grace of which the churches are at best a secondary outcome."[175] A writer for *Living Age* believed that because of James's Gifford lectures, the world was "on the eve of a great revival, whose forerunners are the prophets of psychology." James's work signaled "a time when men will pause in their hot pursuit of evidence, and read each in his own heart 'the Word' which St. John realized to be God."[176] The *New Outlook* offered perhaps the best reason for the book's popular appeal: "William James writes philosophy dramatically because he has the power to put himself in another's place and think his thoughts with him. . . . It is for this reason that his volume . . . is suffused with a glow of feeling and with the power which only feeling can give, such as characterizes the most profoundly religious literature."[177]

In contrast to the praise that popular reviewers heaped upon *Varieties,* professional reviewers—particularly members of the scientific, philosophical, and theological establishment that James assaulted—proved far less enthusiastic. Some faulted James's reliance on "extreme" cases of religious experience, objecting that he slanted the data in his favor—a point James himself dealt with in the book's preface.[178] A reviewer for the philosophical journal *Mind,* for example, chided James for disparaging reason in favor of extreme religious phenomena: "The world cannot be sharply divided, as Prof. James wants to divide it, into those who possess immediate and self-sufficing insight and those who have had no religious experience at all. There are thousands who will not and cannot trust whatever faculty of moral or spiritual insight they possess unless they are presented with a creed which satisfies their Reason."[179] A writer for *Psychological Review* similarly criticized *Varieties* for the extreme nature of the evidence presented, while also questioning James's reliance upon the "subliminal self" as an avenue for knowledge: "In the subconscious region there may be the open door though which divine influences operate, as Professor James suggests, but it may be also the region of chimeras and delusion. As an hypothesis, it may serve to explain the divine, or equally well, to explain it away." Whatever the case, the subliminal self was certainly no "*rational* justification of religious experiences."[180] Others reviewers were even more taken aback by James's unprofessional ways. "On finding himself removed from the vigilant eyes of an exacting Presbyterian audience," wrote J. H. Muirhead in the *International Journal of Ethics,* James "seems to have discovered that far less was really forthcoming than was needed to satisfy them." The little that was forthcoming, Muirhead continued, was intellectually questionable at best: "Before we reduce our intellectual demands upon the universe to the level that is here required, we may be excused if we demand to be assured by more convincing methods than Professor James has employed."[181]

The popular-professional divide that followed *Varieties* was an extension of the popular-professional divide that had followed James's psychical advocacy. Once again, the divide was not absolute, given that some writers for popular periodicals evaluated the book negatively and some writers for professional periodicals evaluated it positively. But the overall distance between the two camps was clear. And it was not at all surprising—or at least it should not have been. After all, James had called into question much of what professional scientists, philosophers, and theologians had worked hard to establish. In terms of its rhetorical operation, *Varieties* subverted the intellectual edifice that narrow, exclusionary professionals had constructed, and audiences responded accordingly. Nonacademics were excited with their newfound power; academics were annoyed that James tried to take their power away.

Perhaps more remarkable, at least if we view *Varieties* through James's commitment to the art of popular statement, is that the populist intellectual culture he envisioned was remarkably similar to the culture of eloquence of his youth. For James, religious understanding hinged more on personal vision and subjective experience than on specialized training and technical precision. Deductive arguments and academic rigor mattered little when one was inspired by whatever he or she considered divine. Had Ralph Waldo Emerson and Henry James Sr. been alive to hear James's musings on the importance of idiosyncratic vision, personal experience, and spirit influences, they likely would have applauded his efforts. *Varieties* was, then, a brilliant mediation between the intellectual culture in which James operated and the intellectual culture of his youth. It was also a profoundly productive text, as it enabled people to go around the stifling strictures of academic professionalism.

This circumvention of academic professionalism, couched in the language of intellectual populism, is likely one of the reasons *Varieties* has remained influential and captivating for more than a century after James's death. The tensions between experts and nonexperts, between specialists and ordinary individuals, between aristocrats of the mind and "the people," were not peculiar to the early twentieth century.[182] Moreover, the religious aspirations and feelings with which *Varieties* dealt involve questions that every generation attempts to answer.[183] Thus when James penned an ode to the power of religious experience and combined it with populist intellectual appeals, he crafted a text capable of invigorating decades, perhaps even centuries, of readers.

In the arc of James's career, however, the intellectual populism of *Varieties* was just a beginning. The Gifford lectures had focused on the epistemological virtues of experience in religious domains. Yet important issues remained: Could a populist intellectual culture move beyond religious inquiry? Could populist appeals shape other epistemologies and structure other texts? As we shall see in the next chapter, the philosophy of pragmatism helped James answer both questions in the affirmative. This most American of philosophies was nurtured on the lecture circuit and, more importantly, called forth a public of lay philosophers to take back the world of thought from the experts who had abducted it.

CHAPTER SIX

Empowering a Pragmatic Public

⌘

When William James looked back on *The Varieties of Religious Experience* a year after the Gifford lectures were over, he knew that his performance on the Edinburgh stage had played a central role in the book's success. In fact, the act of lecturing had been so central that James considered retiring from Harvard to spend more time speaking to general audiences in America and abroad. Why? Because, as he told F. C. S. Schiller on May 1, 1903, popular statement was "the highest form of art."[1] It was a revealing statement from someone who had once studied to be a painter. More revealing, however, was the fact that a mere two days after penning that letter to Schiller, James told his brother Henry something very different: "Lectures have such an awful side (when not academic) that I myself have foresworn them—it is a sort of prostitution of one's person."[2] Here was an attitudinal chasm. On May 1, popular statement was the highest form of art, something to be pursued with enthusiasm and dedication. On May 3, public lecturing was taxing and contemptible, a prostitution of the mind.

James was nothing if not moody, and his letters to Henry often revealed different sentiments than the sentiments he expressed to others. Nevertheless, the disparate statements of May 1 and May 3 raise an important question: What did James really believe about lecturing to popular audiences? Answering the question based solely on his correspondence does little to settle the matter, given that James celebrated public speaking one day and loathed it the next. But if we compare his correspondence to his practices, the disparity goes away. James often complained about lecturing, yet he returned to the public stage year after year. For whatever academic elitism he expressed to his brother Henry, and for whatever difficulties he knew he would encounter on the lecture circuit, he repeatedly chose to travel the country to foster a distinctive, pluralistic, democratic intellectual culture. As Walter Lippmann, one of James's most prolific students, well understood: "He was simply keeping America's promise: he was actually doing what we, as a nation, proclaimed that we would do. He was tolerant; he was willing to listen to what seems preposterous, and to consider what might, though queer, be true. And he showed that this democratic attitude of mind is every bit as fruitful as the aristocratic determination to ignore new and strange-looking ideas. James was a democrat. He gave all men and all creeds, any idea, any theory, any superstition, a respectful hearing."[3]

Nowhere did James express and encourage this democratic attitude more than on the lecture circuit, and nowhere was this expression and encouragement more evident than in the development of pragmatism. The philosophy, as James presented it, was perfectly suited to the problems and possibilities of American life in the early twentieth century. "Practical, democratic, individualistic, opportunistic, spontaneous, hopeful," writes Henry Steele Commager, "pragmatism was wonderfully adapted to the temperament of the average American. . . . No wonder that, despite the broadsides of more formidable philosophers, pragmatism caught on until it came to be almost the official philosophy of America."[4]

During James's lifetime, broadsides against pragmatism from professional philosophers were frequent and many. Charles Bakewell, for one, complained that pragmatism "lacks body" and "needs the support of some more systematic philosophy than that which" James has "roughly sketched."[5] In the eyes of Bertrand Russell, the pragmatic theory of truth was self-contradictory and "to be condemned on the ground that it does not 'work.'"[6] Though "picturesque," insisted J. E. McTaggart, James's ideas were "very far from lucid" and seemed to confirm the very philosophical doctrines he opposed.[7] Thomas Verner Moore compared pragmatism to "the plea of a skillful attorney for a criminal with every *prima facie* evidence of guilt against him." Once all the evidence was in, Moore reached his verdict: "Pragmatism *is* guilty and deserves the condemnations which so many philosophers have heaped upon it."[8]

The fact that many philosophers derided pragmatism did not stop it from becoming a cultural sensation. It was "well suited to popular treatment," the *Nation* explained, because its position was "essentially that of the average man, of the man in the street."[9] Writing in the *New York Times,* Edwin Bjorkman set the concerns of philosophers aside and praised the fact that pragmatism was "being studied and applied by a large portion of the public to an extent heretofore unexampled." The result was a "wonderful awakening of interest in a dreaded and shunned subject"—that is, philosophy.[10] A writer for the *Duluth News Tribune* further developed the popular angle by explaining that pragmatism would "aid in appreciating Ibsen's creed and in directing energy so that it may be worth conserving and result in an evolution upwards."[11] Calling pragmatism a new "gospel," a commentator for the British magazine *The Academy* noted that while philosophers were skeptical of James's work, the American people were quickly converting to this new way of thinking and acting: "The 'cultured' Bostonian girl who is nothing if not up to date proudly professes herself a pragmatist at the present time."[12] Even the great humorist Finley Peter Dunne found pragmatism notable enough to satirize in *American Magazine.* For Dunne's character Mr. Dooley, pragmatism held that "Th' truth is something that wurruks. If it don't wurruk it ain't th' truth. A truth that is lying off is not half as true as a good wurrukin' lie. . . . Th' rale test iv a truth is its cash value. What can ye get on it? If it ain't anny good to ye, chuck it away."[13]

Much of the scorn professional philosophers heaped on pragmatism and much of the enthusiasm nonphilosophers showed toward it can be traced to the popular lectures James delivered in Boston in 1906 and in New York in 1907. Thousands flocked to hear him speak on the subject, and tens of thousands more dove into the published version of the lectures. By some accounts, in fact, *Pragmatism* sold as well as the popular novels of the day,[14] although James himself seemed somewhat disappointed by the sales.[15] Whether or not the book made him as rich as he had hoped, the number of printings during his lifetime revealed the widespread appeal of his philosophical vision. First published in June 1907, *Pragmatism* sold out in a matter of weeks, prompting the publisher to make two more print runs in July. Three months later, a fourth printing was issued, followed by a fifth a month after that. Two more were needed in 1908, another in 1909, and an additional two by the time of James's death in 1910.[16]

Given the trajectory of James's career, it is unsurprising that the reception of *Pragmatism* followed a popular-professional divide. James well knew that the book was a "very unconventional utterance," breaking most rules of philosophical inquiry.[17] Nevertheless, he was taken aback by the intensity of criticism from many in the academic community. "No one seems rightly to understand" it, he wrote to his brother Henry; they mock it "as a philosophy got up for the use of engineers, electricians and doctors."[18] Ultimately, James felt that because of *Pragmatism,* his colleagues saw him "as 1/2 idiot, 1/2 scoundrel."[19]

In the decades since James's death, the controversy over pragmatism has continued, with some still viewing James as half idiot, half scoundrel. For the current purposes, however, there is no need to delve into the pragmatism debates of the twentieth and twenty-first centuries, debates that other scholars have covered in great detail.[20] But it is important to point out the lack of sustained attention paid to pragmatism as a product of the lecture circuit in America. Of course, scholars have long known that James's pragmatism—the philosophy and the book published in 1907—emerged from popular lectures.[21] But it remains to be seen how the character of James's work depended upon the moments of public engagement that nurtured the philosophy over the course of a decade. Even scholars of rhetoric, who have paid significant attention to the intersection of pragmatism and rhetoric in recent years, have failed to examine the difference that James's commitment to public lecturing made in the tone, texture, appeals, and character of the philosophy.[22] Pragmatism became America's intellectual creed in large part because of the rhetorical choices James made on the lecture circuit from 1898 to 1907.

Tracing those rhetorical choices will not only account for the popular appeal of James's ideas but also reveal how James turned the intellectual populism of *Varieties* into a generalized, far-reaching, and proudly democratic system of knowledge. Like *Varieties*, *Pragmatism* was combative, dismissive, and aimed at tearing down the intellectual edifice that narrow-minded professionals had constructed. But the lectures went far beyond religious inquiry into larger questions of truth, reality, method, perception, language, and authority. *Pragmatism* was the culmination of James's intellectual populism and his pursuit of popular statement because it not only commanded the nation's attention but fostered an intellectual community in which ordinary people could gather together, craft the ideas that would serve their lives, and overthrow the philosophical aristocracy of the day.

Pragmatism's Oratorical Birth

The philosophy of pragmatism was conceived decades before James lectured publicly on the subject, although he was involved from the beginning. In the early 1870s in Cambridge, Massachusetts, a group of restless, relatively well-to-do aspiring intellectuals founded something they called the Metaphysical Club. James, having recently emerged from his scientific studies at Harvard and now struggling with depression and vocational anxiety, hoped the club would foster the kind of relationships he desperately craved at the time.[23] Other members included Charles Sanders Peirce, Oliver Wendell Holmes Jr., Nicholas St. John Green, Joseph Bangs Warner, John Fiske, Francis Ellingwood Abbott, Henry Bowen, C. C. Everett, and Chauncey Wright. The purpose of the Metaphysical Club was to "wrangle grimly," as Henry James Jr. remarked, which essentially meant vigorous, heated discussion of the big ideas of the day. On most occasions, one of the club's members would present a paper on a topic of his choosing, after which time the other members would excoriate the presenter's seemingly poor excuse for scholarship. "It gives me a headache merely to know of it," wrote Henry Jr.[24]

Although records of the Metaphysical Club's discussions do not exist, we know that a few days before November 24, 1872, Peirce read what William James described as "an admirable introductory chapter to his book on logic."[25] In this talk Peirce likely turned his attention to an idea that had been floating around the club for some time—namely, the idea that beliefs were above all purposeful and practical, encouraging people to act in specific ways. Drawing upon a passage in Kant's *Critique of Pure Reason,* Peirce supposedly used the word "pragmatism" to encapsulate this theory about beliefs and practical action.[26] In 1878, years after the Metaphysical Club broke up, Peirce further developed the idea of his 1872 talk in an article entitled "How to Make Our Ideas Clear," which appeared in *Popular Science Monthly*.[27] Though he did not use the word "pragmatism" in the article, he did identify the "essence of belief" as "the establishment of a habit." He then elaborated: "Different beliefs are distinguished by the different modes of action to which they give rise. If beliefs do not differ in this respect, if they appease the same doubt by producing the same rule of action, then no mere differences in the manner of consciousness of them can make them different beliefs."[28]

The choices Peirce made in cultivating this new philosophy signaled the intellectual commitments he found most important. He first explained pragmatism to his friends in the Metaphysical Club—his most immediate "community of inquirers."[29] He then talked around it in *Popular Science Monthly*, writing with the dense, precise prose that would distinguish most of his work. He subsequently set pragmatism aside—or at least he set aside the name. Years later, he would even forget having proposed the term to the Metaphysical Club.[30] The result was that pragmatism went "unnoticed," as James lamented, for more than twenty years.[31] Luckily, bringing notice to new ideas was James's specialty, and when it came to developing pragmatism, he would proceed much differently than Peirce had.[32]

In 1898, James publicly articulated the philosophy of pragmatism in a popular lecture entitled "Philosophical Conceptions and Practical Results." Given that this lecture represents the "opening gun" in an American-born philosophical charge,[33] it seems appropriate to consider at length the situation and strategies that announced pragmatism to the world. Moreover, analyzing the craftsmanship of "Philosophical Conceptions" will provide a window into a discrete instance of James's art of popular statement. The lecture was not part of a larger series, and James did not yet know what the philosophy would become. He only knew that he had the opportunity to engage a popular audience on a set of ideas he considered distinctive and powerful, even revolutionary. In response, he created an inviting, inspiring, oratorically stylized text that perfectly exemplified his collaborative approach to the production of knowledge.

"Philosophical Conceptions and Practical Results" was delivered on August 26, 1898, at the University of California, Berkeley. James had gone to California in part because he wanted to see the Pacific Ocean and to witness the supposedly rugged California lifestyle, but he also planned on lecturing extensively. In fact, his lectures funded the trip. At Stanford, he filled the largest auditorium on campus, speaking to 400 people on

"What Makes a Life Significant."[34] At Berkeley, he addressed 700 people on "Psychology and Relaxation."[35] At the Teacher's Institute of Alameda County, he delivered "Talks to Teachers" before audiences of 500 to 800 people.[36] And at the Berkeley Club of Oakland, he spoke on "Human Immortality," a performance he referred to as "improvised bellowing."[37]

James had no qualms about lecturing to supplement his income, but he also recognized the pedagogical and social function of speaking to general audiences. The burgeoning philosophy of pragmatism was important to him, and, he believed, it was perfect for the kinds of people he addressed on the lecture circuit. Accordingly, he offered to speak without monetary compensation. As he explained to his friend George Howison, "Philosophical Conceptions and Practical Results" was "a sublime and transcendental lecture on Heaven and Hell and all that lies between, which I make a free gift to your Philosophical Union" at Berkeley.[38] James went on to tell Howison that because "technicality" in philosophy meant "failure" in the art of lecturing, he planned to make the talk "sufficiently popular & practical," hoping to attract students and faculty as well as members of the larger community.[39]

Word of the free lecture spread quickly through the Bay Area, and on August 26, 800 people arrived at Berkeley's Harmon Gymnasium to hear "the author of so many works on philosophy," as the *San Francisco Chronicle* reported. The paper further explained that the gymnasium "was packed" long before the lecture's 8:00 P.M. start time, with "standing-room even being eagerly sought." When James took the stage, he was greeted "with an outburst of applause." "From his first word," the paper continued, his "striking personality" shone through, and he brought his auditors "with him through his researches in the various theories covered by his lecture."[40]

As the *San Francisco Chronicle* well understood, "Philosophical Conceptions" was designed to lead the audience—both the academic and nonacademic portions of it—through new philosophical terrain. Yet the terms James used to craft the lecture made it less about philosophy in general than about a philosophy that was perfectly suited to the people of northern California—regardless of their academic training. Pragmatism stood above the intellectual divisions and professional barriers that defined the immediate situation. To prove as much, James began the lecture by confronting the most salient divisions surrounding and structuring the occasion—the first of which was the division between the popular and professional portions of the audience. Because he was addressing philosophers from the University of California as well as people not associated with the institution, James announced that the occasion called for "an absolutely untechnical discourse." He had to "speak of something connected with life rather than with logic," offering his listeners "a practical outcome and an emotional musical accompaniment, so to speak, fitted to interest men as men." Yet he did not want to "disappoint philosophers" in the audience, seeing that philosophers, "let them be as queer as they will, still are men in the secret recesses of their hearts, even here at Berkeley."[41] With this lighthearted characterization of the occasion and audience, James communicated his understanding of professional philosophy's reputation outside of academic institutions. He also positioned himself as someone capable of changing the way people thought about philosophy. The ideas he would offer in the lecture would transcend the division between those inside and those outside the university. He would speak to everyone who craved "life" rather than "logic," and he would attempt to bring philosophers closer to the side of "life."

The second division James confronted in the introduction of the lecture had to do not with division *in* the audience but with division *around* the audience—namely, the division between America's East and West. James, the privileged, proud Bostonian, was new to California when he delivered "Philosophical Conceptions," but he made sure to identify himself—and his philosophy—with the audience's place in the American experience. He thus praised "this wondrous Pacific Coast" and pledged his discourse to "this Eden, not of the mythical antiquity, but of the solid future of mankind." The lecture, he promised in some amount of jest, would unite "our rugged East" with "your Wondrous West."[42]

It was in this playful discussion of East and West that James deployed the most captivating imagery of the entire lecture. But his images were not merely about pleasing aesthetics and engaging the audience's fancy; they were about establishing pragmatism's intellectual persona. True philosophers, James explained, are less like prophets than like poets. Better still, they are "path-finders," and the philosopher's ideas are like "so many spots, or blazes—blazes made by the axe of the human intellect on the trees of the otherwise trackless forest of human experience."[43] For two full paragraphs in the introduction, James developed this outdoorsman imagery, positioning true philosophers as rugged trailblazers who cut new paths through intellectual forests and fields. The upshot was that philosophers stood to the world of ideas in the same way settlers of the West stood to the geography of America. Californians cut new paths to settle the Pacific Coast, and James, the philosopher of the occasion, was prepared to blaze new trails in the spirit of a frontiersman.

James spent the majority of the introduction building connections with the audience and deploying the terms that would transcend the divisions of the occasion. It was not until the relatively brief final paragraph of the introduction that he mentioned the work of "Mr. Charles S. Peirce" and his "principle of practicalism—or pragmatism." Mentioning Peirce oriented the audience to the philosophical subject matter of the lecture, even while James's attention remained on intellectual frontiersmanship. In fact, he was not the only outdoorsman in the auditorium that day; the audience was also there to blaze new paths. For pragmatism marked the "trail of truth," and with it, "we may keep our feet upon the proper trail."[44]

The body of the lecture contained two general parts—an overview of pragmatism and applications of pragmatism to various intellectual problems. James, however, did not devote the same amount of time to each part. He gave only a brief overview of his brand-new philosophy, choosing to spend the bulk of the lecture showing how pragmatism could effectively address, and help the audience address, life's big questions.

James explained pragmatism in two modest paragraphs. After mentioning Peirce's 1878 article in *Popular Science Monthly,* he stated pragmatism's claim that beliefs "are really rules for action; and the whole function of thinking is but one step in the production of habits of action." It was even simpler than that, however: "To attain perfect clearness in our thoughts of an object, then, we need only consider what effects of a conceivably practical kind the object may involve—what sensation we are to expect from it, and what reactions we must prepare. Our conception of these effects, then, is for us the whole of our conception of the object, so far as that conception has positive significance at all." It was a relatively straightforward statement of a brand-new philosophy, and to arrive at it, James needed no grand deductions, no technical maneuvering, no syllogisms, no logic chopping. He needed only a succinct expression. As a philosophy of life, pragmatism emerged boldly, crisply, daringly, ready to be tested in the course of experience. It was something the audience could hold onto without difficulty. "The ultimate test for us of what a truth means," James announced, drawing his listeners into a united view of the issue, "is indeed the conduct it dictates or inspires. . . . I should prefer for our purposes this evening to express Peirce's principle by saying that the effective meaning of any philosophic proposition can always be brought down to some particular consequence, in our future experience."[45] With this surprisingly brief overview of a brand-new philosophy, it was time to test a few propositions.

In applying the pragmatic method to various intellectual issues, James took great pains to give the audience a participatory role in the discourse. Through the terms of the lecture at least, those assembled in Berkeley's Harmon Gymnasium became authoritative interlocutors in philosophical disputes; they became pathfinders of truth: "I sincerely think that if you once grasp" the pragmatic method, "it will shut your steps out from many an old false opening, and head you in the true direction of the trail."[46] As pathfinders, the audience could proceed confidently into philosophical forests, even those forests littered with the verbiage of professional philosophy. Pragmatism authorized listeners to test, judge, accept, or dismiss philosophical disputes as necessary. "It is astonishing to see how many philosophical disputes collapse into insignificance the moment you subject them to this simple test," James announced, underscoring the audience's ability to conduct their own tests. "There can *be* no difference which doesn't *make* a difference—no difference in abstract truth which does not express itself in a difference of concrete fact, and of conduct consequent upon the fact, imposed on somebody, somehow, somewhere, and somewhen."[47]

The first philosophical dispute to which James turned was the dispute between materialism and theism. Instead of simply applying the pragmatic method on his own, however, he invited the audience into a cosmic thought experiment. "Let us therefore put ourselves, in imagination, in a position from which no forecasts of consequence, no dictates of conduct, can possibly be made, so that the principle of pragmatism finds no field of application. Let us, I mean, assume that the present moment is the absolutely last moment of the world, with bare nonentity beyond it, and no hereafter for either experience or conduct."[48] At the end of time, the audience was supposed to see, the dispute between materialism and theism vanished because no future consequences were possible. However, James then instructed his listeners "to place yourselves this time in the real world we live in, the world that has a future," and to assess the practical differences between materialism and theism—with the former meaning "a denial that the moral order is eternal, and the cutting off of ultimate hopes," and the latter meaning "the affirmation of an eternal moral order and the letting loose of hope."

When theism is taken prospectively, James elaborated, God is around "to say the last word," and "tragedy is only provisional and partial."[49]

James's endorsement of theism was notable, especially because endorsing it meant that he adopted the side of the materialism-theism dispute that most members of his audience would likely have adopted. More notable, however, was his willingness to defend the perspective of the "common man" when tracing the consequences of the dispute. In so doing, he linked pragmatism with the perspective that "common men" already held. That is to say, the philosophy became a natural counterpart of the beliefs of ordinary people, who were uncorrupted by the inconsequential wordplay of academic professionalism. For example, James lauded those who instinctively and deliberately "turn their backs on philosophical disputes from which nothing in the line of definite future consequence can be seen to follow." He then chastised the "verbal and empty character" of professional philosophy before echoing the complaint of one of his students at Harvard: "Words, words, words, are all that you philosophers care for."[50] Recognizing and agreeing with this complaint, James offered pragmatism as something different, as the perspective of "the common man and the scientist," both of whom rejected most philosophy as "pompous trifling."[51]

James continued to link pragmatism to the perspective of the common man when he applied the pragmatic method to theological discussions of God and God's attributes. In defending the ordinary-person perspective, however, he also imbued pragmatism with a distinctly nationalist tone. It was more than the perspective of ordinary people; it was the perspective of ordinary *Americans*. After marching through a long list of "the definitions of God made by dogmatic theology," James asked squarely:

> Now in which one of us practical Americans here assembled does this conglomeration of attributes awaken any sense of reality? And if in no one, then why not? Surely because such attributes awaken no responsive active feelings and call for no particular conduct of our own. How does God's "aseity" come home to *you?* What specific thing can I do to adapt myself to his "simplicity"? Or how determine our behavior henceforward if his "felicity" is anyhow absolutely complete?[52]

In this confrontation with dogmatic theology, "practical Americans" stood above specially trained experts, whose work often involved "a shuffling and matching of pedantic dictionary-adjectives, aloof from morals, aloof from human needs." Moreover, "practical Americans" stood above the East-West division with which James opened the lecture. Pragmatism, therefore, was perfectly suited to trailblazers in California, but it was fundamentally a philosophy for workaday Americans who understood religion as "a living practical affair."[53]

The nationalist tone of the lecture continued as James juxtaposed pragmatism's approach to religion with the "old monarchical conception of a Deity with his 'court' and pomp"—a conception, James was sure to note, that had exercised significant influence "over the history of European states."[54] To the extent that dogmatic theology was a European, aristocratic mode of thought, pragmatism became a democratic, American mode of thought. Just as the revolutionaries overthrew monarchical political systems in Europe, the people of northern California had the opportunity to overthrow the aristocratic religious thought of the past. They also had the opportunity to overthrow the systems of professional authority that accompanied aristocratic knowledge structures. As James explained, "One feels that, in the theologians' hands," the attributes of God are "only a set of dictionary-adjectives, mechanically deduced; logic has stepped into the place of vision, professionalism into that of life."[55] By putting vision and life into their rightful places above logic and professionalism, pragmatism emerged as the democratic philosophy of practical Americans.

The final application of pragmatism James offered in the lecture concerned a more technical philosophical problem—the One and the Many. James would end up apologizing to the audience for speaking too technically to them,[56] but by addressing the One and the Many, he hoped to show professional philosophers that pragmatism held something for them as well. He also hoped to show that if they moved closer to a pragmatic perspective—the perspective of practical Americans—many of their conundrums would fall by the wayside. Pragmatism, he explained, could accommodate those who affirm "the One" (Absolute Idealists like Josiah Royce) and those who affirm "the Many" (pluralists like James himself). It could, in other words, transcend one of the most extensive divisions of turn-of-the-twentieth-century philosophy. James himself expressed his belief that "this old quarrel" between idealists and pluralists "might be completely smoothed out to the satisfaction of all claimants, if only the maxim of Peirce were methodically followed here." With pragmatism, "the Many and the One both get their lawful rights."[57]

To conclude the lecture, James wanted his audience to know how revolutionary pragmatism was and how effective it could be in their lives. Accordingly, he reduced the pragmatic method to a few simple, easy-to-deploy questions about the value of concepts. They were questions "to ask yourself right off," he told the audience, emphasizing their newfound control of philosophical disputes: "What is it *known* as? In what facts does it result? What is its *cash-value,* in terms of particular experience? and what special difference would come into the world according as it were true or false?"[58] These "cash-value" questions enabled "practical Americans" to judge the value of the ideas they encountered. By approaching intellectual issues economically, by being proud capitalists of the mind, the people of northern California could simply and easily distinguish worthless from worthwhile conceptions. Pragmatism was their tool for working in and capitalizing on the world of modern thought.

Pragmatism was also, according to James, the audience's pathway to intellectual esteem. With it, they could stand on the same epistemological plane as the great "English-speaking philosophers" of history. By deploying the cash-value question, they could handle philosophical conundrums just as Locke, Berkeley, Hume, Mill (John and James), Bain, and other great minds had handled them.[59] Yet the people of northern California could acquire even more intellectual capital than these great philosophers by disregarding "the circuitous and ponderous artificialities of Kant." Where the great English-speaking philosophers erred, James insisted, was in coming "under the influence of Kant," whose mind was "the rarest and most intricate of all the possible antique bric-a-brac museums."[60] A "mere curio, a 'specimen,'" Kant encouraged philosophical professionalism in its most distracting and detrimental form. The time had come to cut a new path through the forest of thought: "The true line of philosophic progress lies, in short, it seems to me, not so much *through Kant* as *round* him to the point where now we stand."[61]

This statement, according to the *San Francisco Chronicle,* caused "considerable merriment among his hearers."[62] And rightfully so, as it was among the most significant statements of the lecture, picturing James and the audience as already occupying the intellectual ground the rest of the philosophical world needed to reach. "Where now we stand," the terrain of practical Americans, was the goal for those still trifling over Kant. The statement was powerfully dismissive and proudly pragmatic, demonstrating to the audience exactly what they as pragmatists could now do. By the end of the lecture, by the end of the first public articulation of this new philosophy, "the people" had gone beyond the professionals because of their pragmatic instincts. "May I hope," James said at the close, "that on this wonderful Pacific Coast, of which our race is taking possession, the principle of practicalism, in which I have tried so hard to interest you, and with it the whole English tradition in philosophy, will come to its rights, and in your hands help the rest of us in our struggle toward the light."[63] In the audience's practical American hands rested the future of philosophy, and it was up to them to lead the way forward.

"Philosophical Conceptions and Practical Results" was at bottom a collaborative text because it made James's immediate audience leaders in the world of thought. Even those who were not Berkeley philosophers, *especially* those who were not Berkeley philosophers, now possessed a set of pragmatic questions that could fend off inconsequential theorizing and could justify the practical perspective of common people. In the lecture hall that night in northern California, James did not demand that his audience—or the popular portion of it—become pragmatists, for they were pragmatists already. All James did was give them a label and a reason to continue being practical Americans, despite what the philosophical aristocracy claimed. So long as the audience avoided Kantian pitfalls, they could confidently deploy pragmatic calculations and go about their business. This was their philosophy as much as it was James's.

Pragmatism's Oratorical Adolescence

James had begun "Philosophical Conceptions" with the promise that pragmatism would overcome divisions and settle philosophical disputes. But much the opposite transpired, with the lecture fostering division and creating philosophical disputes instead of bringing thinkers together. Charles Sanders Peirce, for example, heard about what James had done with pragmatism in 1898 and was worried. Perhaps there was some connection between what James had said in northern California and what Peirce had been working on methodically with the Metaphysical Club and in the pages of *Popular Science Monthly.* But the more Peirce thought about it, the more he wanted to distance his own project from James's. Eventually, he proposed the term "pragmaticism" as something distinct from James's pragmatism, and he hoped the ugliness of "pragmaticism" would keep it "safe from kidnappers."[64] In Peirce's view, pragmatism was not the rigorous, analytically precise philosophy it needed to be.

Other philosophers agreed with Peirce. As soon as "Philosophical Conceptions and Practical Results" was published—first in Berkeley's *University Chronicle,* then as a stand-alone pamphlet—it received critical attention from academics.[65] Many found an interesting set of ideas but not the ender of philosophical squabbles James had pledged. One philosopher, for example, called pragmatism an expression of certain "tendencies of the science and the criticism and the practice of our day," but concluded that it was not a real "method of philosophy."[66]

This is not to say that James had no allies in promoting the new philosophy. Because of his handiwork, pragmatism began attracting a small but close-knit group of supporters who ranged from California to Italy.[67] But it is to say that when James called philosophers "queer," when he disparaged most philosophical scholarship as inconsequential wordplay, and when he told his colleagues that they should stop worrying about Kant and catch up with practical Americans, most philosophers responded predictably. They were unconvinced, even a little irritated, and they criticized James's work in turn.

How did James respond to the criticism? He defended pragmatism in personal correspondence, and he wrote a brief description of it in J. M. Baldwin's *Dictionary of Philosophy and Psychology.*[68] But primarily, he returned to popular lectures. As the previous chapter has already discussed, *The Varieties of Religious Experience* contained a lengthy account of pragmatism; indeed, the philosophy was a crucial way that James performed his "true American theory." While there is no need to reanalyze James's handling of pragmatism in the Gifford lectures, it is important to note that *Varieties* amplified rather than mitigated the combative, dismissive tone from the end of "Philosophical Conceptions." One might think that, in response to criticism from professional philosophers, James would temper his claims. But Edinburgh presented the perfect opportunity to rededicate pragmatism as a form of popular empowerment. He thus repeated his lament that "verbality has stepped into the place of vision, professionalism into that of life."[69] He chastised the "metaphysical monster," which scholars "offer to our worship," as "an absolutely worthless invention of the scholarly mind."[70] He then promoted pragmatism as a way around such worthlessness. The people of Edinburgh, like the people of northern California, could develop value in their lives by figuring out "what conduct" a given idea "is fitted to produce. . . . To attain perfect clearness in our thoughts of an object, we need then only consider what sensations, immediate or remote, we are conceivably to expect from it."[71] Such thinking would leave the audience with the same set of questions that the people of Berkeley had received: "What is the particular truth in question *known as?* In what facts does it result? What is its cash-value in terms of particular experience?"[72]

James's discussion of pragmatism in *Varieties* did not escape the notice of commentators, and unsurprisingly, popular and professional reviewers of the book evaluated the philosophy quite differently. *The Nation,* for example, salivated at the "tantalizing glimpses" of pragmatism offered in the Giffords, calling it a philosophy "native and congenial to the Anglo-Saxon mind" and "so well calculated to bridge the gulf between knowledge and action, and to expel the paralyzing intellectualism to which so many of our theologians and metaphysicians seem to be enslaved."[73] A reviewer for *Popular Science Monthly* echoed the liberating potential of pragmatism, noting James's "wide sympathies" and "capacity for appreciation" of diverse experiences. "Not by its origin, but by its 'fruits for life,' shall a religion be judged, says Professor James, in accordance with his philosophical pragmatism."[74] In contrast to these enthusiastic assessments, the theologian W. Vesey Hague objected that James's discussion of pragmatism in *Varieties* did not meet "the needs of the *intellect,*" serving only "those of the will and the emotions." "Our demand is for harmony in the intellectual, as well as for harmony in the moral, world," Vesey concluded. "Adopting any form of Pragmatism which falls short of this, we are on dangerous ground."[75] Similarly, C. C. J. Webb cited a "measure of confusion running through the whole of Prof. James's reasoning" on pragmatism, which made it "difficult to extract from" his Gifford lectures "a consistent view." Webb continued: "The philosophy to which the author's conclusions point, does not appear to me adequate to the phenomena described; while to the description itself it may be objected that it is confined too exclusively to cares which seem to have in them something of the extravagant and the morbid."[76]

Such criticisms were becoming familiar and predictable. And while a close-knit group of supporters defended pragmatism from philosophical broadsides, James rededicated himself to developing the philosophy through the art of popular statement. Seven years after launching pragmatism in California and three years after explicating it in Edinburgh, James spoke on "Characteristics of an Individualistic Philosophy" at Wellesley College. The Wellesley series was different from the Gifford lectures in that it was devoted specifically to explaining pragmatism; it was different from the Berkeley lecture in that it explored pragmatism over the course of five lectures as opposed to just one. At Wellesley, James hoped to treat pragmatism "in nothing but big practical strokes" that his audience could easily follow.[77] According to the *Wellesley College News,* he was able to do just that. He spoke with "vivid and quaint language," the paper reported, with a "kindly personality pervading every word," and he avoided the "unreality of absolutism which keeps the common people away from philosophy."[78]

What survives from James's Wellesley lectures are only his speaking notes. Thus it is difficult to tell exactly how he crafted the talks. Yet the outline makes clear two important points: James greatly expanded his treatment of pragmatism, and he carried on his combative tone against philosophical professionalism. In expanding his treatment of the subject, he linked pragmatism explicitly to an "*individualistic attitude*," which served as the central theme of the lectures. He also tied it to the concept of "meliorism" and to a kindred philosophy called "*Radical Empiricism.*"[79] Standing halfway between optimism and pessimism, meliorism was the idea that the world could get better through human effort, as opposed to getting better necessarily (optimism) or never getting better (pessimism). Radical empiricism was a philosophical viewpoint that saw the world as an endless tissue of conjunctive and disjunctive experiences. Pragmatism was related to meliorism and radical empiricism in directing people's attention toward the effort needed to make their ideals real in a world that was always "in the making." For the pragmatist, James said, the "genuine novelty" of the world meant that intellectual "order" had to be fought for and "*won*" by personal effort. A rewarding reality could not be deduced from some grand philosophical system; it had to be "paid for."[80]

In carrying on pragmatism's now-familiar combative tone, James decried the fact that too often, the "class room and the street" had no practical connection. He lamented the "shallowness" of most philosophy seminars, and he spoke against the "smugness" with which philosophers conducted their business. A true philosophy, James said, "must keep in touch with the *character* of reality" and avoid the unhelpful abstractions of abstruse professionals.[81]

Jousting with philosophical professionalism helped James draw the nonacademic portion of his audience further into the lectures. It also helped him show the people of Wellesley that pragmatism was perfectly suited to their needs. "Few of you are going to be professional" philosophers, James told the crowd. Yet it was because they were amateurs that they should embrace pragmatism, for pragmatism was "an opener of horizons," an "air into mind," a "resultant attitude" for those interested in living practically in the world.[82] Less a revolution in abstract thought and more a method for living effectively, pragmatism enabled people to "know a good thing from a bad one," to act as critics of life, and to "hold up the hands of the right champions," particularly when it came to supporting the "role of women," a topic of special concern to the audience at Wellesley.[83]

The Wellesley lectures seemed successful enough,[84] and a few months later, James had an opportunity to repeat the series, this time at the University of Chicago. When James arrived at the university to deliver his first lecture, he discovered that the venue had to be changed at the last minute to accommodate the vast crowd. Almost 800 people—most of whom were teachers from rural communities throughout Illinois—had flocked to the university to listen to him, forcing organizers to move the series to Mandel Hall Chapel. Unprepared for the packed house of educators, James realized that he had "more or less to shout" so everyone could hear him. The lecture, he later lamented, ought "to have been written" instead of being delivered from an outline in his "unpretending conversational method," which sounded "insignificant" before a crowd of that size.[85]

As the lecture series went on, however, James felt himself grow "more limber and ambitious."[86] Much the same thing had happened when James delivered "Talks to Teachers" during the 1890s; the initial distance he felt from the audience was overcome through the act of lecturing, the act of tackling an intellectual problem together. And by the end of his time in Chicago, the gap between speaker and audience had been closed, with the teachers of Illinois "pulling on my string like one fish"—a metaphor James repeated to several correspondents at the time.[87] Despite the fact that he was a privileged New Englander who spent most of his time in the halls of Harvard University, he had managed to connect with "great hulking rustics from prairie farms, with thick hands."[88] These "prairie ploughmen & women," these "sons & daughters of the prairie," James reported, found pragmatism positively exhilarating.[89] Because of the audience's enthusiasm, he was confident that his "pluralistic Weltanschauung" was "capable of being put into thoroughly popular form."[90]

In terms of content, the Chicago lectures retained the same breadth as the Wellesley lectures. They also continued the invective against professional philosophy. "Philosophy!" James exclaimed to begin the series. "*You* are not philosophers," he said, parroting the words of academics who dismissed ordinary Americans because they did not possess professional credentials. In contrast to this dismissal, James tried to show his listeners that they were central to the advancement of modern thought. "However ill adapted" they were to the technical minutia of philosophy, they were "all philosophers" because they possessed a "general *attitude*" and a desire to let "air into the mind." Despite what the academics said, ordinary people were philosophers because they knew "a good thing when [they] saw it."[91] The prairie men and women of Illinois harbored a philosophical instinct that was more attuned to the world than any insight of a specialized research program.

James further tied pragmatism to his listeners by lauding their support of "truer leaders" who promoted collective well-being. In Chicago, James explained, there were no truer leaders than John Dewey. Indeed, Dewey's vision of "Democracy" helped hold the community together.[92] When James spoke at the University of Chicago in the summer of 1905, he spoke a year after Dewey had left that institution for Columbia University, but Dewey's reputation and influence remained powerful, especially among educators in Illinois.[93] Warm feelings for Dewey thus provided James with the opportunity to connect further with his listeners. The people of Illinois should, he said, follow Dewey's lead and keep "the *character* of reality" at the forefront of their minds. In turn, they could avoid falling victim to the problems of abstract, inconsequential philosophizing. Pragmatism, James concluded, was the philosophy of "*this* university," which "it pleases me to give a push."[94]

Before 1905 was over, James would have the opportunity to deliver the pragmatism lecture series at yet another locality. In late July and early August, he spoke at the Glenmore Institute in Essex County, New York. Founded by James's friend Thomas Davidson, the Glenmore Institute was similar to other community schools at the time in that it operated as a "culture resort" that brought together "famous educators and curious laity in relatively unstructured environments."[95] More specifically, Glenmore provided poor immigrants from New York City with a solid education, hosting lectures by some of the best-known thinkers in the country. James himself spoke there on multiple occasions.

Although not much is known about James's 1905 lecture series at Glenmore, it is clear that he thought pragmatism well suited to even the most underprivileged members of American society. Only about a dozen people were in the audience when he spoke, and they seemed to be from some of New York City's poorest communities. In a letter to Peirce, James described his audience as "flabby boarding house old maids, two 'Settlement' jews from N.Y. & two men who can understand philosophy."[96] The description was unabashedly elitist, an uncharitable characterization of immigrants who were trying to advance themselves by attending Glenmore lectures. Yet the exclusionary tone of the statement masked the fact that James *did* lecture at Glenmore; he took the time to address this particular audience on some of the biggest philosophical questions of the day. Why? The money he would earn was not a significant factor, as the pay "would doubtfully cover" the journey from Boston to New York.[97] So aside from the compensation, James spoke at Glenmore because he considered it an important part of civil society. The institute was, he believed, a powerful experiment in education that "ought to stand as a model and inspirer to similar attempts the world over."[98]

For most of the Glenmore lectures, James relied on his outline from the Chicago series. He did, however, rework the first lecture to connect more effectively with his specific audience. At the beginning of the outline, James wrote "Davidson—'individualist.'"[99] Though we cannot know exactly what he said in this regard, we can make an educated guess. Two years before speaking at Glenmore in 1905, James had published an essay honoring his friend Thomas Davidson, the central theme of which was Davidson's individualism. "Hostile to all socialisms and administrative panaceas," James wrote in the essay, Davidson insisted that "Life must be flexible."[100] James likely repeated similar sentiments when opening the pragmatism series at Glenmore, thereby linking the philosophy with Glenmore's founder and introducing the topic of the lectures—namely, "Characteristics of an Individualistic Philosophy." The same spirit that animated Davidson and his experiment in education was at the heart of pragmatism.

The connection between pragmatism and the Glenmore Institute went even deeper, however. As James presented it, pragmatism spoke to the plight of even the most underprivileged, and it was antithetical to the academic abstractions the audience thought of when they thought of philosophy. Whereas most philosophy was filled with "discontinuities, irrelevancies, externalities," James said, pragmatism was an intellectual outlook that made sense for poor immigrants from New York, individuals who knew full well the trials and tribulations of "the street." Avoiding the "smugness" of traditional philosophy and keeping in touch with the "*character* of vulgar reality," pragmatism was a "true philosophy" because it approached life not as a conceptual abstraction but as a series of struggles to find and create meaning. It was something his listeners could use day-to-day as they worked to improve their lots in life.[101]

While the surviving lecture notes from Glenmore, Chicago, and Wellesley leave some ambiguity regarding the exact philosophical and rhetorical choices James made in 1905, it is clear that he crafted the philosophy around the people he addressed. At Wellesley, pragmatism was a boon for those who wanted to support the role of women. In Chicago, it was already the philosophy of the community. And at Glenmore, it was exactly what people of "the street" needed to advance themselves. One could argue that this was simply a matter of audience adaptation, and in many ways it was. But James's commitment to his audiences greatly affected his ideas and his intellectual ethos. By positioning himself as a servant of the people he addressed, he made pragmatism less a radical new philosophy than a set of tools his audiences could use. Together, James and the people of Wellesley, Chicago, and Glenmore could make philosophical knowledge work for them, where they lived, in their particular situations.

After the lecture tour of 1905, James began pondering the future of pragmatism. And the more he thought about it, the more he grew interested in a homecoming performance. The Lowell Institute in Boston, which would be full of familiar faces who held him in high regard, seemed like the perfect place to finalize the series. In December 1905, James wrote to Abbot Lawrence Lowell about delivering a set of Lowell lectures in 1906. His lectures on "individualistic philosophy," he explained, had proven to be "an agreeable experience," but before the people of Boston he knew that he could "treat [the subject] still better" and draw a large crowd.[102] Lowell agreed, and eventually the two men settled on a November 1906 start date for the new series.[103]

On November 14, James delivered the first lecture in a series he was now calling "On Pragmatism in Recent Philosophy."[104] With an eye toward publication, he had expanded the series from five to eight lectures, but that seemed agreeable enough to the audience. Throughout the series attendance ran between 500 and 1,000 people. They were the "intellectual elite of Boston," according to James.[105] The *Boston Evening Transcript* concurred: "Intellectual Boston to the number of an even thousand greeted Professor William James last evening at the initial lecture in his Lowell Institute course on the recent philosophical movement called 'Pragmatism.'" In summarizing the content of the lecture, the paper highlighted the combative tone James had adopted over the years. According to the *Transcript,* James spoke like "a skillful general," proceeding "first to outline the topography of the ground, to define the present positions of the various hosts which are striving to maintain, each one for itself, its own opinions, and to make a general disposition of his invading forces or messengers of peace, whichever they may in the future prove to be."[106]

As the Lowell lectures proceeded, James closely monitored his connection with the audience. He called his listeners "splendid" after the first lecture, but after the second he felt his "exposition of truth [was] confused." Other problems emerged after that. The fourth lecture involved a "poorly given" talk on pluralism. In the fifth he was "nervous and bad."[107] Given the praise James had received over the years for his oratorical abilities, he was likely being too hard on himself. But it is telling that he constantly gauged his effectiveness with the audience. In his mind, pragmatism was closely linked with the impression he left on his listeners. Luckily, by the end of the series, he felt himself an effective speaker once again. The audience was "very attractive" on the final day, he said, and he was proud that his sons Aleck and Harry had come to hear him.[108] He wrote to his brother Henry that the series came to a "prosperous end," and he was "called before the curtain" and given a rousing ovation.[109] The *Boston Evening Transcript* corroborated James's report: "Despite the biting cold the hall was well filled, testifying to the power of the speaker to hold his audiences."[110]

Because of the success in Boston, James knew that the lectures were ready for wide distribution; he knew that they would make "a solid and original little chunk of truth when written out & publisht."[111] In fact, delivering the lectures at the Lowell Institute made him "all aflame" at the possibility that pragmatism would become a new philosophic "school," a "cause" that he and his allies could champion.[112] Soon after the Lowell lectures ended, plans for *Pragmatism* began falling into place.

Nevertheless, the philosophy's time on the lecture circuit had not yet come to an end. Organizers at Columbia University, including John Dewey, had tried for over a year to book James for a series of talks. Eventually, they secured him for early 1907.[113] On January 29, James arrived in New York ready to convert "Columbians into enthusiastic advocates of pragmatism."[114] The lectures were supposed to take place in Schermerhorn Hall, a room with seats for 250 people, but as had happened many times before, the hall was too small to accommodate the crowd. The *New York Tribune* described the scene: "The room was packed so full that janitors had to be stationed at the doors to keep people out, while the hall outside was likewise jammed full with more people coming every minute."[115] Organizers moved the lectures at the last minute to the auditorium of the Horace Mann School, which could hold 1,100 people. As soon as the change of venue was announced, the *Tribune* said, "there was a rush for the door and across the snow of the campus, every one apparently anxious to get a front seat. By the time the lecturer arrived, the auditorium was packed."[116] Over the next ten days, more than a thousand people consistently took their seats in the massive auditorium to hear James. He thought the lectures went "swimmingly."[117]

One account of the lecture series was particularly effective at capturing the connection James made with the people of New York. Writing for the *Los Angeles Times,* Harold Bolee explained how he entered a packed auditorium and found James hunched over his manuscript, the audience devouring his every word. Bolee was amazed that any speaker "could pack a big assembly room in the American metropolis during a bitterly cold afternoon in a blizzard week." But after settling into his seat, Bolee found himself, like the rest of the audience, "being greatly entertained." James clearly knew how to combine humor and insight, entertainment and edification, so as to keep a thousand people rapt. In the end, James's "command over his audience was almost complete. Out of the big gathering only three women left during the long address. Possibly I alone was conscious of their going. The rest of the auditors were straining eyes and ears to absorb every word and expression of the great Pragmatist."[118]

James's reception at Columbia was beyond anything he had experienced before, signaling just how far he had come as a public intellectual. The people of New York "treated [me] quite like a lion," he wrote to a friend.[119] Luckily, he said to his wife, he enjoyed "being a lion."[120] "I seem to be getting 'recognized' as I never was before," he explained to another correspondent, "and feel in consequence as if my place in the world was warmer."[121] Befitting his newly realized place in American society, James filled his free time in New York associating with some of the country's most influential figures. One night he dined with publisher Robert Collier, author Norman Hapgood, attorney William Jerome, humorist Finely Peter Dunne, author Frederick Colby, and the icon of American literature, Mark Twain. Other days he rushed from reception to reception on the "the magnificent space-devouring Subway," as friends and strangers "wagged their tongues" and begged him to explain the wonders of pragmatism. "It was certainly the high tide of my existence," he reported to his brother Henry, "so far as *energizing* and being 'recognized' were concerned."[122]

After Columbia, there was no doubt in James's mind that *Pragmatism* would make intellectual waves, and the following months confirmed his belief. Earlier, James had made plans to publish some of the individual lectures in different periodicals, which seemed like a good way to whet the appetite of readers in anticipation of the book. In March 1907, the first lecture of the series appeared in *Popular Science Monthly.* That same month, lecture 6 appeared in *The Journal of Philosophy, Psychology, and Scientific Methods.* In April, lecture 2 appeared in *Popular Science Monthly.* As the individual lectures were appearing in periodicals, James moved quickly to finalize the book, and on March 20, he handed the manuscript to the printer. Longmans had agreed to publish it even before seeing the final text. In fact, as soon as James completed the manuscript, it was set into type. There was no review or editing before page proofs.[123]

In the preface to *Pragmatism,* James tried to explain to readers the relationship between the book they held in their hands and the lectures he had delivered at the Lowell Institute and at Columbia University. He insisted that his Lowell and Columbia lectures were "printed as delivered, without notes or development," even though surviving textual evidence indicates that James revised the lectures prior to publication.[124] Once again, however, the prefatory statement was meant to prepare readers for the oral discourse they would encounter. Personal pronouns, conversational phrasing, colloquial references, vivid imagery, shifting diction, and clearly communicated structures marked *Pragmatism* as a popularly oriented statement, as something distinct from what other philosophers at the time were offering. As with *Talk to Teachers, Varieties,* and other previous lecture series, James used the elements of orality to create a participatory text.

Pragmatism's Oratorical Maturity

Those who listened to James speak in Boston and New York and those who read the published version of the lectures explored eight topic areas: "The Present Dilemma in Philosophy," "What Pragmatism Means," "Some Metaphysical Problems Pragmatically Considered," "The One and the Many," "Pragmatism and Common Sense," "Pragmatism's Conception of Truth," "Pragmatism and Humanism," and "Pragmatism and Religion." These eight topic areas were built upon a set of appeals and ways of relating that James had developed and refined over the years, beginning with "Philosophical Conceptions." Specifically, the rhetorical power of *Pragmatism* emerged from the interplay of confrontation, invitation, and participation. The book's confrontation was with professional philosophy and the way it was typically carried out—or at least the way James portrayed it as being typically carried out. The invitation of the lecture series involved positioning pragmatism as a perfect intellectual fit for the popular portion of the audience. Ordinary Americans were invited to identify as pragmatists, or, better, to recognize that they were pragmatists already. *Pragmatism*'s participatory appeals extended the experientially based system of knowledge from *Varieties,* turning it into a method for living, not just for religious understanding. Encouraging practical Americans to rely on the pragmatic method in addressing life's questions, big and small, was a way of giving them purchasing power in the world of thought.

Perhaps the best way to begin to understand the interplay of confrontation, invitation, and participation at the heart of *Pragmatism* is to consider the basic structure of the lecture series. *Pragmatism* followed a simple yet powerful line of reasoning that approached contemporary philosophy according to a problem and a solution. The problem was that contemporary philosophy (or James's caricature of it) did not meet the needs of the American people; it hindered rather than helped their attempts to understand the world. The solution was pragmatism, a philosophy that did meet the needs of the American people and would help them live profitably. Following the lead of the Gifford lectures and "Philosophical Conceptions," *Pragmatism* opened with a bold characterization of the distance between professional philosophy and everyday life. Though all human beings "have a philosophy," James stated, their philosophies are, the vast majority of the time, far from a "technical matter." For most people, philosophy means our "individual way of just seeing and feeling the total push and pressure of the cosmos."[125] In other words, there was a big difference between having a philosophy and working as an academic philosopher. The street and the classroom were very different places, so much so that knowledge of one did not readily translate into knowledge of the other.

James continued along these lines by articulating people's common frustrations with the technical nature of professional philosophy. To most Americans, he said, philosophy was a "nebulous concoction." It was "that wooden, that straight-laced thing, that crabbed artificiality, that musty school-room product, that sick man's dream! Away with it. Away with all of them!"[126] Because of the stuffiness of philosophy, he maintained, "most men" balk at metaphysical talk and "turn their backs on philosophical disputes from which nothing in the line of definite future consequences can be seen to follow. The verbal and empty character of philosophy is surely a reproach with which we are but too familiar."[127]

As the lecture series progressed, these frustrations with professional philosophy morphed into James's own frustrations. Aligning his perspective with the perspective of nonprofessionals, he decried the "pompous robe of adjectives" that clouded metaphysical disputes.[128] He mocked the "Absolute"—the creation of idealists like F. H. Bradley and Josiah Royce—as a foolish abstraction, completely foreign to "the man-like God of common people."[129] To illustrate further, he asked his audience to consider the way philosophers viewed common sense and the way ordinary people viewed common sense. "In practical talk," he explained, "a man's common sense means his good judgement, his freedom from eccentricity, his gumption, to use the vernacular word. In philosophy it means something entirely different, it means his use of certain intellectual forms or categories of thought."[130] The trouble was that everybody but philosophers found common sense a wonderfully useful idea, for it "suffices for all the necessary practical ends of life." Turning their backs on practicality, James elaborated, most philosophers looked at common sense with disgust: "Only the highly sophisticated specimens, the minds debauched by learning" have "suspected common sense of not being absolutely true."[131]

To make matters worse, James continued, to make the chasm between the classroom and the street all the more problematic, ordinary people actually like discussing big ideas. By nature, Americans enjoy "hearing deep things talked about"; they feel a "thrill" in "the presence of vastness." James elaborated: "Let a controversy begin in a smoking-room anywhere, about free-will or God's omniscience, or good and evil, and see how everyone in the place pricks up his ears. Philosophy's results concern us all most vitally, and philosophy's queerest arguments tickle agreeably our sense of subtlety and ingenuity."[132] Unfortunately, academic philosophy was not speaking to the audience's concerns and interests. As James explained with a striking image, on one side of the philosophical spectrum was "the trail of the serpent of rationalism, of intellectualism, over everything"; on the other side was a loss of "contact with the concrete parts of life." Both sides were "equally remote and vacuous."[133]

None of these confrontational appeals were new. They had been part of James's public performances since the 1898 Berkeley lecture. But *Pragmatism* offered an extended opportunity to identify James's new philosophy with the frustrations, feelings of division, and sense of eroding public culture that many people experienced amid the rise of professionalism.[134] Academics, according to the logic of the lecture series, did not give people what they needed; they did not give ordinary Americans a way to engage the world of ideas for practical purposes. Indeed, the professionalization of modern thought had left a vacuum in people's lives. But the existence of a vacuum signaled opportunity for William James. His job was to fill the intellectual void, correcting the shortcomings of the academics and giving the audience exactly what they needed. His aim during the lectures was, therefore, to "popularize philosophy" where others had failed to. Popularizing philosophy was a challenge, of course, as it meant overcoming the chasm between professionals and nonprofessionals. It meant talking "like a professor to you who are not students." Nevertheless, James assured the audience, he would use his "professorial intellect" to satiate their appetite for philosophical discussion.[135]

James's mention of his own professorial intellect was strategically important and relatively familiar, given that he had done much the same thing in the 1878 Baltimore and Boston lectures, *Talks to Teachers,* and *The Varieties of Religious Experience*. It was now central to his art of popular statement. When confronted with an intellectual barrier between himself and a popular audience, he had learned to decry academic professionalism in order to connect with the nonacademics he addressed, all the while retaining and reinforcing his own intellectual ethos. While he understood the technical details of modern science, psychology, and philosophy, he also understood the hunger of ordinary Americans for new knowledge, and he would do everything he could to give them what they craved.

In *Pragmatism,* then, James made sure to show his audience that he was a professor and philosopher of a different character. He announced at the beginning of the lecture series that he was going to break the conventions of his profession by treating philosophy as a matter of "human temperaments." This would make his work appear "undignified" to "some of my colleagues," he said, but it would bring the American people back to the pursuit of knowledge. Too often, professional philosophers insisted that their work was a matter of "impersonal reasons," not temperamental interests, as they attempted to appear above the fray of human passion. As James saw the situation, however, now was the time to "break this rule" of impersonality and to create a philosophy based on the power of personal interests.[136]

Pragmatism, of course, was this philosophy of personal interests; it was the solution to the American people's hunger for knowledge because it turned its back upon "the intellectualist point of view altogether."[137] Especially when it came to the question of truth, James said, pragmatists were not like typical philosophers. They were, rather, like ordinary people who defined truth by what "works," by what "passes muster" and "in no way clashes with the reality."[138] Pragmatists knew the world was not "*ready-made and complete from all eternity*"; it was, rather, "*still in the making, and awaits part of its complexion from the future.*" For pragmatists, as for ordinary Americans, reality was "still pursuing its adventures."[139]

Examples of *Pragmatism*'s confrontational appeals could be multiplied over and again, but suffice it to say that portraying contemporary philosophy as ineffective, unrealistic, and disconnected from the lives of people on "the street" was a way for James to align his perspective with that of "common men." He could then offer pragmatism as that which followed a different set of standards than those of the philosophy classroom. It was opposed to existing knowledge structures and moved in a new, decidedly popular direction. Thus James's confrontations with the philosophical establishment were also a way of inviting popular audiences into a new kind of intellectual culture. They could be part of a pragmatically focused world of thought and action because pragmatism abided by their temperaments, interests, and impulses. It was "just the mediating way of thinking that you require."[140]

James's invitational appeals were, however, not limited to his confrontations with professional philosophy. As he had done in "Philosophical Conceptions," he insisted in *Pragmatism* that the perspective of the pragmatist was also the perspective of the ordinary American. For example, just as most Americans were, according to James, partly rationalists and partly empiricists, so pragmatism "can remain religious like the rationalisms, but at the same time, like the empiricisms, it can preserve the richest intimacy with facts." It can "satisfy both kinds of demands."[141] Consequently, James said later, "If you are neither tough nor tender in an extreme and radical sense, but mixed as most of us are, it may seem to you that the type of pluralistic and moralistic religion that I have offered is as good a religious synthesis as you are likely to find. Between the two extremes of crude naturalism on the one hand and transcendental absolutism on the other, you may find that what I take the liberty of calling the pragmatistic or melioristic type of theism is exactly what you require."[142] Pragmatism was exactly what the audience required because it was their natural attitude, only in a different name.

James extended this line of identification by labeling his audience as pragmatists already, even pragmatists from birth. When addressing life's big questions, he said, "as good pragmatists we have to turn our face towards experience, towards 'facts.'"[143] "Our pragmatism," he continued, "has forced us to be friendly to the pluralistic view."[144] Later, he questioned: "Must we as pragmatists be radically tough-minded? or can we treat the absolute edition of the world as a legitimate hypothesis?"[145] As "we plunge forward into the field of fresh experience," James explained in helping the audience better know their pragmatic orientation, "what we notice determines what we do" and "what we do again determines what we experience."[146]

Frequent use of collective pronouns gave James's listeners and readers an identity as pragmatists—or, as *Harper's Weekly* wrote in reviewing the book, "In reading Dr. James one comes to feel that we have all been pragmatists without knowing it."[147] But collective pronouns were only a small part of James's overall invitational approach. Perhaps the most interesting feature of the text, at least when recalling James's command of language, were the images he used to tie the philosophy to his audience. Throughout the lectures James spoke in a way that linked pragmatism with the American experience writ large, with the tones, textures, outlooks, rhythms, and attitudes of life on this side of the Atlantic. Three interconnected images were crucial in creating this linkage. First were terms of the "ground," including land, earth, soil, dirt, and mud. Second were terms of human hands and the work of human hands. Third and most notable were the terms of economics that had been part of the philosophy since 1898. None of these images were exclusively American, of course, but the way James fit them together mimicked popular impressions of American society and culture.

The first part of James's Americana imagery revolved around terms of the ground, which helped create a sense of presence for the audience, a sense that they occupied the "real" world as opposed to the artificial world of abstraction. According to James, pragmatism appreciated the desire of most Americans to shake "philosophy's dust off their feet" and to follow "the call of the wild."[148] Embracing this desire, pragmatism clung to the "tangled, muddy, painful and perplexed" world of "concrete personal experiences" while overthrowing the "simple, clean and noble world" of the "philosophy professor."[149] Privileging mud over cleanliness, pragmatism was a philosophy that kept people in touch with the world around them. It was a philosophy that grew out of the "rich thicket of reality," the "real world of sweat and dirt," and the "dust of our human trials."[150] James elsewhere spoke of "a God who lives in the very dirt of private fact"; of "gross, coarse, crass, muddy" matter in the world; and of bringing useful concepts "into life's thicket" so that there "grows light about us."[151] When James advocated pragmatism's conception of truth, he chastised both rationalism's and sentimentalism's desire to remove knowledge "from the muddy particulars of experience." Pragmatism, in contrast, held fast to the "mother soil in experience."[152] It helped people cling "to our old nurse Nature."[153]

James's imagery of the ground alluded to a powerful sense of class conflict that had long defined the American character. Tied to the mud and dirt of experience, pragmatists were farmers tilling the nation's intellectual soil. Professional philosophers, in contrast, were aristocrats of the mind, locked away in their castles of learning and afraid to get their hands dirty. Pragmatism was thus the philosophy of yeomen farmers who needed to ban together in opposition to the upper-class nobility. Such themes of class conflict were familiar refrains in American public discourse, echoing Thomas Jefferson and others, but they took on further significance in the wake of the Industrial Revolution and the populist movement of the 1890s. Indeed, populist discourse was (and still is) closely connected to agrarian appeals.[154] As the intellectual extension of these appeals, pragmatism offered familiarity in response to the great machines of industry that seemed to threaten American traditions. Born in mud, dirt, and soil, it offered people a way to cultivate the land once again.[155]

Building upon this agrarian ethos were images that depicted the work of human hands and the labor required to till the earth. Sometimes James referred indirectly to human hands; at other times he spoke the language of hands openly. In both cases, however, he reinforced the notion that pragmatism enabled people to take control of their world. Pragmatism, he explained, was a "program for more work"; it was a means for using ideas to "make nature over again by their aid."[156] In the project of making nature over—which was what farmers did when cultivating the earth—pragmatism "clings to facts and concreteness."[157] At the same time, it recognized that the world was "plastic," capable of being molded by our touches.[158] When it came to the doctrine of meliorism, James employed similar language. A compatriot of pragmatism, meliorism "holds up improvement as at least possible; whereas determinism assures us that our whole notion of possibility is born of human ignorance."[159] James then scorned rationalism because "there is so little to take hold of that we hardly know what we mean by it."[160] With pragmatism, in contrast, "we patch and tinker," our knowledge of the world growing more complete as we do.[161] When it came to the idea of agreeing with reality, which James insisted was central to his philosophy, pragmatism took agreement to mean getting *"into such working touch with it as to handle either it or something connected with it better than if we disagreed."*[162] Indeed, many philosophical problems end up seeming insignificant when "you handle them pragmatically."[163] As a result, a statement about reality becomes more or less true depending "on the perspective into which we throw it."[164]

In addition to making these indirect references to the power of human hands, James often used hand imagery explicitly to underscore pragmatism's effectiveness. If people became pragmatists, he said in the second lecture, they could make science and metaphysics "work absolutely hand in hand."[165] A pragmatic approach to common sense would prove similarly empowering, he said. With the categories of common sense "in our hand, we make our plans and plot together, and connect all the remoter parts of experience with what lies before our eyes."[166] James made the point of all this hand imagery clearest toward the end of the lectures: "The world stands really malleable, waiting to receive its final touches at our hands."[167] Such imagery made the audience active agents in the creation and re-formation of the world. They could feel significant because they had the power to touch, to shape, and to mold their surroundings. Whereas other philosophies had purported to be matters of impersonal reasons and universal validity, pragmatism put people to work. Importantly, this was the same theme of labor and productivity that ran throughout the populist discursive tradition.[168]

Building on the imagery of hands and labor was the terminology that stood out most to James's contemporaries—his language of economics. While James received significant criticism for his use of economic terminology, critics overlooked the fact that talk of "cash value" was a natural extension of laboring human hands.[169] Pragmatism, according to James, could help people not only get back to the dirt of experience and seize control of their surroundings but also develop profitable "commerce" with their world.[170] It was a philosophy devoted to exploring an idea's "practical cash-value" and setting "it at work within the stream of your experience."[171] The result was a "rich and active commerce" with life.[172] Pragmatism showed people that an idea was true "so long as to believe it is profitable to our lives."[173] Truth, James insisted, hinged upon individual assessments of conceptual worth and "cash-value in experiential terms."[174] Yet it was not just personal economic assessments that defined truth, for people often borrowed the assessments of others when approaching new ideas. In general, then, truth worked "on a credit system. Our thoughts and beliefs 'pass,' so long as nothing challenges them, just as bank-notes pass so long as nobody refuses them. . . . We trade on each other's truth."[175] With pragmatism, what people believed about the world was "so much experience *funded*," and beliefs became part "of the sum total of the world's experience," part of "the next day's funding operations."[176] Recognizing the commerce of truth, the pragmatist was "willing to live on a scheme of uncertified possibilities, . . . willing to pay with his own person, if need be, for the realization of the ideals which he frames."[177]

During the Gilded Age and Progressive Era, economic concerns were at the forefront of public culture. The nation faced daunting questions about wealth accumulation in the hands of a few, about the social and political power of modern corporations, about ensuring a decent future for workers, about backing the nation's currency with gold or silver, about domestic and foreign spending, and about any number of other economic-related issues. Though there is no evidence that James had such questions in mind when crafting pragmatism, it is the case that his economic terminology meshed well with this larger aspect of the nation's conversation.[178] It is also significant that in an age when monied interests seemed to control society, pragmatism was a philosophy that helped people find and make value in their lives. By employing the language of economics, James followed yet another thread of populist discourse to highlight the individual's worth in American society.[179] Dejected and disempowered by the loss of familiarity and tradition, ordinary Americans could find in pragmatism the promise of exchange value. Far from being a sort of crass materialism, however, it reinserted individuals into the fabric of society and gave them power to control their lives.[180]

Notice the arc of James's invitational imagery. It began with America's agrarian past, moved to pictures of laboring hands, which applied equally well to cultures of rural farming and urban industry, and culminated with portrayals of individuals reclaiming purchasing power in their lives. Thus not only did pragmatism speak to widespread cultural anxieties in the early twentieth century, it encouraged people to reinvest in the world of ideas. That is to say, it encouraged extensive intellectual participation. Indeed, one might argue that the hallmark of *Pragmatism* was its participatory character.[181] But that character was not limited to James's imagery; it was integral to the system of knowledge that defined the pragmatic method. To be a pragmatist and to develop the ideas that would be most profitable in dealing with life's problems, one did not need specialized training, an advanced degree, or the ability to talk an exclusive and technical language. Pragmatism was so simple that anyone could grab hold of its method and participate in the advancement of thought. Here was intellectual populism writ large; here was a philosophy that extended beyond religious inquiry to cover every aspect of life. The pragmatic method was a generalized approach to knowledge that circumvented, even subverted, the problems of the culture of professionalism.

Similar to *Varieties, Pragmatism* made individual perception foundational to inquiry. "The most interesting and important thing about you," James told his audience at the start of the lecture series, "is the way in which" your personal philosophy "determines the perspectives in your several worlds." Put differently, "our more or less dumb sense of what life honestly and deeply means" becomes the jumping off point for philosophical insight.[182] Even those who lacked their own "definitely articulated philosophies" could still participate in the advancement of thought, for "almost everyone has his own peculiar sense of a certain total character in the universe."[183] Pragmatism was thus egalitarian in that it started with the "peculiar sense" of the universe that "almost everyone" possessed. But unlike most philosophies at the time, it did not require that people relinquish their peculiar sense or transcend their idiosyncratic position. Instead, it required using "the everlasting weather of our perceptions" as part and parcel to understanding.[184] In James's pragmatic program, "the flux of our sensations" and "the *relations* that obtain between our sensations or between their copies in our minds" were necessary for grasping the character of reality.[185]

Discussion of individual perception and the flux of sensations was directly tied to the most important populist term in James's work: experience. As was the case in *Varieties*, *Pragmatism* made experience the mechanism for testing, corroborating, and verifying people's perceptions of the world. For example, when James turned to the question of God's existence in *Pragmatism,* he co-opted the language of academic science, putting his audience in control of knowledge acquisition: "On pragmatistic principles, if the hypothesis of God works satisfactorily in the widest sense of the word, it is true. Now whatever its residual difficulties may be, experience shows that it certainly does work, and that the problem is to build it out and determine it, so that it will combine satisfactorily with all the other working truths."[186] But *Pragmatism* went far beyond considerations of religious knowledge. In a pragmatist schema, the very nature of ideas hinged upon what ordinary people needed to fulfill their intellectual aspirations. James italicized the point for extra emphasis: "*Ideas (which themselves are but parts of our experience) become true just in so far as they help you get into satisfactory relation with other parts of our experience.*"[187] To be sure, individuals needed no specialized tools to test ideas in experience. They needed only to live and to pay attention to their world—and everyone was capable of doing that. As James declared toward the end of the lecture series:

> Our acts, our turning-places, where we seem to ourselves to make ourselves and grow, are the parts of the world to which we are closest, the parts of which our knowledge is the most intimate and complete. Why should we not take them at their face-value? Why may they not be the actual turning-places and growing-places which they seem to be, of the world—why not the workshop of being, where we catch fact in the making, so that nowhere may the world grow in any other kind of way than this?[188]

The intellectual populism of *Pragmatism* was perhaps best represented in James's discussion of truth, which had already become the most controversial aspect of the philosophy.[189] Part of the controversy had to do with the perception that James broke the rules of professional truth discussions, that he spoke of something other than truth. But another part of the controversy was related to the fact that James discussed truth in a way that robbed academics of their power to set the terms of the debate. "A new opinion counts as 'true,'" he explained, "just in proportion as it gratifies the individual's desire to assimilate the novel in his experience to his beliefs in stock."[190] Related to individual desire and effort, truth belonged to ordinary people and their experiences. Academic proofs were beside the point. "We plunge forward," James elaborated, "into the field of fresh experience with the beliefs our ancestors and we have made already; these determine what we notice; what we notice determines what we do; what we do again determines what we experience; so from one thing to another, altho the stubborn fact remains that there *is* a sensible flux, what is *true of it* seems from first to last to be largely a matter of our own creation."[191]

James further explained the pragmatist notion of truth with an analogy that the popular portion of the audience could easily understand: "Just as certain foods are not only agreeable to our taste, but good for our teeth, our stomach and our tissues; so certain ideas are not only agreeable to think about, or agreeable as supporting other ideas that we are fond of, but they are also helpful in life's practical struggles."[192] Later in the lecture series, he made a similar point with a more artistic metaphor: "By our inclusions and omissions we trace the field's extent; by our emphasis we mark its foreground and its background; by our order we read it in this direction or in that. We receive in short the block of marble, but we carve the statue ourselves."[193] In a populist intellectual culture, metaphors about truth and power were more effective than any rigorous academic arguments. Pragmatists did not need to play word games with professional philosophers; they could simply move forward and discover—or, better, *create*—the truths that would serve their lives.

As was the case in *Varieties,* James's emphasis on the truth of personal creative experience gave ordinary people a trump card they could play when dealing with rigid, narrow-minded professionals. Any time a philosopher proposed some grand new schema or exclusionary system of knowledge, the American people had a right and a duty to ask: What practical difference will these ideas make in my life? Indeed, "the whole function of philosophy ought to be to find out what definite difference it will make to you and me, at definite instants of our life, if this world-formula or that world-formula be the true one."[194] Repeatedly throughout the lecture series, James demonstrated how the audience could play this pragmatic trump card and thereby participate in the march of ideas. When it came to the grand philosophical and scientific idea of "matter," for example, James told the audience to "apply the pragmatic method. . . . What do we *mean* by matter? What practical difference can it make *now* that the world should run by matter or by spirit?"[195] When it came to the problem of the One and the Many, he told the audience to ask: "What is the oneness known-as? What practical difference will it make?" Asking this pragmatic question "saves us from all feverish excitement over it as a principle of sublimity and carries us forward into the stream of experience with a cool head."[196] When it came to figuring out truth, the audience should ask a similar question: "Grant an idea or belief to be true, . . . what concrete difference will its being true make in anyone's actual life? How will the truth be realized? What experiences will be different from those which would obtain if the beliefs were false? What, in short, is the truth's cash-value in experiential terms?"[197] And when it came to the idea of "the salvation of the world," the audience should question: "What does it pragmatically mean to say that this is possible?"[198]

These pragmatic questions, which had emerged from James's earlier lectures, were integral to the dismissive, combative, practical attitude that defined James's populist program. Indeed, the questions themselves were verbal pathways around Kant and the philosophical professionalism Kant encouraged. Whenever philosophers tried to escape into the world of Kantian mystification, nonphilosophers could, in James's intellectual culture, shut them down or bring them back to reality by asking: What practical difference will your work make in my life? It was a personal question, a subjective question, but one of the most powerful questions given to nonacademics since the onslaught of the culture of professionalism.

The result of it all was, according to James himself, an "alteration in the 'seat of authority.'"[199] Because of pragmatism, "Philosophic questions will fall to be treated by minds of a less abstractionist type than heretofore," meaning that ordinary people were now key agents in the pursuit of knowledge. In that regard, pragmatism was akin to the "protestant reformation" that had rocked the world's systems of religious power centuries ago. "And as, to papal minds, protestantism has often seemed a mere mess of anarchy and confusion, such, no doubt, will pragmatism often seem to ultra rationalist minds in philosophy. It will seem so much sheer trash, philosophically. But life wags on, all the same, and compasses its ends, in protestant countries. I venture to think that philosophic protestantism will compass a not dissimilar prosperity."[200]

If we take James's protestant-pragmatism analogy seriously—and there is no reason we should not—it becomes clear that the new philosophy was about returning intellectual power to the people. Pragmatism overthrew reigning intellectual systems by putting ordinary individuals in control of inquiry, much as the Protestant Reformation had put the laity in control of theological questions. This was James's intellectual version of the revolution pictured at the end of most populist discourse.[201] The new philosophy, nurtured for years with audiences on the lecture circuit, remade the power structures of the world of ideas, giving practical Americans a position of privilege in the pursuit of knowledge. In that regard, James had gone far beyond simply addressing popular audiences on issues of contemporary philosophy. He had built around them a new intellectual culture and had given them control over where it went.

Conclusion

F. H. Bradley read over James's work and decided to speak up on behalf of other serious philosophers: "Assuredly I am not alone in the desire that [James] would turn his back for a time on sporadic articles and on popular lectures, with their incoherence and half-heartedness and more or less plausible ambiguities, and would work in the way in which a man who seriously aims at a new philosophy is condemned to work."[202]

Bradley's criticism was exactly right within the context of philosophical professionalism. The problem, however, was that James was working with a different set of intellectual standards. Through his lectures, from Berkeley to New York, he had denounced the rationalist perspective from which Bradley operated and had offered instead a pragmatic, democratic, experientially grounded method of inquiry, where plausible ambiguities were not only acceptable but welcomed.

In the end, James's disregard for supposedly academic protocols and his abiding interest in flattening intellectual hierarchies were central to pragmatism's legacy. Regardless of whether reviewers agreed with the philosophy, they knew why it was exceedingly popular, even populist. "In leaving his Harvard chair to appeal to a wider audience from platform and press," wrote *The Independent,* "Professor James has shown his faith in pragmatism as a philosophy for the people."[203] As a philosophy for the people, pragmatism seemed to be American above all else, extending to the world of thought the perspective that had distinguished the nation politically, socially, and culturally. "It goes with Benjamin Franklin and Thomas A. Edison," wrote one reviewer of James's book, and it is "likely to be the representative philosophy of America."[204]

In the final years of his life, James began to relish, even to celebrate, the widely perceived link between pragmatism and the American experience. In 1909, he offered perhaps the best indication that pragmatism was a decidedly American philosophy. It was, he explained, so attuned to the concerns of the nation that it could settle a feud as monumental as that between the Chicago Cubs and the Chicago White Sox. James's note on this notorious rivalry arrived at the *Chicago Tribune* via a "special wire" and was published in the paper on July 10. Responding to the argument that pragmatism was "just a pseudo-philosophical way of getting along without any philosophy at all," he told the people of Chicago that they should think about pragmatism in terms of their hometown baseball teams. "The Cubs," he said, "are Pragmatists," while "The Sox are mere Hegelians." The Cubs are pragmatists because they "get results," while the Sox "run too much to mist and moonshine and not enough to muscle." When one steps back and assesses the matter, he concluded, it is clear that the Cubs know the right questions to ask: "What counts? Results. What produces results? Two baggers, with now and then a home run. Spit on your hands and lambaste the ball—that's all."[205]

To readers of the *Tribune,* James's point was clear. In 1908, the Cubs had won the World Series. And they had done so, at least according to James, by being pragmatists.

Conclusion

⌘

One month before his death, knowing that the end was near, William James reflected on his career and perceived a problem. His "system," he believed, was "too much like an arch built only on one side."[1] If it was an arch built only on one side, which side was completed and which side needed more work? James knew, as did those around him, that he had given expression to a new way of looking at the world. With eloquence and conviction, he had outlined a system of knowledge that extended from the perceptions and experiences of ordinary people. But many philosophers thought such a system lacked rigor, precision, and proper explication. James, they believed, had not been professional enough in the way he developed his ideas. The result may have been an eloquent vision of the world, but not the sound structure needed for a new philosophy. One month before his death, James worried that his critics were right; his arch was at risk of falling over.

Most scholars take James's comment about the one-sided arch as evidence of his desire to move in a new direction. To complete the arch, we are told, he needed to leave lecturing behind. He needed, according to one commentator, "to set out his views in systematic shape and not waste his energies on polemical writings."[2] To that end, James published *The Meaning of Truth,* which aimed to combat critics who "labor under an inability almost pathetic, to understand the thesis which they seek to refute."[3] He also began work on *Some Problems of Philosophy,* a manuscript that he hoped would "round out" his unfinished system.[4]

While it is true that James wanted to round out his system, we should not take his comment about the one-sided arch as evidence of a desire to set aside the art of popular statement. He was frustrated with many of his colleagues and with what he saw as academic narrow-mindedness, but he did not cease speaking to and writing for the same kinds of audiences he had been addressing for decades. *Some Problems of Philosophy* offered a change of pace, but he began the project in addition to furthering his epistemological system centered on ordinary people. In fact, *Some Problems of Philosophy* was only published posthumously, largely because James spent the bulk of his time continuing to engage the populace.

After the publication of *Pragmatism,* James traveled to England to deliver the 1908 Hibbert lectures at Manchester College. Nervous as always about lecturing to large audiences, he worried that the lectures would further cement his reputation among academics as a charlatan. "This job condemns me to publish another book written in picturesque and popular style," he remarked to a friend, "when I was settling down to something whose manner would be more streng [*sic*] 'wissenschaftlich,' i.e. concise, dry, and impersonal. My free and easy style in 'Pragmatism' has made me so many enemies in academic & pedantic circles that I hate to go on increasing their number." James's mention of his desire to become "concise, dry, and impersonal" masked the fact that he accepted the lecturing job, fully aware of what it demanded of him. He went to England with open eyes, ready to extend his popular role. "These new lectures will have to be even looser," he elaborated, "for lectures *must* be prepared for audiences; and once prepared, I have neither the strength to re-write them, nor the self-abnegation to suppress them."[5]

James's emphasis on *must* revealed the extent of his dedication to the art of popular statement. As he saw it, the character of the audience was a determining factor in the character of the discourse. In that regard, it mattered little that his colleagues would scoff at him. In the lecture hall, he was bound to his listeners in a common pursuit. Because he was speaking to a group composed primarily of nonacademics, the style, attitude, and appeals of *Pragmatism* would have to continue.

When James finally delivered the Hibbert lectures, he addressed a standing-room-only crowd. "Many stood," recalled Manchester's president, J. E. Carpenter, "and many more sat on the book cases, so that nearly 400 were present, and many could not get in at all."[6] A writer for *Oxford Magazine* further underscored the popularity of the lectures: "The Will to Believe is Will James, and certainly this view would seem to be shared by the multitude, to judge by the number of those who have recently thronged the Library at Manchester College—added to that of the foolish virgins and the philosophic votaries of the Not-in-time who, rumor states, were turned away at the door."[7] Another writer wondered if James's immense popularity meant that philosophical professionalism was on the wane in England:

> Those lectures were of a character to which Oxford is unaccustomed, and this is the point—of a kind quite out of harmony with Oxford's traditional mode of philosophical teaching. Yet Professor James had the largest audience which Oxford has probably ever seen at a philosophical lecture. It was a significant event; and many wondered whether it marked the beginning of a new era, and, if so, how much of the old way, so highly valued and so long cherished, would be likely before long to remain.[8]

The Hibbert lectures, which James repeated at Harvard in November 1908,[9] were just one instance of popular statement in the wake of *Pragmatism*. He also delivered a lecture on "The Social Value of the College-Bred," which was later published in *McClure's Magazine*.[10] The following year he published "Confidences of a Psychical Researcher."[11] Finally, in early 1910, he published an essay that he considered essential for the progress of the world, "The Moral Equivalent of War," which appeared in *International Conciliation*, *McClure's Magazine*, and *Popular Science Monthly*.[12] The essay was his attempt to redirect military impulses, which seemed forever ingrained in people and nations, toward the creation of civilized, morally upright communities that could support the common good. It was a utopian dream, but it was a much-needed dream, and James used his public prominence to give the dream a more tangible shape.

As James continued to practice the art of popular statement in the final years of his life, his visibility spread further. Offers to lecture in various parts of the country and around the world poured into his mailbox. In fact, the number of lecture offers he received became so many that he could not keep up with his responses. At some point, although the exact time is not clear, he printed a standard card that allowed him impersonally to decline lecture invitations.[13] All James had to do was address the card, sign it, and drop it in the mail. It was simply too time consuming to reply to the steady stream of lecture invitations with a handwritten letter.

Eventually, James's health prevented him from lecturing, but by that time his reputation was firmly established. When word of his passing on August 26, 1910, appeared in newspapers across the country, commentators reflected on his significance in the world of thought and in public culture. "Is there left to us in this land a man so great as William James?" questioned *Popular Science Monthly*. "Is there a single one to be placed beside him? He excelled in so many ways, in science, in philosophy, in letters, as a teacher, as a leader in good causes and lost causes, before all as a man." James, the magazine concluded, left a "deep impression" on modern thought, but an even deeper impression on "the world of men."[14] The *New York Tribune* echoed the point: James helped "to clarify philosophical knowledge, to divest it of technicality and mysticism and to bring it as far as possible into touch with the impulses and activities of common life. His gifts of clarity and sanity gave an unusual attractiveness to what he said and wrote. . . . Mr. James was a remarkable mixture of the scholar with the man of the world, of native humor and manliness."[15] The *Richmond Times-Dispatch* went even further, writing that "There are many men in authority who have declared Professor James not only the greatest American scholar, but even 'the greatest American of his time.' In Europe and this country they are legion who are of such opinion."[16]

Regardless of whether James was the "greatest American of his time," the very possibility spoke to his connection with the American experience in the early twentieth century. His pursuit of popular statement had encouraged the perception that he was the quintessential American philosopher, spokesperson for an entire nation's perspective. Disdainful of that which had no bearing on practical matters, dedicated to a widely accessible language, interested in overthrowing the academic aristocracy of the day, and, above all, concerned with helping ordinary people develop conceptual tools for living profitably in the new century, James had articulated an angle of vision that seemed purely and proudly American.

James's legacy, as the preceding chapters have argued, was the result of a decades-long evolution at the intersection of public culture, popular statement, and the pursuit of knowledge. From his work as a book reviewer to his 1878 lectures in Baltimore and Boston to *Talks to Teachers on Psychology* to his psychical advocacy of the 1890s to *The Varieties of Religious Experience* and *Pragmatism,* James eloquently secured a unique place in the history of American thought. In spite of these specific instances of popular statement, however, it seems fitting to consider James's art at a more general level. Now that we are able to perceive the arc of his career, we are in a position to discuss the overall strategies and appeals that helped him connect with the audiences he frequently addressed. The art of popular statement was, to be sure, dynamic and adaptive, able to be adjusted and altered for specific situations and challenges, but it was built on a notable discursive foundation.

It should be reiterated, however, that the following characteristics apply above all to James's interactions with popular audiences. That is to say, the art of popular statement does not encompass every aspect of his career, nor does it serve as a framework for understanding every text he produced. James was a sophisticated rhetor, and when speaking to audiences comprised primarily of professional psychologists or philosophers, he spoke differently than when addressing audiences comprised primarily of nonacademics. Thus the following six elements of James's art are offered only to explain his success when interacting with "common people," as he sometimes called them, in lecture halls and in the pages of popularly directed texts.

Oral Style

As we have seen repeatedly in the preceding chapters, particularly in discussions of *Talks to Teachers*, *Varieties*, and *Pragmatism,* James spoke and wrote in a way that is best characterized as oral. His expressions were inclusive, built upon direct references to those with whom he shared a physical space (listeners in a lecture hall) and those with whom he shared an imagined space (readers who were brought into his texts through the terms "you" and "we"). His diction could, in the space of a sentence, move from the heights of formality to the expanses of the colloquial. His imagery brought his ideas before the audience's eyes—an especially important point for lecture attendees who did not have the text of his remarks in front of them. He communicated the structure of thought clearly and directly, telling his audience what he had said, what he was saying, and what he was going to say. This clearly communicated structure, in turn, ensured that the audience could easily follow his ideas. In addition, it established expectations that James could satisfy as the discourse developed.[17] Even James's slang, clichés, and commonplaces were extensions of an oral communicative culture wherein memory was essential for the movement of thought. In short, James's oral style infused his lectures with liveliness, clarity, and purpose reminiscent of a captivating storyteller.

Many of James's contemporaries understood as much. Even though few commentators labeled his style as oral, they frequently isolated the elements of orality in his speaking and writing. William Allan Neilson, a Harvard professor of English at the time of James's retirement from teaching, provided a representative characterization of James's way with words. In the lecture hall, Neilson explained, James always left his listeners "interested, stimulated, exhilarated," and this communicative energy became integral to the success of his publications:

> The fertility of illustration, the close touch between theory and everyday experience, the frank use of the vernacular, all combine to give his books their unique position with others than professed students of philosophy. . . . Passages almost colloquial in phrasing are succeeded by others of a fine eloquence; blunt statements of fact are lightened by the sparkle of epigram; but both the eloquence and the epigram are spontaneous, not labored. One can see the emotion gather that naturally expresses itself in heightened phrases and a nobler rhythm; one watches the flint and steel strike out the spark, with no suspicion of previous deliberation.[18]

Neilson's characterization captured one of the primary reasons James's oral style connected with popular audiences—namely, the elements of orality presented him as in the act of thinking. Regardless of whether James was working from brief, sentence-fragment notes or from a full-sentence manuscript, he seemed to be spinning ideas in the audience's presence. His philosophy appeared to unfold in the moment, enveloping listeners and readers in phrases, markers, and metaphors designed specifically for them. James was indeed "thinking in public with rhetoric."[19] At the least, he was able to persuade his audiences that they were caught up in a burst of intellectual creativity. The result was a powerful sense of identification. As Neilson explained, James "predisposes the reader to take his point of view by convincing him of his honesty, while charming him by his manner."[20] James's oral style was integral to his art of popular statement because it portrayed him as working with his audiences rather than simply speaking to them.

Topical Breadth

Throughout his career, James moved in and out of—even combined and created—disciplines, subject areas, and fields of inquiry. Taken as a whole, his popular statements mimicked the wide-ranging, visionary spirit that had distinguished the culture of eloquence. As we saw in chapter 1, James grew up at a time when speakers could roam the intellectual landscape, so long as their insights were eloquent and compelling and so long as audiences were willing to pay to hear them. And even though he was trained in a very different intellectual culture, James moved with the same trailblazing spirit as the earlier generation. From anatomy and physiology to psychology and psychical research to religion and pedagogy to philosophy and its various subdisciplines, James's breadth of engagement offered people an intellectual vision, not a specialized research program. Like the figures of the culture of eloquence, he guided "a community of listeners toward a revolutionary new world."[21]

James's wide-ranging, frontiersman-like inquiry demonstrated that eloquent intellectualism was still possible at the turn of the twentieth century. It was difficult, to be sure, and it was not the norm. But his popularity and visibility evidenced a desire within the culture of professionalism for familiarity, even conservatism. In many ways, James's career represented a partial return to a world of thought that once was. It communicated the value of tradition in the midst of social change. His ideas, of course, seemed new and captivating, tied brilliantly to the difficulties of the Gilded Age and Progressive Era. But his manner of presentation relied upon the ideals of old to engage the world at hand. And it gave the American people at least a modicum of familiarity at a time of upheaval.

Professional Ethos

It would be a mistake, however, to portray James as simply extending the culture of eloquence into the twentieth century. He did carry on many of its ideals, but he was a product of and greatly benefited from the culture of professionalism. A specialist, an expert, a technically proficient researcher, James was regularly invited to address popular audiences because of his command of psychology and philosophy. Moreover, the rapidly growing prestige of his home institution, America's premier research university, marked him as a professionally cultivated thinker. He stepped before popular audiences not as a freelance intellectual in the mold of Emerson and Henry Sr. but as a scientist and philosopher who expertly understood the brain and the mind. Even when he altered his audience's perceptions of his work, he was first and foremost a Harvard professor.

James's art of popular statement was greatly strengthened by his ability to play off his prominence in the culture of professionalism. As early as his book reviews and 1878 lectures, he had learned how to use his scientific prestige to relate to listeners. He told the people of Baltimore and Boston, for example, that he taught anatomy, physiology, and psychology, and that such breadth enabled him to survey the entire intellectual landscape. As a result, he could formulate responsible judgments about intellectual disputes, which, in turn, enabled him to help the people of Baltimore and Boston arrive at similarly responsible judgments. In other words, James positioned himself as an expert who stood above the intellectual divisions of his era—in touch with multiple perspectives but beholden to none.

James quickly discovered that standing above intellectuals divisions resulted in a powerful speaking position. Exuding expertise as one of the most prominent psychologists and philosophers of the day, he was nonetheless prepared to distance himself from the academic establishment of which he was a prominent member. The art of popular statement meant using the role of the expert to critique the problems of expertise, thereby building a bridge with those who felt uneasy about the systems of professional dependency that arose during the second half of the nineteenth century.[22] According to the terms of his texts, James was up-to-date on the latest research in psychology, philosophy, and other disciplines, but he was ultimately more interested in the problems his audiences faced. This was precisely the posture that made *Talks to Teachers* so appealing to primary and secondary educators. James knew all about the pedagogical-psychology industry; he knew all about its attempts to mystify and profit from America's schoolteachers with concepts like "apperception." He also knew what psychology could and could not do for the schoolmarms he addressed. For the sake of their professional betterment, then, he explained exactly what they needed to know and how they could best improve their pedagogical art.

This intellectual ethos, this way of presenting his character and credibility to his audiences, underscored James's complex relationship with the culture of professionalism. Whenever he decried the problems of academic professionalism—of verbal mystification, of inconsequential theorizing, of exclusive intellectual enclaves, of inflexible, impersonal, monolithic systems of thought—he did so as an insider, as someone with the credibility of critiquing a culture he knew so well. Nevertheless, he *chose* to speak and think differently for the sake of the American people. He was a philosopher extraordinaire who seemed to care more about the people of Wellesley, Chicago, and Glenmore than about following the rules of philosophical professionalism. Simultaneously representing and criticizing the world of modern thought helped James move closer to those who heard him in lecture halls and read his work with glee.

Intellectual Collaboration

Almost all of James's texts that began as popular lectures were built on the appearance of collaboration between speaker and audience. In *Pragmatism*, *The Varieties of Religious Experience*, and *Talks to Teachers,* to name just three, James made his remarks a matter of the beliefs, desires, and experiences of his listeners. The philosophies and ideas he presented were, according to the logic of his texts, their philosophies and ideas. *Pragmatism* in particular exuded this sense of intellectual collaboration, as James presented a philosophy that was purportedly the audience's philosophy already. The people of Boston and New York, not to mention those who read the published lectures, were living pragmatically in their daily lives and should continue living pragmatically. In fact, they occupied the ground that the rest of the philosophical world needed to reach. James thus adopted the perspective of his listeners (or at least appeared to adopt their perspective) and built a philosophy around their way of seeing and experiencing the world. According to F. C. S. Schiller, such was the brilliance of James's work: "In the America of the nineteenth century the genius who revealed to the American people the meaning of their doings, and so enabled them to go on doing them more intelligently and harmoniously, was William James."[23]

The collaborative spirit of James's art of popular statement stands in contrast to the way his philosophy is often portrayed. James, we are told, was a rugged individualist, and his thought was decidedly individualistic. According to one philosopher, he was "captivated by the ideal of absolutely unentangled and unfettered individuality," which turned his focus away from pressing social issues.[24] Following the same line of reasoning, Cornel West has insisted that James outdid even Emerson in directing philosophical energy "away from the community and back to the individual person."[25] James was "an authentic American intellectual frontiersman, not so much staking land in a wilderness but rather, like Mark Twain's Huckleberry Finn, expanding the moral possibilities of individuals on a raft that floats near land and society yet never really banks for long."[26]

There is no doubt that James was concerned with the individual's place in the modern world, and the primacy of personal experience was a constant theme in his work. But to insist that his emphasis on the individual came at the expense of communal and social concerns misses the point of his work on the lecture circuit and in popular periodicals. James entered the forums and venues he did to build a new type of community and to push society in new directions. Even when he appealed to the primacy of personal experience, his appeals functioned to draw people around him, to create common ground, and to encourage a community of inquirers who were capable of resisting what James called "bigness & greatness in all their forms."[27] The art of popular statement was about creating a community of individuals.[28]

Intellectual Participation

James's emphasis on collaboration implied participation, but collaboration was more a characteristic of his texts, while participation pointed toward the world of thought he hoped to foster. Professionalism had created a chain of cultural trust in which people were encouraged to abide by the knowledge of experts. While this chain of trust was valuable in many regards, it also engendered a sense of passivity and deference among many Americans. The result was a kind of "vertical vision," as Bledstein has put it, wherein people "with professional ambitions began comparing themselves to those of higher status, looking up to the next rung of the social ladder. . . . The vertical vision obstructed any horizontal recognition as middle-class Americans refused to relate to each other as equals."[29] Verticality entailed a cultural hierarchy and strengthened systems of professional authority, especially in the realm of inquiry. For most academics, the pursuit of knowledge proceeded through discourses that defined who could and who could not participate.

James's understanding of intellectual participation followed more of a horizontal vision. While there is no reason to overstate the degree to which James attempted to flatten hierarchies and break chains of authority, it is the case that when addressing popular audiences he demonstrated that the best kind of knowledge emerged from a pluralistic, accessible, egalitarian intellectual culture. The voices of *The Varieties of Religious Experience* came from the greatest religious minds of the past and from unnamed survey respondents of no particular distinction. Institutionally confined lunatics spoke alongside middle-aged women and Jonathan Edwards to help the people of Edinburgh grasp why religious knowledge depended on a rich variety of experiences. The diverse voices of *Varieties* also encouraged audience members to pursue the divine not according to dogmatic argument but according to whatever methods they found compelling. Regardless of their academic training, those who listened to and read James's Gifford lectures could know God as thoroughly and completely as any theologian.

The result was a new level of engagement based upon a horizontal vision. People not normally interested in science, theology, and philosophy were given the opportunity to participate in scientific, theological, and philosophical conversations. And this point was not lost on reviewers of James's work. Many reviewers of *Pragmatism,* for example, noted that the text resulted in a new level of engagement among ordinary people. At a time when "ponderousness, opacity, and a technical terminology of elephantine clumsiness" were the defining traits of academic inquiry, wrote one reviewer, pragmatism was "likely to be adopted by more and more persons for whom the formal religions afford no support, and the current philosophies are but the re-winnowing of chaff."[30] Another reviewer stated that "Men and women who have gathered their entire stock of knowledge in the rough school of real existence are today heard to utter the word 'pragmatism' with a fervor and a reverence, falling little short of the feelings displayed by recent religious converts."[31] Still another reviewer concluded that pragmatism offered all people a chance to get rid of the "barren pursuit" of contemporary philosophy. "Facts are notoriously repugnant to dialectic, and this radical demand to test all things, dialectic included, by the concrete practical consequences they involve, is very much the introduction of a bull into a china shop. Upon the horns of fact the pretty, fragile systems are shattered; the porcelain idols of dialectic are knocked to pieces."[32] With fragile systems shattered and porcelain idols broken, nonacademics were able to determine what counted as real, valuable, and profitable.

Personal Empowerment

The hallmark of James's art of popular statement, and perhaps the primary reason people seemed enthralled with his work, was his basic message of empowerment. In addition to picturing a collaborative, participatory community, James insisted from his earliest days on the lecture circuit that individuals retained control over their lives. Despite the power of industry, despite the problems of the Gilded Age and Progressive Era, despite the rise of Science, Theology, and Philosophy, James's message was surprisingly simple and consistent: Individuals still shaped their world. They were, in fact, responsible for determining the character of their world.

In every instance of popular statement analyzed in the preceding chapters, James articulated some version of this message. In 1878 in Baltimore and Boston, he told the audience that despite modern evolutionary science and the emergence of chemical, physiological determinism, they were "not impotent, paralytic spectators" but "real combatants in life's arena."[33] In the 1890s he told schoolteachers not to worry about "those unreal experimental tests, those pedantic elementary measurements" that purported to dictate effective pedagogy; instead, they should know that the best teaching comes from individuals "with eyes in their heads and common sense, and some feeling for the concrete facts of human nature in their hearts."[34] In advocating psychical research he explained that members of the SPR and those who believed in paranormal forces were justified in pursuing their beliefs because "The only form of thing that we directly encounter, the only experience that we concretely have, is our own personal life."[35]

James's message of personal intellectual empowerment was strongest in *Varieties* and *Pragmatism*. In Edinburgh he chastised those who "say that the egoistic elements of experience should be suppressed." To liberate those elements, he declared: "That unshareable feeling which each one of us has of the pinch of his individual destiny as he privately feels it rolling out on fortune's wheel may be disparaged for its egotism, may be sneered at as unscientific, but it is the one thing that fills up the measure of our concrete actuality, and any would-be existent that should lack such a feeling, or its analogue, would be a piece of reality only half made up."[36] In *Pragmatism,* James became even more combative, explaining:

> A pragmatist turns his back resolutely and once for all upon a lot of inveterate habits dear to professional philosophers. He turns away from abstraction and insufficiency, from verbal solutions, from bad *a priori* reasons, from fixed principles, closed systems, and pretended absolutes and origins. He turns towards concreteness and adequacy, towards facts, towards action, and towards power. That means the empiricist temper regnant, and the rationalist temper sincerely given up. It means the open air and possibilities of nature, as against dogma, artificiality, and the pretense of finality in truth.[37]

What *Pragmatism* made crystal clear, if it had not been clear from James's previous popular statements, was that personal empowerment entailed opposition to the stifling aspects of academic professionalism—that is, to those aspects that thwarted and discouraged the efforts of ordinary people. This message of personal empowerment became, over the course of years, intellectual populism; it became James's way of relating to the people he addressed and of letting them know that scientists, psychologists, theologians, and philosophers did not have the final say about what counted as true knowledge and a valuable experience. Of course, practical Americans already knew as much, for they were pragmatists already, happily turning their backs on the "inveterate habits dear to professional philosophers" and turning "towards concreteness and adequacy, towards facts, towards action, and towards power."

Intellectual populism did not define every aspect of James's career, nor did it structure every text he published in the final decade of his life.

But it did animate a host of other interactions with popular audiences. In *A Pluralistic Universe,* for example, James energetically berated "*vicious intellectualism*" and the absolutist thinkers who "fly to violent extremes," denying ordinary people the opportunity to contribute their idiosyncratic experiences and peculiar personalities to the pursuit of knowledge.[38] In response to this denial of individuals, James dedicated himself to ensuring that "intellectualism's edge is broken." Because intellectualism "can only approximate to reality," it becomes "inapplicable to our inner life, which spurns its vetoes and mocks at its impossibilities."[39] *A Pluralistic Universe,* like *Varieties* and *Pragmatism,* authorized ordinary people to spurn and mock intellectualism's rather feeble attempt to discuss what was most important in life—namely, the inner mystery of experience.

It is even possible to trace this theme of personal empowerment, and the other characteristics of the art of popular statement, to interactions with general audiences from earlier in James's career. "The Will to Believe" was nothing if not a precursor to the intellectual populism that emerged more fully in *Varieties* and *Pragmatism.* Dismissing "the logic by which our scientific absolutists pretend to regulate our lives," James told his listeners that "we have the right to believe at our own risk any hypothesis that is live enough to tempt our will."[40] He also lovingly described an "intellectual republic" in which "No one of us ought to issue vetoes to the other, nor should we bandy words of abuse. We ought, on the contrary, delicately and profoundly to respect one another's mental freedom," fostering a spirit of "live and let live, in speculative as well as in practical things."[41] Similar attitudes and appeals can be found in James's writings on imperialism, which were the political extensions of his pragmatic empowerment.[42] For James, the reason to oppose intellectual absolutism and to support pragmatism was the same reason to oppose imperialism and to support the self-determination of foreign nations. Individuals, in whatever local, communal, or national contexts they occupied, had to be given the chance to shape their world.[43]

Detailed analyses of James's anti-imperialist writings, of "The Will to Believe," and of *A Pluralistic Universe* fall outside the parameters of this project. Moreover, as an incredibly active lecturer and writer, James left behind a trove of texts that must also be set aside for the time being. But suffice it to say that his art of popular statement provides a starting point for understanding the times he worked collaboratively with audiences to tackle common problems, to increase opportunities for participation in intellectual culture, and to reconfigure the world of thought so it better served the interests and needs of men and women on "the street."

Popular statement, whether or not it is the highest form of art, certainly helped James interact with people who would not have otherwise found science, psychology, and philosophy entirely applicable to their lives. It also helped him interact with persistent themes of the American experience. Eloquence and professionalism, exclusion and inclusion, the powerful and the powerless, activity and passivity, academics and nonacademics, popular and expert knowledge, to name only some, remain significant parts of our cultural conversations. And as these conversations persist, James will continue to speak with the same visionary eloquence, the same message of empowerment, that carried him into the pantheon of American thought.

Notes

⌘

Introduction

1. William James to Ferdinand Canning Scott Schiller, May 1, 1903, *Corr.* 10:243.
2. "The Review Table," *Bismarck Daily Tribune*, January 20, 1887, 4.
3. "Leaves from Literature," *Galveston Daily News*, January 29, 1888, 7.
4. "The New Psychology," *Daily Picayune*, July 12, 1891, 12.
5. "High School Art Funds Lectures," *Springfield Daily Republican*, November 15, 1898, 4.
6. E. C. Martin, "Literary Outlook," *Los Angeles Times*, January 22, 1899, 31.
7. Joseph Jacobs, "Truth as a Working Hypothesis," *New York Times*, August 31, 1907, BR527.
8. "Distinguishing Qualities of William James," *Los Angeles Times*, August 28, 1910, II4.
9. "William James," *Chicago Tribune*, August 28, 1910, B4.
10. "William James," *New York Times*, September 3, 1910, BR6.

11. See Thomas Bender, *Intellect and Public Life: Essays on the Social History of Academic Intellectuals in the United States* (Baltimore: Johns Hopkins University Press, 1993), especially 30–46.
12. "An American Philosopher," *Springfield Daily Republican*, June 20, 1909, 6.
13. Edwin Bjorkman, "Pragmatism—What It Is—By Professor William James," *New York Times*, November 3, 1907, SM8.
14. James's oral style is discussed in detail in chapter 3.
15. Three biographies stand out as particularly admirable: Ralph Barton Perry, *The Thought and Character of William James*, 2 vols. (Boston: Little, Brown, 1935); Gay Wilson Allen, *William James: A Biography* (New York: Viking Press, 1967); and Robert D. Richardson, *William James in the Maelstrom of American Modernism* (Boston: Houghton Mifflin, 2006).
16. The number of commentaries on James's work is too great to list any large proportion of them, but a good overview of his work can be found in Gerald E. Myers, *William James: His Life and Thought* (New Haven: Yale University Press, 1986).
17. Howard M. Feinstein, *Becoming William James* (Ithaca, NY: Cornell University Press, 1984).
18. Paul Jerome Croce, *Science and Religion in the Era of William James*, vol. 1: *Eclipse of Certainty, 1820–1880* (Chapel Hill: University of North Carolina Press, 1995).
19. John J. McDermott, *The Culture of Experience: Philosophical Essays in the American Grain* (Prospect Heights, IL: Waveland Press, 1976); John J. McDermott, *Streams of Experience: Reflections on the History and Philosophy of American Culture* (Amherst: University of Massachusetts Press, 1986).
20. Francesca Bordogna, *William James at the Boundaries: Philosophy, Science, and the Geography of Knowledge* (Chicago: University of Chicago Press, 2008).
21. Deborah Blum, *Ghost Hunters: William James and the Search for Scientific Proof of Life After Death* (New York: Penguin, 2006).
22. Ross Posnock, *The Trial of Curiosity: Henry James, William James, and the Challenge of Modernity* (New York: Oxford University Press, 1991), 15.
23. George Cotkin, *William James, Public Philosopher* (Urbana: University of Illinois Press, 1989), 73.
24. Frederick J. Ruf, *The Creation of Chaos: William James and the Stylistic Making of a Disorderly World* (Albany: State University of New York Press, 1991).
25. Allen, *William James*, vii–viii.
26. This is not to say that Cotkin does not succeed in his project of portraying James as a public philosopher. In fact, Cotkin's work lays much of the philosophical groundwork for the present study. But it is to say that Cotkin is concerned more with the way James's inward, psychological turmoil was rendered in outward form than with the way James developed intellectual bonds with specific publics.

27. See, for example, Gerard A. Hauser, *Vernacular Voices: The Rhetoric of Publics and Public Spheres* (Columbia: University of South Carolina Press, 1999); Robert Asen and Daniel C. Brouwer, eds., *Counterpublics and the State* (Albany: State University of New York Press, 2001); and Michael Warner, *Publics and Counterpublics* (New York: Zone Books, 2002).
28. See Michael C. McGee, "In Search of 'The People': A Rhetorical Alternative," *Quarterly Journal of Speech* 61 (1975): 235–249.
29. In general, see Cotkin, *William James, Public Philosopher;* and Bordogna, *William James at the Boundaries.*
30. Burton J. Bledstein, *The Culture of Professionalism: The Middle Class and the Development of Higher Education in America* (New York: W. W. Norton, 1978).
31. Barbara A. Misztal, *Intellectuals and the Public Good: Creativity and Civil Courage* (Cambridge: Cambridge University Press, 2007).
32. Russell Jacoby, *The Last Intellectuals: American Culture in the Age of Academe* (New York: Noonday Press, 1987), 5.
33. Richard Posner, *Public Intellectuals: A Study of Decline* (Cambridge: Harvard University Press, 2001), 3.
34. See Jeremy Jennings, "Deaths of the Intellectual: A Comparative Autopsy," in *The Public Intellectual*, ed. Helen Small (Oxford: Blackwell, 2002), 110–130; and Stefan Collini, "'Every Fruit-Juice Drinker, Nudist, Sandal-Wearer . . .': Intellectuals as Other People," in *The Public Intellectual*, 203–223.
35. See Jeremy Jennings and Tony Kemp-Welch, eds., *Intellectuals in Politics: From the Dreyfus Affair to Salman Rushdie* (London: Routledge, 1997); and Mark Lilla, *The Reckless Mind: Intellectuals in Politics* (New York: New York Review Books, 2001).
36. See Edward W. Said, *Representations of the Intellectual* (New York: Vintage, 1994); and Carl Boggs, *Intellectuals and the Crisis of Modernity* (Albany: State University of New York Press, 1993).
37. See Ross Posnock, *Color & Culture: Black Writers and the Making of the Modern Intellectual* (Cambridge: Harvard University Press, 1998); and Houston A. Baker, *Betrayal: How Black Intellectuals Have Abandoned the Ideals of the Civil Rights Era* (New York: Columbia University Press, 2008).
38. Perhaps the most active current writer on questions of intellectual duty and public culture is Stanley Fish. See, in addition to his numerous articles in the *New York Times, Professional Correctness: Literary Studies and Political Change* (Cambridge: Harvard University Press, 1995).
39. See Posnock, *Color & Culture*, 21–22; and John Patrick Diggins, "The Changing Role of the Public Intellectual in American History," in *The Public Intellectual: Between Philosophy and Politics*, ed. Arthur M. Melzer, Jerry Weinberger, and M. Richard Zinman (Lanham, MD: Rowman & Littlefield, 2003), 91–108.

40. In "The Wise Man," for example, Ingersoll declared: "The intellectual should lead, with loving hands, the mental poor" (Robert Green Ingersoll, "The Wise Man," in *Prose-Poems and Selections from the Writings and Sayings of Robert G. Ingersoll* [New York: C. P. Farrell, 1888], 132). For other American uses of "intellectual" that predate James, see Posnock, *The Trial of Curiosity*, 6–12.
41. For an overview, see Jeremy Jennings and Tony Kemp-Welch, "The Century of the Intellectual: From the Dreyfus Affair to Salman Rushdie," in Jennings and Kemp-Welch, *Intellectuals in Politics*, 1–21.
42. William James to William Mackintire Salter, September 11, 1899, *Corr.* 9:41.
43. William James to William Dean Howells, November 16, 1900, *Corr.* 9:361–362.
44. William James, "The Social Value of the College-Bred," *McClure's Magazine* 30 (February 1908): 419–422; reprinted in *ECR*, 106–112.
45. Jacoby, *The Last Intellectuals*, 5.
46. James was often instrumental in arranging for Peirce's lectures, given that Peirce had tremendous difficulty securing work for himself. For a revealing series of letters between James and Peirce regarding the possibility of Peirce delivering lectures at Harvard, see William James to Charles Sanders Peirce, December 1897, *Corr.* 8:324–325; Charles Sanders Peirce to William James, December 13, 1897, *Corr.* 8:325–326; William James to Charles Sanders Peirce, December 22, 1897, *Corr.* 8:326–327; Charles Sanders Peirce to William James, December 16, 1897, *Corr.* 8:329–331; Charles Sanders Peirce to William James, January 4, 1898, *Corr.* 8:334–335; Charles Sanders Peirce to William James, January 21, 1898, *Corr.* 8:337; William James to Charles Sanders Peirce, January 23, 1898, *Corr.* 8:338; Charles Sanders Peirce to William James, January 26, 1898, *Corr.* 8:339–340; Charles Sanders Peirce to William James, January 30, 1898, *Corr.* 8:340–341.
47. Randall Collins, *The Sociology of Philosophies: A Global Theory of Intellectual Change* (Cambridge: Belknap Press of Harvard University Press, 1998), 20.
48. For a fuller discussion of chains of associations, see Collins, *The Sociology of Philosophies*, 19–79.
49. For more on this notion of "contexts of reception," see Steven Mailloux, *Reception Histories: Rhetoric, Pragmatism, and American Cultural Politics* (Ithaca, NY: Cornell University Press, 1998).
50. Kenneth Burke, *A Rhetoric of Motives* (Berkeley: University of California Press, 1969), 43.
51. Donald C. Bryant, "Rhetoric: Its Functions and Its Scope," *Quarterly Journal of Speech* 39 (1953): 413.
52. Aristotle, *Rhetoric*, Book I, chapter 2.26, trans. W. Rhys Roberts, in *The Rhetoric and the Poetics of Aristotle* (New York: Modern Library, 1954).
53. I. A. Richards, *The Philosophy of Rhetoric* (New York: Oxford University Press, 1965), 3.

54. Much of this conception of rhetoric comes from Thomas B. Farrell, *Norms of Rhetorical Culture* (New Haven: Yale University Press, 1993).
55. Robert Danisch, *Pragmatism, Democracy, and the Necessity of Rhetoric* (Columbia: University of South Carolina Press, 2007), 1.
56. Nathan Crick, "Rhetoric, Philosophy, and the Public Intellectual," *Philosophy & Rhetoric* 39 (2006): 131.
57. Steven Mailloux, "Thinking in Public with Rhetoric," *Philosophy & Rhetoric* 39 (2006): 140.
58. For another perspective on the connection between public intellectuals and the art of rhetoric, see Steve Fuller, "The Public Intellectual as Agent of Justice: In Search of a Regime," *Philosophy & Rhetoric* 39 (2006): 147–156. Also see Steve Fuller, *The Intellectual* (Cambridge: Icon Books, 2005).
59. Most notably, see James Albert Winans, *Public Speaking*, rev. ed. (New York: Century Company, 1917), especially 50–75; William E. Utterback, "A Psychological Approach to the Rhetoric of Speech Composition," *Quarterly Journal of Speech* 10 (1924): 17–23; and William Norwood Brigance, "Can We Redefine the James-Winans Theory of Persuasion?" *Quarterly Journal of Speech* 21 (1935): 19–26.
60. Even philosophers seemed uninterested in James's work during the middle part of the twentieth century. In the afterword to the twelve-volume *Correspondence of William James*, for example, John McDermott notes how difficult it was to get the series off the ground in the early 1970s: "We were rebuffed by the American Philosophical Association on the grounds that the thought of William James was no longer a matter of interest and concern!" (*Corr.* 12:577).
61. For examples of the intersection of rhetoric and pragmatism that pay special attention to James, see Alan Brinton, "William James and the Epistemic View of Rhetoric," *Quarterly Journal of Speech* 68 (1982): 158–169; Steven Mailloux, *Rhetorical Power* (Ithaca, NY: Cornell University Press, 1989); Gage Chapel and Richard Jensen, "Synthesizing Jamesian Pragmatism and Platonic Idealism in Nineteenth-Century America: The Discourse of Mary Baker Eddy's Christian Science," *Journal of Communication & Religion* 23 (2000): 95–112; Paul Schollmeier, "Pragmatic Method and Its Rhetorical Lineage," *Philosophy & Rhetoric* 35 (2002): 368–381; Danisch, *Pragmatism, Democracy, and the Necessity of Rhetoric;* Paul Stob, "'Terministic Screens,' Social Constructionism, and the Language of Experience: Kenneth Burke's Utilization of William James," *Philosophy & Rhetoric* 41 (2008): 130–152; and Paul Stob, "Pragmatism, Experience, and William James's Politics of Blindness," *Philosophy & Rhetoric* 44 (2011): 227–249. For work on the intersection of pragmatism, James, and communication studies writ large, see Lenore Langsdorf and Andrew R. Smith, eds., *Recovering Pragmatism's Voice: The Classical Tradition, Rorty, and the Philosophy of Communication* (Albany: State University of New York Press, 1995); and David K. Perry, ed., *American Pragmatism and Communication Research* (Mahwah, NJ: Lawrence Erlbaum, 2001).

62. Mailloux, *Reception Histories*, 61.
63. Danisch, *Pragmatism, Democracy, and the Necessity of Rhetoric*, 16.
64. Danisch, *Pragmatism, Democracy, and the Necessity of Rhetoric*, 19.
65. Danisch, *Pragmatism, Democracy, and the Necessity of Rhetoric*, 37.
66. Frederick J. Antczak, *Thought and Character: The Rhetoric of Democratic Education* (Ames: Iowa State University Press, 1985), 166.
67. Cotkin, *William James, Public Philosopher*, 123–151.
68. See, for example, M. C. Otto, "On a Certain Blindness in William James," *Ethics* 53 (1943): 184–191; Henry Steele Commager, *The American Mind: An Interpretation of American Thought and Character Since the 1880s* (New Haven: Yale University Press, 1950), 98–100; and Cornel West, *The American Evasion of Philosophy: A Genealogy of Pragmatism* (Madison: University of Wisconsin Press, 1989), 54–55.
69. See, for example, Bordogna, *William James at the Boundaries*, 13–15. More generally, see Joshua I. Miller, *Democratic Temperament: The Legacy of William James* (Lawrence: University Press of Kansas, 1997); and Kenneth Ferguson, *William James: Politics in the Pluriverse* (Lanham, MD: Rowman & Littlefield, 2007).

Chapter One. Eloquence and Professionalism in the Nineteenth Century

1. Henry Adams, *The Education of Henry Adams: An Autobiography* (Boston: Houghton Mifflin, 1918), 53.
2. While the Civil War did not mark a clean break in the style of intellectual practice, the social, cultural, economic, and political changes that accompanied it surely hastened the changes already under way. For more, see Roger L. Geiger's introduction to *The American College in the Nineteenth Century*, ed. Roger L. Geiger (Nashville, TN: Vanderbilt University Press, 2000), 1–36.
3. The phrases come from two works: James Perrin Warren, *Culture of Eloquence: Oratory and Reform in Antebellum America* (University Park: Pennsylvania State University Press, 1999); and Burton J. Bledstein, *The Culture of Professionalism: The Middle Class and the Development of Higher Education in America* (New York: W. W. Norton, 1978). For other discussions of the shift from eloquence to professionalism, see Bruce A. Kimball, *Orators & Philosophers: A History of the Idea of Liberal Education* (New York: Teachers College Press, 1986), 114–204; Kenneth Cmiel, *Democratic Eloquence: The Fight over Popular Speech in Nineteenth-Century America* (New York: William Morrow, 1990); and Gregory Clark and S. Michael Halloran, "Introduction: Transformations of Public Discourse in

Nineteenth Century America," in *Oratorical Culture in Nineteenth-Century America: Transformations in the Theory and Practice of Rhetoric*, ed. Gregory Clark and S. Michael Halloran (Carbondale: Southern Illinois University Press, 1993), 1–26.

4. For more on this theme, see Bruce Kuklick, "American Philosophy and Its Lost Public," in *Pragmatism: From Progressivism to Postmodernism*, ed. Robert Hollinger and David Depew (Westport, CT: Praeger, 1999), 142–152.
5. Francesca Bordogna, *William James at the Boundaries* (Chicago: University of Chicago Press, 2008).
6. Warren, *Culture of Eloquence*, 45.
7. Clark and Halloran, introduction to *Oratorical Culture in Nineteenth-Century America*, 8.
8. Barnet Baskerville, "19th Century Burlesque of Oratory," *American Quarterly* 20 (1968): 726.
9. Clark and Halloran, introduction to *Oratorical Culture in Nineteenth-Century America*, 7.
10. Edward G. Parker, *The Golden Age of American Oratory* (Boston: Whittemore, Niles, and Hall, 1857).
11. Robert Alexander Kraig, "The Second Oratorical Renaissance," in *Rhetoric and Reform in the Progressive Era*, ed. J. Michael Hogan (East Lansing: Michigan State University Press, 2003), 8.
12. George William Curtis, "Lectures and Lecturing," *Harper's Monthly Magazine* 14 (1856): 123.
13. Donald M. Scott, "The Popular Lecture and the Creation of a Public in Mid-Nineteenth-Century America," *Journal of American History* 66 (1980): 793.
14. Thomas Wentworth Higginson, "The American Lecture-System," *Macmillan's Magazine* 18 (1868): 56.
15. Scott, "The Popular Lecture," 799.
16. For the history of the lyceum, see Carl Bode, *The American Lyceum: Town Meeting of the Mind* (Carbondale: Southern Illinois University Press, 1968); and Angela G. Ray, *The Lyceum and Public Culture in the Nineteenth-Century United States* (East Lansing: Michigan State University Press, 2005).
17. It should be noted, however, that the lyceum movement promoted a specific type of cultural consciousness. Because the lyceum emerged largely from the work of middle- and upper-class New Englanders, the cultural values spreading across the country were, by and large, New England values. As one scholar describes, the lyceum was "a mechanism to affirm a specific New England culture as the national norm." Ray, *The Lyceum and Public Culture in the Nineteenth-Century United States*, 7.
18. See Ray, *The Lyceum and Public Culture*, especially 113–172, for examples of people who disturbed racial and gender lines.

19. Nan Johnson, *Nineteenth-Century Rhetoric in North America* (Carbondale: Southern Illinois University Press, 1991), 246.
20. Edward T. Channing, *Lectures Read to the Seniors in Harvard College* (Boston: Ticknor and Fields, 1856), 17.
21. Warren, *Culture of Eloquence*, 16.
22. Josiah Holland, "The Popular Lecture," *Atlantic Monthly* 15 (1865): 363.
23. For more on the lecturer's relation to the audience, see Bode, *The American Lyceum*, 27–37.
24. Eugene Taylor, *William James on Consciousness beyond the Margin* (Princeton, NJ: Princeton University Press, 1996), 12–13.
25. For an overview of Emerson's vocational development, see Herbert A. Wichelns, "Ralph Waldo Emerson," in *A History and Criticism of American Public Address*, vol. 2, ed. William Norwood Brigance (New York: Russell & Russell, 1960), 501–525.
26. See Peter S. Field, "'The Transformation of Genius into Practical Power': Ralph Waldo Emerson and the Public Lecture," *Journal of the Early Republic* 21 (2001): 467–493.
27. Robert D. Richardson, *Emerson: The Mind on Fire* (Berkeley: University of California Press, 1995), 418. Also see Cameron C. Nickels, "'Roaring Ralph': Emerson as Lecturer," *New England Quarterly* 76 (2003): 116–123.
28. In general, see Mary Kupiec Cayton, "The Making of an American Prophet: Emerson, His Audiences, and the Rise of the Culture Industry in Nineteenth-Century America," *American Historical Review* 92 (1987): 597–620.
29. Quoted in Cayton, "The Making of an American Prophet," 611.
30. The best resource for information on Henry James Sr. and his struggles growing up is Alfred Habegger, *The Father: A Life of Henry James Sr.* (New York: Farrar, Straus and Giroux, 1994). Also see Paul Fisher, *House of Wits: An Intimate Portrait of the James Family* (New York: Henry Holt, 2008); Howard M. Feinstein, *Becoming William James* (Ithaca, NY: Cornell University Press, 1984); and Ralph Barton Perry, *The Thought and Character of William James*, vol. 1 (New York: Little, Brown, 1935).
31. See Feinstein, *Becoming William James*, 58–75.
32. Henry James Jr., *A Small Boy and Others* (New York: Charles Scribner's Sons, 1913), 30.
33. Quoted in Habegger, *The Father*, 194.
34. Quoted in Habegger, *The Father*, 195.
35. James, *A Small Boy and Others*, 8.
36. Henry James Sr. to Ralph Waldo Emerson, undated letter of 1843, reprinted in Perry, *The Thought and Character of William James*, 1:41–43.
37. Habegger, *The Father*, 204.

38. Habegger, *The Father*, 211.
39. Quoted in Habegger, *The Father*, 265.
40. For coverage of these lectures, see Habegger, *The Father*, 243, 250–251, 265, 272–273, 292–294, 295, 324.
41. In general, see William T. Stafford, "Emerson and the James Family," *American Literature* 24 (1953): 433–461.
42. Henry James Jr., *Notes of a Son and Brother* (New York: Charles Scribner's Sons, 1914), 205.
43. For more on the Albany and Van Buren connection, see James, *A Small Boy and Others*, 8–15.
44. James, *A Small Boy and Others*, 51.
45. James, *A Small Boy and Others*, 50–51.
46. Habegger, *The Father*, 343.
47. Quoted in Habegger, *The Father*, 339.
48. Adam G. De Gurowski, *America and Europe* (New York: D. Appleton, 1857), 329.
49. Quoted in Rollo Ogden, ed., *The Life and Letters of Edwin Lawrence Godkin*, vol. 2 (New York: Macmillan, 1907), 118.
50. William James, "Introduction to *The Literary Remains of the Late Henry James*," *ECR*, 4.
51. On the inside cover of James's copies of *Miscellanies: Nature and Addresses* and *Essays: First Series* is the date July 5, 1871. Several other volumes of Emerson's work followed these two. For more details, see Frederic I. Carpenter, "William James and Emerson," *American Literature* 11 (1939): 40–42.
52. Henry Sr. had a habit of reading Emerson aloud to the family, and it is not unreasonable to think that the young William took some of Emerson's writings from Henry Sr.'s shelf and worked his way through them. See Carpenter, "William James and Emerson," 41–42.
53. Ralph Waldo Emerson, "Nature," in *Nature, Addresses, and Lectures: The Complete Works of Ralph Waldo Emerson*, vol. 1 (Boston: Houghton, Mifflin, 1903), 4–5.
54. Emerson, "Nature," 21–22.
55. Emerson, "Nature," 29.
56. Ralph Waldo Emerson, "The American Scholar," in *Nature, Addresses, and Lectures*, 103.
57. Emerson, "The American Scholar," 103.
58. Ralph Waldo Emerson, "Literary Ethics," in *Nature, Addresses, and Lectures*, 166.
59. Emerson, "Literary Ethics," 182.
60. William James to Henry James Jr., May 3, 1903, *Corr.* 3:234.
61. William James to Henry James Jr., October 2, 1869, *Corr.* 1:102.
62. William James to Henry James Jr., October 2, 1869, *Corr.* 1:102.

63. Henry James Sr., *Lectures and Miscellanies* (New York: Redfield, 1852), 118, 124.

64. James, *Lectures and Miscellanies*, 125.

65. James, *Lectures and Miscellanies*, 126.

66. Henry James Sr., *The Social Significance of Our Institutions: An Oration* (Boston: Ticknor and Fields, 1861), 14.

67. For a similar sentiment, see Henry James Sr., *Society the Redeemed Form of Man, and the Earnest of God's Omnipotence in Human Nature* (Boston: Houghton, Osgood, 1879), particularly 476.

68. William James to Alice Howe Gibbens James, December 20, 1882, *Corr.* 5:342.

69. Kimball, *Orators & Philosophers*, 146–156.

70. Bledstein, *The Culture of Professionalism*, 78–79.

71. Gregory Clark and S. Michael Halloran, afterword to *Oratorical Culture in Nineteenth-Century America*, 248.

72. See, for example, Bledstein, *The Culture of Professionalism*, 90–92, 121–128.

73. David E. Shi, *Facing Facts: Realism in American Thought and Culture, 1850–1920* (New York: Oxford University Press, 1995), 66.

74. Shi, *Facing Facts*, 67.

75. For a good overview of the way scientific communication developed in conjunction with the rise of professionalism, see James Secord, "How Scientific Conversation Became Shop Talk," in *Science in the Marketplace: Nineteenth-Century Sites and Experiences*, ed. Aileen Fyfe and Bernard Lightman (Chicago: University of Chicago Press, 2007), 23–59.

76. See Christopher D. Green, Marlene Shore, and Thomas Teo, eds., *The Transformation of Psychology: Influences of 19th-Century Philosophy, Technology, and Natural Science* (Washington, DC: American Psychological Association, 2001). For James's role in the transformation of psychology, see Bordogna, *William James at the Boundaries*, 21–90.

77. For a thorough discussion of science, philosophy, and uncertainty in the context of James's life, see Paul Jerome Croce, *Science and Religion in the Era of William James*, vol. 1: *The Eclipse of Certainty, 1820–1880* (Chapel Hill: University of North Carolina Press, 1995).

78. See Bledstein, *The Culture of Professionalism*, 309–331.

79. Kimball, *Orators & Philosophers*, 161–162.

80. Christopher J. Lucas, *American Higher Education: A History* (New York: St. Martin's Griffin, 1994), 140.

81. In general, see Laurence R. Veysey, *The Emergence of the American University* (Chicago: University of Chicago Press, 1965).

82. Julie A. Reuben, *The Making of the Modern University: Intellectual Transformation and the Marginalization of Morality* (Chicago: University of Chicago Press, 1996), 61.

83. At Harvard's Lawrence Scientific School James first studied chemistry under Eliot. But he was unsure of chemistry and unsure of Eliot, at least as a professor, so he soon switched to the study of anatomy and physiology. For more detail, see Croce, *Science and Religion*, 134–138.
84. Lucas, *American Higher Education*, 179.
85. Clark and Halloran, introduction to *Oratorical Culture in Nineteenth-Century America*, 18.
86. Bledstein, *The Culture of Professionalism*, 88.
87. Daniel Coit Gilman, "Report of the President," in *First Annual Report of the Johns Hopkins University* (Baltimore: William K. Boyle & Son, 1876), 21.
88. Thomas Bender, *Intellect and Public Life: Essays on the Social History of Academic Intellectuals in the United States* (Baltimore: Johns Hopkins University Press, 1993), 12.
89. John Dewey, *The Quest for Certainty*, vol. 4 of *The Later Works of John Dewey*, ed. Jo Ann Boydston (Carbondale: Southern Illinois University Press, 1988).
90. William James, "The Ph.D. Octopus," *Harvard Monthly* 36 (1903): 1–9; reprinted in *ECR*, 67–73.
91. Lucas, *American Higher Education*, 180.
92. Bledstein, *The Culture of Professionalism*, 90.
93. For more on the technical sphere of argumentation, see G. Thomas Goodnight, "The Personal, Technical, and Public Spheres of Argument: A Speculative Inquiry into the Art of Public Deliberation," *Journal of the American Forensic Association* 18 (1982): 214–227.
94. Bender, *Intellect and Public Life*, 43.
95. Bender, *Intellect and Public Life*, 26.
96. See, for example, Kimball, *Orators & Philosophers*, 147–148.
97. In general, see Bender, *Intellect and Public Life*, 49–77.
98. In general, see Bledstein, *The Culture of Professionalism*, 90–99.
99. For a good discussion of the way the rhetoric of expertise demands deference from general audiences, see E. Johanna Hartelius, *The Rhetoric of Expertise* (Lanham, MD: Lexington Books, 2011), especially 23–25.
100. Bledstein, *The Culture of Professionalism*, 99.
101. See Bruce Kuklick, *The Rise of American Philosophy: Cambridge, Massachusetts, 1860–1930* (New Haven: Yale University Press, 1977), 80–126.
102. For details on James's efforts to become a painter, see Feinstein, *Becoming William James*, 117–145.
103. For details, see Fisher, *House of Wits*, 175–189.
104. For more on William's toying with the idea of joining the army, see Linda Simon, *Genuine Reality: A Life of William James* (New York: Harcourt Brace, 1998), 86–88.

105. For detailed accounts of James's turn to science at Harvard, see Daniel W. Bjork, *The Compromised Scientist: William James and the Development of American Psychology* (New York: Columbia University Press, 1983), 15–36. Also see Feinstein, *Becoming William James*, 146–168; and Croce, *Science and Religion*, 67–148.

106. I discuss James and psychical research in chapter 4.

107. A. Lawrence Lowell, "Reminiscences," *American Mathematical Monthly* 32 (1925): 4.

108. W. E. Byerly, "Reminiscences," *American Mathematical Monthly* 32 (1925): 5.

109. Quoted in Edward Waldo Emerson, *The Early Years of the Saturday Club, 1855–1870* (Boston: Houghton Mifflin, 1918), 105.

110. Quoted in Charles W. Eliot, "Reminiscences of Peirce," *American Mathematical Monthly* 32 (1925): 3.

111. Quoted in Emerson, *The Early Years of the Saturday Club*, 97.

112. Quoted in Emerson, *The Early Years of the Saturday Club*, 98.

113. Training in mathematics—particularly algebra, geometry, and trigonometry—was required for aspiring chemists at the Lawrence School. Courses on "Higher Mathematics" and "Analytical and Celestial Mechanics" gave James extended exposure to the precision and intricacy of Peirce's mind. For course requirements, see *Catalogue of the Officers and Students of Harvard University for the Academical Year 1861–62, First Term* (Cambridge, MA: Sever and Francis, 1861).

114. William James to the James family, September 16, 1861, *Corr.* 4:43.

115. For examples of William James and Charles Sander Peirce's exchanges on the nature of intellectual culture, see Charles Sanders Peirce to William James, November 21, 1875, *Corr.* 4:523–524; Charles Sanders Peirce to William James, January 1, 1894, *Corr.* 7:481–482; William James to Charles Sanders Peirce, January 24, 1894, *Corr.* 7:483–484; Charles Sanders Peirce to William James, January 28, 1894, *Corr.* 7:487–488; William James to Charles Sanders Peirce, June 5, 1897, *Corr.* 8:272; William James to Charles Sanders Peirce, December 1897, *Corr.* 8:324–325; Charles Sanders Peirce to William James, December 13, 1897, *Corr.* 8:325–326; William James to Charles Sanders Peirce, December 22, 1897, *Corr.* 8:326–327; Charles Sanders Peirce to William James, December 16, 1897, *Corr.* 8:329–331.

116. Croce, *Science and Religion*, 124.

117. See Ronald L. Numbers, *Darwinism Comes to America* (Cambridge: Harvard University Press, 1998).

118. See A. Hunter Dupree, *Asa Gray, 1810–1888* (Cambridge: Belknap Press of Harvard University Press, 1959), 229.

119. In general, see Croce, *Science and Religion*, 157–176.

120. Bert James Loewenberg, "The Reaction of American Scientists to Darwinism," *American Historical Review* 38 (1933): 694.

121. Quoted in Croce, *Science and Religion*, 129.

122. Asa Gray, review of Darwin's *Theory on the Origin of Species by Means of Natural Selection, American Journal of Science and Arts* 29 (1860): 153–185.

123. Gray, review of Darwin's *Origin of Species*, 156.

124. Gray, review of Darwin's *Origin of Species*, 182.

125. Gray, review of Darwin's *Origin of Species*, 183.

126. Gray, review of Darwin's *Origin of Species*, 185.

127. See Loewenberg, "The Reaction of American Scientists to Darwinism," 694.

128. Asa Gray, *Darwiniana: Essays and Reviews Pertaining to Darwinism* (New York: D. Appleton, 1889), 175–176.

129. I further explore James's take on evolution in chapter 2.

130. For an overview of Wyman's thoughts on evolution, see Toby A. Appel, "Jeffries Wyman, Philosophical Anatomy, and the Scientific Reception of Darwin in America," *Journal of the History of Biology* 21 (1988): 69–94.

131. For a good summary of Wyman's life, educational development, and professional standing, see Toby A. Appel, "A Scientific Career in the Age of Character: Jeffries Wyman and Natural History at Harvard," in *Science at Harvard University: Historical Perspectives*, ed. Clark A. Elliott and Margaret W. Rossiter (Bethlehem, PA: Lehigh University Press, 1992), 96–120.

132. Appel, "A Scientific Career in the Age of Character," 98.

133. Quoted in Croce, *Science and Religion*, 139.

134. Quoted in Croce, *Science and Religion*, 138.

135. For information on Wyman and the Saturday Club, see Emerson, *The Early Years of the Saturday Club*, 420–427.

136. See *Catalogue of the Officers and Students of Harvard University for the Academical Year 1863–64, First Term* (Cambridge, MA: Sever and Francis, 1864), 71.

137. William James to Alice James, September 13, 1863, *Corr.* 4:83–84.

138. For a discussion of compartmentalization and specialized spaces in the culture of professionalism, see Bledstein, *The Culture of Professionalism*, 46–65.

139. Feinstein, *Becoming William James*, 153.

140. I further explore these book reviews in chapter 2.

141. [William James], "Professor Jeffries Wyman," *Harvard Advocate*, October 1, 1874; reprinted in *ECR*, 8.

142. The best source of information on Agassiz's life and influence remains Edward Lurie, *Louis Agassiz: A Life in Science* (Baltimore: Johns Hopkins University Press, 1988).

143. Lurie, *Louis Agassiz*, 164.

144. Feinstein, *Becoming William James*, 151–152.

145. Louis Agassiz, *Methods of Study in Natural History* (Boston: Fields, Osgood, 1871), iii–iv.

146. James announced his plans to attend the lectures in a letter to his mother, Mary Robertson Walsh James, on September 10, 1861, *Corr.* 4:41.

147. Agassiz, *Methods of Study in Natural History*, 14.

148. William James to the James family, September 16, 1861, *Corr.* 4:43. James reported similar sentiments elsewhere. See William James to Henry James Sr. and Mary Robertson Walsh James, April 21, 1865, *Corr.* 4:101–103; William James to Henry James Sr., September 12, 1865, *Corr.* 4:122; and William James to Hugo Münsterberg, May 15, 1892, *Corr.* 7:265–266.

149. William James to the James family, December 25, 1861, *Corr.* 4:63.

150. See Lurie, *Louis Agassiz*, 312–316.

151. See Lurie, *Louis Agassiz*, 314.

152. For Agassiz's plans for the trip and the objectives he hoped to achieve, see Lurie, *Louis Agassiz*, 345–358.

153. James mentioned these lectures in a letter to his mother and father, April 21, 1865, *Corr.* 4:101. Also see Louis Agassiz and Elizabeth Agassiz, *A Journey in Brazil* (Boston: Fields, Osgood, 1871), 1–46.

154. William James to Henry James Sr. and Mary Robertson Walsh James, April 21, 1865, *Corr.* 4:101–103.

155. William James to Henry James Jr., May 3, 1865, *Corr.* 1:6–8.

156. James confronted the lack of pluralism at various points in his career, notably in his defense of psychical research, covered in chapter 4, and in *VRE*, covered in chapter 5. But in general, see *PU*.

157. William James to Henry James Sr., September 12, 1865, *Corr.* 4:122.

158. William James to Henry James Jr., March 9, 1868, *Corr.* 1:39.

159. William James, "Louis Agassiz," *Science* 5 (1897); reprinted in *ECR*, 51.

160. Peter Gibian, *Oliver Wendell Holmes and the Culture of Conversation* (Cambridge: Cambridge University Press, 2001), 48.

161. Eleanor M. Tilton, *Amiable Autocrat: A Biography of Dr. Oliver Wendell Holmes* (New York: Henry Schuman, 1947), 206.

162. Tilton, *Amiable Autocrat*, 209.

163. Gibian, *Oliver Wendell Holmes and the Culture of Conversation*, 1. For more on Holmes's popular rise, see Edwin P. Hoyt, *The Improper Bostonian: Dr. Oliver Wendell Holmes* (New York: William Morrow, 1979), 38–45.

164. Emerson, *The Early Years of the Saturday Club*, 148.

165. For Holmes, conversation was the key. As Peter Gibian points out, "Doctor Oliver Wendell Holmes was perhaps the era's key spokesman for such a conversational ideal, and his life and work can tell us a great deal about the ways in which models of talk developed in eighteenth-century England and France would

be transformed to suit the needs of the mobile, diverse, democratic culture of mid-nineteenth-century America." Gibian, *Oliver Wendell Holmes and the Culture of Conversation*, 47.

166. For Holmes's medical accomplishments, see Neille Shoemaker, "The Contemporaneous Medical Reputation of Oliver Wendell Holmes," *New England Quarterly* 26 (1953): 477–493.
167. Edward O. Otis, "The Medical Achievements of Dr. Holmes," *Boston Medical and Surgical Journal* 161 (1909): 953.
168. Emerson, *The Early Years of the Saturday Club*, 147.
169. Quoted in E. E. Brown, *Life of Oliver Wendell Holmes* (Akron, OH: Salfield, 1903), 284.
170. William James to Henry James Jr., February 12, 1868, *Corr.* 1:30.
171. [William James], review of *Rapport sur les progrès et la marche de la physiologie générale en France*, by Claude Bernard, *ECR*, 226.
172. William James to Henry James Jr., June 12, 1869, *Corr.* 1:82.
173. See, for example, the untitled article in *Helena Daily Independent*, February 28, 1898, 2; "About People," *New Outlook*, March 19, 1898, 742; and "Men of Note," *Los Angeles Times*, April 24, 1898, 30. Also see William James's letter to William James Jr., June 18, 1903, *Corr.* 10:271; and Henry James, *Charles W. Eliot: President of Harvard University, 1869–1909*, vol. 1 (Boston: Houghton Mifflin, 1930), 276.
174. William James to Oliver Wendell Holmes Jr., October 9, 1894, *Corr.* 7:554.
175. Quoted in Hoyt, *The Improper Bostonian*, 11–12.
176. For more on James's neurasthenic problems, see Feinstein, *Becoming William James*, 182–205. For James's later recognition of the problems, see William James to Frank Abauzit, June 1, 1904, *Corr.* 10:619.
177. The first to bring the crisis passages to light was Perry in *The Thought and Character of William James*, 1:320–332. Since Perry's discussion, the passages have been considered central to telling the story of James's life and thought. See, for example, *The Writings of William James: A Comprehensive Edition*, ed. John J. McDermott (Chicago: University of Chicago Press, 1977), 6–8.
178. William James, *Diary, 1868–1873*, Houghton Library, Harvard University, bMS Am 1092.9 (4550).
179. James, *Diary, 1868–1873*, Houghton Library, Harvard University, bMS Am 1092.9 (4550).
180. For an interpretation of the communicative dimensions of James's depression and recovery, see Gregory J. Shepherd, "Pragmatism and Tragedy, Communication and Hope: A Summary Story," in *American Pragmatism and Communication Research*, ed. David K. Perry (Mahwah, NJ: Lawrence Erlbaum, 2001), 237–250.
181. The characterization of people from "the street" is James's own. See *Prag.*, 17–18.

Chapter Two. Engaging Science and Society

1. For a case study of the importance of institutional backing in the culture of professionalism, see Bruce Kuklick, *The Rise of American Philosophy: Cambridge, Massachusetts, 1860–1930* (New Haven: Yale University Press, 1977), 80–103.
2. See Howard M. Feinstein, *Becoming William James* (Ithaca, NY: Cornell University Press, 1984), 206–222.
3. William James to Alice James, July 27, 1872, *Corr.* 4:426. For further elaboration on the change in James's spirits, see William James to Henry James Jr., February 13, 1873, *Corr.* 1:192; and Robert D. Richardson, *William James in the Maelstrom of American Modernism* (Boston: Houghton Mifflin, 2006), 146–147.
4. William James to Alice James, July 27, 1872, *Corr.* 4:426.
5. Richardson, *William James in the Maelstrom*, 141.
6. See, for example, Richardson, *William James in the Maelstrom*, 117–147.
7. For more on the concept of rhetorical invention, see Bruce E. Gronbeck, "Rhetorical Invention in the Regency Crisis Pamphlets," *Quarterly Journal of Speech* 58 (1972): 418–430; Karen Burke LeFevre, *Invention as a Social Act* (Carbondale: Southern Illinois University Press, 1987); Richard E. Young and Yameng Liu, eds., *Landmark Essays on Rhetorical Invention in Writing* (Davis, CA: Hermagoras Press, 1994); Walter Jost and Wendy Olmsted, eds., *Rhetorical Invention & Religious Inquiry: New Perspectives* (New Haven: Yale University Press, 2000); and Stephen R. Yarbrough, *Inventive Intercourse: From Rhetorical Conflict to the Ethical Creation of Novel Truth* (Carbondale: Southern Illinois University Press, 2006).
8. For more on the science, rhetoric, and invention of disciplinary power, see Herbert W. Simons, ed., *Rhetoric in the Human Sciences* (London: Sage, 1989).
9. For more on the rhetoric of inquiry, particularly as it relates to modern science, see John S. Nelson, Allan Megill, and Donald N. McCloskey, eds., *The Rhetoric of the Human Sciences: Language and Argument in Scholarship and Public Affairs* (Madison: University of Wisconsin Press, 1987).
10. In one letter, James reported earning $5 for a review. In another, he reported earning $10. His brother Henry reported earning upwards of $50 for a review, so it is likely that William earned above $10 at various times, but his correspondence does not report amounts that high. See William James to Henry James Jr., March 22, 1869, *Corr.* 1:62; and William James to Henry James Jr., February 13, 1873, *Corr.* 1:190.
11. [William James], review of *The Bones, Ligaments, and Muscles of the Domestic Cat*, by Henry S. Williams, *Nation* 21 (October 14, 1875); reprinted in *ECR*, 314–315.
12. For more on the notion of public knowledge and its relation to rhetoric, see Lloyd F. Bitzer, "Rhetoric and Public Knowledge," in *Rhetoric, Philosophy, and Literature:*

An Exploration, ed. Don M. Burks (West Lafayette, IN: Purdue University Press, 1978), 67–93; and Michael Calvin McGee and Martha Anne Martin, "Public Knowledge and Ideological Argumentation," *Communication Monographs* 50 (1983): 47–65.

13. See Ignas K. Skrupskelis, introduction to *ML*, xxxviii; and Linda Simon, introduction to *Corr.* 5:xxi.
14. Ralph Barton Perry, *The Thought and Character of William James*, vol. 1 (New York: Little, Brown, 1935), 378. See also Gay Wilson Allen, *William James: A Biography* (New York: Viking Press, 1967), 224.
15. Paul Jerome Croce, "Physiology as the Antechamber to Metaphysics: The Young William James's Hope for a Philosophical Psychology," *History of Psychology* 2 (1999): 302–323.
16. Croce, "Physiology as the Antechamber to Metaphysics," 302.
17. For an overview of the changes that led to the new print culture, see Sheila McVey, "Nineteenth Century America: Publishing in a Developing Country," *Annals of the American Academy of Political and Social Science* 421 (1975): 67–80; and Susan Belasco Smith and Kenneth M. Price, "Introduction: Periodical Literature in Social and Historical Context," in *Periodical Literature in Nineteenth-Century America*, ed. Kenneth M. Price and Susan Belasco Smith (Charlottesville: University Press of Virginia, 1995), 3–16.
18. See Janice A. Radway, "Learned and Literary Print Cultures in an Age of Professionalization and Diversification," in *A History of the Book in America*, vol. 4, ed. Carl F. Kaestle and Janice A. Radway (Chapel Hill: University of North Carolina Press, 2009), 197–233. Also see Marcel Chatkowski LaFollette, "Crafting a Communications Infrastructure: Scientific and Technical Publishing in the United States," in Kaestle and Radway, *A History of the Book in America*, 4:234–259.
19. Eric Lupfer, "The Business of American Magazines," in *A History of the Book in America*, vol. 3, ed. Scott E. Casper, Jeffrey D. Groves, Stephen W. Nissenbaum, and Michael Winship (Chapel Hill: University of North Carolina Press, 2007), 249.
20. Margaret Fuller, *Papers on Literature and Art* (New York: Fowler and Wells, 1852), 137–138.
21. Patricia Okker, *Social Stories: The Magazine Novel in Nineteenth-Century America* (Charlottesville: University of Virginia Press, 2003), 28. Also see Isabell Lehuu, *Carnival on the Page: Popular Print Media in Antebellum America* (Chapel Hill: University of North Carolina Press, 2000); and Louise Henson, Geoffrey Cantor, Gowan Dawson, Richard Noakes, Sally Shuttleworth, and Jonathan R. Topham, eds., *Culture and Science in the Nineteenth-Century Media* (Burlington, VT: Ashgate, 2004).
22. Lupfer, "The Business of American Magazines," 251.
23. See Ronald J. Zboray, *A Fictive People: Antebellum Economic Development and the American Reading Public* (New York: Oxford University Press, 1993), especially 83–109.

24. For a detailed discussion of technological advancements that changed the literary marketplace, see Michael Winship, "Manufacturing and Book Production," in Casper et al., *A History of the Book in America*, 3:40–69. For a discussion of distribution practices, see Michael Winship, "The National Book Trade System: Distribution and Trade," in Casper et al., *A History of the Book in America*, 3:117–130.
25. In general, see Sarah Wadsworth, *In the Company of Books: Literature and Its "Classes" in Nineteenth-Century America* (Amherst: University of Massachusetts Press, 2006).
26. Lupfer, "The Business of American Magazines," 255.
27. Belasco, "The Cultural Work of National Magazines," in Casper et al., *A History of the Book in America*, 3:267.
28. For an overview of the tension between William and Henry regarding Henry's early literary success, see Gerald Myers's introduction to *Corr.* 1:xliv–l.
29. Croce, "Physiology as the Antechamber to Metaphysics," 303.
30. [William James], review of *Lectures on the Elements of Comparative Anatomy*, by Thomas Huxley, *North American Review* 100 (January 1865); reprinted in *ECR*, 197–205.
31. In general, see Paul White, *Thomas Huxley: Making the "Man of Science"* (Cambridge: Cambridge University Press, 2003).
32. [James], review of *Lectures on the Elements of Comparative Anatomy*, *ECR*, 197.
33. [James], review of *Lectures on the Elements of Comparative Anatomy*, *ECR*, 198.
34. James's participation in the Thayer Expedition is discussed in chapter 1.
35. [William James], review of *The Variation of Animals and Plants under Domestication*, by Charles Darwin, *North American Review* 107 (July 1868); reprinted in *ECR*, 234–235.
36. [William James], "The Progress of Anthropology," *Nation* 6 (February 6, 1868); reprinted in *ECR*, 217–218.
37. [William James], review of *Responsibility in Mental Disease*, by Henry Maudsley, *Atlantic Monthly* 34 (September 1874); reprinted in *ECR*, 283.
38. [William James], "Recent Works on Mental Hygiene," *Nation* 19 (July 16, 1874); reprinted in *ECR*, 277.
39. For more on the rhetorical construction of an imagined audience or auditor, see Edwin Black, "The Second Persona," *Quarterly Journal of Speech* 56 (1970): 109–119.
40. [William James], "Herbert Spencer's Data of Ethics," *Nation* 29 (September 11, 1879); reprinted in *ECR*, 348.
41. For an excellent discussion of James's interactions with the new "spaces of knowledge" of the late nineteenth century, see Francesca Bordogna, *William James at*

the Boundaries: Philosophy, Science, and the Geography of Knowledge (Chicago: University of Chicago Press, 2008).

42. [James], review of *Responsibility in Mental Disease, ECR*, 283.
43. [James], "Herbert Spencer's Data of Ethics," *ECR*, 352–353.
44. [William James], "The Unseen Universe," *Nation* 20 (May 27, 1875); reprinted in *ECR*, 294.
45. James's interest in generating audience participation speaks to Johanna Hartelius's distinction between experts that demand deference and invitational experts, who operate through broad identification with general audiences and "offer themselves as the alternative to an established form of expertise." E. Johanna Hartelius, *The Rhetoric of Expertise* (Lanham, MD: Lexington Books, 2011), 25.
46. [William James], review of *Rapport sur les progrès et la marche de la physiologie générale en France*, by Claude Bernard, *North American Review* 107 (July 1868); reprinted in *ECR*, 227.
47. [William James], review of *Grundzüge der physiologischen Psychologie*, by Wilhelm Wundt, *North American Review* 121 (July 1875); reprinted in *ECR*, 296.
48. For more on god terms, see Kenneth Burke, *A Grammar of Motives* (Berkeley: University of California Press, 1969), 355–356.
49. For more on the turn to expert discourse, see Kenneth Cmiel, *Democratic Eloquence: The Fight over Popular Speech in Nineteenth-Century America* (New York: William Morrow, 1990), particularly 148–175.
50. [James], "The Progress of Anthropology," *ECR*, 218.
51. [James], review of *Lectures on the Elements of Comparative Anatomy*, *ECR*, 199.
52. [William James], review of *The Borderlands of Insanity*, by Andrew Wynter, *Nation* 21 (November 18, 1875); reprinted in *ECR*, 316.
53. [William James], "Bain and Renouvier," *Nation* 22 (June 8, 1876); reprinted in *ECR*, 325.
54. [William James], review of *Problems of Life and Mind*, by George Henry Lewes, *Atlantic Monthly* 36 (September 1875); reprinted in *ECR*, 303.
55. [James], review of *The Variation of Animals and Plants under Domestication*, by Charles Darwin, *ECR*, 239.
56. [William James], review of *L'Anthropologie*, by Paul Topinard, *Nation* 22 (March 16, 1876); reprinted in *ECR*, 321.
57. [William James], "Clifford's Lectures and Essays," *Nation* 29 (November 6, 1879); reprinted in *ECR*, 357.
58. [William James], "The Mind and the Brain," *Nation* 24 (June 14, 1877); reprinted in *ECR*, 337.
59. In general, see Robert H. Wiebe, *The Search for Order, 1877–1920* (New York: Hill and Wang, 1967).
60. William James to Henry James Jr., September 26, 1867, *Corr.* 1:18.

61. For more on style in James's work, see Frederick J. Ruf, *The Creation of Chaos: William James and the Stylistic Making of a Disorderly World* (Albany: State University of New York Press, 1991).

62. Perhaps the most notable account of the way rhetoric builds bridges and erects barriers at the same time can be found in Kenneth Burke, *Language as Symbolic Action: Essays on Life, Literature, and Method* (Berkeley: University of California Press, 1966), 44–62. For a discussion of Burke's debt to James in this regard, see Paul Stob, "'Terministic Screens,' Social Constructionism, and the Language of Experience: Kenneth Burke's Utilization of William James," *Philosophy and Rhetoric* 41 (2008): 130–152.

63. [William James], review of *Voltaire*, by John Morley, *Atlantic Monthly* 30 (November 1872); reprinted in *ECR*, 263–264.

64. [William James], review of *The Anesthetic Revelation*, by Benjamin Paul Blood, *Atlantic Monthly* 34 (November 1874); reprinted in *ECR*, 287–288.

65. [William James], "Renouvier's Contribution to *La Critique Philosophique*," *Nation* 16 (February 6, 1873); reprinted in *ECR*, 266.

66. [James], review of *The Variation of Animals and Plants under Domestication*, *ECR*, 229.

67. [William James], review of *Principles of Mental Physiology*, by William B. Carpenter, *Atlantic Monthly* 34 (October 1874); reprinted in *ECR*, 275.

68. [William James], review of *The Physiology of the Circulation in Plants, in the Lower Animals, and in Man*, by J. Bell Pettigrew, *Nation* 19 (July 23, 1874); reprinted in *ECR*, 279.

69. [William James], "Renan's Dialogues," *Nation* 23 (August 3, 1876); reprinted in *ECR*, 327.

70. [James], "Clifford's Lectures and Essays," *ECR*, 360–361.

71. [James], review of *The Anesthetic Revelation*, *ECR*, 287.

72. [James], review of *Grundzüge der physiologischen Psychologie*, *ECR*, 298.

73. [William James], review of *Der moderne Pessimismus*, by Edmund Pfleiderer, *Nation* 21 (October 7, 1875), reprinted in *ECR*, 314; [William James], review of *The Theory of Color in Its Relation to Art and Art-Industry*, by Wilhelm von Bezold, *Nation* 23 (November 9, 1876), reprinted in *ECR*, 331; and [William James], review of *A Defence of Philosophic Doubt*, by Arthur James Balfour, *Nation* 29 (October 23, 1879), reprinted in *ECR*, 354.

74. [William James], review of *The Physiology of Mind*, by Henry Maudsley, *Nation* 24 (June 14, 1877), reprinted in *ECR*, 334; and [William James], review of *The Jukes*, by Richard L. Dugdale, *Atlantic Monthly* 41 (March 1878), reprinted in *ECR*, 347.

75. [William James], review of *Contributions to Mental Pathology*, by Isaac Ray, *Atlantic Monthly* 31 (June 1873); reprinted in *ECR*, 267.

76. [William James], review of *Women's Suffrage*, by Horace Bushnell, and *The Subjection of Women*, by John Stuart Mill, *North American Review* 109 (October 1869); reprinted in *ECR*, 246.
77. [James], review of *Women's Suffrage, ECR*, 250.
78. [James], review of *The Subjection of Women, ECR*, 246.
79. For the division between Chauncey Wright and "common people," see James's unpublished "Against Nihilism," Houghton Library, Harvard University, bMS Am 1092.9 (4422).
80. One of the most telling debates between James and Peirce regarding the idea of "popular philosophy" occurred after James published a tribute to Chauncey Wright. For James's tribute, see [William James], "Chauncey Wright," *Nation* 21 (September 23, 1875), 194; reprinted in *ECR*, 15–17. For Peirce's response, see Charles Sanders Peirce to William James, November 21, 1875, *Corr.* 4:523–524.
81. William James to Henry James Jr., February 12, 1868, *Corr.* 1:30–31.
82. William James to Henry James Jr., August 24, 1872, *Corr.* 1:166.
83. William James to Henry James Jr., October 10, 1872, *Corr.* 1:172.
84. William James to Henry James Jr., November 24, 1872, *Corr.* 1:176.
85. William James to Henry James Jr., July 5, 1876, *Corr.* 1:267.
86. William James to Henry James Jr., October 25, 1902, *Corr.* 3:220.
87. William James to Henry James Jr., October 22, 1905, *Corr.* 3:301.
88. William James to Henry James Jr., May 4, 1907, *Corr.* 3:338.
89. See Paul Fisher, *House of Wits: An Intimate Portrait of the James Family* (New York: Henry Holt, 2008), 174–175.
90. See David E. Shi, *Facing Facts: Realism in American Thought and Culture, 1850–1920* (New York: Oxford University Press, 1995), 275–302.
91. For James's discussion of the pressure to publish more formal academic work, see his letter to George Croom Robertson, January 1878, *Corr.* 5:1.
92. James was elected to the Harvard Natural History Society on December 2, 1875. On December 7, he lectured on the dissection of a three-month-old fetus. He also lectured to the society on December 21, 1875, on an unidentified machine invented by an Austrian physician; on February 1, 1876, he lectured on the causes of vertigo; and on February 20, 1877, he lectured on the hypnotism of frogs. See *ML*, xxvi.
93. See *ML*, xxvi.
94. Coverage of the Sanders Theater lecture did appear in the *Boston Daily Advertiser*, March 2, 1877.
95. In general, see Burton J. Bledstein, "Noah Porter versus William Graham Sumner," *Church History* 43 (1974): 340–350. Also see Richard Hofstadter, *Social Darwinism in American Thought* (Boston: Beacon Press, 1955), 51–66. For a more general view of the shift in modern higher education, see Julie A. Reuben,

The Making of the Modern University: Intellectual Transformation and the Marginalization of Morality (Chicago: University of Chicago Press, 1996).

96. Ultimately, Porter's and Sumner's positions proved irreconcilable. See John D. Heyl and Barbara S. Heyl, "The Sumner-Porter Controversy at Yale: Pre-paradigmatic Sociology and Institutional Crisis," *Sociological Inquiry* 46 (1976): 41–49.
97. Hugh Hawkins, *Pioneer: A History of Johns Hopkins University, 1874–1889* (Ithaca, NY: Cornell University Press, 1960), 71.
98. See Hawkins, *Pioneer*, 293–315.
99. James originally proposed the course in a letter to Harvard president Charles William Eliot on December 2, 1875, *Corr.* 4:527–528. For some of James's lecture notes from the course, see *ML*, 126–129.
100. See Richardson, *William James in the Maelstrom*, 178–179.
101. The evidence of Bowen's attempt to stop James from using Spencer appears primarily in George Herbert Palmer to William James, December 25, 1900, *Corr.* 9:393–396.
102. Francis Bowen, *Modern Philosophy, From Descartes to Schopenhauer and Hartmann* (New York: Scribner, Armstrong, 1877), vi–vii. Also see Bowen's review of *On the Origin of Species by Means of Natural Selection*, by Charles Darwin, *North American Review* 90 (1860): 474–506; and Francis Bowen, *Gleanings from A Literary Life, 1838–1880* (New York: Charles Scribner's Sons, 1880).
103. Quoted in Perry, *The Thought and Character of William James,* 1:476.
104. William James to Daniel Coit Gilman, April 23, 1877, *Corr.* 4:557–558.
105. James spoke at 4:00 P.M. from February 11 to February 22 to an audience of approximately sixty people and was paid $500. See James and Gilman's correspondence of December 30, 1877, *Corr.* 4:588–589; January 4, 1878, *Corr.* 5:2; January 7, 1878, *Corr.* 5:2; and January 11, 1878, *Corr.* 5:547.
106. *ML*, 448, note 3.3.
107. *ML*, 449, note 3.3.
108. Quoted in Ralph Barton Perry, *The Thought and Character of William James*, vol. 2 (New York: Little, Brown, 1935), 27.
109. *ML*, 451, note 16.26.
110. James explained to Gilman that President Eliot had told him that he would eventually earn a professorship in philosophy at Harvard. See William James to Daniel Coit Gilman, January 18, 1879, *Corr.* 5:35–36.
111. William James to Augustus Lowell, May 19, 1878, *Corr.* 5:11–12.
112. "The Lowell Institute," *Boston Daily Advertiser*, October 16, 1878, D.
113. "Local Miscellany," *Boston Daily Advertiser*, October 23, 1878, 1.
114. "Letter from Boston," *Worchester Daily Spy*, October 29, 1878, 2.

115. See "Lowell and Baltimore Lectures," Houghton Library, Harvard University, bMS Am 1092.9 (4395–4401). The drafts and outlines are reprinted in *ML*, 3–43.

116. See *ML*, 452, note 16.26.

117. Bordogna, *William James at the Boundaries*, 69.

118. *ML*, 30–31.

119. *ML*, 3.

120. *ML*, 32.

121. *ML*, 32.

122. *ML*, 4.

123. See, for example, [James], review of *Responsibility in Mental Disease*, *ECR*, 283; and [James], review of *Grundzüge der physiologischen Psychologie*, *ECR*, 296.

124. *ML*, 3.

125. For more on the idea of intellectual translation, see Richard Posner, *Public Intellectuals: A Study of Decline* (Cambridge: Harvard University Press, 2001), 20–21.

126. *ML*, 3.

127. *ML*, 31.

128. *ML*, 30.

129. *ML*, 4.

130. *ML*, 5.

131. See, for example, [James], review of *The Variation of Animals and Plants under Domestication*, *ECR*, 234–235; and [James], review of *Lectures on the Elements of Comparative Anatomy*, *ECR*, 198.

132. *ML*, 23.

133. *ML*, 4.

134. *ML*, 6.

135. See, for example, James's discussion of "Attention" in *PP* 1:380–433.

136. *ML*, 6.

137. See, for example, [James], review of *Responsibility in Mental Disease*, *ECR*, 282–284; [James], "The Unseen Universe," *ECR*, 290–294; and [James], "Bain and Renouvier," *ECR*, 321–326.

138. *ML*, 9.

139. *ML*, 37.

140. *ML*, 30.

141. For example: "If this be a moral world, there are cases in which any indecision about its being so must be death to the soul. . . . If our choice be truly free, then the only possible way of getting at that truth is by the exercise of the freedom which it implies." To be alive, we must "voluntarily take the alternative of faith." [James], "Bain and Renouvier," *ECR*, 326.

142. *ML*, 32.

Chapter Three. Talking to Teachers

1. William James to Augustus Lowell, February 27, 1879, *Corr.* 5:42.
2. Henry Holt to William James, June 8, 1878, *Corr.* 5:14.
3. "Just Odds and Ends," *Macon Weekly Telegraph*, March 25, 1900, 12; Untitled, *Bismarck Daily Tribune*, March 11, 1891, 2; "The New Psychology," *Daily Picayune*, July 12, 1891, 12.
4. James McKeen Cattell, "Our Psychological Association and Research," *Science* 45 (1917): 276.
5. Quoted in Gerard E. Myers, *William James: His Life and Thought* (New Haven: Yale University Press, 1986), 485.
6. William Dean Howells, "Editor's Study," *Harper's New Monthly Magazine* 83 (1891): 314.
7. [George Santayana], "James's Psychology," *Atlantic Monthly* 67 (1891): 556.
8. William James to Henry James Jr., August 22, 1890, *Corr.* 2:146.
9. Between 1878 and 1890, James delivered lectures in places that included the Harvard Natural History Society; the Unitarian Ministers' Institute in Princeton, Massachusetts; the Summer School of Philosophy in Concord, Massachusetts; the Harvard Total Abstinence League; and the New England Normal School Teachers' Association in Boston.
10. See George Cotkin, *William James, Public Philosopher* (Urbana: University of Illinois Press, 1989), 73.
11. For an overview of the success of the book, see Gerald E. Myers, introduction to *TT*, xi–xxvii.
12. Some of the best evidence for the book's popularity appears in the ledgers of Longmans, Green, publisher of the British edition. Between 1899 and 1910, the year of James's death, Longmans recorded sales of almost 25,000 copies. Because the book was remarkably more popular at home than abroad, the 25,000 copies sold in England were likely dwarfed by the number of copies sold in America. For details, see *TT*, 254–255.
13. See the special section "William James's *Talks to Teachers:* 100 Years of Advice," which appeared in the journal *Teaching of Psychology.* The articles in the special section were as follows: Charles L. Brewer, "William James's Talks about Teaching," *Teaching of Psychology* 30 (2003): 34–38; Randall D. Wight, "More Than Mere Weather: James's Talks to Students about Life," *Teaching of Psychology* 30 (2003): 38–40; Wilbert J. McKeachie, "William James's Talks to Teachers (1899) and McKeachie's Teaching Tips (1999)," *Teaching of Psychology* 30 (2003): 40–43; and James H. Korn, "The Teaching Spirit of William James," *Teaching of Psychology* 30 (2003): 44–45.

14. Linda Simon, *Genuine Reality: A Life of William James* (New York: Harcourt Brace, 1998), 264.
15. Myers, *William James*, 11.
16. Burke writes: "You persuade a man only insofar as you can talk his language by speech, gesture, tonality, order, image, attitude, idea, *identifying* your ways with his. . . . The rhetorician may have to change an audience's opinion in one respect; but he can succeed only insofar as he yields to that audience's opinions in other respects." Kenneth Burke, *A Rhetoric of Motives* (Berkeley: University of California Press, 1969), 55–56.
17. James Gilbert, *Designing the Industrial State: The Intellectual Pursuit of Collectivism in America, 1880–1940* (Chicago: Quadrangle Books, 1972), 16.
18. In general, see Daniel T. Rodgers, *The Work Ethic in Industrial America, 1850–1920* (Chicago: University of Chicago Press, 1978).
19. Robert H. Wiebe, *The Search for Order, 1877–1920* (New York: Hill and Wang, 1967), 111–132.
20. The list comes from Burton J. Bledstein, *The Culture of Professionalism: The Middle Class and the Development of Higher Education in America* (New York: W. W. Norton, 1978), 85.
21. In general, see Joseph F. Kett, *The Pursuit of Knowledge Under Difficulties: From Self-Improvement to Adult Education in America, 1750–1990* (Stanford: Stanford University Press, 1994). Also see Bruce A. Kimball, *The "True Professional Ideal" in America: A History* (Lanham, MD: Rowman and Littlefield, 1995); and Alexandra Oleson and John Voss, eds., *The Organization of Knowledge in Modern America, 1860–1920* (Baltimore: Johns Hopkins University Press, 1979).
22. Eliot Freidson, *Professional Powers: A Study of the Institutionalization of Formal Knowledge* (Chicago: University of Chicago Press, 1986), 32–33.
23. For an overview of the tension between popular periodicals and professional journals, see David D. Hall, "Erudition and Learned Culture," in *A History of the Book in America*, vol. 3, ed. Scott E. Casper, Jeffrey D. Groves, Stephen W. Nissenbaum, and Michael Winship (Chapel Hill: University of North Carolina Press, 2007), 347–360. Also see Janice A. Radway, "Learned and Literary Print Cultures in an Age of Professionalization and Diversification," in *A History of the Book in America*, vol. 4, ed. Carl F. Kaestle and Janice A. Radway (Chapel Hill: University of North Carolina Press, 2009), 197–233.
24. Wiebe, *The Search for Order*, 117.
25. Kett, *The Pursuit of Knowledge Under Difficulties*, 164.
26. For an overview of the struggles to modernize teaching, see Christopher J. Lucas, *Teacher Education in America: Reform Agendas for the Twenty-First Century* (New York: St. Martin's Press, 1997), 29–47.
27. Albert Bushnell Hart, "The Teacher as Professional Expert," *School Review* 1 (1893): 4–14.

28. Walter Ballou Jacobs, "The Training of Teachers for Secondary Schools," *School Review* 5 (1897): 386.
29. E. E. Higbee, "The Training of Teachers," *Science* 9 (1887): 72.
30. Henry A. Hayes, "Aims and Methods in Teachers' Institutes," *Southern Educational Journal* 10 (1897): 154.
31. Wiebe, *The Search for Order*, 147.
32. Thomas Jefferson Morgan, *Studies in Pedagogy* (Boston: Silver, Burdett, 1892), 335, 337–338.
33. Vernon C. Hall, "Educational Psychology from 1890 to 1920," in *Educational Psychology: A Century of Contributions*, ed. Barry J. Zimmerman and Dale H. Schunk (Mahwah, NJ: Lawrence Erlbaum Associates, 2003), 3.
34. In 1881, for example, the *Daily Inter Ocean* published an article that summarized the work of a German scientist and educator who deemed pedagogy "but a mere part of psychology." This view, the paper continued, should become the view of educators in the United States. See "Pedagogy as a Science," *Daily Inter Ocean*, May 20, 1881, 10.
35. James McKeen Cattell, "The Progress of Psychology," *Popular Science Monthly* 43 (October 1893): 783–784.
36. Daniel J. Wilson, *Science, Community, and the Transformation of American Philosophy, 1860–1930* (Chicago: University of Chicago Press, 1990), 76.
37. C. H. Thurber, review of *Talks to Teachers on Psychology and to Students on Some of Life's Ideals*, by William James, *School Review* 7 (1899): 434–435.
38. For an overview, see Hall, "Educational Psychology from 1890 to 1920," 3–39.
39. "Pedagogy," *Boston Daily Advertiser*, April 25, 1881, 1.
40. For a discussion of James's influence on the formation of educational psychology, see Frank Pajares, "William James: Our Father Who Begat Us," in Zimmerman and Schunk, *Educational Psychology*, 41–64.
41. William James to Theodore Flournoy, August 30, 1896, *Corr.* 8:190–191.
42. Simon, *Genuine Reality*, 264.
43. In reality, Harvard was following the lead of other universities. For a summary of the rise of pedagogy positions at American universities, see the untitled article in *Science* 14 (1889): 26.
44. William James to Paul Henry Hanus, April 6, 1891, *Corr.* 7:148.
45. See *TT*, 234.
46. Francis Albert Christie to William James, November 6, 1891, *Corr.* 7:585; and Mary Elizabeth Litchfield to William James, November 16, 1891, *Corr.* 7:223.
47. The first report by John Pierce appeared in the issue of November 19, 1891, and the final report appeared in the issue of January 21, 1892. The reports are reprinted in *TT*, 216–217.
48. See, for example, *Corr.* 7:518–519, 523.

49. To my knowledge, *William James and the Art of Popular Statement* is the first published work to verify the Brooklyn Institute iteration of the lectures. Materials recently made available on Google Books have made this verification possible. For announcements of the lectures, see "Notes from the Field," *Pratt Institute Monthly* 3 (1894): 37. For confirmation that James delivered the lectures, see Franklin W. Hooper, "The Brooklyn Institute of Arts and Sciences," in *Lend a Hand: A Record of Progress* 15 (1895): 201.
50. The dates and topics for the lectures were as follows: October 6, "Mind and Environment, Innate Mental Structure, Interests and Impulses"; October 13, "Habit and Character"; October 27, "Association and Memory"; November 3, "Attention"; November 10, "Conception and Reason"; November 17, "The Will." The list can be found in *The Seventh Year Book of the Brooklyn Institute of Arts and Sciences, 1894–5* (Brooklyn: Brooklyn Institute of Arts and Sciences, 1895), 179, 253.
51. See "The Columbian Reading Union," *Catholic World* 60 (1894): 857.
52. William James to Henry James Jr., December 12, 1894, *Corr.* 2:331.
53. The material is actually spread across two notebooks. See "Psychology for Teachers," Houghton Library, Harvard University, bMS Am 1092.9 (4536 and 4537).
54. William James to Rosina Hubley Emmet, July 16, 1895, *Corr.* 8:55. Plans for his summer tour took place in January and February 1895. See William James to G. B. Turnbull, February 6, 1895, in *TT*, 236.
55. See *Report of the Board of Education of the State of Connecticut to the Governor* (Hartford: Case, Lockwood & Brainard, 1896), 42–55.
56. William James to Rosina Hubley Emmet, July 16, 1895, *Corr.* 8:55.
57. William James to Sarah Wyman Whitman, July 18, 1895, *Corr.* 8:57.
58. William James to Rosina Hubley Emmet, July 16, 1895, *Corr.* 8:55.
59. William James to Alice Howe Gibbens James, July 17, 1895, *Corr.* 8:569.
60. William James to Henry James III, July 22, 1895, *Corr.* 8:58–59.
61. See Frederick J. Down Scott, "William James's 1895 Visit to Colorado," *San Jose Studies* 5 (1979): 33–38.
62. William James to Alice Howe Gibbens James, August 1, 1895, *Corr.* 8:59.
63. William James to Alice Howe Gibbens James, August 1, 1895, *Corr.* 8:59.
64. William James to Alice Howe Gibbens James, August 4, 1895, *Corr.* 8:60–61.
65. William James to Alice Howe Gibbens James, August 6, 1895, *Corr.* 8:62. James also reflected on his connection to the community in a letter to his brother Henry, August 6, 1895, *Corr.* 2:372–373.
66. William James to Henry James Jr., August 6, 1895, *Corr.* 2:372–373.
67. William James to Alice Howe Gibbens James, August 8, 1895, *Corr.* 8:66. He repeated the sentiment in other letters. See, for example, William James to Rosina Hubley Emmet, August 11, 1895, *Corr.* 8:571; and William James to Theodore Flournoy, August 13, 1895, *Corr.* 8:71.

68. William James to Alice Howe Gibbens James, August 9, 1895, *Corr.* 8:67.
69. William James to Alice Howe Gibbens James, August 8, 1895, *Corr.* 8:65.
70. See, for example, William James to Henry William Rankin, June 21, 1896, *Corr.* 8:155–156; and William James to Charles William Eliot, June 22, 1896, *Corr.* 8:157.
71. William James to Alice Howe Gibbens James, July 17, 1896, *Corr.* 8:167.
72. William James to Alice Howe Gibbens James, July 16, 1896, *Corr.* 8:166–167.
73. William James to Alice Howe Gibbens James, July 17, 1896, *Corr.* 8:167.
74. William James to Alice Howe Gibbens James, July 19, 1896, *Corr.* 8:169.
75. See *TT*, 97–98.
76. William James to Alice Howe Gibbens James, July 23, 1896, *Corr.* 8:169.
77. William James to Alice Howe Gibbens James, July 17, 1896, *Corr.* 8:168.
78. William James to Henry James Jr., August 15, 1896, *Corr.* 2:406.
79. William James to Alice Howe Gibbens James, July 23, 1896, *Corr.* 8:170.
80. William James to Alice Howe Gibbens James, July 29, 1896, *Corr.* 8:177.
81. William James to Henry James Jr., August 15, 1896, *Corr.* 2:406.
82. William James to Alice Howe Gibbens James, September 4, 1896, *Corr.* 8:199–200.
83. William James to Richard Hodgson, August 28, 1896, *Corr.* 8:188.
84. William James to Alice Howe Gibbens James, September 4, 1896, *Corr.* 8:199–200. Also see William James to Henry James Jr., September 6, 1896, *Corr.* 2:410.
85. William James to Theodore Flournoy, August 30, 1896, *Corr.* 8:190–191.
86. William James to Alice Howe Gibbens James, September 2, 1896, *Corr.* 8:585.
87. William James to Alice Howe Gibbens James, July 10, 1897, *Corr.* 8:283.
88. William James to Alice Howe Gibbens James, July 13, 1897, *Corr.* 8:600.
89. William James to Alice Howe Gibbens James, October 19, 1898, *Corr.* 8:620.
90. William James to George Holmes Howison, January 14, 1897, *Corr.* 8:217.
91. See, for example, William James to George Holmes Howison, April 5, 1897, *Corr.* 8:255–257; William James to George Holmes Howison, July 2, 1897, *Corr.* 8:282; and William James to George Holmes Howison, October 27, 1897, *Corr.* 8:319.
92. William James to George Holmes Howison, January 14, 1897, *Corr.* 8:217.
93. See William James to George Holmes Howison, April 16, 1898, *Corr.* 8:355–356.
94. William James to George Holmes Howison, April 5, 1897, *Corr.* 8:255–257.
95. See *TT*, 241–242.
96. "Innovation for Teachers," *San Francisco Call*, April 16, 1898, 9.
97. William James to Alice Howe Gibbens James, September 15, 1898, *Corr.* 8:436.
98. See Frederick J. Down Scott, "William James's 1898 Visit to California," *San Jose Studies* 3 (1977): 7–22.

99. William James to Alice Howe Gibbens James, September 12, 1898, *Corr.* 8:618.
100. William James to Alice Howe Gibbens James, September 15, 1898, *Corr.* 8:436.
101. William James to Henry James Jr., September 22, 1898, *Corr.* 3:40–41.
102. William James to Henry James Jr., September 22, 1898, *Corr.* 3:40–41.
103. Quoted in *TT*, 245. Also see William James to Alice Howe Gibbens James, October 19, 1898, *Corr.* 8:620.
104. See *TT*, 250.
105. William James to Henry Holt, November 5, 1898, *Corr.* 8:450.
106. Quoted in *TT*, 246.
107. For an overview, see *TT*, 250–266.
108. In general, see *TT*, 244–250.
109. Quoted in *TT*, 251.
110. Review of *Talks to Teachers on Psychology and to Students on Some of Life's Ideals*, by William James, *Boston Evening Transcript*, July 5, 1899, 12.
111. Thurber, review of *Talks to Teachers on Psychology and to Students on Some of Life's Ideals*.
112. Henry Holt to William James, January 9, 1900, *Corr.* 9:587.
113. See Henry Holt to William James, July 18, 1900, *Corr.* 9:602; Henry Holt to William James, September 4, 1900, *Corr.* 9:607; Henry Holt to William James, October 8, 1900, *Corr.* 9:612.
114. Henry Holt to William James, February 11, 1902, *Corr.* 10:581.
115. *Twelfth Biennial Report of the Superintendent of Public Instruction of the State of Colorado* (Denver: Smith-Brooks Printing, 1900), 622.
116. *Report of the Superintendent of Public Instruction of the Commonwealth of Pennsylvania for the Year Ending June 3, 1901* (Philadelphia: William Stanley Ray, 1901), 143.
117. William James to Frances Rollins Morse, December 23, 1899, *Corr.* 9:104.
118. William James to Henry Lee Higginson, June 5, 1901, *Corr.* 9:497.
119. See William James to Katharine Outram Rodgers, May 1, 1903, *Corr.* 10:242.
120. See William James to Alice Howe Gibbens James, September 2, 1896, *Corr.* 8:585.
121. See William James to Henry James Jr., September 25, 1898, *Corr.* 3:42.
122. *TT*, 3.
123. *TT*, 4.
124. See Walter J. Ong, *Orality and Literacy: The Technologizing of the World* (London: Routledge, 1982), 31–76; and Walter J. Ong, *Rhetoric, Romance, and Technology: Studies in the Interaction of Expression and Culture* (Ithaca, NY: Cornell University Press, 1971), 23–47. It should be noted that Ong used "oral residue" to refer more to the discourse of entire cultures than to the discourse of individual

writers. Nevertheless, the phrase aptly characterizes what readers experienced when they picked up James's work.

125. For a discussion of primary versus secondary orality, see Ong, *Rhetoric, Romance, and Technology*, 284–303. Also see Kathleen E. Welch, *Electric Rhetoric: Classical Rhetoric, Oralism, and a New Literacy* (Cambridge: MIT Press, 1999).
126. Carroll C. Arnold, "Oral Rhetoric, Rhetoric, and Literature," *Philosophy & Rhetoric* 1 (1968): 194.
127. Arnold, "Oral Rhetoric, Rhetoric, and Literature," 199.
128. *TT*, 108.
129. For various discussions of the elements of oral style, see Robert J. Connors, "Greek Rhetoric and the Transition from Orality," *Philosophy & Rhetoric* 19 (1986): 38–65; Timothy W. Crusius, "Orality in Kenneth Burke's Dialectic," *Philosophy & Rhetoric* 21 (1988): 116–130; Michael Gagarin, "The Orality of Greek Oratory," in *Signs of Orality: The Oral Tradition and Its Influence in the Greek and Roman World*, ed. E. Anne Mackay (Leiden, the Netherlands: Brill, 1999), 163–180; and Brett Lunceford, "The Science of Orality: Implications for Rhetorical Theory," *Review of Communication* 7 (2007): 83–102.
130. *TT*, 19.
131. *TT*, 27.
132. *TT*, 61–62.
133. See, for example, Ong, *Rhetoric, Romance, and Technology*, 23–47.
134. *TT*, 16.
135. *TT*, 28.
136. *TT*, 38.
137. *TT*, 56.
138. *TT*, 63.
139. *TT*, 47.
140. *TT*, 53.
141. In general, see Frederick J. Ruf, *The Creation of Chaos: William James and the Stylistic Making of a Disorderly World* (Albany: State University of New York Press, 1991).
142. *TT*, 77.
143. *TT*, 107.
144. Ong, *Orality and Literacy*, 67–69.
145. Arnold, "Oral Rhetoric, Rhetoric, and Literature," 197.
146. Thomas D. Zlatic, "The 'Seeing Eye' and the 'Creating Mouth': Literacy and Orality in Mark Twain's Joan of Arc," *CLIO* 21 (1992): 291.
147. Alexis Tadié, *Sterne's Whimsical Theatres of Language: Orality, Gesture, Literacy* (Hants, England: Ashgate, 2003), 15.

148. L. Graham Crozier, review of *Talks to Teachers on Psychology and to Students on Some of Life's Ideals*, by William James, *Southern Education Journal* 13 (1900): 373.
149. *TT*, 14–15.
150. *TT*, 15.
151. *TT*, 15.
152. *TT*, 94.
153. *TT*, 95.
154. *TT*, 21–22.
155. *TT*, 97.
156. *TT*, 69.
157. *TT*, 17.
158. *TT*, 25.
159. *TT*, 27.
160. *TT*, 45.
161. *TT*, 62.
162. *TT*, 63.
163. *TT*, 72.
164. *TT*, 84.
165. *TT*, 110.
166. *TT*, 114.
167. *TT*, 26, 48.
168. *TT*, 113.
169. *TT*, 90.
170. *TT*, 13.
171. *TT*, 100.
172. *TT*, 41.
173. *TT*, 52.
174. *TT*, 53.
175. *TT*, 54.
176. For good discussions of citizenship and classical education, see Teresa Morgan, *Literate Education in the Hellenistic and Roman Worlds* (Cambridge: Cambridge University Press, 1998); Takis Poulakos, *Speaking for the Polis: Isocrates' Rhetorical Education* (Columbia: University of South Carolina Press, 1997); Takis Poulakos and David Depew, eds., *Isocrates and Civic Education* (Austin: University of Texas Press, 2004).
177. B. Edward McClellan, *Moral Education in America: Schools and the Shaping of Character from Colonial Times to the Present* (New York: Teachers College Press, 1999), 23.

178. William J. Reese, *America's Public Schools: From the Common School to "No Child Left Behind"* (Baltimore: Johns Hopkins University Press, 2005), 12.
179. *TT*, 45.
180. *TT*, 69.
181. *TT*, 40.
182. *TT*, 84.
183. *TT*, 70.
184. Edward W. Said, *Representations of the Intellectual* (New York: Vintage, 1994).

Chapter Four. Speaking Up for Spirits

1. William James to Henry James Jr., July 11, 1885, *Corr.* 2:21.
2. James recounted his introduction to Leonora Piper and his mother-in-law's visit in a letter to Frederic Myers, subsequently published as "A Record of Observations of Certain Phenomena of Trance," *Proceedings of the Society for Psychical Research* 6 (December 1890); reprinted in *EPR*, 79–88.
3. James, "A Record of Observations of Certain Phenomena of Trance," *EPR*, 80.
4. Prior to arriving at Piper's house, James explained to his wife that their visit had to be in strict accord with the principles of scientific investigation. For details, see Deborah Blum, *Ghost Hunters: William James and the Search for Scientific Proof of Life After Death* (New York: Penguin, 2006), 98–100.
5. James, "A Record of Observations of Certain Phenomena of Trance," 80.
6. James, "A Record of Observations of Certain Phenomena of Trance," 81.
7. William James, "Address of the President Before the Society for Psychical Research," *Proceedings of the Society for Psychical Research* 12 (June 1896); reprinted in *EPR*, 131.
8. For an overview of the relationship between science and the rhetoric of inquiry, see John S. Nelson, Allan Megill, and Donald N. McCloskey, eds., *The Rhetoric of the Human Sciences: Language and Argument in Scholarship and Public Affairs* (Madison: University of Wisconsin Press, 1987); and Herbert W. Simons, ed., *Rhetoric in the Human Sciences* (London: Sage, 1989).
9. Martin Willis, *Mesmerists, Monsters, & Machines: Science Fiction & the Cultures of Science in the Nineteenth Century* (Kent, OH: Kent State University Press, 2006), 10.
10. Marlene Shore, "Psychology and Memory in the Midst of Change: The Social Concerns of Late-19th-Century North American Psychologists," in *The Transformation of Psychology: Influences of 19th-Century Philosophy, Technology, and*

Natural Science, ed. Christopher D. Green, Marlene Shore, and Thomas Teo (Washington, DC: American Psychological Association, 2001), 72.

11. Shore, "Psychology and Memory in the Midst of Change," 68.
12. Hugo Münsterberg, "Psychology and Mysticism," *Atlantic Monthly* 83 (January 1899): 85.
13. Joseph Jastrow, "The Problems of 'Psychical Research,'" *Harper's New Monthly Magazine* 79 (1889): 77.
14. Charles Sedgwick Minot, "The Psychical Comedy," *North American Review* 160 (1895): 217–218.
15. "Men of Newspaper Fame," *Atchison Daily Globe*, April 14, 1888, 1.
16. "Still They Believe in Ghosts in Boston," *Baltimore Sun*, March 25, 1890, 2.
17. "Modern Ghosts," *Current Literature*, October 25, 1890, 1; "Wonders of the Trance State," *Chicago Daily Tribune*, January 21, 1892, 10; "Facts on Phantoms," *Daily Picayune*, September 10, 1892, 2; "A Trio of Ghost Stories," *Kansas City Star*, August 26, 1892, 8; "Hypnotism as a 'Fad,'" *Morning Oregonian*, October 27, 1892, 9; "Temporary Absence of the Soul," *Chicago Daily Tribune*, February 24, 1895, 34.
18. The most notable exceptions are Eugene Taylor, *William James on Exceptional Mental States: The 1896 Lowell Lectures* (New York: Charles Scribner's Sons, 1982); Eugene Taylor, *William James on Consciousness Beyond the Margin* (Princeton, NJ: Princeton University Press, 1996); Francesca Bordogna, *William James at the Boundaries* (Chicago: University of Chicago Press, 2008); and Blum, *Ghost Hunters*.
19. Ralph Barton Perry, *The Thought and Character of William James*, vol. 2 (Boston: Little, Brown, 1935), 155.
20. George Cotkin, *William James, Public Philosopher* (Urbana: University of Illinois Press, 1989).
21. For a succinct explanation of the differences between the Spiritualist movement of the 1850s and the general idea of spiritualism, see John J. Kucich, *Ghostly Communion: Cross-Cultural Spiritualism in Nineteenth-Century American Literature* (Hanover, NH: Dartmouth College Press, 2004), xi–xxxii.
22. The history of Spiritualism in this section comes from Slater Brown, *The Heyday of Spiritualism* (New York: Hawthorn Books, 1970); Howard Kerr, *Mediums, and Spirit-Rappers, and Roaring Radicals: Spiritualism in American Literature, 1850–1900* (Urbana: University of Illinois Press, 1972); R. Laurence Moore, *In Search of White Crows: Spiritualism, Parapsychology, and American Culture* (New York: Oxford University Press, 1977); Bret E. Carroll, *Spiritualism in Antebellum America* (Bloomington: Indiana University Press, 1997); Robert S. Cox, *Body and Soul: A Sympathetic History of American Spiritualism* (Charlottesville: University of Virginia Press, 2003); and Blum, *Ghost Hunters*.
23. For a discussion of the Fox Sisters and a general treatment of the role of women in the Spiritualist movement, see Ann Braude, *Radical Spirits: Spiritualism and*

Women's Rights in Nineteenth-Century America, 2nd ed. (Bloomington: Indiana University Press, 2001).

24. For incidents described in this paragraph, see Brown, *The Heyday of Spiritualism*, 150–166.
25. Moore, *In Search of White Crows*, 43.
26. See Cox, *Body and Soul*, 2.
27. Carroll, *Spiritualism in Antebellum America*, 1.
28. Kucich, *Ghostly Communion*, xii.
29. Carroll, *Spiritualism in Antebellum America*, 3–4.
30. Carroll, *Spiritualism in Antebellum America*, 94.
31. For more on the Spiritualist view of heaven, see Carroll, *Spiritualism in Antebellum America*, 60–84.
32. Moore, *In Search of White Crows*, 36.
33. In general, see Moore, *In Search of White Crows*, 14–39.
34. Joel Tiffany, *Spiritualism Explained: Being a Series of Twelve Lectures Delivered before the New York Conference of Spiritualists* (New York: Graham and Ellinwood, 1856), 12.
35. Cox, *Body and Soul*, 87.
36. See John W. Edmonds and George T. Dexter, *Spiritualism* (New York: Partridge and Brittan, 1853).
37. For a discussion of the testimonial style of Spiritualist discourse and the reaction of more conventional scientists, see Moore, *In Search of White Crows*, 3–39.
38. Moore, *In Search of White Crows*, 65.
39. Kerr, *Mediums, and Spirit-Rappers, and Roaring Radicals*, 108.
40. The founding of the society is discussed in Ivor Grattan-Guinness, ed., *Psychical Research: A Guide to its History, Principles and Practices* (Wellingborough, Northamptonshire, England: Aquarian Press, 1982).
41. Blum, *Ghost Hunters*, 80.
42. For an overview of Spiritualism, psychical research, and the changing scientific culture of the second half of the nineteenth century, see Eugene Taylor, *Shadow Culture: Psychology and Spirituality in America* (Washington, DC: Counterpoint, 1999), 157–183. Also see Janet Oppenheim, *The Other World: Spiritualism and Psychical Research in England, 1850–1914* (Cambridge: Cambridge University Press, 1985), especially 199–325.
43. Some of the earliest work of the SPR, for example, resulted in the widely celebrated and publicized debunking of the medium Madame Blavatsky. For a discussion, see Blum, *Ghost Hunters*, 85–92.
44. See, in general, Oppenheim, *The Other World*, 2–3, 63–158.
45. See William James to Alice Howe Gibbens James, December 16, 1882, *Corr.* 5:332.

46. Blum, *Ghost Hunters*, 13.
47. See Alfred Habegger, *The Father: A Life of Henry James, Sr.* (New York: Farrar, Straus and Giroux, 1994), 269–272.
48. For the place of Swedenborg's thought in the Spiritualist movement, see Brown, *The Heyday of Spiritualism*, 43–55; and Carroll, *Spiritualism in Antebellum America*, 16–34.
49. Habegger, *The Father*, 311.
50. "Circulars of the American Society for Psychical Research," *EPR*, 7.
51. "Mediums Wanted," *Boston Daily Advertiser*, April 10, 1885, 4.
52. "The American Society of Psychical Research," *Springfield Daily Republican*, January 17, 1890, 4.
53. "Hallucinations," *New York Times*, May 12, 1890, 4. For the requests in other parts of the country, see the untitled mention in the *St. Louis Republic*, May 13, 1890, 4; and "Hallucinations," *Galveston Daily News*, May 23, 1890, 2.
54. Taylor, *William James on Consciousness Beyond the Margin*, xi–xii.
55. William James to Frederic Myers, January 30, 1891, *Corr.* 7:139.
56. William James to Nora Sidgwick, May 15, 1892, *Corr.* 7:270.
57. William James to Frederic Myers, January 30, 1891, *Corr.* 7:139.
58. For coverage of the ASPR's downfall, see Blum, *Ghost Hunters*, 105–156.
59. William James, "The Hidden Self," *Scribner's Magazine* 7 (March 1890); reprinted in *EP*, 247–268.
60. William James, "What Psychical Research Has Accomplished," *Forum* 13 (August 1892); reprinted in *EPR*, 89–106.
61. *EP*, 248.
62. *EPR*, 101.
63. *EPR*, 91.
64. *EP*, 268.
65. *EPR*, 100.
66. *EPR*, 91.
67. *EPR*, 102.
68. *EP*, 259.
69. *EPR*, 104.
70. *EPR*, 89.
71. *EPR*, 93.
72. *EPR*, 90.
73. *EPR*, 91.
74. *EPR*, 89–90.
75. *EP*, 261.

76. *EPR*, 95.
77. *EPR*, 98.
78. *EPR*, 102.
79. *EP*, 268.
80. *EPR*, 100.
81. See "Notes and Magazines," *Magazine of Christian Literature*, March 1890, 408; R. W. Felkin, "Hypnotism, or Psycho-Therapeutics," *Edinburgh Medical Journal* 35 (May 1890): 1031; Sarah E. Post, "The Borderland," *New York Medical Journal* 52 (July 12, 1890): 44; and "Some American Magazines," *Review of Reviews*, March 1890, 220. Also see "Literary Notes," *Philadelphia Inquirer*, February 17, 1890, 6; "Woman in a Trance," *Worchester Sunday Spy*, March 2, 1890, 5; and "Wonders of the Trance State," *Chicago Daily Tribune*, January 21, 1892, 10.
82. "Results of Psychical Research," *New York Times*, September 4, 1892, 4.
83. "Psychical Research," *Daily Picayune*, August 21, 1892, 12.
84. For example, see "Psychical Research," *Baltimore Sun*, July 29, 1892, 4; "Treatment of 'Spiritual Phenomena,'" *Galveston Daily News*, August 8, 1892, 7; and an untitled article in *Southwestern Christian Advocate*, August 11, 1892, 8. One of the few somewhat negative responses came from *The Critic*, which found it "curious" that James did "not show any very positive results" when it came to the work of the SPR. "Magazine Notes," *The Critic*, July 30, 1892, 68.
85. Frederic Myers to William James, October 10, 1893, *Corr.* 7:461–462.
86. Frederic Myers to William James, November 16, 1893, *Corr.* 7:468.
87. William James to Frederic Myers, December 17, 1893, *Corr.* 7:474.
88. See William James to Frederic Myers, September 29, 1894, *Corr.* 7:550–552.
89. William James to Frederic Myers, September 29, 1894, *Corr.* 7:551.
90. William James to Oliver Lodge, October 4, 1894, *Corr.* 7:553.
91. Henry Sidgwick, "Eusapia Paladino," *Journal of the Society for Psychical Research* 7 (1895): 148.
92. "Psychical Research and Eusapia Palladino," *Boston Medical and Surgical Journal* 133 (December 12, 1895): 602. For a similar comment on the Palladino incident, see W. L. Alden, "Wisdom Let Loose," *Pearson's Magazine*, February 1896, 180–181.
93. William James to Henry Sidgwick, November 8, 1895, *Corr.* 8:97–98.
94. See "The Text of *Essays in Psychical Research*," *EPR*, 468–472.
95. William James to Henry James Jr., January 26, 1896, *Corr.* 2:389.
96. William James to Frederic Myers, February 5, 1896, *Corr.* 8:133.
97. William James, "Address of the President before the Society for Psychical Research," *Proceedings of the Society for Psychical Research* 12 (June 1896): 2–10.

98. The address appeared in *Science* 3 (June 19, 1896): 881–888. For a discussion of James and Cattell's opposition throughout their careers, see Daniel W. Bjork, *The Compromised Scientist: William James in the Development of American Psychology* (New York: Columbia University Press, 1983), 105–125.
99. William James to Frederic Myers, February 5, 1896, *Corr.* 8:133.
100. *EPR*, 128.
101. *EPR*, 129.
102. *EPR*, 128.
103. For an overview of the importance of scientific method in the pursuit of knowledge at the end of the nineteenth century, as well as James's place in scientific and philosophical culture at the time, see Daniel J. Wilson, *Science, Community, and the Transformation of American Philosophy, 1860–1930* (Chicago: University of Chicago Press, 1990), 56–97.
104. *EPR*, 132.
105. *EPR*, 131.
106. *EPR*, 132.
107. *EPR*, 129.
108. *EPR*, 133. Emphasis mine.
109. *EPR*, 132.
110. *EPR*, 134.
111. *EPR*, 135.
112. *EPR*, 136.
113. *EPR*, 136.
114. "Notice of 'Address of the President before the Society for Psychical Research,'" *Psychological Review* 3 (September 1896); reprinted in *EPR*, 442.
115. *EPR*, 138.
116. *EPR*, 139.
117. *EPR*, 140.
118. *EPR*, 139.
119. For a thorough list of the SPR's most eminent supporters, see Oppenheim, *The Other World*, 135–136.
120. For a good comparison of psychical research in England and America, including the relative opposition it faced in each country, see Moore, *In Search of White Crows*, 133–168.
121. Bjork, *The Compromised Scientist*, 121.
122. William James to August Lowell, April 18, 1896, *Corr.* 8:141.
123. For a student's recollection of these visits and of James's view of their importance, see Dickinson Sargeant Miller, "A Memory of William James," in *William James*

Remembered, ed. Linda Simon (Lincoln: University of Nebraska Press, 1996), 125–130.

124. William James to Alice Howe Gibbens James, May 23, 1894, *Corr.* 7:505.
125. The best discussion of James's view on the relationships among conventional psychology, abnormal psychology, and psychical research appears in Taylor, *William James on Exceptional Mental States.* Also see Bjork, *The Compromised Scientist*, 145–162.
126. William James to Augustus Lowell, April 18, 1896, *Corr.* 8:141–142.
127. See Taylor, *William James on Exceptional Mental States*, 4–5.
128. See Taylor, *William James on Exceptional Mental States*, 1–14.
129. *ML*, 63.
130. *ML*, 64.
131. *ML*, 83.
132. *ML*, 64–69.
133. *ML*, 67.
134. *ML*, 69.
135. *ML*, 69.
136. *ML*, 71.
137. *ML*, 71.
138. *ML*, 72.
139. *ML*, 72.
140. *ML*, 76.
141. *ML*, 77.
142. *ML*, 75.
143. *ML*, 76.
144. James often disputed the conventional sense of "real," arguing that something was real if it affected human experience. Perhaps the clearest expression of this view appeared in James's philosophy of radical empiricism. See in particular "The Thing and Its Relations," *ERE*, 45–59.
145. "Exceptional Mental States," *Daily Inter Ocean*, November 21, 1896, 16.
146. "Prof. James's Lowell Lectures," *Boston Evening Transcript*, November 17, 1896. For all the reports of James's lectures by the *Transcript*, see *ML*, 519–525.
147. In particular, James subtly wove psychical research and abnormal psychology throughout *The Varieties of Religious Experience*, as we will see in chapter 5.
148. Eugene Taylor explains James's shift to the Gifford lectures after completing the Lowell lectures in *William James on Exceptional Mental States*, 7–10.
149. James McKeen Cattell, "Mrs. Piper, the Medium," *Science* 7 (April 15, 1898): 534–535.

150. William James, "Letter on Mrs. Piper, the Medium," *Science* 7 (May 6, 1898); reprinted in *EPR*, 184–185.
151. James McKeen Cattell, untitled, *Science*, May 6, 1898; reprinted in *EPR*, 186.
152. E. B. Titchener, "The Feeling of Being Stared At," *Science* 8 (December 23, 1898): 895–897.
153. William James, "Lehmann and Hansen on Telepathy," *Science* 9 (May 15, 1899); reprinted in *EPR*, 171–172.
154. "Harvard Leader Talks to Spirit?" *Chicago Tribune*, July 8, 1909, 5.
155. "Prof. James Bets 'Twas Dr. Hodgson," *New York Times*, July 8, 1909, 1.
156. "R.H. and His Victims," *New York Times*, July 9, 1909, 6.
157. William James, "The Confidences of a 'Psychical Researcher,'" *American Magazine* 68 (October 1909); reprinted in *EPR*, 361–375.
158. *EPR*, 362.
159. *EPR*, 370–371.
160. *EPR*, 374.
161. "William James," *New York Times*, August 28, 1910, 8.

Chapter Five. Religious Experience and the Appeals of Intellectual Populism

1. William James to James McKeen Cattell, May 4, 1898, *Corr.* 8:363–364.
2. William James to James McKeen Cattell, May 8, 1898, *Corr.* 8:364–365.
3. "A Great Psychologist," *San Francisco Call*, August 25, 1898, 14.
4. See Alice James to Henry James Jr., February 4, 1899, quoted in *VRE*, 522.
5. William James, "The Gospel of Relaxation," *TT*, 117–131.
6. Ralph Barton Perry notes that James's Gifford lectures were partly the fulfillment of a pledge to pursue religious subjects that James made shortly after Henry James Sr. died. See *The Thought and Character of William James*, vol. 2 (Boston: Little, Brown, 1935), 323.
7. T. D. A. Cockerell, "Varieties of Religious Experience," *Dial* 33 (November 16, 1902): 323.
8. Unsigned review of *The Varieties of Religious Experience*, by William James, *Catholic World* 75 (September 1902): 824.
9. Edwin D. Starbuck, "The Varieties of Religious Experience," *Biblical World* 24 (August 1904): 111.
10. See Dinitia Smith, "Another Top 100 List: Now It's Nonfiction," *New York Times*, April 30, 1999, E45.

11. Eugene Taylor, "Metaphysics and Consciousness in James's *Varieties:* A Centenary Lecture," in *William James and "The Varieties of Religious Experience": A Centenary Celebration,* ed. Jeremy Carrette (London: Routledge, 2005), 12.
12. John E. Smith, introduction to *VRE*, xi.
13. For various interpretations, see Henry Samuel Levinson, *The Religious Investigations of William James* (Chapel Hill: University of North Carolina Press, 1981); Ann Taves, *Fits, Traces, & Visions: Experiencing Religion and Explaining Experience from Wesley to James* (Princeton, NJ: Princeton University Press, 1999); Wayne Proudfoot, ed., *William James and a Science of Religions: Reexperiencing "The Varieties of Religious Experience"* (New York: Columbia University Press, 2004); and the essays in Carrette, *William James and "The Varieties of Religious Experience."*
14. For a recent look at Populism—the capitalized version—see Joe Creech, *Righteous Indignation: Religion and the Populist Revolution* (Urbana: University of Illinois Press, 2006).
15. Michael Kazin, *The Populist Persuasion: An American History* (New York: Basic Books, 1995), 1.
16. For discussions of these and other themes of populist rhetoric, see Kazin, *The Populist Persuasion,* 9–25; Michael J. Lee, "The Populist Chameleon: The People's Party, Huey Long, George Wallace, and the Populist Argumentative Frame," *Quarterly Journal of Speech* 92 (2006): 355–378; Lloyd Rohler, "Conservative Appeals to the People: George Wallace's Populist Rhetoric," *Southern Communication Journal* 64 (1999): 316–322; Rhys H. Williams and Susan M. Alexander, "Religious Rhetoric in American Populism: Civil Religion as Movement Ideology," *Journal for the Scientific Study of Religion* 33 (1994): 1–15; Ronald Lee, "The New Populist Campaign for Economic Democracy: A Rhetorical Exploration," *Quarterly Journal of Speech* 72 (1986): 274–289; and Howard S. Erlich, "Populist Rhetoric Reassessed: A Paradox," *Quarterly Journal of Speech* 63 (1977): 140–150.
17. William James remembered hearing Henry James Sr. read aloud from a Boston newspaper about the aim of Gifford's fortune, and he recounted the incident while delivering the Gifford lectures. See *VRE,* 161.
18. For a general history of the Gifford lectures, see Larry Witham, *The Measure of God: Our Century-Long Struggle to Reconcile Science and Religion* (San Francisco: HarperSanFrancisco, 2005). For the text of Gifford's will, along with a discussion, see Stanley L. Jaki, *Lord Gifford and His Lectures: A Centenary Retrospect* (Edinburgh: Scottish Academic Press, 1986). Gifford's will is also published on the website for the Gifford Lectures: giffordlectures.org.
19. Jaki, *Lord Gifford and His Lectures,* 74.
20. Jaki, *Lord Gifford and His Lectures,* 72.

21. It should be noted that before James received his Aberdeen invitation, a faculty member at the University of Edinburgh had unofficially raised the possibility of bringing him there for the Gifford lectures. See William James to Andrew Seth Pringle-Pattison, January 25, 1897, *Corr.* 8:223–224.
22. For Edinburgh's significance at the time, see Witham, *The Measure of God*, 9–27.
23. William James to Andrew Seth Pringle-Pattison, January 25, 1897, *Corr.* 8:223–224.
24. William James to Andrew Seth Pringle-Pattison, February 7, 1897, *Corr.* 8:231.
25. See William James to Andrew Seth Pringle-Pattison, February 7, 1897, *Corr.* 8:231.
26. William James to Andrew Seth Pringle-Pattison, January 25, 1897, *Corr.* 8:224.
27. *VRE*, 343.
28. For a general discussion of Royce and the Gifford lectures, see John Clendenning, *The Life and Thought of Josiah Royce*, rev. ed. (Nashville, TN: Vanderbilt University Press, 1999), 222–254.
29. Alice James to Henry James Jr., February 4, 1899, quoted in *VRE*, 522.
30. Andrew Seth Pringle-Pattison to William James, January 12, 1898, *Corr.* 8:608.
31. William James to Henry James Jr., February 21, 1898, *Corr.* 3:23.
32. William James to Alice Howe Gibbens James, July 9, 1898, *Corr.* 8:390–391.
33. William James to Alice Howe Gibbens James, July 9, 1898, *Corr.* 8:390.
34. "Harvard Professor Ill," *New York Times*, December 25, 1900, 1. For more on James's medical situation during this time, see Robert D. Richardson, *William James in the Maelstrom of American Modernism* (Boston: Houghton Mifflin, 2006), 385–406.
35. William James to Henry William Rankin, January 16, 1899, *Corr.* 8:488.
36. William James to Andrew Seth Pringle-Pattison, August 13, 1899, *Corr.* 9:573.
37. See William James to Henry James III, December 21, 1899, *Corr.* 9:585; and Andrew Seth Pringle-Pattison to William James, January 12, 1900, *Corr.* 9:123–124.
38. Clendenning, *The Life and Thought of Josiah Royce*, 225.
39. Josiah Royce to Mary Gray Ward Dorr, August 7, 1898, *The Letters of Josiah Royce*, ed. John Clendenning (Chicago: University of Chicago Press, 1970), 378.
40. Josiah Royce to Mary Gray Ward Dorr, August 7, 1898, *The Letters of Josiah Royce*, 378.
41. Josiah Royce to William James, January 12, 1899, *The Letters of Josiah Royce*, 381.
42. Josiah Royce to William James, February 7, 1900, *The Letters of Josiah Royce*, 401.
43. Josiah Royce to William James, June 21, 1901, *The Letters of Josiah Royce*, 419.
44. Descriptions of Royce, along with recollections by those who knew him, appear in Clendenning, *The Life and Thought of Josiah Royce*, 117–118, 270–272; and Robert V. Hine, *Josiah Royce: From Grass Valley to Harvard* (Norman: University of Oklahoma Press, 1992), 53, 120–123.
45. Quoted in Hine, *Josiah Royce*, 123.

46. Bruce Kuklick, *Josiah Royce: An Intellectual Biography* (Indianapolis: Bobbs-Merrill, 1972), 99.
47. Clendenning, *The Life and Thought of Josiah Royce*, 236.
48. Josiah Royce, *The World and the Individual, First Series: The Four Historical Conceptions of Being* (New York: Macmillan, 1900), 5–6.
49. See Clendenning, *The Life and Thought of Josiah Royce*, 240.
50. For an overview, see Richardson, *William James in the Maelstrom*, 389–391.
51. See, for example, Josiah Royce to William James, March 1899, *The Letters of Josiah Royce*, 382–388.
52. William James to Josiah Royce, September 26, 1900, *Corr.* 9:320.
53. William James to Henry James Jr., June 21, 1899, *Corr.* 3:64.
54. William James to Andrew Seth Pringle-Pattison, September 27, 1900, *Corr.* 9:323.
55. Andrew Seth Pringle-Pattison to William James, October 3, 1900, *Corr.* 9:329.
56. See William James to Andrew Seth Pringle-Pattison, September 27, 1900, *Corr.* 9:322–324; Andrew Seth Pringle-Pattison to William James, October 9, 1900, *Corr.* 9:612; and Andrew Seth Pringle-Pattison to William James, December 16, 1900, *Corr.* 9:616.
57. See Deborah Blum, *Ghost Hunters: William James and the Search for Scientific Proof of Life After Death* (New York: Penguin, 2006), 249–252.
58. The account appears in Axel Munthe, *The Story of San Michelle* (New York: E. P. Dutton, 1929), 371–372.
59. William James to Eleanor Mildred Sidgwick, January 20, 1901, *Corr.* 9:412.
60. William James to Frances Rollins Morse, May 15, 1901, *Corr.* 9:483.
61. Larry Witham sets the stage the nicely in *The Measure of God*, 81.
62. *Scotsman*, May 17, 1901; quoted in *VRE*, 540–541.
63. William James to Henry James Jr., May 16, 1901, *Corr.* 3:170.
64. *Scotsman*, June 18, 1901; quoted in *VRE*, 544.
65. For an overview, see *VRE*, 544–547.
66. See "Scotch Degrees for Americans," *New York Times*, April 12, 1902, 9.
67. William James to Henry James Jr., May 12, 1902, *Corr.* 3:200.
68. *Scotsman*, May 14, 1902; quoted in *VRE*, 548.
69. William James to Ferdinand Canning Scott Schiller, May 17, 1902, *Corr.* 10:43.
70. William James to Frances Rollins Morse, June 3, 1902, *Corr.* 10:52.
71. See William James to Theodore Flournoy, June 9, 1902, *Corr.* 10:55.
72. *Harvard Graduate Magazine* 11 (September 1902); quoted in *VRE*, 550.
73. The description first appeared in the *Boston Evening Transcript*, June 10, 1902, and was later reprinted in the *Harvard Graduates' Magazine* 11 (September 1902). See *VRE*, 549–550.

74. For an overview, see *VRE*, 544–547.
75. *VRE*, 409–411.
76. For more details on the relationship between the book and the lectures, see *VRE*, 544–582.
77. The chapters were titled according to the lecture or lectures they contained.
78. *VRE*, 11.
79. See chapter 3.
80. George Coe, review of *The Varieties of Religious Experience*, by William James, *Philosophical Review* 12 (1903): 62.
81. Unsigned review of *The Varieties of Religious Experience*, by William James, *American Ecclesiastical Review* 7 (December 1902): 680–681.
82. "A Study of Man," *New York Times*, August 9, 1902, BR13.
83. *VRE*, 12.
84. See, for example, David W. Wulff, "Listening to James a Century Later: The *Varieties* as a Resource for Renewing the Psychology of Religion," in Carrette, *William James and "The Varieties of Religious Experience,"* 47–57.
85. Jacob A. Belzen, "The *Varieties*, the *Principles* and the Psychology of Religion: Unremitting Inspiration from a Different Source," in Carrette, *William James and "The Varieties of Religious Experience,"* 63.
86. *VRE*, 34.
87. *VRE*, 38, 153.
88. *VRE*, 13, 20.
89. *VRE*, 20.
90. *VRE*, 21.
91. *VRE*, 19.
92. *VRE*, 30.
93. *VRE*, 102.
94. *VRE*, 262–263.
95. *VRE*, 342.
96. See Kazin, *The Populist Persuasion*, 15–16; and Williams and Alexander, "Religious Rhetoric in American Populism," 9.
97. *VRE*, 25.
98. *VRE*, 250.
99. *VRE*, 276.
100. *VRE*, 406.
101. *VRE*, 410.
102. See, for example, William James to Leslie Stephen, June 10, 1902, *Corr.* 10:56.
103. *VRE*, 30.

104. *VRE*, 39.
105. *VRE*, 104.
106. *VRE*, 66.
107. *VRE*, 67.
108. *VRE*, 360.
109. *VRE*, 359.
110. *VRE*, 33.
111. *VRE*, 34.
112. *VRE*, 344.
113. *VRE*, 153.
114. See Martin Jay, *Songs of Experience: Modern American and European Variations on a Universal Theme* (Berkeley: University of California Press, 2005), 261–311.
115. Richard Rorty, "Some Inconsistencies in James's *Varieties*," in Proudfoot, *William James and a Science of Religions*, 86–97.
116. See Russell B. Goodman, *American Philosophy and the Romantic Tradition* (Cambridge: Cambridge University Press, 1990); Roger Lundin, *From Nature to Experience: The American Search for Cultural Authority* (Lanham, MD: Rowman & Littlefield, 2005); and Andrea Knutson, *American Spaces of Conversion: The Conductive Imaginaries of Edwards, Emerson, & James* (Oxford: Oxford University Press, 2011).
117. See *VRE*, 34.
118. *VRE*, 39.
119. *VRE*, 36–37.
120. *VRE*, 394–395.
121. See Kazin, *The Populist Persuasion*, 16–17; and Lee, "The Populist Chameleon," 362.
122. *VRE*, 66.
123. *VRE*, 67.
124. *VRE*, 71.
125. *VRE*, 84.
126. *VRE*, 102–103.
127. *VRE*, 261.
128. *VRE*, 46.
129. *VRE*, 80.
130. *VRE*, 131.
131. *VRE*, 216.
132. *VRE*, 229.
133. *VRE*, 395.

134. David A. Hollinger, "'Damned for God's Glory': William James and the Scientific Vindication of Protestant Culture," in Proudfoot, *William James and a Science of Religions*, 14.
135. *VRE*, 25–26.
136. *VRE*, 56.
137. *VRE*, 88–89.
138. *VRE*, 192.
139. *VRE*, 386.
140. In a letter to Frank Abauzit on June 1, 1904, James revealed that the testimony on the "sick soul" from an unnamed French writer was actually his own. See *Corr.* 10:619.
141. *VRE*, 367.
142. Chaïm Perelman and Lucie Olbrechts-Tyteca, *The New Rhetoric: A Treatise on Argumentation*, trans. John Milkinson and Purcell Weaver (Notre Dame: University of Notre Dame Press, 1969), 351.
143. See Kathleen Glenister Roberts, "Liminality, Authority, and Value: Reported Speech in Epideictic Rhetoric," *Communication Theory* 14 (2004): 264–284.
144. *VRE*, 223.
145. *VRE*, 57–58, 59, 63.
146. *VRE*, 143, 155, 158–160.
147. *VRE*, 187.
148. *VRE*, 55.
149. *VRE*, 197.
150. F. C. S. Schiller, review of *The Varieties of Religious Experience*, by William James, *Proceedings of the Society for Psychical Research* 45 (February 1903): 403–404.
151. For these characterizations of James's voice and manner of presentation, see Linda Simon, ed., *William James Remembered* (Lincoln: University of Nebraska Press, 1996), 13, 138, 236.
152. *VRE*, 11.
153. *VRE*, 12.
154. *VRE*, 25.
155. *VRE*, 34.
156. *VRE*, 74–76.
157. See *VRE*, 522–524. Also see Starbuck's discussion of the material in Simon, *William James Remembered*, 168–171.
158. *VRE*, 164.
159. *VRE*, 65.
160. *VRE*, 165.

161. Jay, *Songs of Experience*, 4.
162. For elaboration, see Jay, *Songs of Experience*, especially 102–110; and Martin Kusch, *Psychologism: A Case Study in the Sociology of Knowledge* (London: Routledge, 1995).
163. *VRE*, 341.
164. *VRE*, 350–351.
165. The name of James's 1898 lecture was "Philosophical Conceptions and Practical Results," which we shall discuss in detail in chapter 6.
166. *VRE*, 351.
167. *VRE*, 351–352.
168. *VRE*, 350.
169. We shall discuss James's use of economic terminology in advancing pragmatism more fully in chapter 6.
170. *VRE*, 352.
171. *VRE*, 353.
172. *VRE*, 393–395.
173. William James to William James Jr., January 26, 1903, *Corr.* 10:185.
174. William James to Giulio Cesare Ferrari, October 13, 1902, *Corr.* 10:144.
175. Cockerell, "Varieties of Religious Experience," 322.
176. "Mr. William James on Religious Conversion," *Living Age*, August 23, 1902, 506.
177. "The Varieties of Religious Experience," *New Outlook*, December 27, 1902, 993.
178. See *VRE*, 5–6.
179. H. Rashdall, review of *The Varieties of Religious Experience*, by William James, *Mind* 12 (1903): 250.
180. John Grier Hibben, review of *The Varieties of Religious Experience*, by William James, *Psychological Review* 10 (1903): 185.
181. J. H. Muirhead, review of *The Varieties of Religious Experience*, by William James, *International Journal of Ethics* 13 (1903): 246.
182. The classic statement on these intellectual tensions in American history is Richard Hofstadter, *Anti-intellectualism in American Life* (New York: Vintage, 1963). For a more rhetorical perspective, see E. Johanna Hartelius, *The Rhetoric of Expertise* (Lanham, MD: Lexington Books, 2011).
183. For two views on the continuing importance of *Varieties*, see Charles Taylor, *Varieties of Religion Today: William James Revisited* (Cambridge: Harvard University Press, 2002); and Lynn Bridgers, *Contemporary Varieties of Religious Experience: James's Classic Study in Light of Resiliency, Temperament, and Trauma* (Lanham, MD: Rowman & Littlefield, 2005).

Chapter Six. Empowering a Pragmatic Public

1. William James to Ferdinand Canning Scott Schiller, May 1, 1903, *Corr.* 10:243.
2. William James to Henry James Jr., May 3, 1903, *Corr.* 3:233.
3. Walter Lippmann, "An Open Mind: William James," in *William James Remembered*, ed. Linda Simon (Lincoln: University of Nebraska Press, 1996), 255.
4. Henry Steele Commager, *The American Mind: An Interpretation of American Thought and Character Since the 1880s* (New Haven: Yale University Press, 1950), 97.
5. Charles M. Bakewell, review of *Pragmatism*, by William James, *Philosophical Review* 16 (1907): 634.
6. Bertrand Russell, "Transatlantic 'Truth,'" *Albany Review* 2 (1908): 410.
7. J. Ellis McTaggart, review of *Pragmatism*, by William James, *Mind* 17 (1908): 104.
8. Thomas Verner Moore, "The Pragmatism of William James," *Catholic World* 40 (1909): 341.
9. "Official Pragmatism," *Nation* 85 (1907): 57.
10. Edwin Bjorkman, "Pragmatism—What It Is," *New York Times*, November 3, 1907, 8.
11. "New and Old Philosophies," *Duluth News Tribune*, June 30, 1907, 8.
12. "The Gospel of Pragmatism," *Academy* 73 (1907): 772.
13. Finley Peter Dunne, "Mr. Dooley on Philosophers," *American Magazine* 65 (1908): 543–544.
14. See Marion Hamilton Carter to William James, November 13, 1907, *Corr.* 11:479.
15. See William James to Charles Augustus Strong, December 31, 1908, *Corr.* 12:139.
16. For documentation on the number of printings, see *Prag.*, 194.
17. William James to Henry James Jr., May 4, 1907, *Corr.* 3:339.
18. William James to Henry James Jr., September 8, 1907, *Corr.* 3:344.
19. William James to Ferdinand Canning Scott Schiller, January 17, 1908, *Corr.* 11:522.
20. For an overview of the debates regarding pragmatism, in James's time and since, see John J. Stuhr, ed., *100 Years of Pragmatism: William James's Revolutionary Philosophy* (Bloomington: Indiana University Press, 2010). Also see Morris Dickstein, ed., *The Revival of Pragmatism: New Essays on Social Thought, Law, and Culture* (Durham, NC: Duke University Press, 1998).
21. See, for example, Ralph Barton Perry, *The Thought and Character of William James*, vol. 2 (Boston: Little, Brown, 1935), 441–451; Gay Wilson Allen, *William James: A Biography* (New York: Viking Press, 1967), 450–459; Robert D. Richardson, *William James in the Maelstrom of American Modernism* (Boston: Houghton Mifflin, 2006), 484–488. Perhaps the best contextualist account of *Pragmatism*

comes from George Cotkin, but even his discussion fails to account for how the context shaped the rhetorical character of the work. See George Cotkin, *William James, Public Philosopher* (Urbana: University of Illinois Press, 1989), 152–176. For a fuller discussion of the style of the work, though one that is largely decontextualized, see Beverly Lawn, "From Temple to Streets: The Style of Pragmatism," *New England Quarterly* 45 (1972): 526–540.

22. For examples of the intersection of rhetoric and pragmatism, see Alan Brinton, "William James and the Epistemic View of Rhetoric," *Quarterly Journal of Speech* 68 (1982): 158–169; Steven Mailloux, *Reception Histories: Rhetoric, Pragmatism, and American Cultural Politics* (Ithaca, NY: Cornell University Press, 1998); Paul Schollmeier, "Pragmatic Method and Its Rhetorical Lineage," *Philosophy & Rhetoric* 35 (2002): 368–381; Paul Stob, "Kenneth Burke, John Dewey, and the Pursuit of the Public," *Philosophy & Rhetoric* 38 (2005): 226–247; Robert Danisch, *Pragmatism, Democracy, and the Necessity of Rhetoric* (Columbia: University of South Carolina Press, 2007); Paul Stob, "'Terministic Screens,' Social Constructionism, and the Language of Experience: Kenneth Burke's Utilization of William James," *Philosophy & Rhetoric* 41 (2008): 130–152; Scott R. Stroud, "John Dewey and the Question of Artful Communication," *Philosophy & Rhetoric* 41 (2008): 153–183; Mats Bergman, "Experience, Purpose, and the Value of Vagueness: On C. S. Peirce's Contribution to the Philosophy of Communication," *Communication Theory* 19 (2009): 248–277; Scott R. Stroud, "Pragmatism and the Methodology of Comparative Rhetoric," *Rhetoric Society Quarterly* 39 (2009): 353–379; Scott R. Stroud, "What Does Pragmatic Meliorism Mean for Rhetoric?" *Western Journal of Communication* 74 (2010): 43–60; Nathan Crick, *Democracy and Rhetoric: John Dewey on the Arts of Becoming* (Columbia: University of South Carolina Press, 2010); and Paul Stob, "Pragmatism, Experience, and William James's Politics of Blindness," *Philosophy & Rhetoric* 44 (2011): 227–249.

23. See Louis Menand, *The Metaphysical Club: A Story of Ideas in America* (New York: Farrar, Straus and Giroux, 2001).

24. Quoted in Menand, *The Metaphysical Club*, 203.

25. William James to Henry James Jr., November 24, 1872, *Corr.* 1:177.

26. Menand, *The Metaphysical Club*, 227.

27. Charles Sanders Peirce, "How to Make Our Ideas Clear," *Popular Science Monthly* 12 (1878): 286–302.

28. Peirce, "How to Make Our Ideas Clear," 291.

29. For a good overview of the Metaphysical Club as Peirce's "community of inquirers," see Joseph Brent, *Charles Sanders Peirce: A Life* (Bloomington: Indiana University Press, 1993), 82–119.

30. For Peirce's confusion about the term, see Charles Sanders Peirce to William James, November 10, 1898, *Corr.* 9:355–356.

31. *Prag.*, 29.

32. It should be noted that James was discussing pragmatism with his Harvard classes years before he addressed nonacademic audiences on the subject. See, for example, W. E. B. Du Bois's recollections in David Levering Lewis, *W. E. B. Du Bois: Biography of a Race, 1868–1919* (New York: Henry Holt, 1993), 96.
33. See the editorial comments proceeding "Philosophical Conceptions and Practical Results" in *Prag.*, 255.
34. See William James to Alice Howe Gibbens James, September 6, 1898, *Corr.* 8:428.
35. See William James to Alice Howe Gibbens James, September 12, 1898, *Corr.* 8:618.
36. See William James to Henry James Jr., September 22, 1898, *Corr.* 3:40.
37. William James to Alice Howe Gibbens James, September 15, 1898, *Corr.* 8:435.
38. William James to George Holmes Howison, April 15, 1897, *Corr.* 8:256.
39. William James to George Holmes Howison, July 24, 1898, *Corr.* 8:398.
40. "Philosophy at Berkeley," *San Francisco Chronicle*, August 27, 1898, 7.
41. *Prag.*, 257.
42. *Prag.*, 257.
43. *Prag.*, 258.
44. *Prag.*, 258.
45. *Prag.*, 259.
46. *Prag.*, 259.
47. *Prag.*, 260.
48. *Prag.*, 260.
49. *Prag.*, 264.
50. *Prag.*, 261.
51. *Prag.*, 261–262.
52. *Prag.*, 264–265.
53. *Prag.*, 265.
54. *Prag.*, 265.
55. *Prag.*, 265.
56. *Prag.*, 268.
57. *Prag.*, 268.
58. *Prag.*, 268.
59. *Prag.*, 268–269.
60. *Prag.*, 269.
61. *Prag.*, 269.
62. "Philosophy at Berkeley," *San Francisco Chronicle*, August 27, 1898, 7. For similar coverage, see the untitled article in the *Kansas City Journal*, September 21, 1898, 4.

63. *Prag.*, 270.

64. Charles Sanders Peirce, "What Pragmatism Is," *Monist* 15 (1905): 166. For an overview of Peirce's thinking on this issue, see Christopher Hookway, "Logical Principles and Philosophical Attitudes: Peirce's Response to James's Pragmatism," in *The Cambridge Companion to William James*, ed. Ruth Anna Putnam (Cambridge: Cambridge University Press, 1997), 145–165.

65. The *University Chronicle*, Berkeley's newspaper, reprinted the entire address, and the Berkeley Philosophical Union published it as a stand-alone pamphlet. See William James, "Philosophical Conceptions and Practical Results," *University Chronicle* 1 (September 1898): 287–310; William James, *Philosophical Conceptions and Practical Results* (Berkeley: University of California Press, 1898). Also see William James, "The Pragmatic Method," *Journal of Philosophy, Psychology, and Scientific Methods* 1 (1904): 673–687.

66. W. Caldwell, "Pragmatism," *Mind* 36 (1900): 455–456.

67. For an overview of pragmatism's supporters around this time, see Perry, *The Thought and Character of William James*, 2:452–636.

68. William James, "Pragmatic and Pragmatism," in *Dictionary of Philosophy and Psychology*, vol. 3, ed. J. M. Baldwin (New York: Macmillan, 1902), 321.

69. *VRE*, 352.

70. *VRE*, 353.

71. *VRE*, 351.

72. *VRE*, 350.

73. Review of *The Varieties of Religious Experience*, by William James, *Nation*, August 21, 1902, 155.

74. "Psychology of Religion," *Popular Science Monthly* 62 (1902): 89.

75. W. Vesey Hague, "What is a Reasonable Faith?" *Irish Ecclesiastical Record* 14 (1903): 271.

76. C. C. J. Webb, "Psychology and Religion," *Journal of Theological Studies* 4 (1903): 68.

77. William James to Harald Höffding, March 9, 1905, *Corr.* 10:565.

78. "Dr. James's Lectures," *Wellesley College News*, March 15, 1905; reprinted in *Prag.*, 276.

79. *Prag.*, 282. Whether or not radical empiricism is a kindred philosophy of pragmatism is an issue up for debate. In the Wellesley, Chicago, and Glenmore lectures of 1905, James tied the two philosophies together as counterparts in the same intellectual project. Yet later in his career, he explicitly denied a connection between radical empiricism and pragmatism. When I link pragmatism and radical empiricism, I do so because James did so in his 1905 lectures.

80. *Prag.*, 284.

81. *Prag.*, 280–281.

82. *Prag.*, 280.
83. *Prag.*, 280.
84. For James's brief evaluation of the Wellesley lectures, see William James to Henry James Jr., March 3, 1905, *Corr.* 3:290.
85. William James to Alice Howe Gibbens James, June 29, 1905, *Corr.* 11:68.
86. William James to Alice Howe Gibbens James, July 6, 1905, *Corr.* 11:70.
87. See, for example, William James to Margaret Mary James, July 11, 1905, *Corr.* 11:75; William James to Henry James Jr., July 12, 1905, *Corr.* 3:296; William James to Alexander Agassiz, July 12, 1905, *Corr.* 11:76; William James to Charles William Eliot, July 12, 1905, *Corr.* 11:77.
88. William James to Henry James Jr., July 12, 1905, *Corr.* 3:296.
89. William James to Alexander Agassiz, July 12, 1905, *Corr.* 11:76; William James to Thomas Mitchell Shackleford, July 23, 1905, *Corr.* 11:84–85.
90. William James to Harald Höffding, July 21, 1905, *Corr.* 11:80.
91. *Prag.*, 285.
92. *Prag.*, 285.
93. Dewey had founded the Chicago Laboratory Schools, which were based on the principle of "learning by doing." He had also delivered two highly regarded lecture series on education: *The School and Society* (1899) and *The Child and the Curriculum* (1902). By the time James spoke in Chicago in 1905, Dewey was an unquestioned authority on education in Illinois, and he served as a perfect way for James to link pragmatism with the audience's predicament. For a detailed discussion of Deweyan pragmatism in the area, see Andrew Feffer, *The Chicago Pragmatists and American Progressivism* (Ithaca, NY: Cornell University Press, 1993).
94. *Prag.*, 295.
95. Joseph F. Kett, *The Pursuit of Knowledge Under Difficulties: From Self-improvement to Adult Education in America, 1750–1990* (Stanford: Stanford University Press, 1994), 167.
96. William James to Charles Sanders Peirce, August 1, 1905, *Corr.* 11:86.
97. William James to Charles Sanders Peirce, August 1, 1905, *Corr.* 11:86.
98. William James, "A Knight-Errant of the Intellectual Life," *McClure's Magazine* 25 (May 1905); reprinted in *ECR*, 92.
99. *Prag.*, 296.
100. James, "A Knight-Errant of the Intellectual Life," 92.
101. *Prag.*, 297–298.
102. William James to Abbott Lawrence Lowell, December 15, 1905, *Corr.* 11:122–123.
103. See Abbott Lawrence Lowell to William James, December 16, 1905, *Corr.* 11:578. Also see James's diary entry for May 27, 1906, in "Diary, 1906 (2)," Houghton Library, Harvard University, bMS Am 1092.9 (4555).

104. See James's diary entry for May 27, 1906, "Diary, 1906 (2)," Houghton Library, Harvard University, bMS Am 1092.9 (4555). The remaining lectures in the series took place on November 17, 21, 24, 28, and December 1, 5, and 8.

105. William James to Henry James Jr., December 9, 1906, *Corr.* 3:330.

106. "Pragmatism Considered," *Boston Evening Transcript*, November 15, 1906, 12.

107. For James's reactions to the lectures, see "Diary, 1906 (2)," Houghton Library, Harvard University, bMS Am 1092.9 (4555).

108. See "Diary, 1906 (2)," Houghton Library, Harvard University, bMS Am 1092.9 (4555).

109. William James to Henry James Jr., December 9, 1906, *Corr.* 3:330.

110. "Pragmatism is Theistic," *Boston Evening Transcript*, December 10, 1906, 12.

111. William James to Henry James Jr., December 9, 1906, *Corr.* 3:330.

112. William James to Theodore Flournoy, January 2, 1907, *Corr.* 11:299.

113. See James's diary entry for January 24, 1906, in "Diary, 1906 (2)," Houghton Library, Harvard University, bMS Am 1092.9 (4555).

114. William James to James McKeen Cattell, January 1, 1907, *Corr.* 11:296–297.

115. "A Race for the Immaterial," *New York Tribune*, January 39, 1907, 14.

116. "A Race for the Immaterial," *New York Tribune*, January 39, 1907, 14. Also see James's diary entry for January 29, 1907, in "Diary, 1907," Houghton Library, Harvard University, bMS Am 1092.9 (4556).

117. William James to Alice Howe Gibbens James, February 1, 1907, *Corr.* 11:311.

118. Harold Bolee, "Thrusts Right and Left," *Los Angeles Times*, February 24, 1907, VI11.

119. William James to John George Piddington, February 13, 1907, *Corr.* 11:320.

120. William James to Alice Howe Gibbens James, February 5, 1907, *Corr.* 11:315.

121. William James to George Angier Gordon, January 24, 1907, *Corr.* 11:307.

122. William James to Henry James Jr., February 14, 1907, *Corr.* 3:333.

123. *Prag.*, 193.

124. *Prag.*, 5. The surviving manuscript pages for *Pragmatism* are preserved in the William James collection, Houghton Library, Harvard University, bMS Am 1092.9 (4543). For an overview of the changes James made, see *Prag.*, 185–194.

125. *Prag.*, 9.

126. *Prag.*, 25.

127. *Prag.*, 52.

128. *Prag.*, 62.

129. *Prag.*, 70.

130. *Prag.*, 84.

131. *Prag.*, 89.

132. *Prag.*, 10.
133. *Prag.*, 16–17.
134. See Burton J. Bledstein, *The Culture of Professionalism: The Middle Class and the Development of Higher Education in America* (New York: W. W. Norton, 1976), 46–79.
135. *Prag.*, 10.
136. *Prag.*, 11.
137. *Prag.*, 62.
138. *Prag.*, 96.
139. *Prag.*, 123.
140. *Prag.*, 26.
141. *Prag.*, 23.
142. *Prag.*, 144.
143. *Prag.*, 81.
144. *Prag.*, 81–82.
145. *Prag.*, 127.
146. *Prag.*, 122.
147. Quoted in "The Pragmatist Microbe," *Current Literature* 43 (October 1907): 420.
148. *Prag.*, 18.
149. *Prag.*, 17–18.
150. *Prag.*, 39–40.
151. *Prag.*, 44, 49, 61.
152. *Prag.*, 110.
153. *Prag.*, 140.
154. For an overview of the agrarian and producer appeals of the populist tradition, see Michael Kazin, *The Populist Persuasion: An American History* (New York: Basic Books, 1995), 27–46.
155. For more on the general relationship between pragmatism and agrarianism, see Paul B. Thompson and Thomas C. Hilde, eds., *The Agrarian Roots of Pragmatism* (Nashville, TN: Vanderbilt University Press, 2000).
156. *Prag.*, 32.
157. *Prag.*, 38.
158. *Prag.*, 35.
159. *Prag.*, 61.
160. *Prag.*, 65.
161. *Prag.*, 83.
162. *Prag.*, 102.
163. *Prag.*, 109.

164. *Prag.*, 118.
165. *Prag.*, 31.
166. *Prag.*, 88.
167. *Prag.*, 123.
168. See Kazin, *The Populist Persuasion*, 27–46.
169. For contemporaneous discussions of James's economic terminology, see "Pragmatism," *Spectator*, July 6, 1907, 9; John Grier Hibben, "The Test of Pragmatism," *Philosophical Review* 17 (1908): 369; and Paul Carus, "Pragmatism," *Monist* 18 (1908): 325.
170. *Prag.*, 24.
171. *Prag.*, 32.
172. *Prag.*, 39.
173. *Prag.*, 42.
174. *Prag.*, 97.
175. *Prag.*, 100.
176. *Prag.*, 107.
177. *Prag.*, 142–143.
178. For a slightly more personal explanation of James's use of economic terminology, see George Cotkin, "William James and the Cash-Value Metaphor," *ETC: A Review of Semiotics* 42 (1985): 37–46.
179. For a good discussion of the theme of individual worth in populist discourse, see Rhys H. Williams and Susan M. Alexander, "Religious Rhetoric in American Populism: Civil Religion as Movement Ideology," *Journal for the Scientific Study of Religion* 33 (1994): 1–15.
180. For more on the rhetorical function of economic terminology at the turn of the twentieth century, see Paul Stob, "Louis Brandeis and the Rhetoric of Transactional Morality," *Rhetoric & Public Affairs* 14 (2011): 261–290.
181. As George Cotkin writes, "*Pragmatism* explodes with the strenuosity of [James's] discourse of heroism. Its possibilities begin with his unmasking of the *tedium vitae* inscribed into the rationalist conception of the universe. In contrast to this constrained view, his pluralistic metaphysics offered an arena necessitating heroic struggle and moral action. This discourse of heroism thus constitutes yet another public message within *Pragmatism*'s enduring philosophical content." Cotkin, *William James, Public Philosopher*, 169.
182. *Prag.*, 9.
183. *Prag.*, 25.
184. *Prag.*, 85.
185. *Prag.*, 117–118.
186. *Prag.*, 143.

187. *Prag.*, 34.
188. *Prag.*, 138.
189. The fury over pragmatic truth was so intense that James felt compelled to publish a companion volume to *Pragmatism*, titled *The Meaning of Truth* and directed at academic objections. In the preface he pointed specifically to "the anti-pragmatist contentions which I try to meet in this volume," and he objected to the way his enemies tried to dismiss him as making "a concession to popular prejudice." *MT*, 8–9.
190. *Prag.*, 36.
191. *Prag.*, 122.
192. *Prag.*, 42.
193. *Prag.*, 119.
194. *Prag.*, 30.
195. *Prag.*, 50.
196. *Prag.*, 73.
197. *Prag.*, 97.
198. *Prag.*, 136.
199. *Prag.*, 62.
200. *Prag.*, 62.
201. For discussion of the revolution component of populist discourse, see Michael J. Lee, "The Populist Chameleon: The People's Party, Huey Long, George Wallace, and the Populist Argumentative Frame," *Quarterly Journal of Speech* 92 (2006): 355–378.
202. F. H. Bradley, "On the Ambiguity of Pragmatism," *Mind* 17 (1908): 231.
203. "Pragmatism," *Independent* 63 (1907): 631.
204. "The Pragmatic Philosophy," *Springfield Sunday Republican*, June 23, 1907, 31.
205. William James, "The White Sox," *Chicago Daily Tribune*, July 10, 1909, 8.

Conclusion

1. The statement appeared in a memorandum James wrote to his friend Horace Kallen, who was charged with the task of completing James's unfinished manuscript, *Some Problems of Philosophy.* The memorandum was quoted in the preface to the manuscript when it was finally published posthumously. See *SPP*, 5.
2. Ignas K. Skrupskelis, introduction to *Corr.* 12:xliii.
3. *MT*, 10.
4. Quoted in the preface to *SPP*, 5.
5. William James to F. C. S. Schiller, January 4, 1908, *Corr.* 11:505.

6. J. E. Carpenter, letter dated June 14, 1908; reprinted in *PU*, 220–221.
7. Unsigned report, *Oxford Magazine* 26 (1907–08); reprinted in *PU*, 221–223.
8. See "Pragmatism at Oxford," *Boston Evening Transcript* (November 4, 1908); reprinted in *PU*, 223.
9. See *PU*, 223–224.
10. William James, "The Social Value of the College-Bred," *McClure's Magazine* 30 (February 1908); reprinted in *ECR*, 106–112.
11. William James, "The Confidences of a 'Psychical Researcher,'" *American Magazine* 68 (October 1909); reprinted in *EPR*, 361–375.
12. William James, "The Moral Equivalent of War," *International Conciliation*, Leaflet No. 27 (February 1910); *McClure's Magazine* 35 (August 1910); *Popular Science Monthly* 77 (October 1910); reprinted in *ERM*, 162–173.
13. See Robert D. Richardson, *William James in the Maelstrom of American Modernism* (Boston: Houghton Mifflin, 2006), 499.
14. "William James," *Popular Science Monthly* 77 (October 1910): 413–414.
15. "William James," *New York Tribune*, August 28, 1910, 6.
16. "William James," *Richmond Times-Dispatch*, August 29, 1910, 4.
17. For more on the idea of creating and then satisfying audience expectations, see Kenneth Burke, *Counter-Statement* (Berkeley: University of California Press, 1968), especially 29–44.
18. William Allan Neilson, "William James as Lecturer and Writer," *Harvard Illustrated Magazine* 8 (February 1907): 99.
19. Steven Mailloux, "Thinking in Public with Rhetoric," *Philosophy & Rhetoric* 39 (2006): 140–146.
20. Neilson, "William James as Lecturer and Writer," 99.
21. James Perrin Warren, *Culture of Eloquence: Oratory and Reform in Antebellum America* (University Park: Pennsylvania State University Press, 1999), 42.
22. See, for example, Burton J. Bledstein, *The Culture of Professionalism: The Middle Class and the Development of Higher Education in America* (New York: W. W. Norton, 1978), 98–105.
23. F. C. S. Schiller, "William James," in *William James Remembered*, ed. Linda Simon (Lincoln: University of Nebraska Press, 1996), 152.
24. M. C. Otto, "On a Certain Blindness in William James," *Ethics* 53 (1943): 189. For a similar account, see Henry Steele Commager, *The American Mind: An Interpretation of American Thought and Character Since the 1880s* (New Haven: Yale University Press, 1950), 98–100.
25. Cornel West, *The American Evasion of Philosophy: A Genealogy of Pragmatism* (Madison: University of Wisconsin Press, 1989), 54.
26. West, *The American Evasion of Philosophy*, 55.

27. William James to Sarah Wyman Whitman, June 7, 1899, *Corr.* 8:546.
28. I borrow the phrase "community of individuals" from John Lachs, *A Community of Individuals* (New York: Routledge, 2003). In the book Lachs himself builds on many of James's ideas.
29. Bledstein, *The Culture of Professionalism*, 106.
30. "Professor James's 'Pragmatism,'" *Harvard Graduates' Magazine* 16 (1907): 23.
31. Edwin Bjorkman, "Pragmatism—What It Is," *New York Times*, November 3, 1907, 8.
32. Horace M. Kallen, "What is Pragmatism?" *Boston Evening Transcript*, September 21, 1907, 5.
33. *ML*, 30.
34. *TT*, 84.
35. *EPR*, 136.
36. *VRE*, 393.
37. *Prag.*, 31.
38. *PU*, 32, 38.
39. *PU*, 130–131.
40. *WTB*, 29, 32.
41. *WTB*, 33.
42. See Paul Stob, "Pragmatism, Experience, and William James's Politics of Blindness," *Philosophy & Rhetoric* 44 (2011): 227–249.
43. James's most extensive public utterance on imperialism and anti-imperialism was his 1903 "Address on the Philippine Question" before the New England Anti-Imperialist League. For the text of the address, see *ECR*, 81–86. For a discussion of the relationship between James's anti-imperialism and the philosophy of pragmatism, see George Cotkin, *William James, Public Philosopher* (Urbana: University of Illinois Press, 1989), 123–151.

Bibliography

⌘

Those who study William James's life and work are fortunate to have access to a trove of primary documents. In general, three collections contain James's extant texts. The William James Papers at Harvard's Houghton Library house the majority of known documents. To make these documents available to the scholarly community and to contextualize them, the editors of two different book series have spent decades selecting, compiling, and publishing most of what is housed at Houghton Library. The twenty-volume *Works of William James* (1975–1988) contains critically edited editions of everything James published as well as most of his unpublished manuscripts. The twelve-volume *Correspondence of William James* (1992–2004) reproduces most of James's letters and summarizes those that are not reproduced in full. These three collections have been the basis of primary documentation for this book.

Given my focus on James's art of popular statement, four bibliographic subcategories are helpful in organizing the primary documents used in this book: manuscript collection, book reviews by William

James, lectures and speeches by William James, and books and essays by William James. The first of these provides the details of the James papers at Harvard's Houghton Library. Because of the central role book reviews played in James's early intellectual development, I have placed his reviews together in their own category. Similarly, I have grouped his lectures and speeches in their own category because of my overall emphasis on James's public speaking. The final primary document category contains a list of his books and essays—not only the volumes of *The Works of William James* that I have utilized extensively but also the original publication information of James's prominent texts.

The bibliographic category below lists the works I have referenced by everyone other than James. This includes works by James's contemporaries and by current scholars.

Manuscript Collection

William James Papers, 1842–1910. 57 linear ft. Houghton Library, Harvard University, Cambridge, Massachusetts. bMS Am 1092.9–1092.12.

Book Reviews by William James

Review of *Lectures on the Elements of Comparative Anatomy*, by Thomas Huxley. *North American Review* 100 (January 1865): 290–298.

"The Progress of Anthropology." *Nation* 6 (February 6, 1868): 113–115.

Review of *Rapport sur les progrès et la marche de la physiologie générale en France*, by Claude Bernard. *North American Review* 107 (July 1868): 322–328.

Review of *The Variation of Animals and Plants under Domestication*, by Charles Darwin. *North American Review* 107 (July 1868): 362–368.

Review of *Women's Suffrage*, by Horace Bushnell, and *The Subjection of Women*, by John Stuart Mill. *North American Review* 109 (October 1869): 556–565.

Review of *Voltaire*, by John Morley. *Atlantic Monthly* 30 (November 1872): 624–625.

"Renouvier's Contribution to *La Critique Philosophique*." *Nation* 16 (February 6, 1873): 94.

Review of *Contributions to Mental Pathology*, by Isaac Ray. *Atlantic Monthly* 31 (June 1873): 748–750.

"Recent Works on Mental Hygiene." *Nation* 19 (July 16, 1874): 43.

Review of *The Physiology of the Circulation in Plants, in the Lower Animals, and in Man*, by J. Bell Pettigrew. *Nation* 19 (July 23, 1874): 63.

Review of *Responsibility in Mental Disease*, by Henry Maudsley. *Atlantic Monthly* 34 (September 1874): 364–365.

Review of *Principles of Mental Physiology*, by William B. Carpenter. *Atlantic Monthly* 34 (October 1874): 495.

Review of *The Anesthetic Revelation*, by Benjamin Paul Blood. *Atlantic Monthly* 34 (November 1874): 627–629.

"The Unseen Universe." *Nation* 20 (May 27, 1875): 366–367.

Review of *Grundzüge der physiologischen Psychologie*, by Wilhelm Wundt. *North American Review* 121 (July 1875): 195–201.

Review of *Problems of Life and Mind*, by George Henry Lewes. *Atlantic Monthly* 36 (September 1875): 361–363.

Review of *Der moderne Pessimismus*, by Edmund Pfleiderer. *Nation* 21 (October 7, 1875): 233–234.

Review of *The Bones, Ligaments, and Muscles of the Domestic Cat*, by Henry S. Williams. *Nation* 21 (October 14, 1875): 252.

Review of *The Borderlands of Insanity*, by Andrew Wynter. *Nation* 21 (November 18, 1875): 330.

Review of *L'Anthropologie*, by Paul Topinard. *Nation* 22 (March 16, 1876): 180.

"Bain and Renouvier." *Nation* 22 (June 8, 1876): 367–369.

"Renan's Dialogues." *Nation* 23 (August 3, 1876): 78–79.

Review of *The Theory of Color in Its Relation to Art and Art-Industry*, by Wilhelm von Bezold. *Nation* 23 (November 9, 1876): 289.

"The Mind and the Brain." *Nation* 24 (June 14, 1877): 355–356.

Review of *The Physiology of Mind*, by Henry Maudsley. *Nation* 24 (June 14, 1877): 355–356.

Review of *The Jukes*, by Richard L. Dugdale. *Atlantic Monthly* 41 (March 1878): 405.

"Herbert Spencer's Data of Ethics." *Nation* 29 (September 11, 1879): 178–179.

Review of *A Defence of Philosophic Doubt*, by Arthur James Balfour. *Nation* 29 (October 23, 1879): 280.

"Clifford's Lectures and Essays." *Nation* 29 (November 6, 1879): 312–313.

Lectures and Speeches by William James

"The Senses and the Brain and Their Relation to Thought." Johns Hopkins University, Baltimore, Maryland. February 11–22, 1878.

"The Brain and the Mind." Lowell Institute, Boston, Massachusetts. October 15–November 1, 1878.

"Topics of Psychology of Interest to Teachers." Harvard University, Cambridge, Massachusetts. October 27, 1891–January 21, 1892.

"Psychology as Applied to Teaching." Brooklyn Institute of Arts and Sciences, Brooklyn, New York. October 6–November 17, 1894.

"Psychology as Applied to Teaching." Schoolhouse on the Corner of St. Botolph and Cumberland, Boston, Massachusetts. November 12–December 24, 1894.

"Talks to Teachers on Psychology." Norwich Free Academy, Norwich, Connecticut. July 15–17, 1895.

"Talks to Teachers on Psychology." Harvard University, Cambridge, Massachusetts. July 18–31, 1895.

"Talks to Teachers on Psychology." Colorado College, Colorado Springs, Colorado. August 1–9, 1895.

"Address of the President before the Society for Psychical Research." Society for Psychical Research, Boston, Massachusetts. January 31, 1896.

"Address of the President before the Society for Psychical Research." Society for Psychical Research, New York, New York. February 1, 1896.

"Talks to Teachers on Psychology." Harvard University, Cambridge, Massachusetts. July 1–12, 1896.

"Talks to Teachers on Psychology." Harvard University, Cambridge, Massachusetts. July 2–15, 1896.

"Talks to Teachers on Psychology." University of Buffalo, Buffalo, New York. July 16–22, 1896.

"Talks to Teachers on Psychology." University of Chicago, Chicago, Illinois. September 1–4, 1896.

"Exceptional Mental States." Lowell Institute, Boston, Massachusetts. October 21–November 14, 1896.

"Philosophical Conceptions and Practical Results." University of California, Berkeley, California. August 26, 1898.

"What Makes a Life Significant." Stanford University, Stanford, California. September 5, 1898.

"Psychology and Relaxation." University of California, Berkeley, California. September 12, 1898.

"Talks to Teachers on Psychology." Teacher's Institute of Alameda County, Alameda, California. September 12–15, 1898.

"Human Immortality: Two Supposed Objections to the Doctrine." Berkeley Club, Oakland, California. September 15, 1898.

"The Varieties of Religious Experience." University of Edinburgh, Edinburgh, Scotland. May 16–June 17, 1901, May 13–June 9, 1902.

"Characteristics of an Individualistic Philosophy." Wellesley College, Wellesley, Massachusetts. February 28–March 10, 1905.

"Characteristics of an Individualistic Philosophy." University of Chicago, Chicago, Illinois. June 30–July 7, 1905.

"Characteristics of an Individualistic Philosophy." Glenmore Institute, Keene, New York. July 27–August 3, 1905.

"Pragmatism." Lowell Institute, Boston, Massachusetts. November 14–December 8, 1906.

"Pragmatism." Columbia University, New York, New York. January 29–February 8, 1907.

"The Social Value of the College-Bred." Radcliffe College, Cambridge, Massachusetts. November 26, 1907.

"A Pluralistic Universe." Manchester College, Oxford, England. May 4–28, 1908.

"A Pluralistic Universe." Harvard University, Cambridge, Massachusetts. November 6–30, 1908.

Books and Essays by William James

"Address of the President before the Society for Psychical Research." *Science* 3 (June 19, 1896): 881–888.

"Chauncey Wright." *Nation* 21 (September 23, 1875): 194.

"The Confidences of a 'Psychical Researcher.'" *American Magazine* 68 (October 1909): 580–589.

The Correspondence of William James. 12 vols. Edited by Ignas K. Skrupskelis and Elizabeth M. Berkeley. Charlottesville: University Press of Virginia, 1992–2004.

Essays in Psychical Research (*The Works of William James*). Cambridge: Harvard University Press, 1986.

Essays in Psychology (*The Works of William James*). Cambridge: Harvard University Press, 1983.

Essays in Radical Empiricism (*The Works of William James*). Cambridge: Harvard University Press, 1976.

Essays in Religion and Morality (*The Works of William James*). Cambridge: Harvard University Press, 1982.

Essays, Comments, and Reviews (*The Works of William James*). Cambridge: Harvard University Press, 1987.

"The Hidden Self." *Scribner's Magazine* 7 (March 1890): 361–373.

"Introduction." In *The Literary Remains of the Late Henry James*, edited by William James. Boston: Houghton Mifflin, 1884.

"A Knight-Errant of the Intellectual Life." *McClure's Magazine* 25 (May 1905): 3–11.

"Lehmann and Hansen on Telepathy." *Science* 9 (May 15, 1899): 654–655.

"Letter on Mrs. Piper, the Medium." *Science* 7 (May 6, 1898): 640–641.

"Louis Agassiz." *Science* 5 (1897): 285–289.

Manuscript Lectures (*The Works of William James*). Cambridge: Harvard University Press, 1988.

The Meaning of Truth (*The Works of William James*). Cambridge: Harvard University Press, 1975.

The Meaning of Truth. New York: Longmans, Green, 1909.

"The Moral Equivalent of War." *International Conciliation*, Leaflet No. 27 (February 1910); *McClure's Magazine* 35 (August 1910): 463–468; *Popular Science Monthly* 77 (October 1910): 400–412.

"The Ph.D. Octopus." *Harvard Monthly* 36 (1903): 1–9.

"Philosophical Conceptions and Practical Results." *University Chronicle* 1 (September 1898): 287–310.

A Pluralistic Universe (*The Works of William James*). Cambridge: Harvard University Press, 1977.

A Pluralistic Universe. New York: Longmans, Green, 1909.

"The Pragmatic Method." *Journal of Philosophy, Psychology, and Scientific Methods* 1 (1904): 673–687.

"Pragmatic and Pragmatism." In *Dictionary of Philosophy and Psychology*, vol. 3, edited by J. M. Baldwin. New York: Macmillan, 1902: 321.

Pragmatism (*The Works of William James*). Cambridge: Harvard University Press, 1975.

Pragmatism: A New Name for Some Old Ways of Thinking. New York: Longmans, Green, 1907.

The Principles of Psychology, 3 vols. (*The Works of William James*). Cambridge: Harvard University Press, 1981.

The Principles of Psychology, 2 vols. New York: Henry Holt, 1890.

"Professor Jeffries Wyman." *Harvard Advocate*, October 1, 1874, 8–9.

"A Record of Observations of Certain Phenomena of Trance." *Proceedings of the Society for Psychical Research* 6 (December 1890): 651–659.

"Report on Mrs. Piper's Hodgson-Control." *Proceedings of the Society for Psychical Research* 23 (June 1909): 2–121.

"The Social Value of the College-Bred." *McClure's Magazine* 30 (February 1908): 419–422.

Some Problems of Philosophy (The Works of William James). Cambridge: Harvard University Press, 1979.

Some Problems of Philosophy: A Beginning of an Introduction to Philosophy. New York: Longmans, Green, 1911.

Talks To Teachers on Psychology and to Students on Some of Life's Ideals (The Works of William James). Cambridge: Harvard University Press, 1983.

Talks to Teachers on Psychology: And to Students on Some of Life's Ideals. New York: Henry Holt, 1899.

The Varieties of Religious Experience (The Works of William James). Cambridge: Harvard University Press, 1985.

The Varieties of Religious Experience: A Study in Human Nature. New York: Longmans, Green, 1902.

"What Psychical Research Has Accomplished." *Forum* 13 (August 1892): 727–742.

Other Sources

Adams, Henry. *The Education of Henry Adams: An Autobiography*. Boston: Houghton Mifflin, 1918.

Agassiz, Louis. *Methods of Study in Natural History.* Boston: Fields, Osgood, 1871.

Agassiz, Louis, and Elizabeth Agassiz. *A Journey in Brazil*. Boston: Fields, Osgood, 1871.

Alden, W. L. "Wisdom Let Loose." *Pearson's Magazine*, February 1896, 180–181.

Allen, Gay Wilson. *William James: A Biography*. New York: Viking Press, 1967.

Antczak, Frederick J. *Thought and Character: The Rhetoric of Democratic Education*. Ames: Iowa State University Press, 1985.

Appel, Toby A. "Jeffries Wyman, Philosophical Anatomy, and the Scientific Reception of Darwin in America." *Journal of the History of Biology* 21 (1988): 69–94.

———. "A Scientific Career in the Age of Character: Jeffries Wyman and Natural History at Harvard." In *Science at Harvard University: Historical*

Perspectives, edited by Clark A. Elliott and Margaret W. Rossiter. Bethlehem, PA: Lehigh University Press, 1992: 96–120.

Arnold, Carroll C. "Oral Rhetoric, Rhetoric, and Literature." *Philosophy & Rhetoric* 1 (1968): 191–210.

Asen, Robert, and Daniel C. Brouwer, eds. *Counterpublics and the State*. Albany: State University of New York Press, 2001.

Baker, Houston A. *Betrayal: How Black Intellectuals Have Abandoned the Ideals of the Civil Rights Era*. New York: Columbia University Press, 2008.

Bakewell, Charles M. Review of *Pragmatism*, by William James. *Philosophical Review* 16 (1907): 624–634.

Barnard, G. William. "*The Varieties of Religious Experience*: Reflections on Its Enduring Value." *Journal of Consciousness Studies* 9 (2002): 57–77.

Baskerville, Barnet. "19th Century Burlesque of Oratory." *American Quarterly* 20 (1968): 726–743.

Belasco, Susan. "The Cultural Work of National Magazines." In *A History of the Book in America*, vol. 3, edited by Scott E. Casper, Jeffrey D. Groves, Stephen W. Nissenbaum, and Michael Winship. Chapel Hill: University of North Carolina Press, 2007: 258–270.

Belzen, Jacob A. "The *Varieties*, the *Principles* and the Psychology of Religion: Unremitting Inspiration from a Different Source." In *William James and "The Varieties of Religious Experience": A Centenary Celebration*, edited by Jeremy Carrette. London: Routledge, 2005: 54–71.

Bender, Thomas. *Intellect and Public Life: Essays on the Social History of Academic Intellectuals in the United States*. Baltimore: Johns Hopkins University Press, 1993.

Bergman, Mats. "Experience, Purpose, and the Value of Vagueness: On C. S. Peirce's Contribution to the Philosophy of Communication." *Communication Theory* 19 (2009): 248–277.

Bitzer, Lloyd F. "Rhetoric and Public Knowledge." In *Rhetoric, Philosophy, and Literature: An Exploration*, edited by Don M. Burks. West Lafayette: Purdue University Press, 1978: 67–93.

Bjork, Daniel W. *The Compromised Scientist: William James and the Development of American Psychology*. New York: Columbia University Press, 1983.

Bjorkman, Edwin. "Pragmatism—What It Is." *New York Times*, November 3, 1907: 8.

Black, Edwin. "The Second Persona." *Quarterly Journal of Speech* 56 (1970): 109–119.

Bledstein, Burton J. *The Culture of Professionalism: The Middle Class and the Development of Higher Education in America*. New York: W. W. Norton, 1978.

———. "Noah Porter versus William Graham Sumner." *Church History* 43 (1974): 340–350.

Blum, Deborah. *Ghost Hunters: William James and the Search for Scientific Proof of Life After Death.* New York: Penguin Press, 2006.

Bode, Carl. *The American Lyceum: Town Meeting of the Mind.* Carbondale: Southern Illinois University Press, 1968.

Boggs, Carl. *Intellectuals and the Crisis of Modernity.* Albany: State University of New York Press, 1993.

Bordogna, Francesca. *William James at the Boundaries: Philosophy, Science, and the Geography of Knowledge.* Chicago: University of Chicago Press, 2008.

Bowen, Francis. *Gleanings from A Literary Life, 1838–1880.* New York: Charles Scribner's Sons, 1880.

———. *Modern Philosophy, From Descartes to Schopenhauer and Hartmann.* New York: Scribner, Armstrong, 1877.

———. Review of *On the Origin of Species by Means of Natural Selection*, by Charles Darwin. *North American Review* 90 (1860): 474–506.

Bradley, F. H. "On the Ambiguity of Pragmatism." *Mind* 17 (1908): 226–237.

Braude, Ann. *Radical Spirits: Spiritualism and Women's Rights in Nineteenth-Century America*, 2nd ed. Bloomington: Indiana University Press, 2001.

Brent, Joseph. *Charles Sanders Peirce: A Life.* Bloomington: Indiana University Press, 1993.

Brewer, Charles L. "William James's Talks about Teaching." *Teaching of Psychology* 30 (2003): 34–38.

Bridgers, Lynn. *Contemporary Varieties of Religious Experience: James's Classic Study in Light of Resiliency, Temperament, and Trauma.* Lanham, MD: Rowman & Littlefield, 2005.

Brigance, William Norwood. "Can We Redefine the James-Winans Theory of Persuasion?" *Quarterly Journal of Speech* 21 (1935): 19–26.

Brinton, Alan. "William James and the Epistemic View of Rhetoric." *Quarterly Journal of Speech* 68 (1982): 158–169.

Brouwer, Daniel C., and Catherine R. Squires. "Public Intellectuals, Public Life, and the University." *Argumentation & Advocacy* 39 (2003): 201–213.

Brown, E. E. *Life of Oliver Wendell Holmes.* Akron: Salfield Publishing, 1903.

Brown, Slater. *The Heyday of Spiritualism.* New York: Hawthorn Books, 1970.

Bryant, Donald C. "Rhetoric: Its Functions and Its Scope." *Quarterly Journal of Speech* 39 (1953): 401–424.

Burke, Kenneth. *Attitudes Toward History.* 3rd ed. Berkeley: University of California Press, 1959.

———. *Counter-Statement.* Berkeley: University of California Press, 1968.

———. *A Grammar of Motives.* Berkeley: University of California Press, 1969.

———. *Language as Symbolic Action: Essays on Life, Literature, and Method.* Berkeley: University of California Press, 1966.

———. *A Rhetoric of Motives.* Berkeley: University of California Press, 1969.

Burks, Don M., ed. *Rhetoric, Philosophy, and Literature: An Exploration.* West Lafayette, IN: Purdue University Press, 1978.

Byerly, W. E. "Reminiscences." *American Mathematical Monthly* 32 (1925): 5–7.

Caldwell, W. "Pragmatism." *Mind* 36 (1900): 433–456.

Carpenter, Frederic I. "William James and Emerson." *American Literature* 11 (1939): 39–57.

Carrette, Jeremy, ed. *William James and "The Varieties of Religious Experience": A Centenary Celebration.* London: Routledge, 2005.

Carroll, Bret E. *Spiritualism in Antebellum America.* Bloomington: Indiana University Press, 1997.

Carus, Paul. "Pragmatism." *Monist* 18 (1908): 321–362.

Casper, Scott E., Jeffrey D. Groves, Stephen W. Nissenbaum, and Michael Winship, eds. *A History of the Book in America*, vol. 3. Chapel Hill: University of North Carolina Press, 2007.

Catalogue of the Officers and Students of Harvard University for the Academical Year 1861–62, First Term. Cambridge: Sever and Francis, 1861.

Catalogue of the Officers and Students of Harvard University for the Academical Year 1863–64, First Term. Cambridge: Sever and Francis, 1864.

Cattell, James McKeen. "Notice of 'Address of the President before the Society for Psychical Research.'" *Psychological Review* 3 (September 1896): 582–583.

———. "Mrs. Piper, the Medium." *Science* 7 (April 15, 1898): 534–535.

———. "The Progress of Psychology." *Popular Science Monthly* 43 (October 1893): 779–785.

———. "Our Psychological Association and Research." *Science* 45 (1917): 273–284.

Cayton, Mary Kupiec. "The Making of an American Prophet: Emerson, His Audiences, and the Rise of the Culture Industry in Nineteenth-Century America." *American Historical Review* 92 (1987): 597–620.

Channing, Edward T. *Lectures Read to the Seniors in Harvard College.* Boston: Ticknor and Fields, 1856.

Chapel, Gage, and Richard Jensen. "Synthesizing Jamesian Pragmatism and Platonic Idealism in Nineteenth-Century America: The Discourse of Mary Baker Eddy's Christian Science." *Journal of Communication & Religion* 23 (2000): 95–112.

Clark, Gregory, and S. Michael Halloran, eds. *Oratorical Culture in Nineteenth-Century America: Transformations in the Theory and Practice of Rhetoric*. Carbondale: Southern Illinois University Press, 1993.

Clark, Gregory, and S. Michael Halloran. Afterword to *Oratorical Culture in Nineteenth-Century America: Transformations in the Theory and Practice of Rhetoric*, edited by Gregory Clark and S. Michael Halloran. Carbondale: Southern Illinois University Press, 1993: 247–250.

———. "Introduction: Transformations of Public Discourse in Nineteenth-Century America." In *Oratorical Culture in Nineteenth-Century America: Transformations in the Theory and Practice of Rhetoric*, edited by Gregory Clark and S. Michael Halloran. Carbondale: Southern Illinois University Press, 1993: 1–26.

Clendenning, John. *The Life and Thought of Josiah Royce*, rev. ed. Nashville, TN: Vanderbilt University Press, 1999.

Cmiel, Kenneth. *Democratic Eloquence: The Fight over Popular Speech in Nineteenth-Century America*. New York: William Morrow, 1990.

Cockerell, T. D. A. "Varieties of Religious Experience." *Dial* 33 (November 16, 1902): 322–323.

Coe, George. Review of *The Varieties of Religious Experience*, by William James. *Philosophical Review* 12 (1903): 62–67.

Collini, Stefan. "'Every Fruit-Juice Drinker, Nudist, Sandal-Wearer . . .': Intellectuals as Other People." In *The Public Intellectual*, edited by Helen Small. Oxford: Blackwell, 2002: 203–223.

Collins, Randall. *The Sociology of Philosophies: A Global Theory of Intellectual Change*. Cambridge: Belknap Press of Harvard University Press, 1998.

"The Columbian Reading Union." *Catholic World* 60 (1894): 857.

Commager, Henry Steele. *The American Mind: An Interpretation of American Thought and Character Since the 1880s.* New Haven: Yale University Press, 1950.

Connors, Robert J. "Greek Rhetoric and the Transition from Orality." *Philosophy & Rhetoric* 19 (1986): 38–65.

Cotkin, George. *William James, Public Philosopher.* Urbana: University of Illinois Press, 1989.

———. "William James and the Cash-Value Metaphor." *ETC: A Review of Semiotics* 42 (1985): 37–46.

Cox, Robert S. *Body and Soul: A Sympathetic History of American Spiritualism.* Charlottesville: University of Virginia Press, 2003.

Creech, Joe. *Righteous Indignation: Religion and the Populist Revolution.* Urbana: University of Illinois Press, 2006.

Crick, Nathan. *Democracy and Rhetoric: John Dewey on the Arts of Becoming.* Columbia: University of South Carolina Press, 2010.

———. "Rhetoric, Philosophy, and the Public Intellectual." *Philosophy & Rhetoric* 39 (2006): 127–139.

Croce, Paul Jerome. "Physiology as the Antechamber to Metaphysics: The Young William James's Hope for a Philosophical Psychology." *History of Psychology* 2 (1999): 302–323.

———. *Science and Religion in the Era of William James*, vol. 1: *Eclipse of Certainty, 1820–1880*. Chapel Hill: University of North Carolina Press, 1995.

Crozier, L. Graham. Review of *Talks to Teachers on Psychology and to Students on Some of Life's Ideals*, by William James. *Southern Education Journal* 13 (1900): 373–374.

Crusius, Timothy W. "Orality in Kenneth Burke's Dialectic." *Philosophy & Rhetoric* 21 (1988): 116–130.

Curtis, George William. "Lectures and Lecturing." *Harper's Monthly Magazine* 14 (1856): 122–125.

Danisch, Robert. *Pragmatism, Democracy, and the Necessity of Rhetoric*. Columbia: University of South Carolina Press, 2007.

De Gurowski, Adam G. *America and Europe.* New York: D. Appleton, 1857.

Dewey, John. *The Quest for Certainty,* vol. 4 of *The Later Works of John Dewey*, edited by Jo Ann Boydston. Carbondale: Southern Illinois University Press, 1988.

Dickstein, Morris, ed. *The Revival of Pragmatism: New Essays on Social Thought, Law, and Culture.* Durham, NC: Duke University Press, 1998.

Diggins, John Patrick. "The Changing Role of the Public Intellectual in American History." In *The Public Intellectual: Between Philosophy and Politics*, edited by Arthur M. Melzer, Jerry Weinberger, and M. Richard Zinman. Lanham, MD: Rowman & Littlefield, 2003: 91–108.

Dunne, Finley Peter. "Mr. Dooley on Philosophers." *American Magazine* 65 (1908): 543–544.

Dupree, A. Hunter. *Asa Gray, 1810–1888*. Cambridge: Belknap Press of Harvard University Press, 1959.

Edmonds, John W., and George T. Dexter. *Spiritualism.* New York: Partridge and Brittan, 1853.

Eliot, Charles W. "Reminiscences of Peirce." *American Mathematical Monthly* 32 (1925): 1–3.

Elliott, Clark A., and Margaret W. Rossiter, eds. *Science at Harvard University: Historical Perspectives*. Bethlehem, PA: Lehigh University Press, 1992.

Emerson, Edward Waldo. *The Early Years of the Saturday Club, 1855–1870.* Boston: Houghton Mifflin, 1918.

Emerson, Ralph Waldo. "The American Scholar." In *Nature, Addresses, and Lectures: The Complete Works of Ralph Waldo Emerson*, vol. 1. Boston: Houghton, Mifflin, 1903: 79–116.

———. "Literary Ethics." In *Nature, Addresses, and Lectures: The Complete Works of Ralph Waldo Emerson*, vol. 1. Boston: Houghton, Mifflin, 1903: 153–188.

———. *Nature, Addresses, and Lectures: The Complete Works of Ralph Waldo Emerson*, vol. 1. Boston: Houghton, Mifflin, 1903.

Erlich, Howard S. "Populist Rhetoric Reassessed: A Paradox." *Quarterly Journal of Speech* 63 (1977): 140–150.

Farrell, Thomas B. *Norms of Rhetorical Culture*. New Haven: Yale University Press, 1993.

Feffer, Andrew. *The Chicago Pragmatists and American Progressivism*. Ithaca, NY: Cornell University Press, 1993.

Feinstein, Howard M. *Becoming William James*. Ithaca, NY: Cornell University Press, 1984.

Felkin, R. W. "Hypnotism, or Psycho-Therapeutics." *Edinburgh Medical Journal* 35 (May 1890): 1031.

Ferguson, Kenneth. *William James: Politics in the Pluriverse*. Lanham, MD: Rowman & Littlefield, 2007.

Field, Peter S. "'The Transformation of Genius into Practical Power': Ralph Waldo Emerson and the Public Lecture." *Journal of the Early Republic* 21 (2001): 467–493.

Fish, Stanley. *Professional Correctness: Literary Studies and Political Change*. Cambridge: Harvard University Press, 1995.

Fisher, Paul. *House of Wits: An Intimate Portrait of the James Family*. New York: Henry Holt, 2008.

Freidson, Eliot. *Professional Powers: A Study of the Institutionalization of Formal Knowledge*. Chicago: University of Chicago Press, 1986.

Fuller, Margaret. *Papers on Literature and Art*. New York: Fowler and Wells, 1852.

Fuller, Steve. *The Intellectual*. Cambridge: Icon Books, 2005.

———. "The Public Intellectual as Agent of Justice: In Search of a Regime." *Philosophy & Rhetoric* 39 (2006): 147–156.

Fyfe, Aileen, and Bernard Lightman, eds. *Science in the Marketplace: Nineteenth-Century Sites and Experiences*. Chicago: University of Chicago Press, 2007.

Gagarin, Michael. "The Orality of Greek Oratory." In *Signs of Orality: The Oral Tradition and Its Influence in the Greek and Roman World*, edited by E. Anne Mackay. Leiden, the Netherlands: Brill, 1999: 163–180.

Geiger, Roger L., ed. *The American College in the Nineteenth Century*. Nashville, TN: Vanderbilt University Press, 2000.

———. Introduction to *The American College in the Nineteenth Century*, edited by Roger L. Geiger. Nashville, TN: Vanderbilt University Press, 2000: 1–36.

Gibian, Peter. *Oliver Wendell Holmes and the Culture of Conversation*. Cambridge: Cambridge University Press, 2001.

Gilbert, James. *Designing the Industrial State: The Intellectual Pursuit of Collectivism in America, 1880–1940*. Chicago: Quadrangle Books, 1972.

Gilman, Daniel Coit. "Report of the President." In *First Annual Report of the Johns Hopkins University*. Baltimore: William K. Boyle & Son, 1876: 7–25.

Goodman, Russell B. *American Philosophy and the Romantic Tradition*. Cambridge: Cambridge University Press, 1990.

Goodnight, G. Thomas. "The Personal, Technical, and Public Spheres of Argument: A Speculative Inquiry into the Art of Public Deliberation." *Journal of the American Forensic Association* 18 (1982): 214–227.

"The Gospel of Pragmatism." *Academy* 73 (1907): 772–773.

Grattan-Guinness, Ivor, ed. *Psychical Research: A Guide to its History, Principles and Practices*. Wellingborough, Northamptonshire, England: Aquarian Press, 1982.

Gray, Asa. *Darwiniana: Essays and Reviews Pertaining to Darwinism*. New York: D. Appleton, 1889.

———. "Review of Darwin's Theory on the Origin of Species by Means of Natural Selection." *American Journal of Science and Arts* 29 (1860): 153–185.

Green, Christopher D., Marlene Shore, and Thomas Teo, eds. *The Transformation of Psychology: Influences of 19th-Century Philosophy, Technology, and Natural Science*. Washington, DC: American Psychological Association, 2001.

Gronbeck, Bruce E. "Rhetorical Invention in the Regency Crisis Pamphlets." *Quarterly Journal of Speech* 58 (1972): 418–430.

Habegger, Alfred. *The Father: A Life of Henry James, Sr.* New York: Farrar, Straus and Giroux, 1994.

Hague, W. Vesey. "What is a Reasonable Faith?" *Irish Ecclesiastical Record* 14 (1903): 254–272.

Hall, David D. "Erudition and Learned Culture." In *A History of the Book in America*, vol. 3, edited by Scott E. Casper, Jeffrey D. Groves, Stephen W. Nissenbaum, and Michael Winship. Chapel Hill: University of North Carolina Press, 2007: 347–360.

Hall, Vernon C. "Educational Psychology from 1890 to 1920." In *Educational Psychology: A Century of Contributions*, edited by Barry J. Zimmerman and Dale H. Schunk. Mahwah, NJ: Lawrence Erlbaum Associates, 2003: 3–39.

Hart, Albert Bushnell. "The Teacher as Professional Expert." *School Review* 1 (1893): 4–14.

Hartelius, E. Johanna. *The Rhetoric of Expertise*. Lanham, MD: Lexington Books, 2011.

Hauser, Gerard A. *Vernacular Voices: The Rhetoric of Publics and Public Spheres*. Columbia: University of South Carolina Press, 1999.

Hawkins, Hugh. *Pioneer: A History of Johns Hopkins University, 1874–1889*. Ithaca, NY: Cornell University Press, 1960.

Hayes, Henry A. "Aims and Methods in Teachers' Institutes." *Southern Educational Journal* 10 (1897): 152–155.

Henson, Louise Cantor, Geoffrey Cantor, Gowan Dawson, Richard Noakes, Sally Shuttleworth, and Jonathan R. Topham, eds., *Culture and Science in the Nineteenth-Century Media*. Burlington: Ashgate, 2004.

Heyl, John D., and Barbara S. Heyl. "The Sumner-Porter Controversy at Yale: Pre-Paradigmatic Sociology and Institutional Crisis." *Sociological Inquiry* 46 (1976): 41–49.

Hibben, John Grier. "The Test of Pragmatism." *Philosophical Review* 17 (1908): 365–382.

Higbee, E. E. "The Training of Teachers." *Science* 9 (1887): 71–72.

Higginson, Thomas Wentworth. "The American Lecture-System." *Macmillan's Magazine* 18 (1868): 48–56.

Hochmuth, Marie, and Richard Murphy. "Rhetorical and Elocutionary Training in Nineteenth-Century Colleges." In *History of Speech Education in America: Background Studies*, edited by Karl Wallace. New York: Appleton-Century-Crofts, 1954: 153–177.

Hofstadter, Richard. *Anti-intellectualism in American Life*. New York: Vintage, 1963.

———. *Social Darwinism in American Thought*. Boston: Beacon Press, 1955.

Hogan, J. Michael, ed. *Rhetoric and Reform in the Progressive Era*. East Lansing: Michigan State University Press, 2003.

Holland, Josiah. "The Popular Lecture." *Atlantic Monthly* 15 (1865): 362–371.

Hollinger, David A. "'Damned for God's Glory': William James and the Scientific Vindication of Protestant Culture." In *William James and a Science of Religions: Reexperiencing "The Varieties of Religious Experience,"* edited by Wayne Proudfoot. New York: Columbia University Press, 2004: 9–30.

Hollinger, Robert, and David Depew, eds. *Pragmatism: From Progressivism to Postmodernism*. Westport, CT: Praeger, 1999.

Hookway, Christopher. "Logical Principles and Philosophical Attitudes: Peirce's Response to James's Pragmatism." In *The Cambridge Companion to William James*, edited by Ruth Anna Putnam. Cambridge: Cambridge University Press, 1997: 145–165.

Hooper, Franklin W. "The Brooklyn Institute of Arts and Sciences." *Lend a Hand: A Record of Progress* 15 (1895): 193–201.

Howells, William Dean. "Editor's Study." *Harper's New Monthly Magazine* 83 (July 1891): 314.

Hoyt, Edwin P. *The Improper Bostonian: Dr. Oliver Wendell Holmes*. New York: William Morrow, 1979.

Hine, Robert V. *Josiah Royce: From Grass Valley to Harvard.* Norman: University of Oklahoma Press, 1992.

Ingersoll, Robert Green. *Prose-Poems and Selections from the Writings and Sayings of Robert G. Ingersoll.* New York: C. P. Farrell, 1888.

Jacobs, Walter Ballou. "The Training of Teachers for Secondary Schools." *School Review* 5 (1897): 375–386.

Jacoby, Russell. *The Last Intellectuals: American Culture in the Age of Academe.* New York: Noonday Press, 1987.

Jaki, Stanley L. *Lord Gifford and His Lectures: A Centenary Retrospect.* Edinburgh: Scottish Academic Press, 1986.

James, Henry Sr. *Lectures and Miscellanies*. New York: Redfield, 1852.

———. *The Social Significance of Our Institutions: An Oration*. Boston: Ticknor and Fields, 1861.

———. *Society the Redeemed Form of Man, and the Earnest of God's Omnipotence in Human Nature*. Boston: Houghton, Osgood, 1879.

James, Henry Jr. *Notes of a Son and Brother.* New York: Charles Scribner's Sons, 1914.

———. *A Small Boy and Others*. New York: Charles Scribner's Sons, 1913.

James, Henry. *Charles W. Eliot: President of Harvard University, 1869–1909*, vol. 1. Boston: Houghton Mifflin, 1930.

Jastrow, Joseph. "The Problems of 'Psychical Research.'" *Harper's New Monthly Magazine* 79 (1889): 76–82.

Jay, Martin. *Songs of Experience: Modern American and European Variations on a Universal Theme.* Berkeley: University of California Press, 2005.

Jennings, Jeremy, and Tony Kemp-Welch. "The Century of the Intellectual: From the Dreyfus Affair to Salman Rushdie." In *Intellectuals in Politics: From the Dreyfus Affair to Salman Rushdie*, edited by Jeremy Jennings and Tony Kemp-Welch. London: Routledge, 1997: 1–21.

———, eds. *Intellectuals in Politics: From the Dreyfus Affair to Salman Rushdie.* London: Routledge, 1997.

Jennings, Jeremy. "Deaths of the Intellectual: A Comparative Autopsy." In *The Public Intellectual*, edited by Helen Small. Oxford: Blackwell, 2002: 110–130.

Johnson, Nan. *Nineteenth-Century Rhetoric in North America.* Carbondale: Southern Illinois University Press, 1991.

Jost, Walter, and Wendy Olmsted, eds. *Rhetorical Invention & Religious Inquiry: New Perspectives.* New Haven: Yale University Press, 2000.

Kaestle, Carl F., and Janice A. Radway, eds. *A History of the Book in America*, vol. 4. Chapel Hill: University of North Carolina Press, 2009.

Kallen, Horace M. "What is Pragmatism?" *Boston Evening Transcript*, September 21, 1907: 5.

Kazin, Michael. *The Populist Persuasion: An American History*. New York: Basic Books, 1995.

Kerr, Howard. *Mediums, Spirit-Rappers, and Roaring Radicals: Spiritualism in American Literature, 1850–1900.* Urbana: University of Illinois Press, 1972.

Kett, Joseph F. *The Pursuit of Knowledge Under Difficulties: From Self-Improvement to Adult Education in America, 1750–1990.* Stanford: Stanford University Press, 1994.

Kimball, Bruce A. *Orators & Philosophers: A History of the Idea of Liberal Education*. New York: Teachers College Press, 1986.

———. *The "True Professional Ideal" in America: A History.* Lanham, MD: Rowman & Littlefield, 1995.

Knutson, Andrea. *American Spaces of Conversion: The Conductive Imaginaries of Edwards, Emerson, & James.* Oxford: Oxford University Press, 2011.

Korn, James H. "The Teaching Spirit of William James." *Teaching of Psychology* 30 (2003): 44–45.

Kraig, Robert Alexander. "The Second Oratorical Renaissance." In *Rhetoric and Reform in the Progressive Era*, edited by J. Michael Hogan. East Lansing: Michigan State University Press, 2003: 1–48.

Kucich, John J. *Ghostly Communion: Cross-Cultural Spiritualism in Nineteenth-Century American Literature.* Hanover, NH: Dartmouth College Press, 2004.

Kuklick, Bruce. "American Philosophy and Its Lost Public." In *Pragmatism: From Progressivism to Postmodernism*, edited by Robert Hollinger and David Depew. Westport, CT: Praeger, 1999: 142–152.

———. *Josiah Royce: An Intellectual Biography.* Indianapolis: Bobbs-Merrill, 1972.

———. *The Rise of American Philosophy: Cambridge, Massachusetts, 1860–1930.* New Haven: Yale University Press, 1977.

Kusch, Martin. *Psychologism: A Case Study in the Sociology of Knowledge.* London: Routledge, 1995.

Lachs, John. *A Community of Individuals.* New York: Routledge, 2003.

LaFollette, Marcel Chatkowski. "Crafting a Communications Infrastructure: Scientific and Technical Publishing in the United States." In *A History of the Book in America*, vol. 4, edited by Carl F. Kaestle and Janice A. Radway. Chapel Hill: University of North Carolina Press, 2009: 234–259.

Langsdorf, Lenore, and Andrew R. Smith, eds. *Recovering Pragmatism's Voice: The Classical Tradition, Rorty, and the Philosophy of Communication.* Albany: State University of New York Press, 1995.

Lawn, Beverly. "From Temple to Streets: The Style of Pragmatism." *New England Quarterly* 45 (1972): 526–540.

Lee, Michael J. "The Populist Chameleon: The People's Party, Huey Long, George Wallace, and the Populist Argumentative Frame." *Quarterly Journal of Speech* 92 (2006): 355–378.

Lee, Ronald. "The New Populist Campaign for Economic Democracy: A Rhetorical Exploration." *Quarterly Journal of Speech* 72 (1986): 274–289.

LeFevre, Karen Burke. *Invention as a Social Act.* Carbondale: Southern Illinois University Press, 1987.

Lehuu, Isabell. *Carnival on the Page: Popular Print Media in Antebellum America.* Chapel Hill: University of North Carolina Press, 2000.

Levinson, Henry Samuel. *The Religious Investigations of William James.* Chapel Hill: University of North Carolina Press, 1981.

Lewis, David Levering. *W. E. B. Du Bois: Biography of a Race, 1868–1919.* New York: Henry Holt, 1993.

Lilla, Mark. *The Reckless Mind: Intellectuals in Politics.* New York: New York Review Books, 2001.

Loewenberg, James. "The Reaction of American Scientists to Darwinism." *American Historical Review* 38 (1933): 687–701.

Lowell, A. Lawrence. "Reminiscences." *American Mathematical Monthly* 32 (1925): 4–5.

Lucas, Christopher J. *American Higher Education: A History.* New York: St. Martin's Griffin, 1994.

———. *Teacher Education in America: Reform Agendas for the Twenty-First Century.* New York: St. Martin's Press, 1997.

Lunceford, Brett. "The Science of Orality: Implications for Rhetorical Theory." *Review of Communication* 7 (2007): 83–102.

Lundin, Roger. *From Nature to Experience: The American Search for Cultural Authority.* Lanham, MD: Rowman & Littlefield, 2005.

Lupfer, Eric. "The Business of American Magazines." In *A History of the Book in America*, vol. 3, edited by Scott E. Casper, Jeffrey D. Groves, Stephen W. Nissenbaum, and Michael Winship. Chapel Hill: University of North Carolina Press, 2007: 248–258.

Lurie, Edward. *Louis Agassiz: A Life in Science.* Baltimore: Johns Hopkins University Press, 1988.

Mackay, E. Anne. *Signs of Orality: The Oral Tradition and Its Influence in the Greek and Roman World*. Leiden, the Netherlands: Brill, 1999.

Mailloux, Steven. *Reception Histories: Rhetoric, Pragmatism, and American Cultural Politics*. Ithaca, NY: Cornell University Press, 1998.

———. *Rhetorical Power*. Ithaca, NY: Cornell University Press, 1989.

———. "Thinking in Public with Rhetoric." *Philosophy & Rhetoric* 39 (2006): 140–146.

McClellan, B. Edward. *Moral Education in America: Schools and the Shaping of Character from Colonial Times to the Present.* New York: Teachers College Press, 1999.

McDermott, John J. *The Culture of Experience: Philosophical Essays in the American Grain*. Prospect Heights: Waveland Press, 1976.

———. *The Drama of Possibility: Experience as Philosophy of Culture*, edited by Douglas R. Anderson. New York: Fordham University Press, 2007.

———. *Streams of Experience: Reflections on the History and Philosophy of American Culture*. Amherst: University of Massachusetts Press, 1986.

McDermott, John J., ed. *The Writings of William James: A Comprehensive Edition*. Chicago: University of Chicago Press, 1977.

McGee, Michael C. "In Search of 'The People': A Rhetorical Alternative." *Quarterly Journal of Speech* 61 (1975): 235–249.

McGee, Michael Calvin, and Martha Anne Martin. "Public Knowledge and Ideological Argumentation." *Communication Monographs* 50 (1983): 47–65.

McKeachie, Wilbert J. "William James's *Talks to Teachers* (1899) and McKeachie's *Teaching Tips* (1999)." *Teaching of Psychology* 30 (2003): 40–43.

McTaggart, J. Ellis. Review of *Pragmatism*, by William James. *Mind* 17 (1908): 104–109.

McVey, Sheila. "Nineteenth Century America: Publishing in a Developing Country." *Annals of the American Academy of Political and Social Science* 421 (1975): 67–80.

Melzer, Arthur M. "What Is an Intellectual?" In *The Public Intellectual: Between Philosophy and Politics*, edited by Arthur M. Melzer, Jerry Weinberger, and M. Richard Zinman. Lanham, MD: Rowman & Littlefield, 2003: 3–14.

Menand, Louis. *The Metaphysical Club: A Story of Ideas in America.* New York: Farrar, Straus and Giroux, 2001.

Miller, Joshua I. *Democratic Temperament: The Legacy of William James.* Lawrence: University Press of Kansas, 1997.

Minot, Charles Sedgwick. "The Psychical Comedy." *North American Review* 160 (1895): 217–230.

Misztal, Barbara A. *Intellectuals and the Public Good: Creativity and Civil Courage.* Cambridge: Cambridge University Press, 2007.

Moore, R. Laurence. *In Search of White Crows: Spiritualism, Parapsychology, and American Culture.* New York: Oxford University Press, 1977.

Moore, Thomas Verner. "The Pragmatism of William James." *Catholic World* 40 (1909): 341–350.

Morgan, Teresa. *Literate Education in the Hellenistic and Roman Worlds.* Cambridge: Cambridge University Press, 1998.

Morgan, Thomas Jefferson. *Studies in Pedagogy.* Boston: Silver, Burdett, 1892.

"Mr. William James on Religious Conversion." *Living Age*. August 23, 1902: 504–506.

Muirhead, J. H. Review of *The Varieties of Religious Experience*, by William James. *International Journal of Ethics* 13 (1903): 236–246.

Münsterberg, Hugo. "Psychology and Mysticism." *Atlantic Monthly* 83 (January 1899): 67–85.

Munthe, Axel. *The Story of San Michelle.* New York: E. P. Dutton, 1929.

Myers, Gerard E. *William James: His Life and Thought.* New Haven: Yale University Press, 1986.

Neibuhr, Richard R. "William James on Religious Experience." In *The Cambridge Companion to William James*, edited by Ruth Anna Putnam. Cambridge: Cambridge University Press, 1997: 214–236.

Neilson, William Allan. "William James as Lecturer and Writer." *Harvard Illustrated Magazine* 8 (February 1907): 97–99.

Nelson, John S., Allan Megill, and Donald N. McCloskey, eds. *The Rhetoric of the Human Sciences: Language and Argument in Scholarship and Public Affairs.* Madison: University of Wisconsin Press, 1987.

Nickels, Cameron C. "'Roaring Ralph': Emerson as Lecturer." *New England Quarterly* 76 (2003): 116–123.

"Notes from the Field." *Pratt Institute Monthly* 3 (1894): 37.

Numbers, Ronald L. *Darwinism Comes to America*. Cambridge: Harvard University Press, 1998.

"Official Pragmatism." *Nation* 85 (1907): 57–58.

Ogden, Rollo, ed. *The Life and Letters of Edwin Lawrence Godkin*, vol. 2. New York: Macmillan, 1907.

Okker, Patricia. *Social Stories: The Magazine Novel in Nineteenth-Century America.* Charlottesville: University of Virginia Press, 2003.

Oleson, Alexandra, and John Voss, eds. *The Organization of Knowledge in Modern America, 1860–1920.* Baltimore: Johns Hopkins University Press, 1979.

Ong, Walter J. *Orality and Literacy: The Technologizing of the World*. London: Routledge, 1982.

———. *Rhetoric, Romance, and Technology: Studies in the Interaction of Expression and Culture.* Ithaca, NY: Cornell University Press, 1971.

Oppenheim, Janet. *The Other World: Spiritualism and Psychical Research in England, 1850–1914*. Cambridge: Cambridge University Press, 1985.

Otis, Edward O. "The Medical Achievements of Dr. Holmes." *Boston Medical and Surgical Journal* 161 (1909): 951–957.

Otto, M. C. "On a Certain Blindness in William James." *Ethics* 53 (1943): 184–191.

Pajares, Frank. "William James: Our Father Who Begat Us." In *Educational Psychology: A Century of Contributions*, edited by Barry J. Zimmerman and Dale H. Schunk. Mahwah, NJ: Lawrence Erlbaum, 2003: 41–64.

Parker, Edward G. *The Golden Age of American Oratory.* Boston: Whittemore, Niles, and Hall, 1857.

Peirce, Charles Sanders. "How to Make Our Ideas Clear." *Popular Science Monthly* 12 (1878): 286–302.

Perelman, Chaïm, and Lucie Olbrechts-Tyteca. *The New Rhetoric: A Treatise on Argumentation*. Translated by John Milkinson and Purcell Weaver. Notre Dame: University of Notre Dame Press, 1969.

Perry, David K., ed. *American Pragmatism and Communication Research*. Mahwah, NJ: Lawrence Erlbaum, 2001.

Perry, Ralph Barton. *The Thought and Character of William James*. 2 vols. New York: Little, Brown, 1935.

Posner, Richard. *Public Intellectuals: A Study of Decline*. Cambridge: Harvard University Press, 2001.

Posnock, Ross. *Color & Culture: Black Writers and the Making of the Modern Intellectual*. Cambridge: Harvard University Press, 1998.

———. *The Trial of Curiosity: Henry James, William James, and the Challenge of Modernity.* New York: Oxford University Press, 1991.

Post, Sarah E. "The Borderland." *New York Medical Journal* 52 (July 12, 1890): 44–45.

Poulakos, John. *Sophistical Rhetoric in Classical Greece*. Columbia: University of South Carolina Press, 1995.

Poulakos, Takis. *Speaking for the Polis: Isocrates' Rhetorical Education*. Columbia: University of South Carolina Press, 1997.

Poulakos, Takis, and David Depew, eds. *Isocrates and Civic Education*. Austin: University of Texas Press, 2004.

"Pragmatism." *Spectator*, July 6, 1907: 9–11.

Price, Kenneth M., and Susan Belasco Smith, eds. *Periodical Literature in Nineteenth-Century America*. Charlottesville: University Press of Virginia, 1995.

"Professor James's 'Pragmatism.'" *Harvard Graduates' Magazine* 16 (1907): 20–24.

Proudfoot, Wayne, ed. *William James and a Science of Religions: Reexperiencing "The Varieties of Religious Experience."* New York: Columbia University Press, 2004.

Proudfoot, Wayne. "Pragmatism and 'an Unseen Order' in *Varieties*." In *William James and a Science of Religions: Reexperiencing "The Varieties of Religious Experience,"* edited by Wayne Proudfoot. New York: Columbia University Press, 2004: 31–47.

"Psychical Research and Eusapia Palladino." *Boston Medical and Surgical Journal* 133 (December 12, 1895): 602.

"Psychology of Religion." *Popular Science Monthly* 61 (November 1902): 89–90.

Putnam, Ruth Anna, ed. *The Cambridge Companion to William James*. Cambridge: Cambridge University Press, 1997.

Radway, Janice A. "Learned and Literary Print Cultures in an Age of Professionalization and Diversification." In *A History of the Book in America*, vol. 4, edited by Carl F. Kaestle and Janice A. Radway. Chapel Hill: University of North Carolina Press, 2009: 197–233.

Rashdall, H. Review of *The Varieties of Religious Experience*, by William James. *Mind* 12 (1903): 245–250.

Ray, Angela G. *The Lyceum and Public Culture in the Nineteenth-Century United States*. East Lansing: Michigan State University Press, 2005.

Reese, William J. *America's Public Schools: From the Common School to "No Child Left Behind."* Baltimore: Johns Hopkins University Press, 2005.

Report of the Board of Education of the State of Connecticut to the Governor. Hartford: Case, Lockwood & Brainard, 1896.

Report of the Superintendent of Public Instruction of the Commonwealth of Pennsylvania for the Year Ending June 3, 1901. Philadelphia: William Stanley Ray, 1901.

Reuben, Julie A. *The Making of the Modern University: Intellectual Transformation and the Marginalization of Morality.* Chicago: University of Chicago Press, 1996.

Review of *Talks to Teachers on Psychology and to Students on Some of Life's Ideals*, by William James. *Boston Evening Transcript*, July 5, 1899: 12.

Review of *The Varieties of Religious Experience*, by William James. *Nation* 75 (August 21, 1902): 155.

Review of *The Varieties of Religious Experience*, by William James. *American Ecclesiastical Review* 7 (December 1902): 680–681.

Review of *The Varieties of Religious Experience*, by William James. *Catholic World* 75 (September 1902): 824.

Richards, I. A. *The Philosophy of Rhetoric.* New York: Oxford University Press, 1965.

Richardson, Robert D. *Emerson: The Mind on Fire.* Berkeley: University of California Press, 1995.

———. *William James in the Maelstrom of American Modernism.* Boston: Houghton Mifflin, 2006.

Roberts, Kathleen Glenister. "Liminality, Authority, and Value: Reported Speech in Epideictic Rhetoric." *Communication Theory* 14 (2004): 264–284.

Roberts, W. Rhys, trans. *The Rhetoric and the Poetics of Aristotle.* New York: Modern Library, 1954.

Rodgers, Daniel T. *The Work Ethic in Industrial America, 1850–1920.* Chicago: University of Chicago Press, 1978.

Rohler, Lloyd. "Conservative Appeals to the People: George Wallace's Populist Rhetoric." *Southern Communication Journal* 64 (1999): 316–322.

Rorty, Richard. "Some Inconsistencies in James's *Varieties.*" In *William James and a Science of Religions: Reexperiencing "The Varieties of Religious Experience,"* edited by Wayne Proudfoot. New York: Columbia University Press, 2004: 86–97.

Royce, Josiah. *The Letters of Josiah Royce,* edited by John Clendenning. Chicago: University of Chicago Press, 1970.

———. *The World and the Individual, First Series: The Four Historical Conceptions of Being.* New York: Macmillan, 1900.

Ruf, Frederick J. *The Creation of Chaos: William James and the Stylistic Making of a Disorderly World.* Albany: State University of New York Press, 1991.

Russell, Bertrand. "Transatlantic 'Truth.'" *Albany Review* 2 (1908): 393–410.

Said, Edward W. *Representations of the Intellectual.* New York: Vintage, 1994.

Santayana, George. "James's Psychology." *Atlantic Monthly* 67 (1891): 556.

Schiller, F. C. S. Review of *The Varieties of Religious Experience,* by William James. *Proceedings of the Society for Psychical Research* 45 (February 1903): 403–411.

Schollmeier, Paul. "Pragmatic Method and Its Rhetorical Lineage." *Philosophy & Rhetoric* 35 (2002): 368–381.

Scott, Donald M. "The Popular Lecture and the Creation of a Public in Mid-Nineteenth-Century America." *Journal of American History* 66 (1980): 791–809.

Scott, Frederick J. Down. "William James's 1895 Visit to Colorado." *San Jose Studies* 5 (1979): 33–38.

———. "William James's 1898 Visit to California." *San Jose Studies* 3 (1977): 7–22.

Secord, James. "How Scientific Conversation Became Shop Talk." In *Science in the Marketplace: Nineteenth-Century Sites and Experiences,* edited by

Aileen Fyfe and Bernard Lightman. Chicago: University of Chicago Press, 2007: 23–59.

Seventh Year Book of the Brooklyn Institute of Arts and Sciences, 1894–5. Brooklyn: Brooklyn Institute of Arts and Sciences, 1895.

Shepherd, Gregory J. "Pragmatism and Tragedy, Communication and Hope: A Summary Story." In *American Pragmatism and Communication Research*, edited by David K. Perry. Mahwah, NJ: Lawrence Erlbaum, 2001: 237–250.

Shi, David E. *Facing Facts: Realism in American Thought and Culture, 1850–1920*. New York: Oxford University Press, 1995.

Shoemaker, Neille. "The Contemporaneous Medical Reputation of Oliver Wendell Holmes." *New England Quarterly* 26 (1953): 477–493.

Shore, Marlene. "Psychology and Memory in the Midst of Change: The Social Concerns of Late-19th-Century North American Psychologists." In *The Transformation of Psychology: Influences of 19th-Century Philosophy, Technology, and Natural Science*, edited by Christopher D. Green, Marlene Shore, and Thomas Teo. Washington, DC: American Psychological Association, 2001: 63–86.

Sidgwick, Henry. "Eusapia Paladino." *Journal of the Society for Psychical Research* 7 (1895): 148–159.

Simon, Linda. *Genuine Reality: A Life of William James*. New York: Harcourt Brace, 1998.

———, ed. *William James Remembered*. Lincoln: University of Nebraska Press, 1996.

Simons, Herbert W., ed. *Rhetoric in the Human Sciences.* London: Sage, 1989.

Smith, Susan Belasco, and Kenneth M. Price. "Introduction: Periodical Literature in Social and Historical Context." In *Periodical Literature in Nineteenth-Century America*, edited by Kenneth M. Price and Susan Belasco Smith. Charlottesville: University Press of Virginia, 1995: 3–16.

Stafford, William T. "Emerson and the James Family." *American Literature* 24 (1953): 433–461.

Starbuck, Edwin D. "The Varieties of Religious Experience." *Biblical World* 24 (August 1904): 100–111.

Stob, Paul. "Kenneth Burke, John Dewey, and the Pursuit of the Public." *Philosophy & Rhetoric* 38 (2005): 226–247.

———. "Louis Brandeis and the Rhetoric of Transactional Morality." *Rhetoric & Public Affairs* 14 (2011): 261–290.

———. "Pragmatism, Experience, and William James's Politics of Blindness." *Philosophy & Rhetoric* 44 (2011): 227–249.

———. "'Terministic Screens,' Social Constructionism, and the Language of Experience: Kenneth Burke's Utilization of William James." *Philosophy & Rhetoric* 41 (2008): 130–152.

Stroud, Scott R. "John Dewey and the Question of Artful Communication." *Philosophy & Rhetoric* 41 (2008): 153–183.

———. "Pragmatism and the Methodology of Comparative Rhetoric." *Rhetoric Society Quarterly* 39 (2009): 353–379.

———. "What Does Pragmatic Meliorism Mean for Rhetoric?" *Western Journal of Communication* 74 (2010): 43–60.

Stuhr, John J., ed. *100 Years of Pragmatism: William James's Revolutionary Philosophy.* Bloomington: Indiana University Press, 2010.

Tadié, Alexis. *Sterne's Whimsical Theatres of Language: Orality, Gesture, Literacy.* Hants, England: Ashgate, 2003.

Taves, Ann. *Fits, Traces, & Visions: Experiencing Religion and Explaining Experience from Wesley to James.* Princeton, NJ: Princeton University Press, 1999.

Taylor, Charles. *Varieties of Religion Today: William James Revisited.* Cambridge: Harvard University Press, 2002.

Taylor, Eugene. "Metaphysics and Consciousness in James's *Varieties*: A Centenary Lecture." In *William James and "The Varieties of Religious Experience": A Centenary Celebration*, edited by Jeremy Carrette. London: Routledge, 2005: 11–26.

———. *Shadow Culture: Psychology and Spirituality in America.* Washington, DC: Counterpoint, 1999.

———. *William James on Consciousness Beyond the Margin.* Princeton, NJ: Princeton University Press, 1996.

———. *William James on Exceptional Mental States: The 1896 Lowell Lectures.* New York: Charles Scribner's Sons, 1982.

Thompson, Paul B., and Thomas C. Hilde, eds. *The Agrarian Roots of Pragmatism.* Nashville, TN: Vanderbilt University Press, 2000.

Thurber, C. H. Review of *Talks to Teachers on Psychology and to Students on Some of Life's Ideals*, by William James. *School Review* 7 (1899): 434–435.

Tiffany, Joel. *Spiritualism Explained: Being a Series of Twelve Lectures Delivered before the New York Conference of Spiritualists.* New York: Graham and Ellinwood, 1856.

Tilton, Eleanor M. *Amiable Autocrat: A Biography of Dr. Oliver Wendell Holmes.* New York: Henry Schuman, 1947.

Titchener, E. B. "The Feeling of Being Stared At." *Science* 8 (December 23, 1898): 895–897.

Twelfth Biennial Report of the Superintendent of Public Instruction of the State of Colorado. Denver: Smith-Brooks Printing, 1900.

Utterback, William E. "A Psychological Approach to the Rhetoric of Speech Composition." *Quarterly Journal of Speech* 10 (1924): 17–23.

"The Varieties of Religious Experience." *New Outlook.* December 27, 1902: 991–995.

Veysey, Laurence R. *The Emergence of the American University*. Chicago: University of Chicago Press, 1965.

Wadsworth, Sarah. *In the Company of Books: Literature and Its "Classes" in Nineteenth-Century America*. Amherst: University of Massachusetts Press, 2006.

Warner, Michael. *Publics and Counterpublics*. New York: Zone Books, 2002.

Warren, James Perrin. *Culture of Eloquence: Oratory and Reform in Antebellum America*. University Park: Pennsylvania State University Press, 1999.

Webb, C. C. J. "Psychology and Religion." *Journal of Theological Studies* 4 (1903): 46–68.

Welch, Kathleen E. *Electric Rhetoric: Classical Rhetoric, Oralism, and a New Literacy.* Cambridge: MIT Press, 1999.

West, Cornel. *The American Evasion of Philosophy: A Genealogy of Pragmatism.* Madison: University of Wisconsin Press, 1989.

White, Paul. *Thomas Huxley: Making the "Man of Science."* Cambridge: Cambridge University Press, 2003.

Wight, Randall D. "More Than Mere Weather: James's Talks to Students about Life." *Teaching of Psychology* 30 (2003): 38–40.

Wichelns, Herbert A. "Ralph Waldo Emerson." In *A History and Criticism of American Public Address*, vol. 2, edited by William Norwood Brigance. New York: Russell & Russell, 1960: 501–525.

Wiebe, Robert H. *The Search for Order, 1877–1920.* New York: Hill and Wang, 1967.

Williams, Rhys H. and Susan M. Alexander. "Religious Rhetoric in American Populism: Civil Religion as Movement Ideology." *Journal for the Scientific Study of Religion* 33 (1994): 1–15.

Willis, Martin. *Mesmerists, Monsters, & Machines: Science Fiction & the Cultures of Science in the Nineteenth Century.* Kent, OH: Kent State University Press, 2006.

Wilson, Daniel J. *Science, Community, and the Transformation of American Philosophy, 1860–1930.* Chicago: University of Chicago Press, 1990.

Winans, James Albert. *Public Speaking*, rev. ed. New York: Century Company, 1917.

Winship, Michael. "Manufacturing and Book Production." In *A History of the Book in America,* vol. 3, edited by Scott E. Casper, Jeffrey D. Groves, Stephen W. Nissenbaum, and Michael Winship. Chapel Hill: University of North Carolina Press, 2007: 40–69.

———. "The National Book Trade System: Distribution and Trade." In *A History of the Book in America,* vol. 3, edited by Scott E. Casper, Jeffrey D. Groves, Stephen W. Nissenbaum, and Michael Winship. Chapel Hill: University of North Carolina Press, 2007: 117–130.

Witham, Larry. *The Measure of God: Our Century-Long Struggle to Reconcile Science and Religion*. San Francisco: HarperSanFrancisco, 2005.

Wulff, David W. "Listening to James a Century Later: *The Varieties* as a Resource for Renewing the Psychology of Religion." In *William James and "The Varieties of Religious Experience": A Centenary Celebration*, edited by Jeremy Carrette. London: Routledge, 2005: 47–57.

Yarbrough, Stephen R. *Inventive Intercourse: From Rhetorical Conflict to the Ethical Creation of Novel Truth*. Carbondale: Southern Illinois University Press, 2006.

Young, Richard E., and Yameng Liu, eds. *Landmark Essays on Rhetorical Invention in Writing*. Davis, CA: Hermagoras Press, 1994.

Zboray, Ronald J. *A Fictive People: Antebellum Economic Development and the American Reading Public*. New York: Oxford University Press, 1993.

Zimmerman, Barry J. and Dale H. Schunk, eds. *Educational Psychology: A Century of Contributions*. Mahwah, NJ: Lawrence Erlbaum, 2003.

Zlatic, Thomas D. "The 'Seeing Eye' and the 'Creating Mouth': Literacy and Orality in Mark Twain's Joan of Arc." *CLIO* 21 (1992): 285–304.

Index

⌘

William James is indicated with WJ.